*Heidegger and Marx*

# *Heidegger and Marx*

A PRODUCTIVE DIALOGUE OVER THE LANGUAGE OF HUMANISM

*Laurence Paul Hemming*

NORTHWESTERN UNIVERSITY PRESS / EVANSTON, ILLINOIS

Northwestern University Press
www.nupress.northwestern.edu



Printed in the United States of America

10 9 8 7 6 5 4 3 2 1

**Library of Congress Cataloging-in-Publication Data**

Hemming, Laurence Paul.
Heidegger and Marx : a productive dialogue over the language of humanism / Laurence Paul Hemming.
p. cm.
Includes bibliographical references and index.
ISBN 978-0-8101-2875-0 (pbk. : alk. paper)
1. Heidegger, Martin, 1889–1976. 2. Marx, Karl, 1818–1883. 3. Hegel, Georg Wilhelm Friedrich, 1770–1831. 4. Nietzsche, Friedrich Wilhelm, 1844–1900. 5. Humanism. I. Title.
B3279.H49H38245 2013
193—dc23

2012027984

♾ The paper used in this publication meets the minimum requirements of the American National Standard for Information Sciences—Permanence of Paper for Printed Library Materials, ANSI Z39.48-1992.

*for Bogdan*
*in friendship*

Und wie steht es mit Marx und Nietzsche?
Treten sie schon aus der Bahn der neuzeitlichen Philosophie heraus?
Wenn nicht, wie ist ihr Standort zu bestimmen?

And how does it stand with Marx and Nietzsche?
Do they already step out of the course of modern philosophy?
If not, how is their standpoint to be determined?
—Martin Heidegger, *Qu'est-ce que la philosophie*? (1956), from a lecture at Cerisy-la-Salle, Normandy, August 28, 1955

Τάνταλος
θυμός ποθ' ἁμὸς οὐρανῷ κυρῶν ἄνω
ἔραξε πίπτει καὶ με προσφωνεῖ τάδε
—γίγνωσκε τἀνθρώπεια μὴ σέβειν ἄγαν—

Tantalus: "A human heart, once having reached up to the ruling heavens
is thrown down to the earth, and addresses me thus:
'Learn not to be in awe of what lies within the reach of man.'"
—Aeschylus, *Tantalus* (*Fragment*)

# Contents

# Preface

This book began as a series of public lectures in the spring of 2010 from the Institute of Advanced Studies in Lancaster University (where I was awarded a research fellowship in 2008), and as seminars in the research training program of the university's Faculty of Arts and Social Sciences and the Management School. The idea for the lectures was hatched with two colleagues, Bogdan Costea and Mick Dillon, without whose encouragement and help they could not have come to fruition. I owe a profound and powerful debt to Bogdan Costea for his many suggestions for improvement and clarification of the book as it was being written. No scholar can be accorded greater kindness or a higher privilege than this. Together with others who attended some parts of the series, three colleagues, Norman Fairclough, Gavin Hyman, and Kostas Amiridis, and thirteen student participants, Huw Fearnall-Williams, Eleanor Fitton, Chris Fletcher, Adam Gregory, Ralph Guth, Eleanor Lamb, Alex (Cary) Monreal-Clark, Dunja Njaradi, Andrea Rossi, Ruth Slater, Susan Starling, Diana Stypinska, and Peter Watt, formed the core of what was one of the most invigorating intellectual experiences of my work so far. Their enthusiasm and commitment to the matters at hand were a formidable spur to what emerged. A number of the students offered invaluable comments and suggestions on earlier drafts of the manuscripts: special thanks are due for this to Huw Fearnall-Williams for his many careful observations on a late draft, and to Adam Gregory for his helpful corrections. To this must be added my thanks to Uta Papen and Michaela Scott for their help in organizing the seminars. As always, I am in debt to Ferdinand Knapp, whose unswerving affection, and whose patience with my German, has now stretched over sixteen years. Gratitude is also owed to Fred Dallmayr, emeritus of Notre Dame University, and Stuart Elden, of Durham University, for encouraging the Northwestern University Press to publish this book, and for their important and helpful observations on the text, and to those at the Press, especially Henry Carrigan, Jr. and Peter Raccuglia, who have done so much to bring the book to publication

When quoting Martin Heidegger, I have referred predominantly to the

Heidegger *Gesamtausgabe* and only deviated where material is not, or not yet, available in that collection. The relevant volume number is in each case indicated by the initials *GA* and the volume number. The *Gesamtausgabe* is scheduled to run to a total of 102 volumes by the time it is complete, of which just under 80 volumes have so far appeared. The schema and the basis for the *Gesamtausgabe* was laid down by Heidegger himself, and the first volume to be published, twenty-fourth in the schema, appeared two years before his death.[1] The Heidegger *Gesamtausgabe* is anything but a critical edition and is certainly not without its scholarly difficulties. Heidegger really only ever wrote one book, *Sein und Zeit,* and even that is incomplete, in ways that are important for this study. All the other books he published in his lifetime were either redactions of lectures, lecture courses (such as the *Kantbuch* or the two volumes compiled from his lectures between 1937 and 1944 on Friedrich Nietzsche),[2] or collections of essays. In the *Gesamtausgabe* editions of the works that were also published in his lifetime, Heidegger's marginal notes to his own copies have been reproduced as footnotes and comments. Rarely do we have a date for these remarks, especially in those cases where the same text or sentence occasioned more than one, sometimes several, remarks. In addition, and especially with his manuscripts, Heidegger often reworked his material, so that the "authentic" date of the exact word, or the precisely periodized thought, is all too often impossible to determine (even if this were a worthy scholarly goal). An exact "chronometry" of the development of Heidegger's thought, a concern of some Heidegger scholars and commentators, is almost impossible—if not pointless—to reconstruct. Robert Bernasconi has wisely cautioned that "Heidegger scholars should be used by now to finding what had seemed to be late developments firmly located in earlier texts."[3]

Heidegger specifically refused the production of a "critical edition" of his writings. Many of the volumes of his university lecture courses and seminars are in fact reconstructed not only from his own notes but also from the verbatim or protocol reports of students who attended them, reports which were often circulated, having been typed up and then cyclostyled (before the advent of photocopying). Heidegger himself at times kept and circulated copies of these transcripts. While at times the precise word, the precise wording, of a thought is decisive, at others it is not. Paradoxically, the peda-

1. Martin Heidegger, *Die Grundprobleme der Phänomenologie* (*GA*24).

2. Martin Heidegger, *Kant und das Problem der Metaphysik* (*GA*3). The two volumes of extracts from Heidegger's lectures on Nietzsche did not appear until 1961, published by Günther Neske (*GA*6.1 and *GA*6.2). The full texts of the lecture courses and discussions on which these two *Gesamtausgabe* volumes were based can be found in *GA*43, *GA*44, *GA*46–*GA*48, and *GA*50 (see the bibliography for a full explanation).

3. Robert Bernasconi, "The Greatness of the Work of Art," 115, n. 4.

gogical voice often emerges from these compilations more effectively than if every volume had been approved and "settled" by the author—although at times and in cases Heidegger did exercise this intensity of editorial control.

A recurring question in this book concerns how the texts of the authors with which it deals are to be read. This question was sharply present before the authors in question. The character and need to interpret Nietzsche's ironic voice is well known, but the *for whom* and *to whom* is always in play. The lectures and exercises Heidegger laid out for his students are motivated pedagogically, but at times (especially when there were Nazi spies in the lecture hall) even these withdraw into a cryptic or coded language. If *Being and Time* (1927) is the book which, of all his work, Heidegger intended to have the widest reach, the *Beiträge zur Philosophie* (Contributions to Philosophy, 1989), first of the personal notebooks which we will discuss in some detail, is addressed thus: "for the few—for the rare."[4] Heidegger spoke in different voices and at different times: at times he concealed most from those who would have thought themselves his intellectual peers: the most arcane material he at times put before the least academic audiences (as in the case of his *Bremen Lectures* of 1949). Heidegger's voice is often pitched as one to which the hearer has to find his own way.

It is perhaps necessary to comment on one set of publications in more detail. Heidegger's lectures on Nietzsche were edited by him and published by Günther Neske in two volumes in 1961: the original texts from which they were edited have only appeared later (although these are the ones I have cited, unless I have remarked otherwise in the text), and I have tried to provide in the bibliography as full notes as possible to enable the edited 1961 texts to be coordinated to their earlier manuscript and reported forms. Are the earlier texts more authentic? And even if we were to say that they are, do I subscribe to the view that Heidegger was, in the 1961 material, "covering up" certain matters, or making them more palatable for postwar audiences compared to his earlier views? It could well be that in 1961 Heidegger thought that there were matters for which the world was not ready: this is not my concern. What, in any case, is the "authentic" text? Anyone who works with so-called critical editions or historical variations of texts, or historically differentiated texts, knows, or ought to know, that such a thing as the *pure* text, the pure thought, never really exists. We leave these preoccupations to the forensic hygienists of intellectual life. I doubt their impartiality as much as I fear the sterilized prose which seems to be their goal. Despite textual and historical variation, and even the emendations of editors, the original thinker can all too often be caught or heard in just a few of his

4. Martin Heidegger, *Beiträge zur Philosophie* (GA65), 11. "Für die Wenigen—Für die Seltenen."

genuine words. To hear in this way is what lets us into texts; an altogether riskier, more dangerous business, one in which we are required to be interpreters, and for which we ourselves can, and should, ever be held to account. This is the leap into the authentic word. Every encounter with a thinker demands an attitude of interpretation—there is no escape from this requirement; rather it is the very stuff of it, be he Heidegger, Marx, Nietzsche, or the person in the room next door.

There have been two attempts at a *Marx Engels Gesamtausgabe* (*MEGA*), together with an additional collection in between, the *Marx Engels Werke* of the Institut für Marxismus-Leninismus of the Communist Party of the former German Democratic Republic. I have chosen to use the *Marx Engels Werke,* because at present, it is the most complete set of texts, although it omits large quantities of Marx's writings in English (many of which remain unpublished, or hidden in the nineteenth-century editions of the American newspapers in which they originally appeared). Volume numbers of the *Marx Engels Werke* cited are indicated by the initials *MEW* and the volume number. The *MEGA-2,* which has already published fifty-six volumes, is scheduled to run in its entirety to 112 (reduced from an original plan of 170), including the "Excerpt" notebooks toward which the editor of the first *Gesamtausgabe,* David Riazanov, had a forceful, if idiosyncratic, prejudice. The reading of Marx which I propose in these lectures is, perhaps, therefore provisional, or questionable, from the standpoint of the improved texts (especially of *Das Kapital,* the *Economic and Philosophical Manuscripts,* and the *Grundrisse*) of the *MEGA-2,* the more so since its relocation to the International Marx Engels Foundation (IMES), across three national jurisdictions—Berlin, Amsterdam, and Moscow.[5]

A central question in the establishment of the various editions of Marx's works has been the place and editorial role of Friedrich Engels. Jürgen Rojahn, secretary of IMES from its inception in 1990 until 2000, was reported in 1999 as saying: "In the past it was thought that Marx and Engels were intellectual twins, but current research suggests that significant differences separated Marx from Engels."[6] From this the interviewer draws the conclusion (which may mischievously report Rojahn, but did not upset IMES sufficiently to prevent them foregrounding the quotation in their own publicity) that "the MEGA will show in what way Engels altered Marx's text for volumes two and three [of *Das Kapital*]. It appears that it was Engels who revised these texts into a prophecy of inevitable decline of capitalism, whereas

5. See, for an excellent short history of the fate of Marx's published and unpublished works, the appendix to Kevin B. Anderson, *Marx at the Margins,* 247–52.

6. Norman Levine, "What Marx Really Said."

Marx himself never foretold such an ending."[7] There were important differences between Marx and Engels over the various forms and editions of *Das Kapital* (especially the difference between the French editions of 1872 and 1875, translated by Joseph Roy, but edited with important emendations by Marx himself), and discussed between them.[8] It is certainly true that Marx regarded the French edition as definitive in ways that Engels appears to a greater extent to have overlooked in his edited editions of 1886, and in what actually came to be the defining edition of 1890: Marx suggests that "whatever the literary imperfections of this French edition, it possesses a scientific value independent of the original and needs to be consulted even by readers familiar with the German language."[9] The differences, however, are, while important, largely technical and do not alter the fundamental metaphysical comportment of either *Das Kapital* or Marx himself. It is difficult to sustain the argument that they represent a formal or ideological split between the two men (although this thought is now in vogue).

The editors of the *MEGA*-2 appear, however, to favor a "scientific" Marx, free of the meddling Engels, despite that the intellectual friendship of these two men represented perhaps the closest partnership of its kind in modern thought. The enterprise of producing such a Marx at the expense of Engels surely falsifies both, in their persons and in the history of their reception.[10] Inasmuch as Heidegger's most important philosophical developments from 1936 to 1948, and those greatly pertinent to us from 1946 and 1949, arise on the basis of a political engagement, even more so do the works of Marx and his collaborator Engels. No one should attempt to free themselves from the *tone* of Marx's and Engels's writing: always in concert, if not always harmonious, never in any sense antiphonal. At worst, catty, petulant, journalistic, at other times humorous, but at best cool, sharp, and penetratingly thought through to the very end, the sheer urgency of especially Marx's *voice,* as much as the content itself, betrays the vitality with which Marx and

7. Ibid.

8. See, for instance, the letters between Engels and Marx on November 29 and 30, 1873, in Karl Marx and Friedrich Engels, *Briefe Juli 1870 bis Dezember 1874* (*MEW*33), 94–95.

9. Karl Marx and Joseph Roy, "Note des éditeurs," in Karl Marx, *Le Capitale,* 1:9. "Quelles que soient donc les imperfections littéraires de cette édition française, elle possède une valeur scientifique indépendante de l'original et doit être consultée même par les lecteurs familiers avec la langue allemande."

10. Kevin Anderson has considered with nuance the relationship between Marx and Engels, and the issue of Engels's editorial decisions, especially surrounding *Das Kapital,* and the differences between the German and French editions. See Kevin B. Anderson, *Marx at the Margins,* 4–5 and 154–95. As Anderson notes (4), whatever else the intellectual relation between them (and as Engels himself freely acknowledged on more than one occasion) "Engels was not Marx," a wiser and more just observation than any attempt to set them at odds.

Engels wrote and thought, and the urgency of the moment into which they wrote. Marx's voice is almost always addressed to the widest audience. It is not accidental that he, like several other revolutionaries (Lenin and Trotsky are cases in point), was often most at ease with a journalist's voice. At the same time, Marx had direct experience of the Prussian censors in editing the *Rheinische Zeitung.* It was for the sake of attaining a freedom of voice that Marx came to England, and it was not only for the income but also for the possibilities for freedom of expression that led him to publish in the *New York Daily Tribune.* At the same time, the appropriation of Marx by (especially the Soviet) Communist authorities also resulted in a posthumous censorship of his writings—the privileging of some, even the suppression of others—whose consequences are yet fully to be undone. Access to Marx's accessible voice has at times been rigidly policed.

The most productive dialogues are often those conducted in *philia,* which can mean in Greek both friendship and love. Friendship, as we presently conceive it, is never adequate to what *philia* names: the name of love, as it is now too often understood (through categories that mask modern love's sentimentality, its self-consumption, kitsch, and melancholy), can all too easily exceed what it opens up. *Philia* is not the frenzied, incandescent blaze of emerging friendship, a kind of possession that can also lay claim to being love or even eroticism. Rather is *philia* the love that passes instinctively between two who recognize each other as equals and as (long-lasting) friends, even where they clash. It names an equality based not on equalization or an enforced homogeneity, but on mutual understanding given in difference. Only friends can truly comport to each other as equals or the same: for this very reason they need not always, and in the most weighty things might never do. Only between friends can true freedom arise, for freedom is not something we take or attain, but always something that is returned to us: it comes, not as a point of liberation, but as an unfettered, even unexpected, gift. It does not need to be requited, nor need it bring cost or loss to the one giving. *Philia* is in itself appropriate, which means it appropriates those on whom it is bestowed to *charis*—that is, to a divine grace—and in a stable holding that is at the same time a mutual reserve and thankfulness. A common life in friendship provides hope against what passes for the politics that marks our times. This book is grounded in this place of *philia* and *charis* by two particular friendships: Paul Fletcher's, without whom I would not first have come to Lancaster (and whose untimely death in the summer of 2007 we still mourn), and Bogdan Costea's, to whom this work is dedicated and who keeps me in friendship when I am there.

The only person to have attempted a full-scale synthesis of Heidegger's and Marx's thinking is Kostas Axelos. His work was strongly influenced by Heidegger, whom he first met at the country house of Jacques Lacan in 1955.

Axelos was at the same time a committed scholar of Marx and a Marxist, although he had broken with the Communist Party formally in 1946. While in no sense have I tried to follow the path he laid down (discussed in more detail in chapter 1), the depth of his engagement with both Heidegger and Marx was invaluable in attempting to understand and bring to light the "productive dialogue" which is the subject of this book. His death in the small hours of Thursday, February 4, 2010 (at the age of 85), occurred in the middle of the lectures which were the beginning of this book, and we marked his passing and his stature as a thinker of these two giants formally in the week following his death. He represents perhaps the last of that generation of French thinkers—Jean Beaufret, Jean-Paul Sartre, Emmanuel Lévinas, and others as well as Axelos—who (prior to Jacques Derrida's remarkable and powerful confrontation with Heidegger) had first engaged so acutely and in person with Heidegger.[11] Of all of these, Axelos was the one who was most committed to the politics of the Left.

I have throughout translated *der Mensch* as "man" and favored the masculine pronoun to speak of humanity. The text and translations are always intended to be taken inclusively, although I have often eschewed inclusive language where it seems to do violence to the sense or seems clumsy: I have always believed the use of female pronouns by a male author to be a colonization more totalizing than any imbalance it seeks to correct. Of those readers for whom any of this use is a difficulty, I ask forbearance.

We owe the greatest debt to those with whom we learn to think: and so I acknowledge my own indebtedness to the thinkers with whom I have sought to enter dialogue: first Martin Heidegger, from whom I have learned so much of what I know of thinking, and Karl Marx, who influenced me strongly as a young man and in this book represents for me something of a return. Whatever I have said that truly inquires into what they themselves inquired into, I hold for their honor, and for whatever I have failed in and falsified, should be held to my account alone.

11. Axelos discussed both his Marxism and his understanding of Heidegger in an interview with Stuart Elden in "Interview: Kostas Axelos, Mondialisation without the World," 25–28.

*Heidegger and Marx*

# There Is No Justice in Heidegger or for Marx

MARX AND HEIDEGGER EACH understood that what they had to say arose from their own place and time. In this, they are, if in quite different ways, among the most concrete and rigorous of thinkers. More than any other thinkers in the last two hundred years, each, although differently, thought historically and sought to explain history as he understood it. Each is capable of great abstraction, both of them spoke from concrete situations. The situations of both were marked by urgency, and, in contrast to many others of their caliber, their own biography was entangled in what they thought and said. Each has ushered in not one, but a wealth of schools of followers. To attempt to address the thought of either on his own betrays a deal of ambition: to have attempted both, and together, is perhaps to have doomed oneself to failure. This book is not, therefore, an attempt to be a final word: it aims to do no more than identify the main strands of thought that might place these two thinkers within the same dialogue. It is in this sense merely an introductory text—and even that low aim has proved challenge enough, if it succeeds at all.

Peter Gast's manufactured *Preface* to the work he published in Friedrich Nietzsche's name, a work all of whose words were Nietzsche's in a book of which Nietzsche was not the author, the *Will to Power*, opens with the words "what I recount is the history of the next two centuries."[1] This tale alone is evidence enough for how in these two centuries all too often what is thought by one is put to use for the purposes of others.[2] The history is a

1. Friedrich Nietzsche, *Der Wille zur Macht*, 3. "Was ich erzähle, ist die Geschichte der nächsten zwei Jahrhunderte." Gast took the *Preface* from a notebook of Nietzsche's of November 1887–March 1888, from a text which was entitled *Vorrede—Preface* (= Friedrich Nietzsche, vol. 13, *Nachlaß 1887–1889*, 189).

2. The history of the text *Der Wille zur Macht* is explained in Walter Kaufmann's "Editor's Introduction" to his English translation, Walter Kaufmann (ed. and trans.), *Friedrich Nietzsche: The Will to Power*, xiii–xxix; the background to the fiction is given in H. F. Peters, *Zarathustra's Sister: The Case of Elisabeth and Friedrich Nietzsche*. The problematic status of the work

philosophical one: Nietzsche was only able to speak of history and its recounting because of the prevailing way in which philosophy itself had become historical. Prior to him, Karl Marx had concretized and materialized the thought of the one philosopher who had thought through and made possible the historical character of philosophy in the modern age: Georg Friedrich Hegel. Prior to Hegel, the highest philosophy, the philosophy of the absolute and infinite (which Hegel sought to treat), had dealt only with that which is eternal and unchanging: "eternal being," the most extreme pole to which first Plato and then Aristotle had driven thinking in the birth itself of Western philosophy. The Christianization of philosophy, if not from Justin Martyr or Augustine, then certainly from the sixth century onward, had identified *the* eternal being as God. In the move into history, the eternal thought of being left God behind and had itself become the philosophy of, not being, but becoming. Nietzsche dares to write a history of the future, because becoming is above all concerned with what is not yet, or rather, what not yet *is*. Hegel, Marx, and Nietzsche: each gave birth to the philosophy of becoming that is the thought of our age and these centuries, and they materialized that becoming as politics. This book is about how they conceived the materialization of this, a history yet to come.

It is Martin Heidegger who sought to make clear, over a lifetime's thinking, how this history was to be understood as both a history of being and a history of the forgottenness of being. In this he sought to show how (and this means for whom) the "first" and "highest" philosophy had become historical, and what of the "political" had been forgotten in that course. The pursuit of what he called this "path" of thinking brought him increasingly into confrontation with the whole of modernity, in ways for which he has only partially been either understood, or even forgiven. He has been accused of nostalgia, Luddism, and an eccentric "philhellenism" (the word is not mine), or of merely being a peasant farmer with intellectual pretensions: none of which is true. This book is about how that confrontation with modernity is to be understood, and what "being-historical" really means. Heidegger frequently makes a distinction between history (*die Geschichte*) and historiography (*die Historie*)—the latter being the mere assemblage of "facts" and sequences of events constituted self-evidently as historical "knowledge." In *Being and Time,* Heidegger reminds us that philosophy is none of these kinds of "theory" of historiography but is "the interpretation of the properly historical entity [*Seienden*] in its historicality."[3] It did not seem necessary in this work to explore this par-

---

meant that it was left out of the critical edition of Nietzsche's works and *Nachlaß* edited by Giorgio Colli and Mazzino Montinari (see bibliography).

3. Martin Heidegger, *Sein und Zeit* (*GA*2), 14. "Die Interpretation des eigentlich geschichtlich Seienden auf seine Geschichtlichkeit." See especially 518–24.

ticular distinction that Heidegger made (so often for pedagogical purposes), so that throughout, it is taken for granted that in both Heidegger and Marx, "facts" are grounded in interpretation, such that "history [*die Geschichte*] is never necessarily historical [*historisch*]" and that "in the theory of historiography, history holds sway as what cannot be got around."[4]

Marx, far more than Hegel, and perhaps (although perhaps not) even more than Nietzsche, is still the thinker of that epoch in history we name "modernity." Marx's account of the inevitability of progress gives immediate shape to modernity's commitment to technology, to an endless moral, social, political, and economic advancement and development, wherein modernity does not think, but first, and only, acts. For modernity, thinking is disdained as afterthought.

Although primarily concerned with two, this book is really about four figures—Hegel, Marx, Nietzsche, and Heidegger. It is also a book about how we might understand the half (and a bit) of the "next two centuries" of Nietzsche's extravagant claim, through which we have already lived. To be in-midst of something is to find oneself in the most difficult of places for understanding. We neither properly see the end, nor entirely remember the beginning. Yet life itself is this "being in the midst": life rarely, if ever, grants us more than this. And so it is both the most difficult, and the most familiar, and even the most privileged, place from which to think. If we are halfway through, we are in the eye of the tempest. And what tempest there has been. For since the birth of 1888 we have seen a resurgent Germany, the eye of the European storm, crushed not once, but twice. We have seen the mighty empires of Britain and the Soviet Union (if it is correct to understand the latter as an empire) enter their full flower and fade or fall. We have seen another ancient empire come to an end and transform itself into a mighty nation which is communist by name, and seemingly capitalist by nature, and which is locked in a financial, economic, and political brace with its seeming opposite—if this is one way to understand the extraordinary fate of China and its emerging and surprising relations with the United States. It has been said more than once that "the proletariat of the United States is Chinese." And we have seen the United States, a "second Europe" in both size and design, become the guarantor and pinnacle of Western liberal democracy. All of this has been called by Heidegger, and by others around him (Ernst and Georg Jünger, and the circle around the journal *Die Tat*), the planetary, global, reach of Occidental ideas, which had its intellectual and spiritual birth in antiquity, in Greece. This book is also an attempt to grapple with the

4. Martin Heidegger, "Wissenschaft und Besinnung" (*GA*7), 58. "Die Geschichte ist niemals notwendig historisch. . . . In der Theorie der Historie waltet die Geschichte als das Unumgängliche."

mighty phenomena of which I can speak here in only the broadest terms, and which have been unleashed as the first of Nietzsche's next two centuries has ended, and we enter the second.

The two centuries in question are, above all, European, and this book is essentially about Europe. In saying this there is a great danger—that every non-European, or everyone who thinks himself to have overcome the "Eurocentrism" of modern thought, will decide "this book is not for me." To say these centuries are Europe's is to understand the extent to which Europe has overtaken the world. North America, that site of the improvement and overcoming of Europe, is itself an entirely European affair. Karl Marx was in no doubt that Europe—even Germany alone—was the vanguard of progress toward communism: he was no nationalist or provincial thinker. To think that Europe can be, or has been, "overcome" and left behind, is itself a colonization of the worst kind, for to believe that the foremost intellectual ideas are themselves a vanguard which have already reached far beyond the shores of Europe in laying hold of the whole planet through a single grasp is already to be oneself in the grip of the essence of European, Western, thought, and so not its overcoming. Heidegger noted in a lecture in 1957 that—for just three examples—the worlds of ancient India, China, and Japan remained ever more lost to thinking: "this question becomes ever more urgent, as European thinking threatens evermore to become planetary, so that today Indians, the Chinese and Japanese in many cases can only pass on the matter of their experiences in our European manners of thought." In this kind of Eurocentrism, everything becomes a "mishmash" so that we no longer know "whether the ancient Indians were English empiricists or whether Lao-tzu was a Kantian."[5]

Europe is no longer a particular place on the surface of the globe, but rather it is the manner in which all who wield power (often by most denying that they do) seize upon, and attempt to grasp in action and thought, the planet as a whole. Heidegger distinguished the German term *Abendland*—the land of the evening, of the passing of the day, and the preparation for the new beginning (the day that is yet to come), from the word "Europe," by which latter term he meant the entire West and its planetary reach (he even at one time speaks of Europe and Asia as "Eurasian," and a single place, by which he meant to indicate the essential identity and uniformity of Western

5. Martin Heidegger, *Bremer und Freiburger Vorträge* (*GA*79), 145–46. "Diese Frage wird um so brennender, als das europäische Denken auch darin planetarisch zu werden droht, daß die heutigen Inder, Chinesen und Japaner uns das von ihnen Erfahrene vielfach nur noch in unserer europäischen Denkweise zutragen . . . ob die alten Inder englische Empiristen waren und Laotse ein Kantianer."

political forms with "Bolshevism").[6] For this reason I have employed the term "Europe" to speak of what Heidegger terms either Europe or, more rarely, "the Western"; and the word "Occident," denoting the falling or dying away of the sun, for when he specifically refers to the *Abendland,*[7] or "evening land." Heidegger understands that, as the opening toward the "other beginning" of which we will learn something as we proceed, "the evening-land is the future of history,"[8] and so is the promise of what comes *after* the twilight of the end, and what unfolds after we have undergone the rediscovery of the meaning of the darkness of the night. The Occident is, for Heidegger, a word which yields the meaning of our history: by contrast the merely European, or Western, is the drive to seize the planet, to grasp and dominate it through the essence of technology, a drive which occludes the Occidental destiny.

To return to action: does thought give rise to events, or are events the basis for ideas? This is the riddle of metaphysics, from beginning to end. This riddle, this *question,* which lies at the heart of these two centuries, lies at the center of this book. At the same time, the riddle of metaphysics will turn out to be the riddle of subjectivity, as we shall see. Who is the subject of this book, and for whom is it written? The question of subjectivity, of how to understand the human person and what humanity *is* (how the subject thinks and acts) has also formed the basis of the intellectual and spiritual struggle over the future of thinking, and the future of Europe and the planet as a whole, that came to such a refinement in the nineteenth century and has given birth to the ideas of its successor and our own. Even more than René Descartes was Immanuel Kant the thinker of modernity's understanding of subjectivity. Hegel, Marx, Nietzsche, and Heidegger are each responding to questions that are Kant's legacy for modern thinking. Kant is the thinker par excellence of the *Übersinnliche,* the "supersensible," that unity of the subject which constitutes the formal ground and cause of its freedom and is the origin of practical (ethical) action in the human subject, over against the visible appearances of the things of nature. Kant in several places posited a formal, seemingly unbridgeable division between the supersensible and the realm of sense, although he does concede that the power or faculty of judgment, because it can grasp nature as an end (the ground of grasping the planet as a

6. See Martin Heidegger, *Das Ereignis* (*GA*71), 95, §131, "'Abendland' und Europa" and §132 "Das Abendland und Europa."

7. On one occasion at least Heidegger explicitly distinguished the *Abendland* from the Occident, as a way of repudiating the cultural pessimism of Spengler, but to have replicated this in my English translations would have meant leaving the word *Abendland* untranslated, an unsatisfactory solution.

8. Martin Heidegger, *Das Ereignis* (*GA*71), 96. "Das Abendland ist die Zukunft der Geschichte."

whole), can constitute such a bridge.[9] This is not the place to examine Kant's determining of the supersensible (although we will explore it in depth as we proceed), but rather to understand that from Hegel hence, and certainly in Nietzsche's two hundred years, a tireless war has been waged on the supersensible in its every form, through thought and deed. Marx's drive for a fully concrete materialism is born from this war: but not less is Heidegger's determined understanding—expressed as early as 1925—that "philosophical research is and remains atheism,"[10] adding "and precisely in this atheism [it] becomes what a great man once called the 'Gay Science.'"[11] Heidegger speaks here of Nietzsche, in whose *The Gay Science* (*Die Fröhliche Wissenschaft*) is recounted the proclamation of the death of God: his argument is that with the historical *event* of the death of God, the identification of God and being has finally come apart, so that the *question* of being and its meaning is reopened all over again.

The centrality of Marx's writing to modern thought means that Marx's terms are very familiar to us. Marx was not, in any case, a particular innovator of terms, even as he was an innovative thinker. Class, surplus value, commodity fetishism, alienation, realism, "nature," historical and dialectical materialism, humanism (and its counter-essence, antihumanism)—all of these and the character in which Marx (and Engels) speak have become part of the intellectual fabric of Western thought. This is not because we have absorbed Marx and Marxism—unwittingly, as it were—but because Marx spoke, and still speaks, not just to, but *for* and *of* the age in which we *are*. Marx's familiarity to us is because ours is first his voice, when (whatever our "personal" political commitments) we think socially: his voice, as much as Nietzsche's, *is* and *will continue to be* the narrator's, as we live the unfolding history of these two hundred years.

Heidegger's language is altogether more strange. A master of the German language on the level of Martin Luther or Friedrich Nietzsche, Heidegger has often been accused (either approvingly, or with disdain) of coining neologisms to weave a poetic, even mystical, language for thinking. Much of Heidegger's German translates, or has been translated, only poorly into English (which is invariably hardly the fault of the translators, as my own at-

9. See Immanuel Kant, *Kritik der Urteilskraft,* 107 and following. See also Kant's letter to Johann Heinrich Tieftrunk of December 11, 1797, in Immanuel Kant, *Briefwechsel,* §411, 757–61, especially 756.

10. Martin Heidegger, *Prolegomena zur Geschichte des Zeitbegriffs* (*GA*20), 109–10. "Philosophische Forschung ist und bleibt Atheismus."

11. Martin Heidegger, *Prolegomena zur Geschichte des Zeitbegriffs* (*GA*20), 110. "Und gerade in diesem Atheismus wird sie zu dem, was ein Großer einmal sagte, zur 'Fröhlichen Wissenschaft.'"

tempts to translate him have proved to me too frequently). Heidegger himself was aware of how newly arrived the German tongue was to the language of thinking, and he commented on issues of translation in many of his lecture courses and public writings.[12] The tradition of widespread knowledge of classical languages in Germanic centers of study (we should recall that the nation of "Germany" is itself an object of nineteenth-century manufacture, the effect of the statecraft of Otto von Bismarck) lasted for far longer than in France—where revolution and the love of all things new put paid to the learning of antiquity—or England—where education was progressively reordered to producing a colonial civil service or for mercantile and industrial success—neither goal finding much use for classics. We take for granted that a term in one language has an immediate cognate in another. Heidegger was often at pains to point out that translation from one language to another tends to seize upon one meaning in an otherwise polysemic term which, in rendering that well, excludes the others. All too often the very significance of the term and its employment is its polysemy—what it is able to suggest and draw forth in its penumbra, as much as what it directly says. On one occasion, he cites the example of the translation of a phrase employed by Greek mathematicians, *koinai ennoiai,* into German as *allgemeine angenommene Vorstellungen.* Heidegger notes that "Plato was fond of this word; it says: insight, to get insight, and, indeed, with the inner eye."[13]

Reginald Lilly, who translated these passages of Heidegger into English, reads *allgemeine angenommene Vorstellungen* as "universally assumed ideas,"[14] but they could just as well be translated as "generally perceived representations." Plato's *koinai ennoiai,* more literally "things commonly in-minded," does indicate community of knowledge, but not in the sense of an already-agreed meaning (as "universally assumed ideas" might suggest) but as what *might* give you the same insight as I *might* have, were we to be granted the insight that a thing can give to the one well attuned to it and capable of rising up to reach it. This is very far from Gottfried Leibniz's view, as Heidegger understands it, that the *allgemeine angenommene Vorstellungen* are in each case "what is held by all as obvious": aptitude, capacity, alertness, success, and—far from psychological capability—what can be *granted* by

12. Heidegger's discussions of issues of translation are too numerous to cite. Much of the subject matter of the lecture course *Der Satz vom Grund* (*GA*10) is concerned with issues of translation, and the issue is repeatedly discussed in *Was heißt Denken* (*GA*8), where Heidegger says (178) "jede Übersetzung ist aber schon Auslegung" ("each translation is, however, already interpretation").

13. See Martin Heidegger, *Der Satz vom Grund* (*GA*10), 22. "Platon gebraucht das Wort gern; es besagt: Einblick, Einblick nehmen und zwar mit dem geistigen Auge."

14. Martin Heidegger, *The Principle of Reason* (*GA*10), trans. Reginald Lilly, 15.

what is thought *of* (and so also the moment, the mood, the place) are all of far greater consequence.[15] Heidegger's argument is that to deliberate across these meanings allows us slowly to tease out both their possibilities and their history of interpretation, and so to bring ourselves into a thoughtful proximity with both what they mean now, and how we learn to discover what they originally meant. Heidegger concludes that "the possibilities for thoughtful conversation with a tradition that nurtures and invigorates us fails, because instead we consign our speaking in electronic thought- and calculation-machines, an occurrence which will lead modern technology and knowledge to completely new procedures and unforeseen consequences, that perhaps will push aside reflective thinking as something useless and therefore disposable."[16] Anyone who has ever lifted a sentence or definition from an online "community encyclopedia" to embellish an argument or even just a footnote should understand instantly what it is that Heidegger names here.

Heidegger did coin neologisms, but many of these were developments of words either already present in the tradition, or renderings into German of Greek terms. *Dasein,* literally "here-being" (and never "being-there"),[17] can also mean "existence" and "presence," and is a word to be found all over the works of Kant, Hegel, and Marx himself. *Mitsein,* meaning "with-being," which Heidegger (in *Being and Time* especially) expanded into *Miteinandersein,* "being-with-one-another," is a literal rendering of the Greek word *sunousia,* "with-being," "together-being," which can mean community, sociality, society, "society" (in the older English sense of "company"), and (among other meanings) even sexual copulation. Perhaps one of Heidegger's least understood, but most abused, neologisms is "ontotheology," a term he developed specifically in explanation of Hegel's thought, and so which will concern us later. Ontotheology names the whole of metaphysics, and names this whole by naming how every being (Greek *on*) is taken as a "thing" to be inquired into, and so is taken in relation to what is most "beingful" in the thing, which Aristotle had defined as either "first or highest being" and then "theology." The theology in question was at first nothing to do with Abraham

15. Martin Heidegger, *Der Satz vom Grund* (*GA*10), 23, quoting Leibniz's Latin formulation "quae ab omnibus pro manfestis habentur." The Latin literally says "things which are held by all for having been made evident" (compare Leibniz, "Consilium de Encyclopædia nova conscribenda methodo inventoria," 32).

16. Martin Heidegger, *Der Satz vom Grund* (*GA*10), 22. "Weil die Möglichkeiten des denkenden Gesprächs mit einer uns erregenden, fördersamen Überlieferung fehlen, weil wir statt dessen unser Sprechen in die elektronischen Denk- und Rechenmaschinen hineinschicken, ein Vorgang, der die moderne Technik und Wissenschaft zu völlig neuen Verfahrensweisen und unabsehbaren Erfolgen führen wird, die vermutlich das besinnliche Denken als etwas Unnützes und darum Entbehrliches abdrängen."

17. See the discussion of Heidegger's rejection of this translation on 31, n. 44.

and was not Jewish, Christian, or Islamic, but in antiquity named the "essence" of the gods, and so the totality and entirety of what is "most beingful." For Aristotle, it named what of a thing is "divine" and so expressive of the *aei on*—the "being-ever-same" that is the property of the gods. In what Heidegger calls the "christianisation of philosophy" this becomes (the revealed, Abrahamic) God himself, as that one who is "most in being" and so who gives being to all particular beings. This "giving being" is also to be understood as "causing each being to be," a philosophical rendering of the first line of the biblical Book of Genesis "In the beginning God created the heavens and the earth." Ontotheology names the whole tradition of metaphysics from its inception in Plato and Aristotle, through its theistic entanglements, up to Hegel, and so beyond. In this sense, Heidegger first coined the word "Onto-ego-theo-logy," the "ego" in question naming Hegel's "absolute subjectivity," which we will examine in great detail, and which names the whole of metaphysics as both a psychology and the humanism with which divinity, God, and being became wrapped up.

The riddle of subjectivity underpins the whole of the dialogue this book attempts to enter. That riddle is given in the indeterminacy of the subjectivity of the subject in the metaphysics of Hegel and Nietzsche—the metaphysics which Marx and Heidegger confront. The subjectivity of the subject, given in the pure *ego cogito* which accompanies every self-reflexion of the being of being-human, is at the same time empty. The word *cogito* is ordinarily translated as "I think" but can just as well mean "I deliberate" and even "I act": it stands in contrast to the other verb for thinking that Descartes uses, *intelligo:* "I know"; "I understand."

The distinction in two forms of knowledge—*intelligo* and *cogito*—Descartes had in effect received from the origin of philosophy, a distinction described by Aristotle. Aristotle suggests that there are two ways in which something is true. The first, he says, is what is seen for itself: "the seeing of a particular thing is true" (elsewhere he speaks of this as "always" true),[18] and this "seeing" refers to thinking (*nous*) directly, and recognizes the thing in its "being true," its essence,[19] such that this is not some concern about how it is to be described or said.[20] The second, however, concerns speaking of some thing through assertion and denial, such that it is understood with respect to the true and the false.[21] What is said with respect to the true and the false is, for Descartes, always grounded in the will, rather than the intellect. It is for

18. Aristotle, *De anima,* 430b29–30. τὸ ὁρᾶν τοῦ ἰδίου ἀληθές (πᾶς, ἀεὶ).

19. Aristotle, *De anima,* 430b28–29. ὁ τοῦ τί ἐστι κατά τὸ ἦν εἶναι.

20. Aristotle, *De anima,* 430b29. οὐ τὶ κατά τινος.

21. Aristotle, *De anima,* 430b25–26. ἔστι δ'ή μὲν φάσις τι κατὰ τινος, ὥσπερ ἡ κατάφασις, καὶ ἀληθὴς ἢ ψεθδὲς πᾶσα.

this reason that Descartes selects the verb *cogitare* for the establishment of the subjectivity of the subject in the indubitability of the statement *cogito, ergo sum.* This statement is not the result of a proof, or a syllogism, but a matter so self-evident that it is outside the realm of every possible doubt, and so is inerrant. It is the one statement which, belonging to the sphere of what is deliberative (the realm of "the true and the false"), whenever spoken by a subject, must *only* be true.

For Descartes, what the intellect knows, it knows absolutely, and as a matter of fact. However, whereas the will of God cannot err, the will of man not only can, but routinely does err. The human will is, of its very nature, errant. If Descartes can find *one* truth that the will knows and which cannot be said to err, then he has established a connection between the actually infinite will of God and the only potentially infinite will of man. That truth is cogito. *Cogitare* has an active sense: it is *essentially* a productive thought. To cogitate is not to twiddle the thumbs, but *productively* to think the "I"-think, actively to represent the self *to* the self. Such a thinking is also a doing. Several times Heidegger drew attention to the etymology of *cogitare* as *co-agitatio,* from Latin *co-*, meaning "with," "alongside and together," and *agere,* "to act, to do."[22] The riddle of metaphysics—of the question of the relative priority of thinking and acting, acting and thinking—lies at the heart of the establishment of the subjectivity of the subject, and it lies at the heart of what follows from the death of God. We shall see that Marx effortlessly takes over this place of God for the sake of man, when he describes man alone as the creative one, that one who creates by producing his own future. For to produce is to create, and creation, hitherto and in the epoch of theistic metaphysics, is the one action proper to God (which man can only imitate, after the fact of his own creation). As Heidegger himself tersely noted: "the *agere* as *facere, creare.*" We would paraphrase this as: "humanly to act is to make, to create."[23] This is the fundamental connection that comes to be established in the history of thought between Latin *agere* and Greek *ergon*—work, labor, *doing.* The subject produces and creates, in virtue of the will. The will, in thinking, acts. Heidegger shows how "this *co-agitatio* is, therefore, *in itself* already *velle,* willing. With the subjectivity of the subject will comes to appearance as the essence of subjectivity."[24] The will, in acting, thinks. This

22. Compare Martin Heidegger: "Die Zeit des Weltbildes" (*GA*5), 110; "Nietzsches Wort: Gott ist Tot" (*GA*5), 243; "Entwürfe zur Geschichte des Seins als Metaphysik" (*GA*6.2), 426.

23. Martin Heidegger, "Entwürfe zur Geschichte des Seins als Metaphysik" (*GA*6.2), 432. "Die ἐνέργεια wird umgedeutet zur actualitas des actus. Das agere als facere, creare." The first part says "*Energeia* comes to be reinterpreted as the actuality of the thing done."

24. Martin Heidegger, "Nietzsches Wort: Gott ist Tot" (*GA*5), 243. "Die co-agitatio aber ist *in sich* schon velle, wollen. *Mit* der Subjektität des Subjekts kommt als deren Wesen der Wille zum Vorschein" (Heidegger's emphasis).

possibility opens up only in the history of metaphysics as it is thought from Plato and Aristotle up to Marx and Nietzsche. Indeed, in establishing the distinction between factual, "visible" (self-evident) truth and deliberative truth—the distinction on which Descartes draws to establish the subjectivity of the subject—we find Aristotle wondering why this distinction was not noticed by anyone before.[25]

The subjectivity of the subject is two-sided. On the one hand, subjectivity establishes the human being as a pure postulate, a self-representation to itself: as such this postulate is indeterminate in itself. The subject is prior to gender, class, education, history, color, race, sexuality, ability, belief, and so on. On the other hand, in order to bring about its determinations, the subject has to act, or rather *en*act the subjectivity that it *is:* it becomes the things that it *does* or *represents* in the "outer" world. A conventional, and purely psychological account of this enacting determines subjectivity from out of "drives" and "lacks," the fulfillment of "needs." None of this explains the moment of extreme risk and confrontation with nullity undertaken by the acting subject, who wills, to become. Descartes was largely unconcerned with this aspect of subjectivity, but Kant illustrates the essential connection between cogitation and the justification required *for* every cogitation. Kant refers to this as the problem of "how, in particular, subjective conditions of thought can have objective validity": how they might *become.*[26] This, as Heidegger points out, is how "Kant, in his critical foundation of metaphysics thinks the ultimate self-securing of transcendental subjectivity as the *quaestio iuris* of the transcendental deduction"—it is, in other words, how justice, "justification," *for* the subject is secured as "self-justification."[27] Every act of will of the willing subject is subject to justification, and must be justified in order to establish its validity. Risk and nullity are overcome by the justification of the self in self-justification: "I have the right to be, or do, *this* that I am, or enact."

Nietzsche's understanding of justice and justification (*Gerechtigkeit*) is the ground from out of which he establishes the differences between sub-

25. See Aristotle, *De anima,* 427a22–b10. Aristotle mentions Empedocles explicitly, but then goes on to speak of all the "earlier ones" (οἵ ἀρχαῖοι) who preceded him and failed to make this distinction. It seems to elude him (unless he is being ironic) that the distinction was never made because the earlier thinkers were thinking in a quite different way about the nature of ἀλήθεια, "truth," and that Aristotle's distinction is therefore a genuine innovation.

26. Immanuel Kant, *Kritik der reinen Vernunft,* 129 (A89; B123). "Wie nämlich subjektive Bedingungen des Denkens objektive Gültigkeit haben [sollten]."

27. Martin Heidegger, "Nietzsches Wort: Gott ist Tot" (*GA*5), 245. "Kant denkt in seiner kritischen Grundlegung der Metaphysik die letzte Selbstsicherung der transzendentalen Subjektivität als die quaestio iuris der transzendentalen Deduktion. . . . Recht-fertigung . . . Selbst-Gerechtigkeit."

jects. Justice retains its connection with legality only in the sense that justice legitimates and authorizes difference, differentiation as such. Inasmuch as I can lay claim to a justification, I can lay claim to the value on which I am set and it cannot, without justice, be taken from me. Nietzsche argues that "merely to possess the will is in no way sufficient":[28] rather, "truly, no one has a higher claim to our veneration than he who possesses the drive and strength for justice."[29] We must hear this sentence in all its Nietzschean irony, as a reworking of Kant's opening remarks to the section concerning the "Transcendental Deduction" of the *Critique of Pure Reason* with its reference to law and jurists.[30] For if justice has hitherto been a matter of establishing the truth (in law), now the law of the will is to establish the truth by means of justification. Morality is established from out of the justification that any subject can summon in defense of his or her cogitation. Every contemporary politics functions in this manner. Nevertheless, we must understand what this means: for the will to power as Nietzsche understands it is *not* the "will to will" in the most obvious sense of "I must get what I want, all I need is to dare to will, to get it." Justice means that, for instance, every commanding political leader experiences the command to lead from out of the will to power as a *destiny* to which he or she is justified, and to which he has to rise up to attain. Justice confers, not the enactment of a supervenient sense of power, but the attainment to a sense of entitlement. Every leader called into this destiny does so for the sake of all other social relations which flow from that leadership: "I am the one destined to undertake this task for *all your sakes*": "I do this for you: each and all."

The most public and prevailing concept in contemporary political discourse is indeed that of "justice." A battle cry of the Left,[31] it names something so immediately intelligible to the modern world that it is increasingly taken up with equal force in the rhetoric of the Right. It is in this sense that the politics of Left and Right (and every other politics besides—identity politics, ecological politics, the politics of animal rights, and so forth) is on the way to being better explained by Nietzsche than by Marx. Or rather

28. Friedrich Nietzsche, vol. 1, *Unzeitgemäße Betrachtungen,* 287. "Es genügt durchaus nicht, den Willen dazu allein zu haben."

29. Friedrich Nietzsche, vol. 1, *Unzeitmäßige Betrachtungen,* 287. "Wahrlich, niemand hat in höherem Grade einen Anspruch auf unsere Verehrung als der, welcher den Trieb und die Kraft zur Gerechtigkeit besitzt."

30. Compare Immanuel Kant, *Kritik der reinen Vernunft,* 125 (A84; B117).

31. See, for example, the character of Alain Badiou's, in his play *L'incident de Antioch,* and whom he quotes in his *L'hypothèse communiste.* In the name of the revolution, she speaks repeatedly of the "will to justice," "the consciousness that organizes justice," and "the history of justice." Alain Badiou, *L'hypothèse communiste,* 23, 25. "La volonté de justice . . . la conscience, qui organise la justice . . . l'histoire de la justice."

we should say, Nietzsche foresaw what politics would become: justice is not a moral question: rather morality (or, as we would now say, ethics) is to be established through the self-justification of the subjectivity of the subject. Every subjectivity, to exist and appear in the social sphere, must be able to justify its place. To achieve this, my claim to justice must be unassailable: you must give me justice because you can find no reason to deny me. In this, justification retains its essential connection with law as it is understood in contemporary liberal democracy.

If this is Nietzsche's view, then not so Marx,[32] who (in savaging the pretensions of the "socialists" who founded social democracy in Germany) held justice in contempt, describing it as a merely bourgeois concept: "do not the bourgeois assert, that today the distribution of property is 'just'? And is it not in fact the only 'just' distribution on the basis of today's means of production?"[33] Marx asks, "are economic relations regulated through concepts of justice, or do the relations of justice not spring the other way about, from the economic?"[34] The question is rhetorical (anticipating Nietzsche's own reversal of the meaning of justice): for Marx, economic relations determine social relations (like those of justice and right), which is why the *inevitable* development of economic relations is at the same time the inevitable development of the social. In *Das Kapital,* Marx expressly connects relations of will with economic relations. Every contractual, legal relation (relation of justice) is a reflection of the real economic relations that pertain and make them possible: "the contents of this relation of will or justice is given through the economic relation itself."[35]

Heidegger also advances no concept of justice, although he discusses Nietzsche's understanding of justice not once, but repeatedly. An entire division of Heidegger's 1938–39 seminar on the second of Nietzsche's *Untimely Meditations* was devoted to the relation in Nietzsche between justice and truth.[36] If justice is the basis for the establishment and justification of difference between subjects, both Heidegger and Marx (in contradistinction to

32. A. M. Shandro, in attempting to formulate a Marxist theory of justice, provides a good survey of the American, French, and Soviet literature that discusses the extent to which no theory of justice exists in Marx. A. M. Shandro, "A Marxist Theory of Justice?" especially 27–30.

33. Karl Marx, "Kritik des Gothaer Programms" (*MEW*19), 19. "Behaupten die Bourgeois nicht, daß die heutige Verteilung 'gerecht' ist? Und ist sie in der Tat nicht die einzige 'gerechte' Verteilung auf Grundlage der heutigen Produktionsweise?"

34. Karl Marx, "Kritik des Gothaer Programms" (*MEW*19), 19. "Werden die ökonomischen Verhältnisse durch Rechtsbegriffe geregelt, oder entspringen nicht umgekehrt die Rechtsverhältnisse aus den ökonomischen?"

35. Karl Marx, *Das Kapital* (*MEW*23), 99. "Der Inhalt dieses Rechts- oder Willensverhältnisses ist durch das ökonomische Verhältnis selbst gegeben."

36. Compare Martin Heidegger, *Zur Auslegung von Nietzsches II.* Unzeitgemäßer Betrachtung (*GA*46), 157–97.

Hegel and Nietzsche) share a radical rejection of the claims of justice. On the one hand, Marx seeks to show how all differentiation between subjects will be overcome through the highest development of economic relations. This development will result in an absolute equalization of every subject, so that the inequalities of surplus value will be replaced, not by the abolition of value, but by each participating fully in the value he creates. Heidegger, on the other hand, seeks to show how the end of metaphysics is itself the overcoming of subjectivity: in this sense justice as an effect of the will to power is overcome by *dikē* (ordinarily translated from the Greek as "justice"). Heidegger says of *dikē* "just as impossible as the interpretation of the [Greek] polis on the basis of the modern state or the Roman *res publica* is the interpretation of this *dikē* in the sense of modern justice and the Roman *iustitia.*"[37] Heidegger translates *dikē* "as the jointure, which ordains for humanity the relations of its comportments."[38] The word I have translated as "jointure" (*der Fug*) literally means a join (like a dovetail) in a wooden construction that is fixed using no nail or screw. The word has resonance both with what is ordered by fate (*vom Schicksal gefügt*), but also that which is *fügsam,* "obedient." Obedient to what and to whom we will only discover in understanding Heidegger's own political engagement, as we proceed. What Heidegger seeks to convey is a proper "fittedness" of human life, its being held together in its relations without compulsion or constraint, but in proper order.[39] Heidegger does not say so here, but it is clear that in releasing himself into what is ordained for him, Heidegger thinks that man encounters genuine *dikē* as a freedom.

Marx and Heidegger reject the contemporary "juridical" understanding of justice because each understands that what is truly at issue for humanity is not what man wills for himself, but rather what is ordered and ordained for humanity, which then lets humanity truly come to be, that which (although Marx never speaks in these terms) is fated for humanity and into which it grows up, rather than what it simply wills as its choice or desire: in this they both thought alike and yet did not think the same. It is this understanding of "the political," and what Marx and Heidegger understood this to mean, that truly concerns this book and the dialogue it seeks to unfold.

37. Martin Heidegger, *Parmenides* (*GA*54), 142–43. "Gleich unmöglich wie die Deutung der πόλις aus dem neuzeitlichen Staat oder aus der römischen res publica ist die Deutung der δίκη aus der neuzeitlichen Gerechtigkeit und der römischen iustitia."

38. Martin Heidegger, *Parmenides* (*GA*54), 143. "Die δίκη als der Fug, der das Menschentum in die Verhältnisse seines Verhaltens weisend fügt."

39. "Order" is the word chosen by the English translators of this text. Compare André Schuwer and Richard Rojcewicz, *Martin Heidegger: Parmenides* (*GA*54), 96.

*Chapter 1*

# Interpretations of Heidegger and Marx

KARL MARX AND Martin Heidegger are each in their own right among the most commented-on and discussed thinkers of the recent period. Each has had a formative influence on not just one, but many, schools of thought, interpretation, and in Marx's case, political practice. Even among those who would bear the name "Marxist," we find vastly differing interpretations of Marx. On the other hand, those who have attempted to place Marx and Heidegger side by side or put them into dialogue of any kind have been few. Philosophically, both thinkers stand in a strong tradition of writing after Hegel—and of the self-conscious repudiation of Hegel, although for Marx and Heidegger this takes quite different forms. Both are strongly influenced by Aristotle (as indeed, was Hegel), although this book will only glimpse, and only very much later, the confrontation with Aristotle that underlies the dialogue between them. Heidegger apparently only rarely, and then never systematically, engaged with Marx, but as we shall see later, there are constant intimations that his reading of Marx (and other Marxists, Lenin included) ran far deeper than is commonly supposed. This chapter begins with Heidegger's most publicly visible commentary on Marx (a commentary he makes in other places in the same decade)[1] before examining how other thinkers have sought to bring Marx and Heidegger together. This provides the preliminary backdrop of the contrasting understanding of the "productive dialogue" that the following chapters will develop, a dialogue which (to my knowledge) has not been attempted on this scale before.

To bring Marx and Heidegger into proximity in this way immediately brings before us the common language that they share. Marx and Heidegger *both* inquire into, and take up, the range of terms that was established before them, especially in the tradition of German idealism, beginning with Kant, and more fully developed in Hegel and Friedrich Schelling. Marx and Hei-

1. See for just two examples Martin Heidegger, "Zeichen" (*GA*13), 211; "Kants These über das Sein" (*GA*9), 447.

degger both speak of the nation or people (*Volk*), but also *Dasein* (existence, presence), which immediately throws into relief much of the commentary on these two terms in subsequent literature (some of which we will examine) that has understood Heidegger's use of the term *Volk* in *Being and Time* in 1927 to be evidence of his proto-Nazism, or *Dasein* to have been a term unique to Heidegger. It is worth recalling how recently the German language had become a philosophical language—arguably only with Kant. Kant's immediate predecessors, the Silesian Christian Wolff, the Berliner Alexander Baumgarten, and before them the almost pan-European Gottfried Leibniz, had all written the burden of their philosophical work in either Latin, or in Leibniz's case, Latin and French. German had, until the Enlightenment in which Kant, and to a lesser extent Gotthold Lessing, were such central figures, been a demotic, rather than technical, speech. When Marx speaks in 1843 of how Germany assumed only theoretically (and so in its philosophy) the progress that other Western nations had made in practice (and so in fulfilment of their history),[2] he is speaking of a Germany that is *itself* at the time a theoretical rather than geographical unity (attaining its greatest size only in 1870 under Bismarck), and a philosophy that was truly articulated in the German language only within living memory. The freshness and promise of all Marx names with this statement is barely visible to us now, and yet is itself for Marx the very evidence of an upsurge of possibility of vast import, proportion, and vitality.

In 1969 Heidegger raised the question of Marx, as if spontaneously, in a television interview with Richard Wisser.[3] Taking Marx's "Theses on Feuerbach" from a bookshelf adjacent to where he was seated, Heidegger proceeded (without looking up the place) to read the eleventh (last) thesis and to comment on it:[4]

> The question of the demand for world change leads us back to Karl Marx's frequently quoted statement from his "Theses on Feuerbach." I would like to quote it exactly and read out loud: "Philosophers have only *interpreted* the world differently; what matters is to *transform* it." When this statement is cited *and* when it is followed, it is overlooked that changing the world presupposes a change in the *positing of the world*. A positing of the world can only be won by adequately *interpreting* the world. That means: Marx's demand for a "change" is based upon a very definite interpretation of the world, and therefore this statement is proved to be without foundation. It gives the im-

2. See the discussion of this on 130.

3. The interview with Richard Wisser was broadcast on the German television channel ZDF on September 24, 1969, and again the day after Heidegger's death, on May 27, 1976.

4. Karl Marx, "Thesen über Feuerbach" (*MEW*3), 7.

pression that it speaks decisively against philosophy, whereas the second half of the statement presupposes, unspoken, a demand for philosophy.[5]

What appears at first to be so decisive a dismissal of Marx is, of course, nothing of the kind. It is hardly accidental that, in 1969, the question of Marx and the consequences of what he thought should have been to the fore: a little more than a year before there had been a near-social revolution in France, led in part by Marxist influences, and which had repercussions across Europe and especially, for Heidegger, in West Germany, given the widespread student movements that followed it there. The cold war with the Soviet Union, with its concomitant, the constant threat of nuclear annihilation, was the backdrop of international relations. Communism was counterposed to social democracy in every region of the globe: either directly, or in the spirited struggle for influence.

What Heidegger exposes is not the marginal character of Marx, but an ambiguity, one that persists to the present day: does thought produce action, or is every action preparatory for what is to be thought? What does it mean to interpret the world? And in interpreting the world, why does interpretation differ with respect to who interprets, and when? Is there a single interpretation of the world, which is "true," and against which every particular interpretation is ultimately to be measured? Or is all interpretation merely grounded in the particularity of "standpoint," mine, and yours, and theirs? The implication of Marx's statement is that change overcomes difference: transformation is a unifying force. How so? Into this Heidegger inserts his own thinking: from where does the demand for thinking, for philosophy, spring? From the experience of change; or from the need to interpret; or does it spring forth from a decisive standpoint that already holds in view, and so has decided (despite the way the world *is*) how the world *should* be? And in this latter, if we know what should be on the basis of what is *not*, then from whence did that knowledge of what we know *should* pertain spring, given that it did not spring from the conditions of things as they *are*, but rather

5. Martin Heidegger, "Martin Heidegger im Gespräch" (*GA*16), 703. "Die Frage nach der Forderung der Weltveränderung führt auf einen vielzitierten Satz von Karl Marx aus den 'Thesen über Feuerbach' zurück. Ich will ihn ganz zitieren und vorlesen: 'Die Philosophen haben die Welt nur verschieden *interpretiert;* es kömmt darauf an, sie zu *verändern.*' Bei der Zitation dieses Satzes *und* bei der Befolgung dieses Satzes übersieht man, daß eine Weltveränderung eine Änderung der *Weltvorstellung* voraussetzt und daß eine Weltvorstellung nur dadurch zu gewinnen ist, daß man die Welt zureichend *interpretiert.* Das heißt: Marx fußt auf einer ganz bestimmten Weltinterpretation, um seine 'Veränderungen' zu fordern, und dadurch erweist sich dieser Satz als nicht fundierter Satz. Er erweckt den Eindruck, als sei entschieden gegen die Philosophie gesprochen, während im zweiten Teil des Satzes unausgesprochen die Forderung nach einer Philosophie vorausgesetzt ist" (Heidegger's and Wisser's emphases from the published transcripts).

as they are *not*? How *then* do conditions determine "consciousness," where consciousness would function as a name for thinking? Is it at this point that dialectic enters in?

We are again living through a period of economic and political turmoil which threatens new political upheaval and uncertainty on a scale not seen since twice in the twentieth century, when civil turmoil in Europe was plunged into the pursuit of politics by other means: in the worldwide waging of war. Such warfare is so far from being a possibility in the present age that the governments of the West, and globally, now seek with all iron force to manage and assure the future of their political economies (in every resonance of that term) by managing the direction and processes of production while at the same time taking the planet as a whole in hand through every means of technical control and manipulation. For good or ill, we are not witnessing the end of history, but its return with intensified imperative. We learn that the fate of the whole planet is at stake in what comes next. The power of the state, and its abilities to interact with corporations as the means of the global management of political economy in face of this apocalypse, is about to be yet further refined and enhanced, which means all the questions that beset the globe and came to a certain head in the 1930s return in a new and intensified way. Our every good and optimistic intention for a "better" future is co-opted and coerced into a collaboration with a metaphysical and a moral imperative whose ground at the same time remains obscure and difficult to exhibit. This *is* the imperative voice of the renewed state: the moral injunction to avert the end of the world. The power of the state has nothing to do with the size of the state—indeed, it is the very invisibility of this force of management that lends it such power and effectiveness.

The claim to have, or even to desire and so need to acquire, the means to avert the end of the world is itself metaphysical. The attempt to manage, addressed as it is in an apocalyptic voice, and to mass audiences, the "we must" of so much contemporary political rhetoric, is orchestrated as much in public relations exercises and by means of careful interaction and negotiation with the organs of the mass media, as it is in actual actions to be taken or state organs to be established, and in fact represents the means of managing the destiny and future of the world as a whole. Nothing less is at issue than the world history of European thought (of which America is only yet another intensification). Not to understand this is to fail to understand what Heidegger means when he speaks of "metaphysics." To understand this is to understand how metaphysics, as that which speaks from, and of, the "beyond," nevertheless determines a fate and an outcome for all materiality, and so is always a politics.

The phrase "a productive dialogue" is taken from Martin Heidegger's *Letter on Humanism*, sometimes called the *Humanismusbrief*. Heidegger speaks here of the dimension within which a productive dialogue with Marxism becomes possible.[6] To open the way to speak with Marxism, we will concentrate on Heidegger's engagement with Karl Marx. This focus is because Heidegger almost always speaks specifically with respect to the texts and works of Marx, never with Engels, and although he refers to "Marxism" and "Bolshevism" at times, only on the rarest of occasions does he refer to other Marxists.[7] Heidegger's discussion of Marx is fragmentary, and there is no systematic or prolonged treatment of Marx or Marxism in any of Heidegger's works. Remarks and observations are scattered throughout his public lectures and more private notes and notebooks. In prewar Germany, the scope for an engagement with Marxism was extremely limited—after 1933 it could only have taken the form of Nazi-approved polemic. Postwar Germany, with the presence of the German Democratic Republic in the east, and in the light of Heidegger's own Nazi commitments prior to 1945, arguably afforded little additional opportunity. It is outside Germany that Heidegger speaks most freely of Marx, especially when he speaks with his French interlocutors—Beaufret, Sartre, Axelos. Nevertheless, I wish to disavow the truth of Kostas Axelos's claim that "Heidegger does not supply us with the basic outlines of a Marx interpretation"[8] by showing not only where, but also how, it is to be found. There *is* the beginning of a publicly available dialogue as early as the *Letter on Humanism,* nevertheless Heidegger wrapped his "Marx interpretation" up in a language that as much concealed, as made available, how it was to be understood. There is a sense in which this entire book is no more than a commentary on the passages in the *Letter on Humanism* where Heidegger carries this out.

The *Letter on Humanism* was written in the fall of 1946 as a response to a letter to Martin Heidegger by Jean Beaufret, the text of which is not currently in the public domain. The *Letter on Humanism* was first published in 1947, at a time when Europe was at one and the same time in ruins and on the threshold of an extended upswing of optimism and growth that would last for nigh on sixty years. This was the inception of a period marked by the fierce ideological clash between two seemingly antagonistic worldviews—Western capitalism and Soviet communism—that had together inflicted defeat on a third—Nazism and other forms of fascism and "national" socialism. Even before the Second World War, thinkers like Martin Heidegger and Ernst

6. Martin Heidegger, *Brief über den Humanismus* (GA9), 340. See 23, n. 12.

7. In a note in a bundle of slips seemingly from 1940, Heidegger cites Lenin's *Materialism and Empirico-Criticism* from 1909, and adds a quotation which he attributes to the Soviet pedagogical and industrial theorist (sentenced to death in Stalin's show trials in 1939) Alexei Gastev. Compare Martin Heidegger, *Leitgedanken zur Entstehung der Metaphysik* (GA76), 301.

8. Kostas Axelos, *Einführung in ein künftiges Denken: Über Marx und Heidegger,* 8. "Heidegger liefert uns nicht die Grundlinien einer Marx-Interpretation."

Jünger were claiming that these three, together with their related political forms, are to be understood from out of the same metaphysical ground. In 1930 Jünger had argued: "In Fascism, in Bolshevism, in Americanism, in Zionism, in the movements of non-white peoples, advance is made into a progress that would have been formerly unthinkable; in effect it performs a somersault, in order to continue its movement on a very simple level after a circle or circular movement of artificial dialectic."[9] In 1935 Heidegger claimed that "Russia and America are both, metaphysically viewed, the same."[10] Throughout his later public engagement with Jünger, Heidegger names all of this as a planetary "movement of nihilism."[11] How we are to understand that claim will be decisive for us in working out what Heidegger meant by "a productive dialogue."

What is intended by the phrase "a productive dialogue"? We live in an age when everything must, in order to be justifiable, be instrumentalized to a purpose. A productive dialogue therefore "solves" something or allows something to be done, to be achieved: there is always a better outcome ahead. Surely, therefore, we intend to put two "great" thinkers into a dialogue: Heidegger and Marx: Marx and Heidegger. To sit at their feet, and to "learn from" and "absorb" the clash of differences between them. Except that as an ambition nothing could be more shallow, unless we ourselves begin to think. Marx as the thinker of capital, and Heidegger as the thinker of being, surely, have nothing to say to each other? What is at issue in any dialogue? Rather, we should ask, what makes a thinker a *great* thinker? Is a great thinker so because everyone thinks he is great and therefore reads him? How could we enter into such a dialogue except by getting in between? All thinking thinks *of* something. Are we trying to think of Marx and of Heidegger—or are we not, rather, and in dialogue with them, trying to think *of* what they themselves thought *of*? Greatness in thought is that thinking which strives to be adequate to what it thinks of, and so with what it is concerned.

Heidegger's remark concerning a "productive dialogue" in the *Letter on Humanism* makes specific reference to the phenomenologist Edmund Husserl and the existentialist Sartre: "Since, however, neither Husserl, insofar as I can see up until now, nor Sartre recognise[s] the essentiality of

9. Ernst Jünger, "Die Totale Mobilmachung," 27. "Der Patriotismus wird durch einen modernen, stark mit Bewußtseinselementen durchsetzten Nationalismus abgelöst. Im Faschismus, im Bolschewismus, im Amerikanismus, im Zionismus, in den Bewegungen der farbigen Völker setzt der Fortschritt zu Vorstößen an, die man bisher für undenkbar gehalten hätte; er überschlägt sich gleichsam, um nach einem Zirkel der künstlichen Dialektik seine Bewegung auf einer sehr einfachen Ebene fortzusetzen."

10. Martin Heidegger, *Einführung in die Metaphysik* (*GA*40), 40. "Rußland und Amerika sind beide, metaphysisch gesehen, dasselbe."

11. Compare Martin Heidegger, *Zur Seinsfrage* (*GA*9), 386, 391–93, 395.

the historical in being, for that reason neither phenomenology nor existentialism enter into only that dimension within which a productive dialogue [*Gespräch*] with Marxism becomes possible."[12] Phenomenology, as the name for that kind of thinking that named a movement that attempted to follow in the wake of Edmund Husserl, Max Scheler, Karl Jaspers, and Heidegger, had sparked various attempts at dialogue with Marxism in the period before the Nazis came to power in Germany. In October 1945, Sartre had given a lecture to the Club Maintenant, published the following year under the title "Existentialism Is a Humanism," in which Sartre had explicitly sought a dialogue with communists from an atheistic existentialist standpoint (within which he included Martin Heidegger), and in which he asserted (following Francis Ponge) that "man is the future of man."[13] This future which is itself, for Sartre, a production of man is, as we shall see, already metaphysically the same as that future which Marx addresses. For Heidegger, an existentialism of this kind could not enter into a dialogue of *difference* with Marxism on the most essential ground, which Heidegger identifies here as that of history, because it already springs forth from that same ground in too much the same way. There was no difference to be attained. It seems extremely likely, but (to my knowledge) is unknown, whether Heidegger had any version of Sartre's essay to hand when he wrote the *Letter on Humanism.*

Of the three French figures who were closely allied and represented part of the nucleus of the very specific intellectual milieu out of which Sartre was speaking, Sartre, Beaufret, and Axelos, only Kostas Axelos was a formally committed Marxist. Axelos's dissertation, published in 1961 and translated into English in 1976 as *Alienation, Praxis, and Technē in the Thought of Karl Marx,* was the second volume of a trilogy whose overall title is *The Deployment of Errance,* and was strongly influenced by Heidegger (as the overall title suggests).[14] Axelos's most important contribution to Heidegger's dialogue with Marxism is his untranslated *Introduction to a Futural Thinking: On Marx and Heidegger* from 1966,[15] aspects of which he repeated for a French audience in the second of Jean Beaufret's four volumes of essays on

12. Martin Heidegger, *Brief über den Humanismus* (*GA*9), 340. "Weil aber weder Husserl noch, soweit ich bisher sehe, Sartre die Wesentlichkeit des Geschichtlichen im Sein erkennen, deshalb kommt weder die Phänomenologie, noch der Existentialismus in diejenige Dimension, innerhalb deren erst ein produktives Gespräch mit dem Marxismus möglich wird."

13. Jean-Paul Sartre, *L'existentialisme est un humanisme,* 38. For the reference to Heidegger, see Sartre, *L'existentialisme,* 17. Sartre was citing an article by the poet Francis Ponge, "Notes premières de l'homme," in *Les Temps Modernes* 1 (1945).

14. Kostas Axelos, *Le déploiement de l'errance.* The three titles under this heading were *Marx, penseur de la technique; Héraclite et la philosophie* (published in 1962); and *Vers la pensée planétaire* (published in 1964).

15. Kostas Axelos, *Einführung in ein künftiges Denken: Über Marx und Heidegger.*

Heidegger, under the title *The "Dialogue with Marxism" and the "Question of Technology,"* engaging directly with the *Letter on Humanism.*[16]

Axelos knew Heidegger personally through Beaufret, and there are hints in Axelos's texts that Heidegger (as he sometimes did with those who engaged with him) gave Axelos some personal access to material that has only very lately come into the public domain. Axelos interprets Marx as heavily indebted to Hegel's dialectic and logic, and, through a wide engagement with those writings of Heidegger's that were available at the time, Axelos pieces Heidegger's reading of Marx together in the light of Heidegger's suggestion that Hegel and Nietzsche represent the "completion" of metaphysics. "Marx and Heidegger," Axelos claims, "name the same . . . in no way do [they] say the same, their thinking moves itself within 'the same.'"[17] Axelos seeks constantly to show Heidegger's, and Marx's, relation to the "end of metaphysics" and its "overcoming": "Hegel, Marx, Nietzsche, Heidegger: four names; four thinkers, who, each in their own manner, are remarkable in their passage on the same paths."[18] It is this constant constellation of the end of metaphysics, brought together through unfolding of the hidden essence of technology, that Axelos seeks to explain.

In this sense, Axelos exhibits with dexterity one theme central to Heidegger's work from beginning to end, that leaves Axelos himself unable to abandon either his manifest admiration for and commitment to Marx, or his sensitivity to what Heidegger is also seeking to name. Axelos is acutely aware of the place Marx also occupies in Heidegger's critique of subjectivity: "Marx does not get over the representing of subjectivity, in fact it overcomes him,"[19] which leads him to ask, and persist in asking, "does not therefore Marx belong to the epoch of subjectivity, so within the metaphysics of humanism?"[20] In this Axelos betrays a very careful understanding of Heidegger's "history of being." For the history of being as it manifests itself in Marx is the culmination of the history of *the* nothing. From around 1935 Heidegger makes a distinction between being as *das Sein* and (using an archaic, Schwabian Germanic spelling) being as *das Seyn.*[21] If *das Seyn* is be-ing as it is in itself,

16. Kostas Axelos, "Le 'dialogue avec le Marxisme' et la 'question de la technique.'"

17. Kostas Axelos, *Einführung in ein künftiges Denken: Über Marx und Heidegger,* 12, 13. "Marx und Heidegger das Gleiche nennen. . . . [Sie] sagen keineswegs das Gleiche, ihr Denken bewegt sich innerhalb des 'Selben.'"

18. Ibid., 16. "Hegel, Marx, Nietzsche, Heidegger. Vier Namen, vier Denker, die, jeder in einem anderen Schritt, auf demselben Wege gehen und fallen."

19. Ibid., 28. "Marx übersteigt nicht die Vorstellung der Subjektivität, er übersteigt sie sogar."

20. Ibid., 28. "Gehört also nicht Marx der Epoche der Subjektivität, der Metaphysik des Humanismus an?"

21. There is a tendency for some commentators to write "beyng" from an archaic English spelling, which I have eschewed. *Das Seyn* is indicated in the text by the term "be-ing."

being as such, then the history of being (*das Sein*), being manifesting itself historically, is the way *in* to the thinking of being as such. History (as it is thought metaphysically) is, however, characterized by negation: by the cancellation of what went before for the sake of making way for what is yet to come. We will encounter this character of cancellation in both Hegel and Marx as the essential inner working of dialectic in its relation to time (and hence to history), named as "sublation," German *Aufhebung*, which can also be translated variously as cancellation, abolition, revocation, but also preserving, lifting, uprising, and even as transcending. Axelos therefore says "the nothing presences as being . . . the nothing is being itself."[22]

Hegel and Nietzsche each in their own way, for Heidegger, unfold the completion of nihilism and the persistent presence of *the* nothing as at the same time the presencing of being (*das Sein*). This unfolding of the nothing is itself nothing other than the history of being, the forgetfulness *of* being, as both being's "withdrawal," and the historical unfolding of man's forgetting of being. Axelos goes some way to bring Marx and Heidegger side by side: his most basic assertion, that they spring from "the same," is, from Heidegger's perspective at least, fundamentally correct. However, inasmuch as he brings them together, in two short essays and in his highly impressionistic and at times aphoristic style, he is unable to identify "the same," and so to show how an identical ground manifests itself differently in each thinker. A task of this book will be to show what "the same" names, and how we are to understand what is the *same* in each of these thinkers—Hegel, Marx, Nietzsche, and Heidegger.

Axelos avoids the question of Heidegger's own political engagement in his juxtaposition of Marx and Heidegger. This avoidance comes despite the fact that Heidegger's Nazism had emerged as an issue in France as early as 1946 with the publication there of Karl Löwith's denunciation of Heidegger's politics, and the first "Heidegger affair," something Axelos could not have been ignorant of.[23] Axelos, naming Heidegger's suggestion that human being is sexually neutral, argues that, in the same manner, "Heidegger actually says nothing of class struggle, of the proletariat, of capitalist exploitation. He says nothing of it or against it. . . . He attempts to think through a so-called social or political neutrality."[24] Heidegger's political withdrawal after 1945,

22. Kostas Axelos, *Einführung in ein künftiges Denken: Über Marx und Heidegger*, 40, 41. "Das Nichts west als das Sein . . . Das Nichts ist das Sein selbst."

23. Karl Löwith, "Les implications politiques de la philosophie de l'existence chez Heidegger."

24. Kostas Axelos, *Einführung in ein künftiges Denken: Über Marx und Heidegger*, 28. "Heidegger sagt tatsächlich nichts von Klassenkampf, vom Proletariat, von der kapitalistischen Ausbeutung. Er sagt nichts dafür und nichts dagegen. . . . Heidegger versucht auch, die sogenannte gesellschaftliche oder politische Neutralität zu durchdenken."

indeed after 1934, will turn out, as we shall see, to be anything but the neutrality that Axelos suggests, as a kind of lofty indifference. If Heidegger does not think with Marx's categories, this does not mean that Heidegger does not think through the political, nor does it mean that his thought is any kind of political neutrality.

Axelos identifies Marx's strong relation to Hegel by frequently citing Marx's early (1844) text, the *Economic and Philosophical Manuscripts.*[25] One of Axelos's commentators, the veteran American former Marxist and disciple of John Dewey's Sidney Hook, says (derogatorily) of Axelos's writing "this is idealistic metaphysics with a vengeance" and is harshly critical of Axelos's interpretation of subjectivity, commenting: "This 'subject' is obviously a fragment or phase of the Hegelian creative spirit and had very little to do with the subject Marx describes, after repudiating both Hegel and Feuerbach, whose consciousness is determined by his social existence."[26] Hook argues that "Marx was not born a Marxist. Axelos should have at the very least come to grips with the possibility that Marx, as his criticism of the German true socialists in *The Communist Manifesto* shows, subsequently regarded all the talk about alienation in the so-called *Philosophic-Economic Writings of 1844* as 'philosophical nonsense.'"[27] Hook's prejudices against Hegel (and against dialectic,)[28] are insupportable in the light of the presence of the word "alienation" all over later texts of Marx, irrespective of its seeming absence from *Das Kapital* (an absence we will revisit), but Hook's dispute with Axelos indicates what is at issue with the refusal of many Marxists to enter into dialogue with Heidegger.

This refusal is highlighted by David Schweickart, who cites Sartre's summary dismissal of any Marxist reading of Heidegger ("'and there is no

25. Axelos usually refers to this text by the alternative title *Nationalökonomie und Philosophie.* The *Economic and Philosophical Manuscripts* sometimes also go under the title of the *Parisian Manuscripts.*

26. Sidney Hook, *"Alienation, Praxis and Technē in the Thought of Karl Marx by Kostas Axelos,"* 744.

27. Sidney Hook, *"Alienation, Praxis and Technē,"* 744, referring to "der deutsche oder der 'wahre' Sozialismus" ["the German or 'true' socialism"], "Sie schrieben ihren philosophischen Unsinn hinter das französische Original. Z.B. hinter die französische Kritik der Geldverhältnisse schrieben sie 'Entäußerung des menschlichen Wesens'" ("They wrote their philosophical nonsense beneath the French original. For instance, under the French critique of the relations of money they wrote 'alienation of the human being'"). (*Manifest der Kommunistischen Partei* [*MEW*4], 485–88, compare 486).

28. See Sidney Hook, "Dialectic and Nature," 253–84. While Hook undertakes a deft demolition of Engels's use of the term "dialectical," like many who fell under the spell of Anglophone logical analysis, he fails to answer his own question—in this case, just *why* it is that (253) "the philosophy of dialectical materialism is easily one of the most important social doctrines of our times."

longer any Marxist, to my knowledge, who is still capable of doing this'") as the basis for his own relapse into "a truth-condition acceptable even to most Marxists" which must, because of fierce division "be general."[29] Having established this "truth-criterion" acceptable to all Marxists, he then proposes to "recast certain Heideggerian positions—those related to his critique of Marxism—in such a way that they may be tested by this criterion." The superficiality of this alternative need hardly detain us, except to note that it exactly evades Axelos's entirely correct inquiry into "the same," as that from which Heidegger and Marx spring, which is not at the same time mere "common ground," let alone some trivial point of consensus or, worse yet, merely "logical" truth-criterion.

The word "dialogue," translating Heidegger's word *Gespräch,* comes from both the translations into English of the *Letter on Humanism*[30] but might better be translated "conversation." What is the "topic" of the conversation at hand? Heidegger's subsequent remarks make us listen to this seeming adjective "productive" all over again. Marx is primordially concerned with production: both how what is produced *is* produced, and who owns the means of its production. The Greek verb *ergazomai* means "to produce," to labor, to bring forth into the open. This word is strongly related to the verb *ergein,* "to work," which gives us the neuter noun *ergon,* "work," but also "labor" as such. The original Greek should be sounded with the missing digamma, *ϝέργον,* Indo-European **werĝ,* from which German *wirken* (to realize) and English "work" are all derived. Here we must also hear the connection with Aristotle's *energeia* (and we will return to this much later): that which is en-ergized, "set to work," that which we would now call the "real." The *essential,* by which we mean philosophical, counterpart to *energeia* that Aristotle identifies is *dunamis:* not the merely possible, the "potential," but what plenitudiously lets things into being, the from-out-of-which they are, to be realized.

The productive dialogue Heidegger has in mind is not one with an "end," a product, in view, but rather what in itself concerns "the productive." The "productive dialogue" with Marxism immediately and first off concerns a dimension: the dimension from out of which "the productive" speaks, *that* dimension whose origins can be found by thinking through and behind Aristotle's discussion of the pair *energeia-dunamis.* In this, Heidegger both acknowledges the extent to which Marx is himself indebted to Aristotle, and

29. David Schweickart, "Heidegger and Marx: A Framework for Dialogue," 230, citing the English translation of Jean-Paul Sartre's 1957 essay "Question de méthode."

30. See the translation originally by Frank A. Capuzzi in collaboration with J. Glenn Gray as *Letter on Humanism* in *Martin Heidegger: Basic Writings,* 217–265 (compare 243), revised in *Pathmarks,* 239–76 (259).

the extent to which Marx as a thinker brings to light an essential interpretation of a thought as old as the history of Occidental thought itself. Essential here means, an interpretation which presses in on him, and which demands to be brought to description—a thought which cannot be evaded, and from out of which Marx's own thinking both is bound to history and makes an ineluctable claim on him.

It is with this in mind that we can make sense of Heidegger's remarks from the *Letter on Humanism* that immediately follow: "for this [i.e., the conversation] it is certainly necessary that one free oneself from naive conceptions concerning materialism and from the cheap refutations that are supposed to get us out of it. The essence of materialism does not consist in the assertion that everything is mere matter, but rather in the metaphysical determination according to which every being appears as the material of labour."[31]

About the best-known statement of Marx's and Engels's is "a spectre is haunting Europe—the spectre of communism."[32] *The Communist Manifesto* notes that "all powers of the old Europe have bound themselves into a holy chase against this ghost."[33] Not less was Heidegger concerned with this question of the "whereto" of Europe: "the danger, into which the former Europe is ever more strongly pressed into, presumably consists in this, before all else, that its thinking—once its greatness—falls behind the essential course of a dawning world destiny that at the same time in the basic features of its essential provenance remains determinedly European."[34] We should hear here the concern for the destiny and whereto of, not only Europe, but also the planetary reach of European thinking, and so, therefore, of the whole globe. Heidegger emphasizes in the editorial alterations he made between the 1947 edition of the *Letter on Humanism* and the 1976 *Gesamtausgabe* edition, and in his marginal notes to the text (preserved in the German and the revised English translation), that the "danger" that he names, which we

31. Martin Heidegger, *Brief über den Humanismus* (*GA*9), 340. "Hierzu ist freilich auch nötig, daß man sich von den naiven Vorstellungen über den Materialismus und von den billigen Widerlegungen, die ihn treffen sollen, freimacht. Das Wesen des Materialismus besteht nicht in der Behauptung, alles sei nur Stoff, vielmehr in einer metaphysischen Bestimmung, der gemäß alles Seiende als das Material der Arbeit erscheint."

32. Karl Marx and Friedrich Engels, *Manifest der Kommunistischen Partei* in *Marx Engels Werke* (*MEW*4), 461. "Ein Gespenst geht um in Europa—das Gespenst des Kommunismus."

33. Ibid., 461. "Alle Mächte des alten Europa haben sich zu einer heiligen Hetzjagd gegen dies Gespenst verbündet."

34. Martin Heidegger, *Brief über den Humanismus* (*GA*9), 341. "Die Gefahr, in die das bisherige Europa immer deutlicher gedrängt wird, besteht vermutlich darin, daß allem zuvor sein Denken—einst seine Größe—hinter dem Wesensgang des anbrechenden Weltgeschickes zurückfällt, das gleichwohl in den Grundzügen seiner Wesensherkunft europäisch bestimmt bleibt."

will return to later, is "a falling-back of thinking into metaphysics, [which] takes on a new form."[35]

A significant number of Heidegger's students were, at one point or another, Marxists, especially at the time when they studied with him. If Karl Löwith, who later converted to Lutheranism, was one of these, another was perhaps the most often cited Marxist interpreter of Heidegger, Herbert Marcuse. Marcuse wrote his *Habilitationsschrift* (thesis) on Hegel under Heidegger's direction, and it was published in 1932,[36] but never formally granted (apparently as a result of Heidegger's own opposition).[37] Marcuse's early work attempted a critique of the idealism of Marxism from the perspective of what he understood to be the more concrete appeal to experience he recognized in the phenomenology of Heidegger and Husserl.[38] Douglas Kellner has attempted to analyze Marcuse's attraction to Heidegger's thought in some detail[39] but does not really assess how, despite his engagement with Heidegger, Marcuse is not able to engage with the radical and systematically destructive critique of philosophical subjectivity that Heidegger believed himself to be undertaking. After the publication of *Being and Time,* and before 1933, Marcuse enthusiastically took up much of Heidegger's terminology and analysis, in particular Heidegger's term *Dasein.* In discussion Marcuse much later said "we saw in Heidegger what we had first seen in Husserl, a new beginning, the first radical attempt to put philosophy on really concrete foundations—philosophy concerned with human existence, the human

35. Ibid., 341, n. *a* (but compare note *b* on the same page, both prefixed "1. Auflage 1949." "Der Rückfall des Denkens in die Metaphysik nimmt eine neue Form an" ("The relapse of thinking into metaphysics takes on a new form").

36. Herbert Marcuse, *Hegels Ontologie und die Grundlegung einer Theorie der Geschichtlichkeit.* In the German university system, a *Habilitationsschrift* is a further thesis, after the doctoral thesis, publication of which gives the holder the right to teach at a German state university as a *Privatdozent.* Marcuse was never granted that right.

37. Herbert Marcuse, *Hegels Ontologie und die Grundlegung einer Theorie der Geschichtlichkeit.* Richard Wolin reports that "during the 1980s Frankfurt School historian Rolf Wiggershaus found a 1932 letter from Edmund Husserl to University of Frankfurt Rector Kurt Riezler confirming that, for reasons that are still unclear, Heidegger 'blocked' Marcuse's attempt to habilitate" (see Herbert Marcuse, *Heideggerian Marxism,* xxii and n. 25).

38. See Herbert Marcuse, *Heideggerian Marxism.* See also from this period Herbert Marcuse, "Beiträge zu einer Phänomenologie des Historischen Materialismus" ("Contributions to a Phenomenology of Historical Materialism"); "Über konkrete Philosophie"; "Über die philosophischen Grundlagen des wirtschaftswissenschaftlichen Arbeitsbegriffs" ("On the Philosophical Foundation of the Concept of Labor in Economics"); "Zum Problem der Dialektik I" ("On the Problem of the Dialectic").

39. Douglas Kellner, *Herbert Marcuse and the Crisis of Marxism,* 38 and following. Richard Wolin has a useful summary of Marcuse's relationship with Heidegger in *The Heidegger Controversy: A Critical Reader,* 152–60.

condition."[40] In an article in 1928, Marcuse first attempted an integration of phenomenology with Marxism and historical materialism. Explicitly drawing attention to (the then only just published) *Being and Time*, Marcuse argues that a phenomenology of historical materialism entails a revolutionary attitude such that historicality "culminates as the basic determination of human existence [*Dasein*] and with a new understanding of reality [*Wirklichkeit*] we get the possibility of a radically transformative action."[41] Marcuse collapses the relationship between being (*das Sein*) and the entity in being (*das Seiende*) into "human existence [*Dasein*]" when he says of *Being and Time*, "but the whole of the first section that has already appeared treats of the interpretation of a preeminent being [*Sein*], the '*Dasein*,' by which the human *Dasein* is always understood. 'This being [*Seiende*], that we ourselves indeed are . . . which we fix terminologically as *Dasein*.' "[42]

The whole of *Being and Time* turns on the distinction between *das Sein* and *das Seiende*, which Marcuse here collapses into *Dasein*, making each term indistinguishable with respect to it. The problem with this interpretation—even apart from its conflations—is that it inevitably drives the interpretation of the term *Dasein* toward becoming a masked name for the subjectivity of the subject. Marcuse is careful to show how "world" is necessarily a precondition of *Dasein*, and so not secured, as Descartes secures the cogito, through radical doubt, and so cancellation of "world." Marcuse also correctly (in terms of Heidegger's own understanding and claims) identifies that what is missing in the formula *cogito, ergo sum* is any genuinely phenomenological investigation of the *sum*, the being of the "I am."[43] What he lapses into, however, is a concentration on the "human," such that he ends up implicitly positing the formula "every human being is 'a' *Dasein*." This formula is in itself ambiguous, especially in English (where *Dasein* is left untranslated), as we are apt to hear the term *Dasein* as a designator, a proper noun (as in "the" cogito), rather than its ordinary German meaning (in a way used frequently by Marx) as "existence," or Heidegger's own utterly techni-

40. Herbert Marcuse, "Heidegger's Politics: An Interview with Frederick A. Olafson," 165–66.

41. Herbert Marcuse, "Beiträge zu einer Phänomenologie des Historischen Materialismus," 348. "Als der Grundbestimmtheit menschlichen Daseins gipfelt und mit einem neuen Verstehen der Wirklichkeit die Möglichkeit einer radikal verändernden Tat bekommt."

42. Ibid., 358, quoting at the end Martin Heidegger, *Sein und Zeit* (*GA*2), 9. "Aber der ganze bisher erschienene erste Teil behandelt die Interpretation eines vorzüglichen Seins, des 'Daseins,' worunter stets das menschliche Dasein verstanden wird."

43. A point Heidegger himself repeatedly made. See, for instance, Martin Heidegger, *Sein und Zeit* (*GA*2), 33. "What [Descartes] left undetermined with this 'radical' beginning, is the manner of being of the *deliberating thing*, more precisely, the *meaning-of-being of the 'I am.'* " ("Was er aber bei diesem 'radikalen' Anfang unbestimmt läßt, ist die Seinsart der res cogitans, genauer der *Seinssinn des 'sum'* " [Heidegger's emphases].)

cal, specific, ontological, sense of "here-being."[44] It took Heidegger decades to free *Being and Time* from this propensity of interpretation, and indeed many of his interpreters have yet to get free of it even now.

The question is directly germane to Heidegger's interpretation of Marx. In his essay from 1928, Marcuse cited a very early text of Marx's, published for the first time only in 1927,[45] the *Critique of Hegel's Philosophy of Right:* "to be radical is to grasp the root of the thing. The root for man is however man himself."[46] Forty-five years later, in a seminar in Switzerland, Heidegger himself cites this very sentence in the context of a discussion concerning Marx. It seems hardly accidental that Heidegger should draw attention to this passage, even with the distance of these many years, and so it seems we have one of the few examples in print of Heidegger commenting on the interpretations of one of his students, despite not mentioning Marcuse by name (although he does mention Marcuse elsewhere).[47] The protocols of the seminar say that "from this thesis, Heidegger explained, rests the whole of Marxism. Indeed Marxism thinks from out of production: social of society (society produces itself) and self-production of man as a social being."[48] In this seminar and this interpretation, Heidegger explicitly rejects that this sentence of Marx could ever be the basis of a genuinely phenomenological understanding of the being of beings (*das Sein des Seienden*). To show why will be one of the tasks of this book and will entail us examining much more closely how Heidegger really understands the term *Dasein*. There can be no doubt, however, that even as Marcuse embraces the understanding of production as human-self-production (something he explains in much greater detail in a brief essay from 1933, *On the Philosophical Foundations of the Concept of Labor in Economics*),[49] even in 1927, and indeed at no other time in the general sweep of his thought, Heidegger could and did not understand human being as human self-production.

Marcuse foresaw that his own Jewish origins, together with his social-

44. And never, as Heidegger himself specified, with direct reference to Sartre and Karl Löwith (among others), as "being-there" (French "être-là"). Compare Martin Heidegger, quoted by Jean Beaufret in "En chemin avec Heidegger," 212.

45. Marcuse provides a reference to the first *Marx Engels Gesamtausgabe* (see Herbert Marcuse, "Beiträge zu einer Phänomenologie des Historischen Materialismus," 351, n. 3).

46. Karl Marx, "Zur Kritik der Hegelschen Rechtsphilosophie" (*MEW*1), 385. "Radikal sein ist die Sache an der Wurzel fassen. Die Wurzel für den Menschen ist aber der Mensch selbst."

47. See 234.

48. Martin Heidegger, "Seminar in Zähringen" (*GA*15), 387. "Auf dieser These, erläutert Heidegger, beruht der gesamte Marxismus. Der Marxismus denkt nämlich von der Produktion aus: gesellschaftliche Produktion der Gesellschaft (die Gesellschaft produziert sich selbst) und Selbstproduktion des Menschen als soziales Wesen."

49. Herbert Marcuse, "Über die Philosophischen Grundlagen des wirtschaftswissenschaftlichen Arbeitsbegriffs."

ism, would have brought him into immediate conflict with the incoming Nazi regime, and he left Germany in 1933 a few days before Adolf Hitler took power, entering the United States in 1934, where he remained as a career academic until the end of his life, although always (from his involvement with the Frankfurt Institut für Sozialforschung from 1932 onward) closely allied with the Frankfurt school, and so with Theodor Adorno, Max Horkheimer, and their circle. Of greater significance for our study than anything Marcuse wrote in Heidegger's wake was the review Marcuse undertook of Marx's then just-published *Economic and Philosophical Manuscripts* of 1844.[50] Marcuse shared in laying the basis for a wide-scale revision of the interpretation of Marx, by interpreting the later Marx through the newly uncovered earlier work. It is not unlikely that Marcuse was instrumental in drawing Heidegger's attention to the *Economic and Philosophical Manuscripts*, the first (1932) German edition of which was edited by Siegfried Landshut, himself a student of Heidegger's.[51] Certainly Heidegger was reading widely in Marx and Marxism at this time—the period of the publication of Ernst Jünger's *The Worker—Dominion and Form* (*Der Arbeiter—Herrschaft und Gestalt*)[52] and of Heidegger's first series of seminars considering this work in detail.[53] Heidegger had also been lecturing on Hegel's *Phenomenology of Spirit* (*Phänomenologie des Geistes*) in only the previous year (1930–31), the only time he ever provided a full series of lectures at Freiburg on Hegel.[54] These overlaps cannot have been coincidental, and the intimate interconnections between them will, I hope, become very clear as we proceed.

It is Marcuse who is the origin of the accusation that Heidegger never

50. Karl Marx, *Ökonomisch-philosophische Manuskripte aus dem Jahre 1844* (*MEW*40), 467–588. Marcuse's review was published as Herbert Marcuse, "Neue Quellen zur Grundlegung des Historischen Materialismus."

51. See Karl Marx, "Nationalökonomie und Philosophie," in *Der historische Materialismus*, ed. Siegfried Landshut and J. P. Mayer.

52. Ernst Jünger, *Der Arbeiter: Herrschaft und Gestalt.*

53. For Heidegger's margin notes to *Der Arbeiter* and the preparatory notes and remarks for these and the seminars "in einem kleinen Kreis von Universitätslehrern" ("in a small circle of university teachers") held from 1939 to 1940 until their suppression by the Nazis (if Heidegger's claims are correct), see Martin Heidegger, *Zu Ernst Jünger* (*GA*90). Heidegger later said "Man war aber auch nicht überrascht, daß ein Versuch, den 'Arbeiter' zu erläutern, überwacht und schließlich unterbunden wurde" ("One was, however, not surprised when an attempt to explain *Der Arbeiter* was watched and eventually disbanded"). See Martin Heidegger, *Zur Seinsfrage* (*GA*9), especially 390.

54. Martin Heidegger, *Hegels Phänomenologie des Geistes* (*GA*32). There are shorter treatises and reports of seminars on Hegel from 1938–39, 1941, and 1941 published as Martin Heidegger, *Hegel. 1. Die Negativität. 2. Erläuterung der "Einleitung" zu Hegels "Phänomenologie des Geistes"* (*GA*68). The protocols of Heidegger's seminars on Hegel from the mid-1930s have been published as Martin Heidegger, *Seminare: Hegel—Schelling* (*GA*86). Compare also "Hegel und die Griechen" in *Wegmarken* (*GA*9), and "Hegels Begriff der Erfahrung" (*GA*5), as well as others from the 1930s we will also discuss later.

really retracted or apologized for his support of the Nazi regime from May 1933, and maintained a silence and no opposition to the regime from 1933 to 1945.[55] Marcuse's accusations against Heidegger, especially those of May 1948, are (again, as we shall later see) insupportable on the basis of the facts, barely any of which could have been available to Marcuse at the time.[56] Nevertheless the accusations have stuck and formed the basis of much subsequent interpretation.[57]

Others have written on Heidegger and Marxism, although few. Fred Dallmayr's *Heidegger and Marxism* is a case in point, and we will return to Dallmayr's careful and fruitful analyses on more than one occasion.[58] There have been attempts to identify links between György Lukács and Heidegger, which remain unconvincing.[59] Heidegger never once mentioned Lukács in all his writing, and, although (as Tom Rockmore notes) "Lukács and Heidegger are alike in the respect that each tends, although this is more often the case for Heidegger than for Lukács, to conceal the proximate origins of his thought,"[60] nevertheless Lucien Goldmann's attempt to assert Heidegger's dependency on Lukács is, at the very best, wildly improbable, despite the occurrence of the phrase, strongly redolent of Lukács, "reification

55. Herbert Marcuse, "Briefe an Martin Heidegger," letter to Martin Heidegger of August 28, 1947, 465–80. Heidegger replied to this letter on January 20 (*GA*16, 431–32). This view is repeated and amplified in Marcuse's interview with Frederick Olafson.

56. Marcuse's letter of May 1948 chides Heidegger for his claim that the Germans of the eastern territories suffered as much under the Russians as the Jews had under the Nazis (See Martin Heidegger, letter to Herbert Marcuse of January 20, 1948, in *Reden und andere Zeugnisse eines Lebenswegs* [GA16], 431). It might indeed be shocking to make the sufferings of Germans outside the 1949–89 borders of West Germany commensurate with the hideous crime of the Holocaust, but Marcuse could not have known (as Heidegger clearly did) of, for instance, the systematic and deliberate rape of German women and vicious molestation of Germans in general in the territories that are now Russian, Polish, Czech, Hungarian, and "Yugoslavian," from the advance of the Allied forces into former German lands from 1944 onward. For just one example: in the chaos that followed the Nazi defeat in one town in the former German east, liberated inmates of concentration camps (and so victims of the criminality of the Nazis) were lynched and hung by the neck from lampposts with piano wire merely because they were understood by local Czechs to be German. See Giles McDonogh, *After the Reich: From the Liberation of Vienna to the Berlin Airlift,* especially 125–96 and 201–26.

57. The collection of Alan Milchman and Alan Rosenberg, eds., *Martin Heidegger and the Holocaust,* for just one example, is entirely constructed around Heidegger's "silence" over his Nazism and the Holocaust. A more nuanced view—that nevertheless maintains the view that Heidegger was from 1934 onward, and remained, "silent" is Hans Sluga, *Heidegger's Crisis: Philosophy and Politics in Nazi Germany,* especially 234–35.

58. Fred Dallmayr, "Heidegger and Marxism," 207–224.

59. See Lucien Goldmann, *Lukács et Heidegger: Fragments posthumes pour une nouvelle philosophie.*

60. Tom Rockmore, review of William Q. Boelhower, *Lukács and Heidegger: Towards a New Philosophy,* 343.

of consciousness" twice in *Being and Time.*[61] There are always huge dangers in attempting to hammer together interpretations based on the occurrence of a common word or phrase across two authors. Goldmann is unable to ask the question that concerns both Heidegger and Lukács, the question that would tie them together far more closely than any mere commonality in phrases: What is the legacy of Hegel and how does Marx arise on the basis of Hegel's thinking? What does Hegel mean for the destiny of European, and global, thinking, in Marx, in Heidegger, and even now?

Lukács, however, did comment on Heidegger, in his work entitled *Existentialism or Marxism,*[62] but again fails to address sufficiently the critique of subjectivity in the text, interpreting *Dasein* as the figure of the isolated individual, and so as a masked name for the subjectivity of the subject. He dismissed *Being and Time* as merely "polemical writing," even if "of imposing dimensions."[63] Other Soviet writers similarly dismissed Heidegger and the existentialism they associated with him as entirely bourgeois philosophy. One commentator noted in 1965 that "there is also evidence that at least some Soviet philosophers are reading the original existentialist writings, at least for purposes of condemnation," referring to interest in Heidegger.[64] With such prejudices at work, there was hardly much ground for dialogue.

Contrary, it would seem, to what I argued in my book *Heidegger's Atheism* in 2002, that there is no "Heidegger II" over against a "Heidegger I," the schema proposed by William Richardson in 1963,[65] but in fact in conformity with the interpretation I advanced in that book, there is emerging an important "Heidegger II," one of immense significance for this book. Much of the material that Heidegger specified was to be released only after all of his university lecture courses had been published is in the form of notebooks and schemata for what appeared to be possible books. The first of these, comprising writings undertaken between 1936 and 1938, was published on the centenary of his birth (and earlier than he had specified, since the last volume of university lectures has only just appeared)[66] as the *Beiträge zur*

61. Goldmann (*Lukács and Heidegger,* 27), drawing attention to Heidegger's use of the phrase "Verdinglichung des/zu Bewußtseins" ("reification of consciousness") in *Sein und Zeit* (*GA*2), 62 and 576, indicates that Heidegger was citing Lukács. The same argument is made by Rainier Rochlitz, "Lukács et Heidegger—suites d'un débat."

62. A French translation appeared in 1948, followed in 1951 by a German translation. See György Lukács, *Existentialisme ou marxisme?*

63. György Lukács, *Existentialisme ou marxisme?* 118–19.

64. R. T. de George, "Heidegger and the Marxists," 290.

65. See Laurence Paul Hemming, *Heidegger's Atheism: The Refusal of a Theological Voice,* especially 87–97.

66. Martin Heidegger, *Der Anfang der abendländischen Philosophie (Anaximander und Parmenides)* (*The Beginning of Western Philosophy [Anaximander and Parmenides]*) (*GA*35), a lecture course given at Freiburg in the summer semester of 1932.

*Philosophie (vom Ereignis)* (*Contributions to Philosophy* [*from out of the Event*]).[67]

In all, six further volumes of these notebooks (of which five have been published, the most recent having arrived only late in 2009) belong in the *Gesamtausgabe* plan. In the very middle of them, a fact not without significance in itself, is a volume of seminar notes, protocols, and the schemata for lectures given to small, but unspecified, groups, all on Hegel. These focus on "negativity" and the interpretation of the *Phenomenology*.[68] The editor of the most recent, and penultimate of these volumes of notebooks, Friedrich-Wilhelm von Herrmann (also the editor of the *Gesamtausgabe* overall), discusses in the sixth volume only for the first time how they hang together as the "seven major treatises of the history of being," and von Herrmann groups them all under the title of *Das Ereignis* (*The Event*).[69] Until now the *Beiträge* has been regarded as a singular event, to which the appearance of the text *Mindfulness* (*Besinnung*) in 1997 has been understood as a kind of annex (but only to that singularity). As far as I can tell, the other volumes have attracted almost no particular scholarly notice at all. Here for the first time there is formal confirmation that Heidegger's thought of *das Ereignis* functions as a vast series of connected sketches, akin in size and scope to Nietzsche's *Nachlaß*, across the crucial years 1936 (when Heidegger began his formal confrontation with Nietzsche, and after finally having put the year of the Nazi rectorate behind him) up until 1948, the year before the crucial but enigmatic public lectures delivered in Bremen (under the title *Insight into That Which Is*),[70] which really mark his return to public life after the war, the denazification process, and the breakdowns in his mental health.

*Das Ereignis*, "the event," is sometimes translated as the "event of appropriation," a translation popularized by Joan Stambaugh, since Heidegger stresses the *eigen, eignis,* "own/self"-character of the intensive *Er-eignis*. For Heidegger this is the language that does not speak within metaphysics—most specifically, that announces itself *in* the "overcoming" of meta-

67. Martin Heidegger, *Beiträge zur Philosophie (Vom Ereignis)* (*GA*65).

68. The other six volumes are Martin Heidegger: *Besinnung* (*GA*66); *Metaphysik und Nihilismus. 1. Die Überwindung der Metaphysik (1938/39), 2. Das Wesen des Nihilismus (1946–48)* (*GA*67); *Die Geschichte des Seyns. 1. Die Geschichte des Seyns (1938/40). 2. Κοινόν. Aus der Geschichte des Seyns (1939)* (*GA*69), 1998; *Über den Anfang (1941)* (*GA*70); *Das Ereignis (1941/42)* (*GA*71); and *Die Stege des Anfangs (1944)*, scheduled to be published as volume 72 of the Heidegger *Gesamtausgabe*. The Hegel volume is *Hegel* (*GA*68). The seven volumes comprise a multitude of notebooks.

69. Martin Heidegger, *Das Ereignis (1941/42)* (*GA*71), 343. "Sieben große [ ] seinsgeschichtlichen Abhandlungen . . . Zwar handeln alle sieben seins- und ereignisgeschichtlichen Abhandlungen vom Ereignis, doch die jetzt zur Veröffentlichung gelangende sechste Abhandlung trägt eigens den Titel *Das Ereignis*."

70. Published in Martin Heidegger, *Bremer und Freiburger Vorträge* (*GA*79), 5–77.

physics that is the theme of so much of Heidegger's public work, especially from 1944. The seven volumes that come under the title of *Das Ereignis* are the working out of the central understandings of technology, the history of being, and the critique of metaphysics, that produce the discussions of *The Enframing, The Fourfold, The Turning,* and *The Danger.* These were the themes of the Bremen lectures of 1949, which marked Heidegger's return to a public stage. The notebooks are above all a *political* engagement in the years 1936 to 1948, and paved the way for a yet more political engagement even if it was, as we shall later discuss, predicated on the absolute abdication of any actual political involvement of Heidegger's whatsoever after 1934. Any "productive dialogue" for Heidegger with Marx and with Marxism must of necessity take this into account.

The *Letter on Humanism* is by far the most important single text for Heidegger's interpretation of Marx, but for surprising reasons. Near the beginning of the *Letter on Humanism,* Heidegger raised the question of how his central work, *Being and Time,* was to be interpreted. His work, he indicates, was "the adequate execution and completion of this other, subjectivity-abandoning, thinking" made more difficult by the fact that the third division of the first part of *Being and Time* was held back.[71] The third part of the first division was to have been entitled "Time and Being," where, from being and time "here everything turns itself about."[72] Heidegger comments: "The division in question was held back, because thinking failed in the adequate saying of this turn, and so did not succeed with the help of the language of metaphysics."[73]

The standard interpretation of these sentences is that Heidegger believed that *Being and Time,* his own central work, was therefore "a failure of thinking" which took form "in the language of metaphysics." Daniela Vallega-Neu, citing this passage, argues that "in some instances the language of *Being and Time* seems to reaffirm what it means to overcome, namely metaphysical thought."[74] Many other commentators reference this passage in the *Letter on Humanism,* drawing attention to what seems to be its obvious conclusion. These interpretations tend to promote the interpretation of the word *Dasein* that suggests it is itself a masked name for the "subject" of "subjectivity." Richardson thought no differently, when, taking as his cue this very pas-

71. Martin Heidegger, *Brief über den Humanismus* (*GA*9), 327. "Der zureichende Nach- und Mit-vollzug dieses anderen, die Subjektivität verlassenden Denkens."

72. Martin Heidegger, *Brief über den Humanismus* (*GA*9), 328. "Hier kehrt das Ganze um."

73. Ibid., 328. "Der fragliche Abschnitt wurde zurückgehalten, weil das Denken im zureichenden Sagen dieser Kehre versagte und so mit Hilfe der Sprache der Metaphysik nicht durchkam."

74. Daniela Vallega-Neu, "Poietic Saying," 67.

sage for an interpretation of the lecture "On the Essence of Truth" (which Heidegger mentions on the page of the *Letter on Humanism* in question), he says: "How far have we come? Heidegger I becomes Heidegger II . . . the thinking of Being . . . at last!"[75] Thus, if *Being and Time* thinks *Dasein,* the "later" Heidegger thinks being, *Sein.*

Heidegger entitles a section of one of the notebooks of the series *Das Ereignis* " 'Being and Time' and Metaphysics."[76] The notebook dates from 1938–39. Here he argues that if *Being and Time* were simply an "epistemology" of "ontology," asking the question "how is ontology generally possible?," then "*Being and Time* would be an appendix to metaphysics."[77] However, Heidegger says

> But it is *being* [*das Sein*] that stands in question, not "ontology"; so is *Being and Time* perhaps a more original metaphysics, but nevertheless, still metaphysics? No.
>
> In truth here is an entirely more other inception from out of the essencing of be-ing [*das Seyn*] itself.[78]

The question is always one of interpretation: *how* the text is read will determine *how* it will speak, and will decide *who* is reading. Interpreted as epistemology and ontology, *Being and Time* will read as metaphysics. Interpreted from within the question of being, the text will place text and interpreter together into a wholly other departure of thought. However, this question of interpretation is not relative or merely arbitrary: every interpretation springs from an already "having taken the world," as the unity of thinking, in a particular way. The "failure in thinking" is, therefore, simply thinking's need to be yet further drawn in to what *is* to be thought: the failure has to be heard as a "not yet," an absence, rather than a conscious presence (of metaphysical language). The failure is the faltering entry into the yet more other inception.

Even though several years separate this statement from the statement of the *Letter on Humanism,* there is no reason to doubt that Heidegger held

75. William Richardson, *Through Phenomenology to Thought,* 254 (dotted spacing original to the text).

76. Martin Heidegger, *Die Überwindung der Metaphysik* (*GA*67), 125. "§117. 'Sein und Zeit' und die Metaphysik."

77. Ibid., 125. "So wäre 'Sein und Zeit' ein Nachtrag zur Metaphysik."

78. Ibid., 125. "Aber in Frage steht *das Sein,* nicht die 'Ontologie'; dann ist 'Sein und Zeit' vielleicht eine ursprünglichere Metaphysik, aber eben doch Metaphysik? Nein.

'In Wahrheit ist hier ein ganz anderer Anfang aus der Wesung des Seyns selbst' " (Heidegger's emphasis).

a different view in 1938–39 from the view he states in his letter to Beaufret of 1946. In a later notebook concerned with *The Essence of Nihilism* in the same series (and, dating from 1946–48, which much more closely coincides with the writing of the *Letter on Humanism*), Heidegger revisits this question, naming *Being and Time* only once in the treatise itself, in a footnote on the first page. Here he shows how the discussion "of being itself" is "being thought in *Being and Time* as 'time,'" alongside the other ways of thinking it, as "presence, the present, the play of time and space, *Ereignis.*"[79] He asks, "How then does metaphysics relate itself to being [*das Sein*] itself? Does metaphysics think being itself? No and never."[80] However, *Being and Time* asks the *question* concerning being, and so opens the way: as such it is an opening, an inception. *As* an inception and as a questioning, the thinking of *Being and Time* leaves behind and abandons the language of subjectivity. Metaphysics only goes out to question what *is*, the beings themselves: for metaphysics, "being itself is never the interrogated. Therefore being itself remains unthought in metaphysics."[81] Because *Being and Time* raises the question of being, the *Seinsfrage,* its thinking abandons metaphysics and thinks from out of an entirely other beginning.

This idea is confirmed in the supplementary pages to *The Essence of Nihilism,* where Heidegger does now identify *Being and Time* specifically and concludes that "the mindfulness of the essence of nihilism arises from the experience from which the thinking in *Being and Time* is seated."[82] Heidegger stresses here that from the beginning of Occidental thought, being in its truth, and this truth itself in its being, has lain unthought. As such, *Being and Time* is the refusal of this unthought, and so the clear implication is that the thinking that arises within *Being and Time,* correctly understood, is *itself* an occasion of this refusal of "Occidental thinking in the form of metaphysics."[83] This is why *Being and Time* is an entirely more *other* beginning

79. Martin Heidegger, *Das Wesen des Nihilismus* (*GA*67), 177, n. 1. "In der folgenden Abhandlung sagt die Rede 'vom Sein selbst' immer: Das Sein als Sein. Das Sein selbst: 1, Das Sein als Sein (Sein in 'Sein und Zeit' gedacht als 'Zeit,' als Anwesen, Gegenwart, Zeitspielraum, Ereignis); 2. Das Sein selber (Das Selbe, Identität, Wesen der Identität, Ereignis)" ("In the following treatise the talk 'of being itself' is always: being as being. Being itself: 1. Being as being [being in *Being and Time* as 'time,' as presence, as the present, the play of time and space, *Ereignis*]; 2. Being ever [the same, identity, the essence of identity, *Ereignis*]").

80. Martin Heidegger, *Das Wesen des Nihilismus* (*GA*67), 212. "Wie verhält sich also die Metaphysik zum Sein selbst? Denkt die Metaphysik das Sein selbst? Nein und niemals."

81. Ibid., 213. "Das Sein selbst ist nicht das Befragte. Darum bleibt das Sein selbst in der Metaphysik ungedacht."

82. Ibid., 267. "Die Besinnung auf das Wesen des Nihilismus kommt aus der Erfahrung, auf der das Denken in 'Sein und Zeit' beruht."

83. Ibid., 267. "Das abendländische Denken in der Gestalt der Metaphysik."

and inception for thinking, exactly as Heidegger claims in 1938–39. This interpretation shows the remarkable unity of Heidegger's thinking across the whole period of the manuscripts of *Das Ereignis* and indicates that there is no fundamental reorientation between his thinking concerning *Being and Time* from the beginning to the end of this inquiry.

While it is undoubtedly true that Heidegger wanted to indicate, with his statement in the *Letter on Humanism,* a thinking that had not yet attained to a language adequate for the thinking that abandons subjectivity, as *that* thinking which at the same time abandons metaphysics, no one, as far as I can tell, has paid sufficient attention to an important marginal note of Heidegger's on the very first page of the *Letter on Humanism* that was added to the *Gesamtausgabe* edition, indicating a remark Heidegger had added by hand to the title of his personal copy of the 1949 edition of the published text. Heidegger's addition says: "What is said here was not thought out only at the time of writing down, but is based on the course of a path that was begun in 1936, in the 'moment' of an attempt simply to say the truth of being.—The letter still speaks in the language of metaphysics, and indeed knowingly. The other language lies in the background."[84]

Attending to this means we must accept that it is not *Being and Time,* but the *Letter on Humanism* itself that cannot adequately explain *that* thinking which abandons subjectivity. The thinking that abandons subjectivity is the thinking that speaks "the truth of being" simply, and that therefore does not speak with the language of metaphysics. But the *Letter on Humanism* speaks the language of metaphysics, and it does so knowingly. The language that is required for the *other* thinking is contained in the path that began in 1936, that in 1946 (at the time of the writing of the *Letter on Humanism*) was not entirely concluded. This thinking has come to light in its full form only in the seven volumes that live collectively under the title *Das Ereignis* (at the time of writing, only six of these are extant). The *Letter on Humanism* itself (not *Being and Time,* therefore) is the text that *cannot* "succeed with the help of the language of metaphysics."

In the section of the *Letter on Humanism* where Heidegger discusses the central interpretation of *Being and Time,* he adds that "this turn [over into saying simply the truth of being] is not a changing of the standpoint of *Being and Time,* but in it the attempted thinking arrived only in the locality

84. Martin Heidegger, *Brief über den Humanismus* (*GA*9), 313, note *a* on the title. "Das hier Gesagte ist nicht erst zur Zeit der Niederschrift ausgedacht, sondern beruht auf dem Gang eines Weges, der 1936 begonnen wurde, im 'Augenblick' eines Versuches, die Wahrheit des Seins einfach zu sagen.—Der Brief spricht immer noch in der Sprache der Metaphysik, und zwar wissentlich. Die andere Sprache bleibt im Hintergrund."

of the dimension out of which *Being and Time* was experienced, and indeed, experienced from out of the basic experience of the forgetfulness of being."[85] A marginal note is again added in Heidegger's own hand against this term, *Seinsvergessenheit*, "forgetfulness of being," which says "Forgetfulness—*lēthē*—concealing—withdrawal—expropriation—*Ereignis*."[86]

What this means is that the interpretation of Marx advanced in the *Letter on Humanism* must itself be placed within the context of what I have suggested is the real "Heidegger II" that has only yet, and indeed not even yet fully, come to light, in the seven volumes that stand collectively under the title *Das Ereignis*. The *Letter on Humanism* may allow us to unlock the interpretation of Marx contained in Heidegger's work, but only on the basis of itself being unlocked by our interpretative approach to the hidden texts of the years 1936–48.

85. Ibid., 328. "Diese Kehre ist nicht eine Änderung des Standpunktes von 'Sein und Zeit,' sondern in ihr gelangt das versuchte Denken erst in die Ortschaft der Dimension, aus der 'Sein und Zeit' erfahren ist, und zwar erfahren in der Grunderfahrung der Seinsvergessenheit."

86. Ibid., 328, note *d*. "Vergessenheit—λήθη—Verbergung—Entzug—Enteignis: Ereignis."

*Chapter 2*

# The History of Marx and Heidegger

BOTH MARX'S AND HEIDEGGER'S thought are grounded in an understanding of history, and above all, how philosophy itself has become historical. Before Hegel, philosophy had believed itself to be dealing with "the eternal" and unchanging: either, in the case of Plato, the eternity of the ideas, or in Aristotle, the ever-same of being itself, or, with the advent of Christianity as the religion of Europe and Christianity's impact on philosophy, with the eternal creator God who wills what things are to be, and how, through the single and "eternal" act that he is. This chapter examines what understanding of philosophy is at work in Marx, and in Heidegger, and begins to inquire into how philosophy is, after Hegel, historical. The productive dialogue that arises between Heidegger and Marx does so through Hegel, and through the interpretation of history. The question of Hegel's place in Marx's thinking, and Heidegger's own reading of Hegel, will occupy several chapters.

Martin Heidegger's television interview with Richard Wisser raises the question of the demand that philosophy itself lays before thinking. Alasdair MacIntyre argues that "Marx rejected Hegel and Feuerbach . . . [and] by rejecting philosophy, at a stage at which his philosophical enquiries were still incomplete and were still informed by mistakes inherited from his philosophical predecessors, Marx allowed his later work to be distorted by presuppositions which were in key respects infected by philosophical error."[1] MacIntyre adds of Marx that "with his rejection of philosophy in 1845 he lost the opportunity to develop those thoughts systematically and to understand their implications for the relationship of theory to practice."[2] This is to underestimate Marx and to fail to see adequately what Heidegger himself identifies: that Marx's understanding of political economy has already secured a sufficient world-interpretation for itself to proceed as a demand for world-change: moreover, that this demand for world-change, however much

1. Alasdair MacIntyre, "The Theses on Feuerbach: A Road Not Taken," 224.
2. Ibid., 232.

it claims to spring from a rejection of Hegel, in fact is possible only in consequence not of what Hegel claimed, but from out of the *same* as he himself was describing. In this sense, Marx fulfills an understanding that arises only on the basis of what Hegel's phenomenology arises on the basis *of.* We want to read Marx's eleventh thesis on Feuerbach as a rejection of philosophy: it is nothing of the kind. In what is often described by Marxists as Marx's first genuinely "Marxist" text,[3] the *Critique of Hegel's Philosophy of Right: Introduction,* Marx reminds us that "*you cannot exceed philosophy unless you realise it.*"[4] "Exceed" here translates *aufheben,* a word whose philosophical roots are to be found in Kant and which comes to be of absolutely central importance in Hegel, and which we will have to consider in far greater depth as we proceed. Here it would be better translated as "cancel and take-up-and-over." The word "realise" translates *verwirklichen:* we should hear this as "put to work, and *set* to work": as we shall discover over and again, this word contains the essence of *Wirklichkeit,* "reality," which in German already has the sense of something not just standing "there" (where the real would be rendered in German as *Reell*) but as something brought about and realized, "worked." The eleventh thesis has to be read historically, as a statement concerning not the rejection, but the development of philosophy—it lays out what philosophy is to *become,* to remain adequate to its name. If Heidegger repeatedly says philosophy is the most useless discipline, Marx says the opposite: philosophy is realized and put to use through what realizes and works it out.

A phenomenology does not simply bring to adequate description what it knows (and yet, genuinely to speak of the phenomena, it must do this), for the bringing to description in question appears to stand to one side of what is described, as if it were coolly or dispassionately gesturing toward what is to be seen in what is to be said. Every genuine phenomenology at the same time brings to the fore the *one* undertaking the description, and it brings this one to the fore in the midst of what is to be brought to light. This does not mean that Marx is that one brought to the fore: rather it means a particular understanding of some matter—in Marx's case, the particular (and historical) understanding of the subjectivity of the subject that produces the history that it at the same time *is.*

As soon as the texts of the early Marx became available, the status and character of the thought of the early Marx was propelled to the fore as a question, and (as we can see with MacIntyre) has remained so in ways to which we will have to return. Right from the beginning of Marx's and En-

3. See, for instance, Kostas Axelos, *Marx: Penseur de la technique,* 148.

4. Karl Marx, "Zur Kritik der Hegelschen Rechtsphilosophie. Einleitung" (*MEW*1), 384. "*Ihr könnt die Philosophie nicht aufheben, ohne sie zu verwirklichen*" (Marx's emphasis).

gels's political thinking, however—indeed, in the very first recorded exchange between Engels and Marx—the *one* in question, and the manner of its coming to light, arises, as the very basis of Marxism. Engels, writing from the Wuppertal region and energized by the effects of remorseless industrialization on that region, speaks of the social effects of the transformation he witnesses, saying "in short, a splendid soil prepares itself for our principle."[5] The "principle" in question is that which stands out in advance of everything else, one that organizes and lets be seen what is most fundamental, and leads and directs everything else around it. The principle in question is an entirely metaphysical principle. What is this principle? Engels speaks of how the workers and proletariat of Wuppertal have "arrived at the last stage of the old civilisation," and how they protest against the old social organization through taking to violence and crime. The principle is therefore one of transition: from individuals, through communism, to become exemplars of human being in general. Engels says of these workers: "so they will soon come to see that in this manner as *individuals* and violently to protest against the social order is useless." They will therefore *become* something else, "and protest in their general capacity as *human beings* through communism."[6] Protest is a mere means: social transformation indicates a transformation in the essence of being human in itself.

Every thought is therefore to be read off from the means by which this transformation both comes to light, and is actively brought to light. This "bringing to light" is a necessity; it is the exhibiting of an already insistent principle. This is how the *phenomenon* of "the human being in general" (the subjectivity of the subject) comes to be thought, from out of the actions which it undertakes. This is in the most condensed form the metaphysics of Marxism, the metaphysical principle from which every other understanding of Marxism comes to light. There is no failure of philosophy here—rather this is philosophy as an *active* phenomenology, even if it is yet to receive a full and adequate terminological description. Although the description of this process of becoming, and the essence of man transforming itself and producing itself anew *as* the principle of transformation itself, is provided by Engels and not Marx, it is the very essence of Marx's own understanding, and of Marxism itself. The *one* in question is the human being as "subject."

In Heidegger's critique of the presence of a metaphysical outlook in

5. Friedrich Engels, letter to Karl Marx of October 1844 (*MEW*27), 7. "Kurz, hier bereitet sich ein prächtiger Boden für unser Prinzip vor."

6. Friedrich Engels, letter to Karl Marx of October 1844 (*MEW*27), 7. "Auf der letzten Stufe der alten Zivilisation angekommen . . . so werden sie bald einsehen, daß diese Manier, als *Individuen* und gewaltsam gegen die soziale Ordnung zu protestieren, nutzlos ist, und als *Menschen* in ihrer allgemeinen Kapazität durch den Kommunismus protestieren" (Engels's emphases).

Marx, what Heidegger brings to the fore is the *taxis,* the "order in which" things occur. Heidegger points out that Marx has *already* secured the understanding required for the world-transformation on which the understanding of any subsequent action would then depend. Marx argues: "You can see already what is required for the changes that must be carried out! The adequate philosophy on which the demand for change is already present to you and stands before your very eyes as an insistent demand!" What this means is that the vision of everyone who sees adequately is determined from out of the already visible requirement that stands before him: the social transformation in question has the necessity of an imperative which can be resisted or opposed in the particular, but cannot be avoided—it will *over*come all that stands in it way. Most of all, this principle of transformation is to be taken up and completed. It is here that we can understand that the place which one occupies with respect to this demand is itself already directional—either *for* and *able to promote* the already-present requirement for change, or *against,* and *withholding* the requirement for change.

To a certain extent, however, we jump ahead of ourselves. In the television interview, Wisser had spoken of how the current situation (in 1969) is characterized by modern attempts within the social or interpersonal sphere to obtain a reorientation of objectives and a "restructuring" of factual conditions—we would now say, the technical manipulation of personal or social relations for the sake of desired outcomes. Wisser concludes this question by asking of Heidegger, "Do you see a social mission arising from philosophy?"[7] Heidegger replies, in advance of the quotation concerning the "Theses on Feuerbach," "In order to answer this question, one must first ask 'What is society?' and one must pursue this by thinking through that contemporary society is only the absolutising of modern *subjectivity,* and that from here onwards a philosophy which has overcome the standpoint of subjectivity really must not join in this discussion."[8] This sentence is translated quite differently in the two English translations that have been made of the Wisser interview,[9] in each case overlooking the emphasis of the character of the discus-

7. Martin Heidegger, "Martin Heidegger im Gespräch" (*GA*16), 702. "Sehen Sie einen gesellschaftlichen Auftrag der Philosophie?"

8. Ibid., 703. "Wenn man diese Frage beantworten will, muß man zuerst fragen: 'Was ist Gesellschaft?' und muß darüber nachdenken, daß die heutige Gesellschaft nur die Verabsolutierung der modernen *Subjektivität* ist und daß von hier aus eine Philosophie, die den Standpunkt der Subjektivität überwunden hat, überhaupt nicht mitsprechen darf" (Heidegger's emphasis).

9. See "Martin Heidegger in Conversation with Richard Wisser," 82. "A philosophy that has overcome a position of subjectivity therefore has no say in the matter." See also the translation by B. Srinivasa Murthy in *Martin Heidegger in Conversation: Edited by Richard Wisser,* 39. "A philosophy which has overcome the standpoint of philosophy may not join in the discussion at all."

sion which philosophy is to have. Heidegger does not say: philosophy is not to engage with any discussion on the character of what is here being named "the social." Rather he says: philosophy is not to understand itself as having any "mission" (*Auftrag*) in the technical rearrangement of the social and interpersonal for supposedly desirable ends. In this he is in perfect agreement with Marx: the action of transformation of the social order cannot spring from out of a rational plan: it springs from the imperative of the actual occurring of the subjectivity of the subject, of what "human being in its absolutely most general capacity" *is*. The social order that Marxism believes is demanded by the subjectivity of the subject is: communism. Insofar as this is the case, Heidegger correctly and astutely remarks, what one means by "society" (the imperative in question) depends on how the subjectivity of the subject is *already* understood.

We would be tempted, as is indicated precisely by the inclusion of a discussion of the interview by Wisser himself in the volume prepared by one of Heidegger's publishers (and close friend), Günther Neske, entitled *Reply: Martin Heidegger in Conversation*,[10] to assume that what is at issue is Heidegger's own withdrawal from the political, a withdrawal that had been mocked by a colleague, Wolfgang Schadewaldt, bumping into Heidegger in 1934 after his adventure as rector of Freiburg University and resignation from the post at the beginning of the Nazi accession to power with the comment "Back from Syracuse?" Rüdiger Safranski recounts the tale, noting that it was "in Syracuse Plato had intended to realise his State utopia and had thereby only luckily escaped enslavement."[11] In the last chapter, I already noted that the period of Heidegger's thinking under the title *Das Ereignis* is to be understood as a political engagement, but that a political engagement does not entail an engagement in the politics of the moment. Richard Wisser says in his reflections on the circumstances surrounding the television interview that he had discussed with Heidegger the questions he proposed to ask him while waiting for the television crew and technicians to arrive. Heidegger had balked at the question concerning the social mission of philosophy precisely because, as Heidegger had said, to clarify the claim that philosophy is "equal to social philosophy" would require bringing in Marx.[12]

10. Günther Neske and Emil Kettering, eds., *Antwort: Martin Heidegger im Gespräch.*

11. Rüdiger Safranski, *Ein Meister aus Deutschland: Heidegger und seine Zeit*, 313. "'Zurück aus Syrakus?' . . . In Syrakus hatte Platon bekanntlich seine Staatsutopie verwirklichen wollen und war dabei nur mit großem Glück der Sklaverei entronnen."

12. Richard Wisser, "Nachdenkliche Denkarbeit," in *Antwort: Martin Heidegger im Gespräch*, 42. "[Wisser] 'Dann sagen Sie es! Sagen Sie es, warum Sie keinen sehen! Sagen Sie, was heute manch einer hinunterschluckt! Klären Sie das Mißverständnis auf, daß Philosophie gleich Gesellschaftsphilosophie ist!' [Heidegger] 'Da müßte ich weit ausholen, da ist Marx, und Sie wissen . . .'"

Wisser reports Heidegger as concluding the discussion on this "social philosophy" by saying, with regard to the situation of contemporary philosophy, "yes, but what happens today has nothing to do with philosophy, that is sociology."[13]

Heidegger brings us up before the understanding that philosophy, specifically the philosophy of the period *Das Ereignis,* stands in contrast to what passes for philosophy in the contemporary situation. Philosophy that has a "social mission" is not philosophy at all (the adequate bringing to a description of the imperative that is experienced and that presents itself, and in presenting itself, poses the question of the *one* being presented), but in fact is mere sociology. Sociology, by implication, has already secured in advance what the imperative is, using every technical means at one's disposal to bring about with even greater speed the imperative in question.

There is a third indication from the Wisser interview which will help us open up the dialogue with the productive that we seek to undertake. We have already established that for Heidegger, the thinking that thinks *das Ereignis,* the thinking that he suggests here remains on the course of philosophy (although here he speaks in a shorthand, a language itself presented for presentation through a mass medium: elsewhere he is apt to equate philosophy and metaphysics), has overcome "the standpoint of subjectivity," that thinking which has absolutized "subjectivity as society." This raises the *historical* question of philosophy. In what sense is philosophy "historical"—in what sense is it said to have a history? In the *Letter on Humanism,* Heidegger makes the claim that "the Marxist view of history is superior to that of the other historical accounts."[14] This is in consequence of what Marx derived from Hegel, "as the estrangement [alienation] of human beings."[15] Nevertheless the *Letter on Humanism,* you will recall, still speaks, as far as Heidegger is concerned, with the language of metaphysics: the "other language" lies in the background. The other language comes to the fore only in the most condensed form in the Wisser interview.

Wisser suggests to Heidegger that his is an attempt "to see through the former history of philosophy as a history of decline with regard to being."[16] This, as it were, would be to locate Heidegger's thinking in the history of radical conservative critique, the tradition of Ernst Jünger and his brother Friedrich Georg Jünger—what Daniel Morat has called the "activistic logic

13. Richard Wisser, "Nachdenkliche Dankarbeit," 44. "Ja aber was heute geschieht, das hat mit Philosophie nichts zu tun, das ist Soziologie."

14. Martin Heidegger, *Brief über den Humanismus* (*GA*9), 340. "Deshalb ist die marxistische Anschauung von der Geschichte der übrigen Historie überlegen."

15. Ibid., 340. "Als die Entfremdung des Menschen."

16. Martin Heidegger, "Martin Heidegger im Gespräch" (*GA*16), 704. "Die bisherige Philosophiegeschichte als eine Verfallsgeschichte im Blick auf das Sein zu durchschauen."

of the conservative revolution and the New Right,"[17] of the "decisionism" of Carl Schmitt,[18] and above all the "cultural critique" of Oswald Spengler's *Decline of the West.*[19] Heidegger explicitly refuses that the "history of decline" is to be understood negatively in this way, and then continues:

> I do not speak of a history of decline, but only of the fate [*Geschick*] of being insofar as it more and more withdraws itself in comparison to the openness of being to be found in the Greeks—up to the unfolding of being as mere objectivity for the sciences and today as mere material for the technical mastery of the world. Thus, it is not a history of decline, but it is a *withdrawal of being*, in which we stand.
>
> The most characteristic feature for the forgetfulness—and forgetfulness is here *always* to be thought from the Greeks forward, from out of Lethe, that means from the self-concealing, from the self-withdrawing of being—now, the characteristic feature of the fate in which we stand is—as far as I can see overall, the fact that the *question of being*, which I pose, is not yet *understood.*[20]

Wisser finally raised with Heidegger the question of "destroying" (*destruieren*), that is, of the way in which Heidegger had announced in *Being and Time* that the philosophical tradition is to be interpreted as a whole, in order to gain access to it.

The language here remains in the province of the language of *Being and Time,* illustrating yet again the central importance of the question of how *Being and Time* is to be interpreted, the very question that Heidegger himself raises in relation to Marx in the *Letter on Humanism,* and that has

17. Daniel Morat, *Von der Tat zur Gelassenheit: Konservatives Denken bei Martin Heidegger, Ernst Jünger und Friedrich Georg Jünger 1920–1960,* 35–50.

18. See especially Carl Schmitt, *Der Nomos der Erde im Völkerrecht des Jus Publicum Europaeum.*

19. Oswald Spengler, *Der Untergang des Abendlandes: Umrisse einer Morphologie der Weltgeschichte.*

20. Martin Heidegger, "Martin Heidegger im Gespräch" (*GA*16), 704–5. "Ich spreche nicht von einer Verfallsgeschichte, sondern nur vom Geschick des Seins insofern, als es sich mehr und mehr im Vergleich zu der Offenbarkeit des Seins bei den Griechen entzieht—bis zur Entfaltung des Seins als bloßer Gegenständlichkeit für die Wissenschaft und heute als bloßer Bestand für die technische Bewältigung der Welt. Also: es ist nicht eine Verfallsgeschichte, sondern es ist ein *Entzug des Seins,* in dem wir stehen.

"Das am meisten charakterische Merkmal für die Seinsvergessenheit—und Vergessenheit ist hier *immer* zu denken vom Griechischen her, von der Lethe, d.h. vom Sich-Verbergen, vom Sich-Entziehen des Seins her—nun, das charakterische Merkmal des Geschicks, in dem wir stehen, ist—soweit ich das überhaupt übersehe—die Tatsache, daß die *Seinsfrage,* die ich stelle, noch nicht *verstanden* ist" (Heidegger's emphases).

been raised by subsequent commentators with respect to restricting it to the language of metaphysics. There is no doubt that before and up to *Being and Time* Heidegger's language took one form, concentrating, it would seem, on the "preparatory fundamental analysis of existence,"[21] and after 1927 appears to undergo a certain change, with a far stronger emphasis on the question of the truth of being. In Heidegger's letter to William Richardson, addressing the question of whether there is a "Heidegger I" and "Heidegger II," Heidegger replied by saying: "The distinction you make between Heidegger I and II is justified only on the condition that this is kept constantly in mind: only by way of what Heidegger I has thought does one gain access to what is to-be-thought by Heidegger II. But [the thought of] Heidegger I becomes possible only if it is contained in Heidegger II."[22] Frequently in later texts, however, Heidegger reverts to the language of "Heidegger I," and of the analysis of existence (*Dasein*), so that right to the end of his life it is clear that he did not understand the fundamental position of *Being and Time* to have been invalidated or superseded, even if it had been vastly amplified and explained.[23]

What this means for us is that the productive dialogue must itself be

21. This is the title of the first section of the First Division of *Being and Time*. Compare Martin Heidegger, *Sein und Zeit* (*GA*2), 55. "*Die vorbereitende Fundamentalanalyse des Daseins*" (italicized in the German text).

22. William J. Richardson, *Through Phenomenology to Thought,* xxiii. "Ihre Unterscheidung zwischen 'Heidegger I' und 'Heidegger II' ist allein unter der Bedingung berechtigt, daß stets beachtet wird: Nur von dem unter I Gedachten her wird zunächst das unter II zu Denkende zugänglich. Aber I wird nur möglich, wenn es in II enthalten ist."

23. In one of the few places where Heidegger discusses the progress and development of his own thinking, in a report in the third Le Thor seminar of 1969, Heidegger said: "With *Being and Time,* however, the question concerning being receives an entirely other meaning. Here it appears as the question concerning being as being. It becomes thematic in *Being and Time* under the name 'the question concerning the meaning of being.'"

"Later this formulation was given up in favour of the 'question concerning the truth of being'—finally in favour of that of the 'question concerning the place or location of being'—from out of which the name 'topology of being' arose.

"Three words, which, inasmuch as they succeed one another, at the same time indicate three steps along the way of thinking:

"MEANING—TRUTH—PLACE (τόπος)."

Martin Heidegger, *Seminare* (*GA*15), 344. "Mit 'Sein und Zeit' jedoch bekommt 'Frage nach dem Sein' einen ganz anderen Sinn. Hier geht es um die Frage nach dem Sein als Sein. Sie wird in 'Sein und Zeit' unter dem Namen 'Fragen nach dem Sinn von Sein' thematisch.

"Später wird diese Formulierung aufgegeben zugunsten jener 'Frage nach der Wahrheit des Seins'—und schließlich zugunsten jener der 'Frage nach dem Ort oder Ortschaft des Seins'—woraus der Name 'Topologie des Seins' entsprang.

"Drei Worte, die, indem sie einander ablösen, gleichzeitig drei Schritte auf dem Weg des Denkens bezeichnen:

"SINN—WAHRHEIT—ORT (τόπος)."

interpreted with respect to both the "history of being" and to the "forgetfulness of being." The language that Heidegger uses in the Wisser interview remains within the province of *Being and Time,* but it is to be understood from out of that historical understanding that is at the same time given in the meaning of *Das Ereignis:* as the interpretation of a withdrawal of being. What this also means is that our "productive dialogue," the dialogue which will yield the meaning of "the productive as such," will also enable us to understand in what way Marx's own thought arises both within the history of being, and on the basis of the withdrawal of being.

It is here that we should turn briefly to what Marx means by "society," which Heidegger wants to interpret as "the absolutising of subjectivity." We will not be able to conclude this inquiry in this chapter, but we must begin. First, however, having gained a fundamental orientation on the meaning of the term "forgetfulness of being," as essentially connected with *Das Ereignis,* we must take one further directive from Heidegger, this time not from the television interview, but from somewhere quite else.

Marx understands the emergence of the proletariat as a specifically *historical* phenomenon. Marx notes in *Das Kapital* that capital can "itself only come into existence where the owner of the means of production and means of subsistence meets with the free worker as one selling his labour-power in the market, and this one historical condition comprises a world-history. Capital forecloses therefore and from the outset on an epoch in the processes of social production."[24] The freedom of the worker is, as we shall explore later on, Marx's indication of the subjectivity of the subject, *itself* a historical phenomenon which takes shape in the form of the worker only after long centuries of preparation. Marx points out in a footnote to the text of *Das Kapital* that "on the other hand only from this moment on is it a generality that the product of work is a commodity": the appearance of *this* subjectivity of the subject at the same time produces the object-character of objects for this historical event.[25]

Marx explains at a later point in *Das Kapital:* "The reproduction of labour-power, which must incessantly incorporate itself as a means of exploitation, which cannot get free from capital, and whose enslavement to capital is only concealed through the process of exchange with individual capitalists to whom it sells itself, forms in the very fact a moment of the reproduction of

24. Karl Marx, *Das Kapital,* vol. 1 (*MEW*23), 184. "Es entsteht nur wo der Besitzer von Produktions- und Lebensmitteln den freien Arbeiter als Verkäufer seiner Arbeitskraft auf dem Markt vorfindet, und diese eine historische Bedingung umschließt eine Weltgeschichte. Das Kapital kündigt daher von vornherein eine Epoche des gesellschaftlichen Produktionsprozesses an."

25. Ibid., 184, n. 41. "Andrerseits verallgemeinert sich erst von diesem Augenblick die Warenform der Arbeitsprodukte."

capital itself. Accumulation of capital is thus the increase of the proletariat."[26] Marx deliberately and self-consciously turns the meaning of the term "proletarian" against itself. That he is doing so is given by his specific tracing of the historical appearances of this term to Constantin Pecqueur and Wilhelm Roscher at this point in *Das Kapital.*[27] In ancient Rome, the proletariat were the least of the population of the city, contributing nothing to the state but its own physical increase: *proles,* the Latin for "offspring." Marx's employment of the term takes up this etymology, showing how every increase is at the same time an *effect* of the increase of capital, or rather, that capital feeds off and consumes even the increase it generates in the proletariat—who, by implication, are unable to enjoy the increase that they *are.* At every turn, in other words, Marx seeks to concretize and shake loose from all theoretical abstraction that *one* whom he seeks to describe. The proletarian is that one who, most of all, is in the midst, and *is* the very driving force, of the expansion of capital and the history of humanity itself, even if the fruits of that drive are always stripped from him. Even here, the capitalist is merely that one who extracts value from the very driving force, the alienated labor of the engine of the imperative, the work-life of the proletarian.

In loose-leaved notes whose date (best estimated at 1940, from the note on the packet in which it was found) is almost certainly from almost exactly the middle of the period of the development of the understanding of *Das Ereignis,* but not part of these notebooks themselves, Heidegger opens a discussion of that most Marxist of phrases, "the misery of the masses (proletariat)."[28] There is much in this small section that will gain our attention for our productive dialogue, but here I want to examine only two features of it. Exactly as Marx also does, Heidegger understands the emergence of the pro-

26. Ibid., 641–42. "Die Reproduktion der Arbeitskraft, die sich dem Kapital unaufhörlich als Verwertungsmittel einverleiben muß, nicht von ihm loskommen kann und deren Hörigkeit zum Kapital nur versteckt wird durch den Wechsel der individuellen Kapitalisten, woran sie sich verkauft, bildet in der Tat ein Moment der Reproduktion des Kapitals selbst. Akkumulation des Kapitals ist also Vermehrung des Proletariats."

27. Constantin Pecqueur was appointed to the "Luxembourg" Commission of 1848 headed by Louis Blanc and was a distinguished socialist economist of the period, developing a rudimentary theory of class and advocating state ownership of production. Roscher was the founder of the "historical school" of political economy, following Friedrich List, and developed by Roscher, and culminating to an extent in the work of Max Weber.

28. Martin Heidegger, *Leitgedanken zur Entstehung der Metaphysik, der neuzeitlichen Wissenschaft und der modernen Technik* (*GA*76), 299. "Das Elend der Masse (Proletariat)." The notes were in a single collection of 24 manuscripts dating from 1936 to 1955, with one sheet appearing from 1958. Almost all are undated, with the exception of those from which this section, *Τέχνη und Technik* (285–318) are found, which were contained in a wrapper with the date "1940" written on them. Much of the material appears preparatory for the lecture series *Einblick in das was ist* (the "Bremen" lectures) of 1949 (*GA*79).

letariat, of the massification of humanity *into* the proletariat, to have reached a particular stage of *historical* development through the introduction of the machine. The machine represents not simply an enhancement of the tool, but is itself a historical event. Marx is mocking of those mathematicians and mechanicians who see no essential difference between the tool and the machine, adding: "and one finds" that this viewpoint "is recapitulated here and there by English economists."[29]

Heidegger notes that "indeed the masses themselves and their origin are established through the machinic generation of goods; at the same time, however, the masses are the ones who can least do without this means of production."[30] Does Heidegger not therefore suggest that the misery of the masses itself arises on the basis of the historical development of capital, when in a rough and incomplete note that he argues that this development occurs in the following way: "with machine-production—command over men, accumulation of 'capital' and at the same time expansion of the proletariat"?[31]

Heidegger's conclusion runs in another direction, arguing that "technology does not save and make 'work' easier in a particular sense, rather, it only transforms it and through the essential alteration of work it carries out the reinforcement of the forgetfulness of being."[32] Heidegger understands the fundamental connection between work, technology, capital, and their factical historical forms (as the expression of their "essential" forms) to be in consequence of, and expressive of, the forgetfulness of being. Located in the proletariat itself, and in its misery, we can identify the poles of the conversation that we are seeking to unfold. On the one hand in Marx the very existence of the proletariat is the possibility for the expansion and the existence of capital and the driving imperative of history. On the other hand, for Heidegger, this essentially historical development of the existence of the proletariat and its need of technological expansion and advance is itself only in consequence of the withdrawal and forgetfulness of being.

In any conversation of Heidegger's with Marx and Marxism, the ques-

29. Karl Marx, *Das Kapital,* vol. 1 (*MEW*23), 391–92. "Und man findet dies hier und da von englischen Ökonomen wiederholt."

30. Martin Heidegger, *Leitgedanken zur Entstehung der Metaphysik* (*GA*76), 299. "Ja die Masse selbst und ihre Entstehung mitgesetzt durch die maschinenhafte Gütererzeugung; zugleich aber kann die Masse am wenigsten auf diese Art von Produktion verzichten."

31. Ibid., 299. "Mit der Maschinenproduktion—Verfügung über Menschen, Anhäufung des 'Kapitals' und zugleich Wachsen des Proletariats." We should note that Axelos had thought Heidegger could never speak in these terms—and yet inasmuch as he does, he does so entirely privately.

32. Ibid., 299. "Die Technik erspart und erleichtert nicht die 'Arbeit' im eigentlichen Sinne, sie formt sie nur um und vollzieht durch den Wesenswandel der Arbeit erst recht die Verfestigung der Seinsvergessenheit."

tion of history comes to the fore: the Marxist view of history, says Heidegger, attains to superiority over every other so far; at the same time, Heidegger's understanding of being arises on the basis of the history of being in its withdrawal. Philosophy *as* historical, however, is itself a historical development, specifically in the thought of Hegel. Heidegger sets out Hegel's fundamental position in the following way: "Therefore for Hegel philosophy as the self-production of *Geist* toward absolute knowledge and the history of philosophy are identical.[33] No philosopher *before* Hegel had achieved such a fundamental position, one which enabled and required that philosophizing at the same time move itself within its history and that this movement is itself philosophy."[34] Heidegger notes that philosophy has, Hegel says, "truth" as its "goal." Hegel places the subjectivity of the subject into the very center, to become the very site, of both the production and the unfolding of history. Marx's materialism is taken off from this very point, while setting aside the question of the "goal" as truth: so, also from this very point, is Heidegger's understanding of being historical, but from out of the "truth of being," which is the description he gives to his own thinking.

Heidegger cites Hegel, but does not quote the sentence he cites, selecting only the words "goal" and "truth" from Hegel's sentence. In the sentence in question, Hegel says: "The thought of a history of philosophy which we first encounter is that the object itself contains an inner conflict. For philosophy envisages knowing what is unchangeable, eternal, in and for itself: its goal is truth. But history recounts that which has been at one time, at another vanished, being overcome through something else."[35]

Marx rounds on Hegel for asserting the priority of the abstract and ideal over the actual, the phenomena themselves—this is the very basis of his 1843 manuscript, the *Critique of the Hegelian State Order.*[36] In reality

33. We will leave the word *Geist* untranslated for now.

34. Martin Heidegger, "Hegel und die Griechen" (*GA*9), 428–29. "Demnach sind für Hegel die Philosophie als die Selbstentwicklung des Geistes zum absoluten Wissen und die Geschichte der Philosophie identisch. Kein Philosoph *vor* Hegel hat eine solche Grundstellung der Philosophie gewonnen, die es ermöglicht und fordert, daß das Philosophieren sich zugleich in seiner Geschichte bewegt und daß diese Bewegung die Philosophie selbst ist" (Heidegger's emphasis).

35. Compare Martin Heidegger, "Hegel und die Griechen" (*GA*9), 429. Heidegger cites the first section of Hegel's lectures on the history of philosophy. See G. W. F. Hegel, *Vorlesungen über die Geschichte der Philosophie I,* 23. "Der Gedanke, der uns bei einer Geschichte der Philosophie zunächst entgegenkommen kann, ist, daß sogleich dieser Gegenstand selbst einen inneren Widerstreit enthalte. Denn die Philosophie beabsichtigt das zu erkennen, was unvergänglich, ewig, an und für sich ist; ihr Ziel ist die Wahrheit. Die Geschichte aber erzählt solches, was zu einer Zeit gewesen, zu einer anderen aber verschwunden und durch anderes verdrängt worden ist."

36. Compare Karl Marx, *Kritik der Hegelschen Staatsrechts* (*MEW*1), 201–333, not published until 1927 under the editorial work of David Riazanov and the Marxist-Leninist Institute in Moscow. See 218, where Marx comments "Hegel is here a Sophist" ("Hegel ist hier Sophist").

Marx only attacks a possibility of interpretation already present in Hegel's thought: and presses Hegel away from the understanding of being as a formal topic, toward humanity as the formal principle of every "idea" that manifests itself, and so that appears *as* a phenomenon in the real and the actual. In relation to Hegel's understanding of the political constitution of the state, Marx argues that the constitution must advance "stepping forth with consciousness," that is, as consciousness develops historically, with the aim that it advances "in step with real human beings, which is only possible when man as such has become a principle of the constitution."[37] Hegel himself, and especially in the *Philosophy of Right,* emphasizes the extent to which the idea, the Idea itself, becomes phenomenally available only through the actual, through the realization of the idea. In Hegel there is a powerful and constant impulse to overcome the supersensible which Marx at one and the same time refuses to acknowledge and yet in his own writing presses to its furthest degree, that purely ideal realm in which the ideas subsist and the Idea *is.* Hegel stresses that "it is indeed *this positioning of philosophy within reality,* which is struck by misunderstandings . . . philosophy, because it is the *getting to the bottom of the reasonable* is even so the *grasping of the present and real,* not the erection of a *beyond;* God alone knows where that might be."[38]

The "getting to the bottom" (*Ergründen*), emphasized in Hegel's text, evidences his own privileging of the "here," the "actual and "real" *over* the idea. Hegel's attitude (paralleling Nietzsche's "devaluation of the uppermost values for the sake of a revaluation of all values") is for the *grounding* of reason rather than its idealization, its ideation in the "beyond." The word "beyond," *jenseits,* which Hegel employs here, is a direct reference to Plato's term *epekeina,* the "beyond" as the "over there" of the *idea tou agathou,* that place which constitutes the site of the eternal and unchanging in the history of metaphysics, discussed in the *Republic* and to which Hegel himself directly alludes.[39] Hegel, no less than Nietzsche, announces the overcoming of the uppermost of reason with the priority of the here-present, the formal overturning of the hitherto structure of transcendence. It is precisely in this

37. Karl Marx, "Kritik der Hegelschen Staatsrechts" (*MEW*1), 218. "Mit dem Bewußtsein fortzuschreiten; fortzuschreiten mit dem wirklichen Menschen, was erst möglich ist, sobald der 'Mensch' zum Prinzip der Verfassung geworden ist."

38. G. W. F. Hegel, *Grundlinien der Philosophie des Rechts,* 24. "Es ist eben *diese Stellung der Philosophie zur Wirklichkeit,* welche die Mißverständnisse betreffen . . . die Philosophie, weil sie das *Ergründen des Vernünftigen* ist, eben damit das *Erfassen des Gegenwärtigen und Wirklichen,* nicht das Aufstellen eines *Jenseitigen* ist, das Gott weiß, wo sein sollte" (Hegel's emphases).

39. See Plato, *Republic,* 514a2–517a7; 509b. οὐκ οὐσίας ὄντος τοῦ ἀγαθοῦ, ἀλλ' ἔτι ἐπέκεινα τῆς οὐσίας πρεσβείᾳ καὶ δυνάμει ὑπερέχοντος.

way that Hegel transforms the activity of transcending into an actualized historical activity, rather than the formal (and unchanging) structure which is the consequence of an idealized *single* act (the *actus purus* of the eternally unchanging divine mind). In this Hegel emphasizes the formal emptiness of being (as the most general, "uppermost" concept), the source of Hegel's determined claim that being and nothing are the same (which we will examine in greater depth in the next chapter). The real and the actual attain to the idea, but at the same time they produce what they attain to. The idea therefore is the overcoming of the real, but, as Heidegger stresses (quoting a remark of Hegel's added to the original text), "from within"—"the inner remaining-within-itself of *Geist*."[40] The idea *is* only because of the historical, the real and the actual. In the overcoming of the real which is the manifestation of the idea as such, only further reality is produced.

Idealism, which Hegel is supposed to "represent" and which Marx is, with his most strongly argued materialism, supposed to be opposing, never departs from a concern with the material and what is positively given. In the text of a series of lectures from 1942 which were never delivered, Heidegger stresses that all thinking that seeks to represent beings in their beingness and explain them through the division between the sensory and the "supersensible," whether it seeks to explain the supersensible or "overcome" it by combating or rejecting it (in "realism," empiricism," "positivism," and the like), remains within the original region marked out by Plato's understanding of being as *represented* which means represented through the *idea.* The force of philosophy is not whether the philosophy in question is idealism or materialism or all the counter-movements and reversals in between, but rather that every philosophy thinks the ground of beings as *represented.* Idealism and materialism as "opposites" really only function as names for different ways of struggling with this question. Heidegger says "that thinking which represents the being in its beingness is 'philosophy.' 'Philosophy' has been since Plato the name for this understanding that oscillates between the sensory and the supersensible, which strives after the possession of the authoritative knowledge of the ground of the being of beings through being as representation."[41] All of this "understanding" is Platonism, which means inasmuch as idealism is a form of Platonism, at the same time "even materialism is Platonism."[42] In

40. See Martin Heidegger, "Hegel und die Griechen" (*GA*9), 429, citing G. W. F. Hegel, *Grundlinien der Philosophie des Rechts*, 13, n. 5. "Das innere Beisichselbstbleiben des Geistes."

41. Martin Heidegger, *Der Spruch der Anaximander* (*GA*78), 13. "Das Denken, das das Seiende in seiner Seiendheit vorstellt, ist 'Philosophie.' 'Philosophie' wird seit Platon der Name für dieses zwischen dem Sinnlichen und dem Übersinnlichen hin und her gehende Verstehen, das danach strebt, durch das Vorstellen des Seins als des Grundes für das Seiende von Seienden selbst das maßgebende Wissen zu besitzen."

42. Ibid., 13. "Sogar der Materialismus ist Platonismus."

the same place, Heidegger emphasizes that, inasmuch as Nietzsche's philosophy is the reversal of Platonism, it remains in this region of Platonism, and there in the same region "Occidental philosophy is Platonism, as is the philosophy of Aristotle."[43] Philosophy *is* "being as representation"—the question is, "represented through what"? If in Hegel's idealism the idea comes to expression through humanity, as we shall see, Marx's counter-position to Hegel is that humanity materially produces itself as the idea, and thereby brings the idea to representation.

Marx identifies in Hegel a formal ambiguity which he shows Hegel is never finally able to resolve, between the status of the individual and the formal status of humanity taken as a whole.[44] Hegel attempts to resolve this ambiguity through his description of the concrete form of the state, but this is insufficient for Marx, for whom the state is only a relative or provisional form in the hands of particular interests. The existence of this ambiguity, and Hegel's inability to clarify it, is, for Marx, precisely the driving need to disband and destroy formally the place or manifestation of that "whole" as a "beyond" or "other" to humanity. It is not accidental that, following Hegel's own impulses toward materialism, and toward the priority of the "real" and "actual" *over* the ideal, these questions manifest themselves in the character of the political—of the social locus of the individual, in the state, and in the social manifestation of human identity. In his commentary on Hegel's understanding of the state, Marx cites the ambiguity Hegel raises: "The individuals of the mass hold here within themselves their own *geistige* nature of a twofold significance: namely one extreme of *explicit individuality* of knowing and willing and the [other] extreme of *universality* which knows and wills the substantial."[45] *Geistig* here means intellective, intelligent, "spiritual," but also social—the substantial is nothing other than being as such, the truth of which philosophy (the practice of the intellectual and spiritual at the highest) aims at. The ambiguity is itself twofold: not only between the individual and its entirety, but also in the *where* of the manifestation of this universality. Where does it show itself? Is it manifest in the political state or in its consti-

43. Ibid., 12. "Die abendländische Philosophie ist Platonismus, auch die Philosophie des Aristoteles."

44. Heidegger formally identifies this ambiguity as it is presented in Hegel's thought in the all too frequently overlooked penultimate section of *Sein und Zeit.* Compare Martin Heidegger, *Sein und Zeit* (GA2), 572. For Hegel, "So ist das Ich '*Allgemeinheit,*' aber *ebenso* unmittelbar 'Einzelheit.'" ("Thus is the I '*in general*' even *as much* as it is 'individuality.'") (Heidegger's emphases.)

45. Karl Marx, "Kritik der Hegelschen Staatsrechts" (*MEW*1), 208, citing §264 of G. W. F. Hegel, *Grundlinien der Philosophie des Rechts,* 411. "Die Individuen der Menge, da sie selbst geistige Naturen und damit das gedoppelte Moment, nämlich das Extrem der *für sich* wissenden und wollenden *Einzelheit* und das Extrem der das Substantielle wissenden und wollenden *Allgemeinheit* in sich enthalten" (Hegel's original emphases, reproduced in Marx's text).

tution, as the "general will" of the individuals in the polity (or which resolves that general will into something higher and more positive)? Is it exhibited in the supersensible?—which Marx will not allow, but which it would seem Hegel himself is also disavowing? Is it in a new form of individual life in virtue of communism? Where, and so *when,* is it to be seen?

Or is this universal, as Heidegger had argued in *Being and Time* and several other places, in the already given "being-together" (*Mitsein*) of human being, from which the meaning of existence, *Dasein,* is taken off?[46] Or is it not rather, for Heidegger, in being itself, which is nothing abstracted? But which understanding of being? Being as *das Sein,* wherein the fundamental history of being is again a negating, a withdrawal and forgetting of being (both forgetting *by* being and being as *forgotten* by the most fundamental articulations of humanity)? Or is it *das Seyn,* the understanding of be-ing for itself that appears in Heidegger's thinking only after 1934, after the adventure with Hitlerism, and as a formal theme of his philosophical writing really only from 1936? If *das Sein* unfolds historically, as the history of being (itself a history that unfolds as a departure, something marked by a certain negativity, and by the pressing absentedness of *the* nothing), to what extent is *das Seyn* the "in and for itself" of which Hegel speaks, albeit without reference to the Idea, and so not anything abstracted or postulated as "other" or "beyond"? Can it be merely accidental that Heidegger's thought of *das Seyn* appears only after Heidegger's particularly violent confrontation with Hegel's political thinking, as we shall come to see?

If we see the extent to which Hegel also indicates the priority of the actual, it becomes clearer how we can understand Hegel's equation of being and nothingness. For being as the "all," the infinite, is at the same time the "empty," the purely formal. Heidegger's understanding of the nothing turns out to be quite different. Being is precisely not a universal, an absolute, or an infinite, *because* it is characterized by a not-ness: for Heidegger, being is finite, both formally and individually.

Hegel and, following him, Marx, each makes history decisive as the production of the universalized character of humanity: on the one hand, for Hegel, as the abstract idea (even if, as Hegel argues, the abstract idea is "lived," i.e., attained from *within*); on the other hand, for Marx (as we shall explore in far greater depth as we proceed), in the universalizing and so canceling of the differences between individuals in communism. This cancelling *is* a negating of difference. These two movements (as actual historical "unfoldings") involve the fundamental negativity that can be found at the heart of Hegel's and Marx's thinking (what Marx had called the outstanding achieve-

46. I do not propose to discuss Heidegger's understanding of *Mitsein* in detail here. For his own discussion of it, see Martin Heidegger, *Sein und Zeit* (*GA*2), §§26–27, 157–73.

ment of Hegel's *Phenomenology* and its "moving and generating principle"),[47] expressed through the range of meanings of "sublating." The negativity in Marx is never total; it is always for the sake of the positivity of what is to come. Each however is grounded in a universalized understanding of humanity where there is an account of movement, of motion itself through time: the movement of history itself *as* the movement of time *as* a human production which is under way *from* the individuality of the individual into the totality of the universal, the universal, absolute subject. This is exactly what Heidegger rejects: as such, being cannot qualify for Heidegger as the ground or basis of any kind of "universal" essence of humanity, because it is not only the human that is to be found in being. Marx (as we shall see later) says that the whole of nature comes to be represented through humanity: Heidegger argues that although only humanity experiences the fullness of the "worlding" of the world, nevertheless the phenomenon of world is not a purely human affair, nor is it disposed solely by humans (and therefore at their sole disposal).

Heidegger's understanding of being specifically sets aside the concentration on the human: it is through this that the "other thinking" that had remained in the background in the *Letter on Humanism* is able to appear. In his reply to Ernst Jünger of 1955, Heidegger asserts that "the essencing (verbal) of humanity, the 'existence [*Dasein*] in humanity' is nothing human,"[48] and at the same time he cites as proof of where he has worked this out in detail the popularly named "Kant book" of 1929.[49] Heidegger indicates, in other words, that this understanding is basic to his own thought, and runs through it as a continuous thread through near three decades at least, and certainly across the prewar and postwar years. In 1929 we find Heidegger saying: "The existence [*Dasein*] in humanity determines the human as that being who, being [*seiend*] in the midst of beings [*Seienden*] comports himself to them as such and who, as this comporting to beings, is essentially differently determined in his or her own being from all other beings manifest in *Dasein*."[50] What this means will become fully clear only at the very

47. Karl Marx, *Ökonomisch-philosophische Manuskripte aus dem Jahre 1844* (*MEW*40), 574. "Der Dialektik der Negativität als dem bewegenden und erzeugenden Prinzip."

48. Martin Heidegger, *Zur Seinsfrage* (*GA*9), 397. "Aber das Wesen (verbal) des Menschen, 'das Dasein im Menschen' (vgl. *Kant und das Problem der Metaphysik*, §43) ist nichts Menschliches."

49. This text, in many ways developing important themes of *Being and Time*, was worked up from Heidegger's lectures on Kant's *Critique of Pure Reason* of the winter semester of 1927–28 (see also *GA*25).

50. Martin Heidegger, *Kant und das Problem der Metaphysik* (*GA*3), 234. "Das Dasein im Menschen bestimmt diesen als jenes Seiende, das, inmitten von Seiendem seiend, zu diesem als einem solchen sich verhält und als dieses Verhalten zu Seiendem wesenhaft anders in seinem eigenen Sein bestimmt wird denn alles übrige im Dasein offenbare Seiende."

end of this book. Nevertheless, we could not have before us a clearer statement of the very ambiguity in Heidegger's use of the term *Dasein* that I have already drawn attention to: the ambiguity between "existence overall" and "*an* existence." However, Heidegger concludes, "man himself comes forth as a being under being's entirety."[51]

To understand the sheer difficulty and subtlety of what is being said here we have to set aside the usual translations of Heidegger's term *das Seiende* as "a being," the name of a thing, the counterpart to *das Sein,* the "general concept" (as it is commonly understood) of "being." *Seiend* in German, as in English, is a participle—as a noun it always names what is *in* being and is *being* as much as what can therefore be taken as *a* being. Because we hear so easily the "ontological distinction" between *das Sein,* "being as such," and *das Seiende,* "what (ever)-is" (as many earlier translations of Heidegger had it),[52] indicating being as (an) entity, we overlook that the distinction at hand is between "being as such" and "the being of things as a whole, or in general." *Das Seiende* might almost—if clumsily—be translated as "beingness," with all the ambiguities contained in that word. What is at issue here is the understanding of humanity within the whole of being, where humanity does not have all beings at its disposal and in its grasp. In many ways it is this thought that much of the "Green" movement has striven to attain to, while at the same time many within it resort to ever more extreme proposals for the use of technology to lay hold of the whole planet and manipulate it for the sake of its preservation and even salvation.

Heidegger, implicitly no less ferocious a critic of the "supersensible" than Marx (or Nietzsche, for that matter), thinking in consequence of the priority of the historical and "real" or "actual" established by Hegel, does not concentrate the fate of mankind on humanity's own "essence," but rather draws attention to how "essence," the "substantial" as such, *being,* is nothing human. Heidegger transforms the ambiguity implicit in questions of individual existence in its relation to the universal in *Being and Time* by explicating the structures of existence of human being not as the interiorizing of *Geist* as the (psychological) "history of thought finding itself" in self-consciousness becoming absolute, and so in individuality constantly universalizing itself into the singularity of its most general and absolute essence or substantiality, but in the very opposite (antipsychological) manner of *each* human existence individuating itself with respect to the "all," the generality of *Mitsein,* in, and as,

51. Ibid., 235. "Der Mensch selbst kommt als ein Seiendes unter dem übrigen Seienden vor."

52. See, for instance, the translations of "Vom Wesen der Wahrheit" (*GA*9) and *Was ist Metaphysik?* (*GA*9) by R. F. C. Hull and Alan Crick. See also Ralph Manheim's translation *An Introduction to Metaphysics* of *Einführung in die Metaphysik* (*GA*40), which also speaks of *das Seiende* as "the essent."

"temporality." For Heidegger, temporality arises through, and is indicated by, "mood." Mood here does not mean emotional comportment, but rather the opposite—"mood" indicates the way in which the surrounding world gives itself to be understood, its "manner" and character (its "how") in each "giving itself." This character impresses itself upon us, and at the same time itself arises through our capacity for comporting, our own manner of being at the time. Heidegger concludes this discussion in *Being and Time* by noting that he had attained through the analysis of "care" the original interpretation of existence (*Dasein*) that was required: "temporality has been exhibited with a view to the proper possibility for being-in-its-entirety of existence [*Dasein*]."[53] In other words, temporality constitutes the formal relatedness of every individual being to being as a whole. Heidegger accomplished this analysis in *Being and Time* without reference to the political, except, in the most general terms in an aside, by speaking of the consequences of this thought for the notion of the destiny of a people. Heidegger argues that being with one another within a common existence is not the mere occurring together of a multitude of subjects alongside each other, but rather manifests itself as "the happening of the community, of the nation (*Volk*)."[54] A huge amount has been made of this use of the word *Volk* in this place in *Being and Time,* as every attempt is made to scour the text for hints of Heidegger's coming commitment to the Nazi Party, given the nazification of this word by the Hitler regime. It should be clear from what has been said here that this is precisely the point in *Being and Time* where the question of the political is posed: Heidegger's use of the term indicates not so much the presence, as the absence—to the point of avoidance—of any discussion of the political here. He reduces the discussion to a mere reference to the nation or people as a whole. Nothing of Nazism should or need be read into this particular appearance of the term: the term *Volk* is as ordinarily present in the thought of Marx or Hegel in the sense it is used here. We are returned, therefore, in 1927, to the very question that Heidegger had identified to Richard Wisser as one that still requires a *historical* answer: who, or what, or how, is "society"? In *Being and Time* this difficulty not only begs an (ungiven) answer, it also formally throws up the question of history as such,[55] which Heidegger explicitly interprets in *Being and Time* as "*descent,*" which he italicizes in the text. He clarifies this question of history by concluding: "what has 'history' in this way, can

53. Martin Heidegger, *Sein und Zeit* (*GA2*), 492. "Die Zeitlichkeit wurde im Hinblick auf das eigentliche Ganzseinskönnen des Daseins herausgestellt."

54. Ibid., 508. "Das Geschehen der Gemeinschaft, des Volkes." See for discussion of the issue itself, James Phillips, *Heidegger's Volk,* especially 5–6, 11.

55. In German the verb "to happen," *geschehen,* and the verbal substantive, "a happening," *das Geschehnis,* are strongly etymologically related to "history" as such, *die Geschichte.*

at the same time 'make' it. 'Epoch-making' 'presently' determines for itself a 'future.' History signifies here a 'connection' of event and 'effects' which draws itself through 'past,' 'present,' and 'future.' Thus understood, the past has no particular priority."[56]

It is impossible not to hear the Hegelian overtones of this statement: it is impossible not to see how a certain understanding of Marx is not also provided for in what is said. It is impossible not to see the extent to which the question is left unanswered, nor to see how the answer suggested would have to surpass any understanding of history as *that* history which humanity produces for itself.

56. Martin Heidegger, *Sein und Zeit* (*GA2*), 500, 501. "*Herkunft* . . . Was dergestalt eine 'Geschichte' hat, kann zugleich solche 'machen.' 'Epochemachend' bestimmt es 'gegenwärtig' eine 'Zukunft.' Geschichte bedeutet hier einen Ereignis- und 'Wirkungszusammenhang,' der sich durch 'Vergangenheit,' 'Gegenwart' und 'Zukunft' hindurchzieht. Hierbei hat die Vergangenheit keinen besonderen Vorrang" (Heidegger's emphasis).

*Chapter 3*

# The History and Negation of Metaphysics

THE FOLLOWING THREE CHAPTERS are perhaps the most demanding in this book, in seeking to prepare the ground for the productive dialogue suggested by Heidegger with Marx. Each of them endeavors to illustrate an aspect of Hegel's thought. Both Marx and Heidegger enter into a confrontation with Hegel, although the motives for the confrontation are in each case quite different. Marx seeks to radicalize and concretize Hegel's speculative idealism. Part of what follows in these chapters will therefore be my attempt to show how Marx (not uncharacteristically) has, in his drive for this more material thinking, a tendency to cover over the extent to which Hegel is already the most materialist of the German philosophers. It is this second aspect which Heidegger brings to the fore in his own engagement with Hegel.

Heidegger shows on the one hand how Hegel's is the highest and most complete philosophy of subjectivity—in this sense, Hegel is the most ardent of humanists—and on the other hand, how Hegel introduces into philosophy in an entirely new and vital way the experience of history, and so prepares for Heidegger's own investigation of the phenomenon of being as time or "temporality." Hegel is, therefore, the most peculiar kind of "idealist," precisely because he is also an implacable opponent of the "supersensible," that realm of the ideas, celebrated by Kant, and inaugurated by Plato, which is a divine realm and the only realm wherein necessity and freedom are reconciled. For Hegel the idea becomes visible in what it itself is *to* become—which means, become *concrete*, material, reality. This reality is itself "produced" by human *Geist*—which, when referring to Hegel's philosophy, we can only translate as "subjectivity."

The first of these three chapters therefore deals with the question of Hegel's understanding of history, and both Marx's and Hegel's engagement with that understanding. Chapter 4 will examine Hegel's dialectical thought, which Marx develops into what has become known as "dialectical materialism," a term Marx himself did not employ, but which Engels sought to develop and explain. Chapter 5 examines Hegel's theory of the state. This is the most concrete of Hegel's "speculative" philosophical endeavors. It is also the one which both Marx and Heidegger enter into the most violent confrontations with: for Heidegger especially, Hegel's understanding of the state becomes the basis of Heidegger's slowly developing critique and rejection of Nazism and Hitlerism, after the disaster of his period as rector of Freiburg University (from May 1933 to April 1934). Without an understanding of Hegel's theory of the state, it will be impossible to understand Heidegger's own confrontation with Nazism, tainted by it as he was.

The very end of Engels's edition of the third volume of *Das Kapital* contains a question which, it seems, Marx is able to analyze but is unable to answer. Engels concludes the short section in question with the parenthesized comment "(here the manuscript breaks off)."[1] The section is entitled "The Classes," and Marx notes that "in England, it is indisputable that the modern society is developed, in its highest and most classical economic structure. Nevertheless this class structure does not itself emerge as pure here."[2] The historical manifestation of something provides us with the orientation on its meaning, which is at the same time the meaning from out of which the historical manifestation is itself to be interpreted. If, as Marx notes, "intermediate and transitional stages" exist in the class structure, "nevertheless this is immaterial for our analysis."[3] Marx proceeds: "the next question requiring an answer is this: 'What forms a class?' "[4] The verb here, *bilden,* means to form, to constitute, to envisage, but philosophically speaking, indicates the *ideation* (Greek: *eidos*) of a class.

There is no suggestion here that Marx is thinking as if class, or its ideation, were an eternal ideal or type. On the contrary, class is itself an intermediate form, a purely historical phenomenon that appears, strictly speaking, with capitalism and will disappear with capitalism's demise, and so is restricted to a particular epoch of development. As this, class is what is to be overcome. Class exists only in its historical manifestations (if we were thinking in terms of the ancients, this is an inherently "Aristotelian" appeal to universals rather than Platonic). In fact, however, Marx is thinking in consequence of Hegel: in consequence of how the historical constitutes the manifestation of the idea: the *idea itself* is subject to change, to becoming. However, the analysis (*Betrachtung*) is what is at issue here. The historical

1. Karl Marx, *Das Kapital,* vol. 3, ed. Friedrich Engels (*MEW*25), 893. "(Hier bricht das Ms. ab)."

2. Ibid., 892. "In England ist unstreitig die moderne Gesellschaft, in ihrer ökonomischen Gliederung, am weitesten, klassischsten entwickelt. Dennoch tritt diese Klassengliederung selbst hier nicht rein hervor."

3. Ibid., 892. "Mittel- und Übergangs-stufen . . . Indes ist dies für unsere Betrachtung gleichgültig."

4. Ibid., 893. "Die nächst zu beantwortende Frage ist die: Was bildet eine Klasse?"

manifestations, the historical *form* is to be understood from our prior ideation of it, in each case. We can see the *actual* "non-pure" form with respect to the pure form, even though the pure form never exists historically as such. Marx does not think "platonically," but he is forced to think in consequence of what Plato identified with the word *eidos*. Marx thinks, after Plato.

In the text at the end of *Das Kapital*, Marx begins to analyze the specificities of class insofar as they appear as classes—"the infinite splitting-up of interests and places, wherein the separating of societal work splits the worker as much as the capitalists and landlords—the latter, for example, as vineyard-owners, farm-owners, owners of forests, mine-owners, owners of fisheries."[5] *Gesellschaftlichen Arbeit*—"societal work" is the *formal ground*, the ideation as such, of every ideation of class. Society, *Gesellschaft*, and work, *Arbeit*, are formally one and the same thing, in a way that will only become possible to see when we analyze the meaning of work as such. It becomes clear, however, that *gesellschaftlichen Arbeit*—"societal work" *as* the formal definition of society *as* work—is itself an understanding from out of which every other phenomenon is to be explained. It is for this very reason that we presume the manuscript breaks off: to proceed would require a retreat into what Marx himself recognizes as the way philosophy (metaphysics) itself formerly proceeded: the list of classes does not adequately account for class as such, or rather, here Marx is unable to show the connection between the metaphysical occurrence of classes (worker, capitalist) and the multiplicity of class distinctions. Here, with the inquiry into class as the constitution of society as such, "society as work," something entirely new is being said.

We earlier encountered Martin Heidegger's statement that to answer the question whether or not philosophy has a social "mission" (*Auftrag*), one must first ask "What is society?" and one must pursue this by thinking through that contemporary society is only the absolutizing of modern subjectivity.[6] We are seeking the fundamental connections between Marx and Hegel, and Heidegger's own interpretative understanding of Marx as a central figure in the completion and fulfillment of metaphysics. In this, strictly speaking, we have no signposts, no easy orientation, not least because a major interpretative key for Marx which we have already encountered is one that argues that there is *no* metaphysics to be found in Marx. To interpret Marx in this way, Sidney Hook (for just one instance) was forced to split out the Marx of the *Economic and Philosophical Manuscripts* of 1844, with its strong

5. Ibid., 893. "Die unendliche Zersplitterung der Interessen und Stellungen, worin die Teilung der gesellschaftlichen Arbeit die Arbeiter wie die Kapitalisten und Grundeigentümer—letzte z.B. in Weinbergbesitzer, Äckerbesitzer, Waldbesitzer, Bergwerkbesitzer, Fischereibesitzer—spaltet."

6. See 44, and note 8 on that page.

metaphysical overtones, from the Marx of *Das Kapital,* and the theorization of surplus value.

We can find sharp confirmation of what Hook identifies as Marx's antimetaphysical view in another journalistic, disorganized, and polemical text written in part by Marx and in part by Engels, against the "Left Hegelians" and the circle of Bruno Bauer, entitled *The Holy Family, or Critique of Critical Critique.*[7] It was Marx's and Engels's first joint work. This antimetaphysical work was *also* written between September and November 1844 (and so immediately after the *Economic and Philosophical Manuscripts* that were written in the spring and summer of the same year, parts of which Marx included in *The Holy Family*), although it was not published until 1845. The editors of the Marxist-Leninist Institute, in their notes on the English edition of this work, while conceding that the work "was written largely under the influence of the materialistic views of Ludwig Feuerbach" when "the process of the formation of Marxism was not yet completed,"[8] nevertheless argue that it reflects Marx's and Engels's "new materialistic and communistic outlook."[9]

For Hook, as for many others, the "realism" of *Das Kapital,* its mature materialist outlook, is the mark of its opposition to "metaphysics" (in contrast to the residual metaphysics of Feuerbach), precisely because this materialism is "historical." Yet, as the editors of *The Holy Family* pointed out, this is what is indicated by the mocking title of those still yet committed to "idealism" in the thoroughgoingly materialist "critique of critical critique." In 1866 Engels published *Ludwig Feuerbach and the End of Classical German Philosophy,* in which, in the third section (quoted in part by the Marxist-Leninist Institute "Preface"), he noted that the formation of historical materialism was at the same time the overcoming of Feuerbach: "But the step which Feuerbach did not take nevertheless had to be taken. The cult of abstract man, which formed the kernel of the Feuerbachian new religion, had to be replaced by the science of real men and of their historical development. This further development of a Feuerbachian standpoint beyond Feuerbach was inaugurated by Marx in 1845 in *The Holy Family.*"[10]

7. Friedrich Engels and Karl Marx, *Die heilige Familie, oder Kritik der kritischen Kritik: Gegen Bruno Bauer und Konsorten* (*MEW*2), 3–223. The sections written by Engels, and those written by Marx, were each indicated on the contents page (compare *MEW*2, 723–25). I have indicated the author of quotations by citing only the specific author in each case.

8. Karl Marx and Friedrich Engels, *The Holy Family, or Critique of Critical Critique,* 10. "From the institute of Marxism-Leninism."

9. Karl Marx and Friedrich Engels, *The Holy Family,* 279. "Notes."

10. Friedrich Engels, "Ludwig Feuerbach und der Ausgang der klassischen deutschen Philosophie" (*MEW*21), 288. "Aber der Schritt, den Feuerbach nicht tat, mußte dennoch getan werden; der Kultus des abstrakten Menschen, der den Kern der Feuerbachschen neuen Religion bildete,

*The Holy Family* sought to undertake a historical reading of the emergence of materialism in its historical forms. Marx declares that "materialism is the *native* son of *Great Britain.* Already the scholastic Duns Scotus had asked himself '*whether matter might not think.*'"[11] Marx stresses, nevertheless, that it is Francis Bacon who must be considered the real founder of English materialism, and all modern experimental science. This is a time, Marx notes, when "materialism became *hostile to humanity.*"[12] For Marx this is a stage of its historical development: the implication is that in what is yet to come, materialism will overcome through its own historical development this hostility toward being humanity's self-fulfillment.

If, as we have seen, in the Wisser interview Heidegger claims that "contemporary society is only the absolutising of modern *subjectivity,*" Marx understood his criticism of the Left Hegelians also to be a criticism of a certain kind of absolute subjectivity: "Critical Criticism estimates itself as *absolute subject.*"[13] Marx seeks to indicate the difficulty he understands the Left Hegelians to have of inscribing socialist analysis into the language of Hegel's logic by mockingly noting "Critical Criticism in its *absolute* existence [*Dasein*] as Herr *Bruno* has explained humanity in *mass,* the whole of humanity, which is not critically critical, to be its *opposite,* as its *essential object.*"[14] What Marx describes as the "cult" of the absolute subject *over against* the masses is not the attainment of a historical-materialist critique over against a metaphysical one, but the fulfillment of an understanding of history only made possible by Hegel's philosophy.

Earlier we noted Heidegger saying that "the essence of materialism does not consist in the assertion that everything is mere matter," but rather in a metaphysical determination from out of which everything material is to be understood. Heidegger does not elucidate this statement, and we are not yet ready fully to inquire into everything he says even in the *Letter on Humanism* in connection with what he says here, but everything turns here on the meaning of the word "metaphysics."

---

mußte ersetzt werden durch die Wissenschaft von den wirklichen Menschen und ihrer geschichtlichen Entwicklung. Diese Fortentwicklung des Feuerbachschen Standpunkts über Feuerbach hinaus wurde eröffnet 1845 durch Marx in der *Heiligen Familie.*" See also Karl Marx and Friedrich Engels, *Die heilige Familie* (*MEW*2), (translated by R. Dixon), *The Holy Family,* 11.

11. Karl Marx and Friedrich Engels, *Die heilige Familie* (*MEW*2), 135. "Der Materialismus ist der *eingeborne* Sohn *Großbritanniens.* Schon sein Scholastiker *Duns Scotus* fragte sich, '*ob die Materie nicht denken könne*'" (Marx's emphases).

12. Ibid., 137. "Der Materialismus wird *menschenfeindlich*" (Marx's emphasis).

13. Ibid., 152. "Die kritische Kritik gilt sich als *absolute Subjekt*" (Marx's emphasis).

14. Ibid., 152. "Die kritische Kritik in ihrem *absoluten* Dasein als Herr *Bruno* hat die Menschheit in *Masse,* die ganze Menschheit, die nicht kritische Kritik ist, für ihren *Gegensatz* erklärt, für ihren *wesentlichen Gegenstand*" (Marx's emphases).

If by metaphysics is simply meant that which is "beyond" beings, and so which also speaks of God, then historical materialism is as much a refutation of metaphysics as Nietzsche's thought of the death of God. Heidegger is the one who points up that what is at issue for Nietzsche is nothing of the kind. Heidegger takes up Nietzsche's thought of "European" nihilism as "the word for that which Nietzsche himself was the first to recognize, the historical movement that already governed the previous century and was determining for the next century."[15] This nihilism lives out of the death of God, but at the same time is to be understood not as an opinion or viewpoint put forward by some individual (least of all Nietzsche himself). As *recognized* it is already a "situation," the "normal state of affairs."[16] We are to understand this, Heidegger says, "as the history of beings [*Seienden*] themselves . . . Nihilism is rather that long-drawn-out event [*Ereignis*], in which the truth concerning beings as a whole essentially transforms itself and is driven toward an end it determines through itself."[17] Heidegger explains this by saying "the truth concerning beings as a whole has long been called 'metaphysics.'"[18] Heidegger does not speak here of the truth of being (*Sein,* or *Seyn*), but beings (*Seienden*). Metaphysics is, as he repeatedly says, unable to think being as such, it can only think, and speak of, beings. Heidegger consistently argues that nihilism is itself the *Seinsvergessenheit,* the forgetfulness and disappearance of the being of beings *in* their being. Nihilism both is this as a centuries-long forgetfulness, and *as nihilism as such* it is the possibility of the overcoming of metaphysics. How could this be for Marx? Later we will have to examine how *the productive* as such is an effect of the *Seinsvergessenheit* as the annihilation of beings. For now it will have to suffice that this is what we must later show.

Metaphysics concerns "what is in being as a whole." To show how Marx's fundamental philosophical position is *also* an *Ereignis,* an event, in the history of beings, it will be necessary to show how Marx thinks "being as a whole." In the same way that Nietzsche's tireless and incessant assault on

15. Martin Heidegger, *Nietzsche: Der europäische Nihilismus* (*GA*48), 2 (= *GA*6.2, 24). "Das Wort für die von Nietzsche selbst erstmals erkannte, bereits die voraufgehenden Jahrhunderte durchherrschende und das nächste Jahrhundert bestimmende geschichtliche Bewegung."

16. Friedrich Nietzsche, vol. 12, *Nachlaß 1885–1887,* Herbst 1887 9[35], 350 (= *Der Wille zur Macht,* §23, 20). "Der Nihilism ein normaler Zustand" (the word *normaler* is stressed in Nietzsche's actual note).

17. Martin Heidegger, *Nietzsche: Der europäische Nihilismus* (*GA*48), 3 (= *GA*6.2, 25). "Nihilismus ist die Geschichte des Seienden selbst. . . . Der Nihilismus ist vielmehr jenes langhin dauernde Ereignis, in dem sich die Wahrheit über das Seiende im Ganzen wesentlich wandelt und einem durch die selbst bestimmten Ende zutreibt."

18. Martin Heidegger, *Nietzsche: Der europäische Nihilismus* (*GA*48), 3 (= *GA*6.2, 25). "Die Wahrheit über das Seiende im Ganzen heißt von altersher 'Metaphysik.'"

the *Übersinnliche,* the "supersensible" world, the assault that leads him to proclaim in *The Gay Science* and throughout his work that "God is dead,"[19] is interpreted by Heidegger as his fundamentally metaphysical outlook, so also Marx's relentless materialism itself has for Heidegger to be interpreted against itself, in order to disclose within it its fundamentally metaphysical position. In undertaking the productive dialogue suggested by Heidegger, do we not thereby falsify Marx? If we interpret in this way, are we not simply choosing *for* Heidegger *over against* Marx, and so doing violence to Marx's own understanding? Or is something else posed for us: namely to *read* Marx within the whole history of Occidental thinking, to read Marx as Heidegger suggests we read him?

In this must we not ask the question, "why Heidegger?"—what is it that Heidegger will have to give us that we could not get, say, from Lukács, or Adorno, or any other of the interpreters of Marx? Except that the history of thinking, the task of interpretation itself, *to think at all,* and that thoughtfully, does not simply mean to put one "thinker" or school of that thinker's thought, in conversation with another, preferably one most opposed to him (also one of the "greats") and thereby to entertain ourselves by constructing the "conflict" between them. Our task is the reverse: to find out how Marx and Heidegger speak of the "same," that same which also addresses us, and out of which even we might also hope to speak (what is in being as a whole). We are not even seeking "answers" or seeking to prove Marx "right" and Heidegger "wrong" or vice versa, or to show how both fail when measured up to what we think we know *now.* All of these comportments to Marx, to Heidegger, even our self-comportment to ourselves, would be mere "standpoints," mere postures of thinking. Marx and Heidegger both invite us to inquire what is *here* to be thought: what each brought to description in their thinking and speaking.

We have set ourselves the task not simply to inquire into "Marx" or "Heidegger" but to inquire into the essence of Europe and Europe's global consequences. Each of these thinkers takes up the question of the essence of Europe, as the essence of man, either in Marx's case, on the ground of "humanism" (although we have yet to secure what he meant by that), or in the case of Heidegger, through the *Seinsfrage,* the question that goes out after the meaning of being, as the truth of being, inquired into through the being of being human, given in the destiny of the Occident and the path of its thinking, from which "Europe" is taken off.

We enter into dialogue with Heidegger not because of what Heidegger thinks, as if all intellectual life were simply mere conversations and

19. See Friedrich Nietzsche, vol. 3, *Die Fröhliche Wissenschaft,* §125, *Der Tolle Mensch,* 480–82.

differences, but because of what Heidegger thinks *of.* With Heidegger we can, perhaps, think the essence of Europe, and thereby, modern, globalized "world democracy," and understand how he contrasted that with the destiny of the Occident as the history of Europe's confrontation with the planet as a whole. And we enter into dialogue with Marx because Marx (as much as Nietzsche) is the thinking of our age. If, as Heidegger claimed, "from the title 'Hegel and the Greeks,' the whole of philosophy in its history addresses itself to us, and does so now," this is only because, as we have seen Heidegger argue, no philosopher before Hegel attained to such a pitch of historical thinking, *as* philosophy itself.[20] Both Marx and Heidegger—in very different ways—reopen the question of the essence of the Occident, in contrast to the essence of Europe's global reach through communism, through fascism, through world democracy, and through bringing ourselves to understand how these politics arise and what they mean.

If Hegel brings the whole history of philosophy to the fore and is its completion (which brings us before the whole history of modern politics as well as the history of philosophy), who then is Marx, if, as Heidegger had assured us in the *Letter on Humanism,* the Marxist view of history is superior to that of the other historical accounts? Heidegger remarks in *Hegel and the Greeks* that Marx (along with Kierkegaard) "are the greatest of the Hegelians. They are this against their will. The completion [*Vollendung*] of philosophy is neither at its end, nor does it remain in the isolated system of speculative idealism."[21] Marx and Marxism are not an addendum to the end of the history of philosophy, they are the working out of the history of the end.

How do we undertake the task of interpretation posed before us, to dare to read Marx against himself in order to understand what in Marx's thinking is the thinking through of the history of this end? We have before us the texts of Marx and the texts of Heidegger. They are to assist us in thinking through this question of interpretation—indeed, and above all, they are what we have, and to a great extent they are *all* that we have or might even need to think through this end. I have raised before in our discussion the question of the meaning and status of the "text." We who write after Jacques Derrida's grandiloquent claim, "*il n'y a pas de hors-texte*" (which is in itself nothing other than an observation concerning how thinking has come to think at this history of the "end," the full ending, of philosophy),[22] have been taught to

20. Martin Heidegger, "Hegel und die Griechen" (*GA*9), 427, 428–29. "Aus dem Titel 'Hegel und die Griechen' spricht uns das Ganze der Philosophie in seiner Geschichte an und dies jetzt."

21. Ibid., 432–33. "Marx und Kierkegaard sind die Größten der Hegelianer. Sie sind es wider Willen. Die Vollendung der Philosophie ist weder deren Ende, noch besteht sie in dem abgesonderten System des spekulativen Idealismus."

22. Jacques Derrida, *De la grammatologie,* 227 (Derrida's emphasis).

think at one and the same time "that there is only the text" and that "there is no author behind the text, as guarantor or guardian of its meaning." We have trained ourselves, therefore, to read "texts" *against* authors: because there is only the text, and there is nothing beyond it, only the text has anything to tell us at all. And, we say, the author must be measured against the text, such that we can set one text of an author against another so that the author himself can be broken up for the sake of understanding the text and its relation to other texts. Or from now on everything becomes a matter of "development" in the author, of what he was "doing" in such-and-such a period, or on such-and-such an afternoon, as if that was all that needed to be said. And because the text can also be broken open by means of "hermeneutics" or "deconstruction," the text itself need no longer speak as a unity—although we have become entirely impervious as to where the unity of thinking is to be found. This "Marx who was a Feuerbachian of sorts" wrote in 1844, seemingly in a thoroughly metaphysical way, but has nothing to do with the Marx of historical or dialectical materialism, or class struggle, or so on and so on.

As more than one commentator has pointed out, the history of texts is not just their availability, but also what of them, or in them, is held back from us. History itself (and so not just authors and editors) held back central texts of Marx which even now have not seen the light of day—Marx's ethnographical writings, and those concerning the situation and fate of Russia, which did not accord well with the views of Russia's later communist leaders.

Interpretation is not the artificial segmentation of texts or authors on the basis of some exterior theorization about textuality as such, or what the author "meant," or how the text stands against the author so that only the text "means" anything at all. For the sake of interpretation, all that we have is texts, and yet what is given in these texts is often itself already fragmented, or incomplete, or heavily adapted, especially to the circumstances into which they were published. Hegel's published philosophical texts were subject to censorship by the Prussian state, a fact of which Marx was well aware. This did not necessarily mean that Hegel's work was censored: we should not underestimate the extent to which the presence of the censors represented a pressure for self-censorship to evade an even worse interference. Not only Hegel, but Marx also experienced the effect of censorship, especially when editing the *Rheinische Zeitung*,[23] a principal reason for his ending up in London. Without doubt Heidegger, too, felt the pressure of the need to alter

23. Domenico Losurdo cites Marx's letter to Arnold Ruge of January 25, 1843, as evidence of Marx's irritation with the limitation on his freedom of expression in the newspaper: see Karl Marx (*MEW*27), 415. Losurdo devotes most of the first chapter of his book *Hegel e la libertà dei moderni* to the question of censorship in Hegel and Marx (see Domenico Losurdo, *Hegel e la libertà dei moderni* [vol. 1], 27–89, especially 37 and n. 11).

what he was able to say during the Nazi terror, but there is considerable evidence to suggest that after the war, Heidegger shaped and crafted what he said in the light of how it was likely to be interpreted, especially by those who did not understand him or had no sympathy with his work. If there is no direct evidence that Nietzsche experienced interference, or the threat of it, from the censors, nevertheless his ironic tone is itself one that requires to be interpreted: in no sense does Nietzsche write without at one and the same time hiding and masking, as well as making plain, the meaning of much of what he wants to say.

One of the texts most affected by the context into which it was written is Hegel's *Philosophy of Right*, a text that will prove to be central to our considerations in this book. The text was originally published in 1821 (and was Hegel's last published work in his lifetime), but what has come to be the definitive edition is based on that of 1833, and incorporates considerable additions from Hegel's pupil, Eduard Gans. Several Anglophone commentators have been ambiguous toward, or even dismissive of, Gans's additions (citing Gans's general caveat that his own words had at times crept into the material), notably T. M. Knox (who produced the first translation in English of the *Philosophy of Right*, and who simply left much of the additional material out of the translation), and Walter Kaufmann.[24] In fact, there is good evidence that Gans was restoring to the text material from Hegel's lectures on the philosophy of right, where Hegel had been able to speak far more freely. Marx would certainly have been aware of the complexity and difficulties in this text which is so central to his own interpretation of Hegel, and it is clear that Heidegger regarded Gans's interpolations as reporting Hegel's authentic voice.

Our interpretative task is to enter into what the texts speak *of*. Do texts construct the world, so that we reconstruct the world only from texts (a pointless circularity, to which there is no end), or is it that, having nothing other than texts, we must *read off from the text* the *world from out of which the text sprang, of which it speaks,* and which it points out and denotes, knowing that this reading-off at the same time separates us, and occludes as much as opens that of which it speaks? Texts, words, language itself, what Heidegger himself understood as *logos,* both denote and speak of the world, and at the same time they dissemble, and cover over precisely that which they at the same time point out and up in speaking. In each case what is required is the leap into interpretation—to be willing to enter into and take the risk of the interpretative step. At each step we must attend to the text,

24. See Kaufmann's discussion of a passage which we will see Heidegger draw attention to, at least in his seminar notes on Hegel. Walter Kaufmann, *Nietzsche: Philosopher, Psychologist, Antichrist,* 105 and n. 8.

and to the one speaking the text (who may or may not be the author), and to the "whence," the world from out of which text and speaker speaks.

At the very end of *Hegel and the Greeks* Heidegger raises again the question of the "truth" of the whole, but this time thought, not with the word "truth," but the Greek word *alētheia.* I have discussed elsewhere the question of the interpretation and derivation of this word, with its alpha-privative (ἀ-λήθεια),[25] which Heidegger, quite correctly, interprets as "the experience of . . . unconcealment and disclosing."[26] Hegel, Heidegger says, wishes to take in the whole of the history of philosophy such that "Hegel determines as the 'goal' of philosophy 'truth.' This is only attained at the stage of the completion. The stage of Greek philosophy remains in the 'not yet.'"[27] Heidegger remarks that truth is, for Hegel, the absolute certainty of the self-knowing subject, but that for the Greeks, the subject has not yet even arrived. This means that "therefore *alētheia* cannot be determining for truth in the sense of certainty."[28]

Concerning *alētheia* Heidegger concludes by arguing that "Hegel experienced the essence of history out of the essence of being in the sense of absolute subjectivity. To this very hour there has been no experience of history which, seen philosophically, is able to correspond to this experience of history. But the speculative-dialectical determining of history now itself directly has the result, that it remained denied to Hegel to behold *alētheia* and its sway as *the matter for thinking.*"[29] If we were to take at face value the standard English translation (made by Robert Metcalf) of this sentence we would miss entirely the subtle thrust and force of it, such that it accounts for what unfolds in Marx, even if it does not yet let us fully into the content of that unfolding. Where Heidegger speaks of *entsprechen,* which Metcalf translates as "responds,"[30] we have to hear "corresponds." If it is all a mat-

25. See Laurence Paul Hemming, *Postmodernity's Transcending,* 10 and especially n. 6.

26. Martin Heidegger, "Hegel und die Griechen" (*GA*9), 439–40. "Die Erfahrung der . . . Unverborgenheit und Entbergung."

27. Ibid., 438. "Hegel bestimmt als das 'Ziel' der Philosophie: 'die Wahrheit.' Diese wird erst auf der Stufe der Vollendung erreicht. Die Stufe der griechischen Philosophie bleibt im 'Noch nicht.'"

28. Ibid., 439. "Demnach kann die ἀλήθεια nicht das Bestimmende sein für die Wahrheit im Sinne der Gewißheit."

29. Ibid., 441. "Hegel (hat) das Wesen der Geschichte aus dem Wesen des Seins im Sinne der absoluten Subjektivität erfahren. Es gibt bis zur Stunde keine Erfahrung der Geschichte, die, philosophisch gesehen, dieser Geschichtserfahrung entsprechen könnte. Allein die spekulativ-dialektische Bestimmung der Geschichte bringt es nun gerade mit sich, daß es Hegel verwehrt bleib, die ἀλήθεια und deren Walten eigens als *die Sache des Denkens* zu erblicken" (Heidegger's emphasis).

30. See Martin Heidegger, "Hegel and the Greeks" (*GA*9), 333. Metcalf's translation in full reads: "Hegel experienced the essence of history in terms of the essence of being in the sense of

ter of "responses," if we were discussing the next "move" on the chessboard of philosophical practitioners and antagonists (we often hear commentators speak this way, of "the moves" so and so makes, of how he "cashes in" or "cashes out" and all the other dreadful paraphernalia of argumentative jargon that passes so often for thought), then surely what Heidegger says falsifies his earlier claim that the Marxist view of history is superior.

Surely if the Marxist view of history is "superior," then Marx's response to Hegel (and his claim to be reversing Hegel's thinking in some way) "gets over on top of," and so beyond, even Hegel's, so that we get somewhere new, and better, and more up to the moment (we "make" some history for ourselves in seeing this, even as we speak)? Surely Marx *is* progress? Heidegger's expression "to this very hour" brings us up against what it means to progress. This is not a statement of how far we might have got (which "hour" is in question? The hour in which Heidegger wrote this? The hour of the clock as you read this sentence?); rather it is a reminder that *every* "hour" can only be spoken of in that it already represents a kind of horizon, a limit *against which* the moment, the "now," appears and can be measured. Hegel's philosophy lives out of "this very hour"—it lives out of the farthest horizon we can see, *against which* we measure where we are, and, more importantly, where we are striving to be. History, as something whose end can be brought into view through history's becoming itself an *object,* a condition for inquiry, functions in the same way as the gap named in the horizon announced "to this very hour." Yet the essence of Hegel is to understand all becoming as *increase:* every limit, every hour's horizon is succeeded by its extension into the successive hour. Here is the need for the cancellation and negation of the word we translate as "sublation," *Aufhebung.* We enter the next horizon through the overcoming, cancellation, and setting aside of that horizon now being surpassed.

The word *ent-sprechen* means to "speak alongside and together with," and so in this case, "to measure up to." Heidegger argues that to understand Marx properly, we have to understand that Marx is not (as he himself claimed he was) *re*sponding to Hegel, but *co*-responding. To co-respond is to "be alongside and together with," to be within the "same," the same region of thought. This is what it means to be "measured" to Hegel. In understanding how this is—that Marx's thought arises in the same region of thinking and is measured to Hegel's, we pose the question, does he measure up? Measure up to *what*? If Hegel is the *Vollendung,* the completion and fulfill-

---

absolute subjectivity. To this day there has been no experience of history that, seen philosophically, could respond to this experience of history. But the speculative-dialectical determination of history does entail that it remained denied to Hegel to see ἀλήθεια and its holding sway as *the matter of thinking*" (Metcalf's emphasis).

ment, how can there be "more"? The *Vollendung*, however, is the completion and fulfillment of absolute subjectivity in thinking. Marx precisely identifies (this is the thrust of *The Holy Family*) that there has been "to this hour" *no* completed measuring-up: quite the contrary: "Bruno Bauer and co." are altogether a collection of epigones, who fall far short of what is required. When Heidegger says "to this hour there has been no experience of history" he is speaking not of an event in *thought* even though the matter for thinking, "absolute subjectivity," has been laid out: no, what Heidegger speaks of is an actual historical occurrence. There has been no actual historical occurrence, no *event* (we would say, if we were speaking outside Heidegger's own language, no "reality," no "fact") equal to the thought of absolute subjectivity.

The claim that Heidegger makes here is precisely Marx's own position: the contradictions of capitalism have still not yet resulted in capitalism's overcoming with the advent of actual communism, which is for Marx a necessary occurrence. Communism is as yet only a thought. Marx describes what is *yet* to happen, when he says: "If the proletariat in struggle against the bourgeoisie necessarily unites itself as a class, through a revolution [it] makes itself the ruling class, and as ruling class forcibly destroys the old relations of production, thus destroying the conditions for the existence of class antagonisms, thus classes in general, and therewith its own rulership as a class."[31] This at the same time returns us to Heidegger's critique of Marx's eleventh thesis on Feuerbach: to know how to change the world is *already* to have thought through the basis and ground of the change that is required to take place.

To have gone beyond Hegel would mean to have overcome the completion and fulfillment of metaphysics without having completed the *experience* of its fulfillment and completion (in this sense we see again how closely Heidegger interrogates Marx in his discussion of the eleventh thesis). To be equal to Hegel, and to be equal to the completion and fulfillment that Hegel is, Marx must precisely *not yet* to this hour *have* corresponded, but rather must *be the corresponding itself*. It is in this sense that Marx and the Marxism he unleashes is both a historical phenomenon and the *imperative* attempt to attain to that historical experience. Inasmuch as we are being invited to understand this as the place from out of which Marx speaks, corresponding to Hegel (as Heidegger argues), Marx also does not speak out

31. Karl Marx and Friedrich Engels, *Manifest der Kommunistischen Partei* (*MEW*4), 482. "Wenn das Proletariat im Kampfe gegen die Bourgeoisie sich notwendig zur Klasse vereint, durch eine Revolution sich zur herrschenden Klasse macht und als herrschende Klasse gewaltsam die alten Produktionsverhältnisse aufhebt, so hebt es mit diesen Produktionsverhältnissen die Existenzbedingungen des Klassengegensatzes, die Klassen überhaupt, und damit seine eigene Herrschaft als Klasse auf."

of the experience of *alētheia.* The question we must uncover is: in what way does Marx speak from out of absolute subjectivity as this "measuring up" and "corresponding" to the absolute metaphysics in its fulfillment and completion in Hegel?

I have argued that Heidegger's *Letter on Humanism* is itself the basis for Heidegger's confrontation with Marxism, but at the same time that Heidegger himself warned that the *Letter on Humanism* spoke in the language of metaphysics. The language of metaphysics, inasmuch as Heidegger takes it up, is the language of Hegel, the language of absolute subjectivity. The word "humanism" which Heidegger takes up in the letter is itself derived from Marx: specifically, from the *Economic and Philosophical Manuscripts.* Here Marx, in direct dialogue with Hegel, indeed in discussing the "*positive* moments of Hegelian dialectic—within the determining of estrangement [*Entfremdung*],"[32] argues that

> atheism, being the negating of God, is the advent of theoretic humanism, and communism, as the negating of private property, is the vindication of real human life as one's possession and thus the coming into being of practical humanism, or inasmuch as atheism is mediated through the negating of religion, communism is humanism mediated through the negating of private property. Only through the negating of this mediating—which is itself, however, a necessary premise—does the positive of self-producing humanism come into being, *positive* humanism.[33]

In each case the word *negating* translates *Aufhebung:* it is what *is to be attained to, and so undertaken and done,* that which is to be carried out as the historical task. It is the experience which is to be produced by fulfilling the demand, the imperative, of history. This imperative could never be fulfilled by Bauer and co., they are insufficient to the task. *Aufheben* is, as we have seen, the central term of Hegel's phenomenology, as at once negation, cancellation, and the being lifted-up, carried off, into something greater. *Aufheben*—literally, up-heaving—names what transcendence also names, the

32. Karl Marx, *Ökonomisch-philosophische Manuskripte* (*MEW*40), 583. "Die *positiven* Momente der Hegelschen Dialektik—innerhalb der Bestimmung der Entfremdung" (Marx's emphasis).

33. Ibid., 583. "Der Atheismus als Aufhebung Gottes das Werden des theoretischen Humanismus, der Kommunismus als Aufhebung des Privateigentums die Vindikation des wirklichen menschlichen Lebens als seines Eigentums ist, das Wenden des praktischen Humanismus ist, oder der Atheismus ist den durch Aufhebung der Religion, der Kommunismus der durch Aufhebung des Privateigentums mit sich vermittelte Humanismus. Erst durch die Aufhebung dieser Vermittelung—die aber eine notwendige Voraussetzung ist—wird der positiv von sich selbst beginnende, der *positive* Humanismus" (Marx's emphasis).

sublime moment of metaphysics: that negation and cancellation which at the same time is never tragic, never fateful, always open to something greater—indeed is "the greater" as the "ever" and beyond: the *means by which* infinity is attained-to through finite subjectivity. If, as I argued in chapter 2, in German philosophy a new terminology is being forged, which in Marx's and Hegel's own lifetime is an event within living memory, from where does this thought of sublation, *Aufhebung* come and what does it translate?

To answer this question we can supply only the briefest of sketches.[34] In his third *Critique* (the *Critique of the Power of Judgment*) Kant provides an account of the dynamical and mathematical sublime. The "sublime" in German is *das Erhabene,* which has the same etymological root as the verb *aufheben,* from which we take the noun *Aufhebung* (sublation). The root is the verb *heben,* from which we get the English verb "to heave," and which means "to lift up," "raise." *Das Erhabene* is not a literal translation of Latin *sublimitas,* but of the Greek word *hypsos,* from which the Latin term was an interpretation, but which in Greek meant "upliftment." The earliest extant systematic consideration of *hypsos* is by the first-century-AD author Longinus, for whom the term related to the experience of upliftment in literature and art. The Latin term *sublimitas,* to which "sublation" is also related, means literally "to get up to the limit." Getting up to the limit names precisely the horizon Heidegger names in "to this hour": the highest and outermost limit of experience—hence why the Latin term does not render the Greek literally (as the German does), but interprets its meaning in an act of translation. The "limit" in question is the "outermost" of the heavens (which in antiquity were understood to be finite), which in Hegel is precisely transformed into a temporal limit, and (because the "universe" is understood to be neither spatially nor temporally finite), the "limit" in question is of its essence a limit not of "finite" being but "infinite" becoming, or infinity as such. Sublation is the moment when the *infinity* of the "outermost" horizon becomes manifest *in* the finite "now." What is really being named in "upliftment," the sublime, and in sublation is transcendence, but the concrete, material, *human* "experience" of transcendence (hence why in Kant the sublime is primarily an aesthetic category). Hegel takes over this category in aesthetics because in the overcoming of the supersensible for the sake of the privileging of the sensory, *every* experience, technically, is "aesthetic" or has this aesthetic character.[35] Thus in his lectures on aesthetics, we find Hegel asserting that "whatever is sensuous can address itself to [human] *Geist* in

34. There is a fuller consideration of this genealogy in Laurence Paul Hemming, *Postmodernity's Transcending,* especially 39–41.

35. In a sense this is Hegel's own attempt to connect the "aesthetic" with *Geist,* or, in Aristotelian terms, αἴσθησις (sensory experience) with νοῦς (*Geist,* "spirit," "the supersensible").

a variety of ways."[36] This principle is derived from, and permeates, the *Phenomenology:* every human experience of transcendence has the capacity to bring the one experiencing up to—up against—and make manifest for him, the "limit" of the infinite, in the immediately present ("now"). Hegel transforms Kant's understanding of the sublime as transcendence to remove from it the place of God, as that toward which the sublime transcends, so that every experience of the sublime (every sublation) is not into the "noumenal" realm of God but *temporally* into the concrete realm of what is to become "real," what is to "realize" itself, *through* human experience. Marx takes up and concretizes yet further this essential aspect of Hegel's understanding of sublation *as* transcendence.

For Marx, communism is humanism, or rather, it is the *end* of humanism: it is what humanism is to become, and it is what every humanism is striving for and tending toward. Marx is also driven by this understanding of how the "limit," the infinite becomes present in the "now," but this experience is the immediate and present experience of the possibility of communism itself. Humanism, however, is the name in Marx for absolute subjectivity, but taken in a particular way. As absolute subjectivity it is not the "ontotheological"[37] absolute identity of the subject with the infinite, but rather the fulfilment (the infinite as the "end" and "overcoming" of finitude). Marx opens this discussion of Hegel by saying: "*Negation* as the objective movement of alienation [*Entäußerung*] taking-back-into-itself."[38] We will have to return to this Janus-headed term, "alienation," "estrangement," *Entäußerung, Entfremdung,* but for the time being it will suffice to note its essential connection for Marx with *Aufhebung,* negating as such.

Heidegger in *Hegel and the Greeks* asks "must, however, the human being, which is what is being thought here, necessarily be determined as subject?"[39] and replies that we must recall

> that *alētheia,* thought in a Greek way, holds sway in all things for human beings, but the human being remains determined through *logos.* The human

36. G. W. F. Hegel, *Vorlesung über die Ästhetik,* 56. "Was sinnlich ist, kann auf verschiedene Weise zu dem Geiste sich verhalten."

37. See Martin Heidegger, *Hegels Phänomenologie des Geistes* (*GA*32), 183; compare 140–44. Heidegger specifically developed the term "ontotheology" (originally here even as "onto-ego-theo-logy") in the course of interpreting Hegel's *Phenomenology* in lectures given at Freiburg in the winter semester of 1930–31.

38. Karl Marx *Ökonomisch-philosophische Manuskripte* (*MEW*40), 583. "Das *Aufheben,* als gegenständliche, die Entäußerung in sich zurücknehmende Bewegung" (Marx's emphasis).

39. Martin Heidegger, "Hegel und die Griechen" (*GA*9), 442. "Muß jedoch der Mensch, an hier gedacht wird, notwendig als Subjekt bestimmt sein?"

being is the one who says. Saying, in Old High German *sagan,* means showing, letting appear and letting be seen. The human being is the being [*Wesen*—essence] that lets the presencing in its presentness lie before us in saying and takes over that which lies-before. The human being can only speak insofar as he is the sayer.[40]

We should attend most carefully to the phrase "showing, letting appear and letting be seen." These are the things that in setting out to speak the (goal) of truth, Heidegger has already said Hegel is *un*able to attain to, despite being the forerunner of the completion of history as the history of metaphysics. Hegel, in speaking, has not attained to *saying,* and as such, speaks from out of the *Seinsvergessenheit,* the forgetfulness of being: sublation is not "saying," but, in its negativity, "nay-saying" or gainsaying: it denies what the being before us *is* (both in its particularity and as a whole) for the sake of what it is to *become.*[41] To speak from forgetfulness is not to be able to *say* what being demands be said. Hegel remains in the *lēthē* of concealment, in negation, and yet he shows up the whole history of metaphysics both *as* and *in* history and *as* metaphysics. Metaphysics is not counterposed to history in Hegel: history becomes the necessary ground from out of which metaphysics occurs. History becomes the metaphysical possibility of the unity of the *material* of materialism (the "physical"). Inasmuch as the "beyond," the *epekeina,* of metaphysics (the "supersensible") is overcome, it is overcome by its reversal *into* the historical. The historical as such, taken as a whole, becomes the ground which the supersensible "beyond" once fulfilled as the grounding possibility of the physical appearances, the "beings."

Inasmuch as *alētheia* is uncovered by speaking, and that speaking speaks from the overcoming of metaphysics (from "a philosophy which has overcome the standpoint of subjectivity"),[42] Heidegger seeks also to be a

40. Ibid., 442–43. "daß die ἀλήθεια, griechisch gedacht, allerdings für den Menschen waltet, der Mensch aber durch den λόγος bestimmt bleibt. Der Mensch ist der Sagende. Sagen, althochdeutsch sagan, bedeutet: zeigen, erscheinen- und sehen-lassen. Der Mensch ist das Wesen, das sagend das Anwesende in seiner Anwesenheit vorliegen läßt und das Vorliegende vernimmt. Der Mensch kann nur sprechen, insofern er der Sagende ist."

41. In *Postmodernity's Transcending* I demonstrated how this "nay-saying" is the essential feature of Kant's understanding of transcendence and the sublime (183): "What Kant is naming as a power and an instrument is transcendence itself, but as that power and instrument to *negate* beings in favour of being in general, being as God. Upliftment, as the reading-off from beings to being as such *is* a negating. Upliftment is an instrument of the nihilation of beings, and so, insofar as the gulf that he posits between the world of beings and the ideas is achieved through this nihilation, is a kind of annihilation of beings so that the ideas themselves can be 'seen'" (my original emphasis).

42. See 44.

sayer, to speak from out of what is there to be spoken *of:* to enter once again into *alētheia* as the uncovering and unconcealment of beings *in* their being. As such, he says, "*alētheia* has come before the history of philosophy."[43] As the before, the outside, *alētheia* as proper saying lets the history of philosophy be seen and appropriated. In this understanding of *alētheia* Heidegger says, the clearing (*die Lichtung*), the "realm of unconcealment" lets itself be seen and appears.[44] Heidegger concludes that "only where this [i.e., the realm of unconcealment] already holds sway can something become sayable, seeable, indicable, apprehendable."[45]

We have still not answered our question, however, concerning whether Heidegger is inconsistent in claiming superiority for the Marxist view of history. Surely if Marx is yet to attain to the measuring-up of the completion and fulfillment of the metaphysical realm, the history of philosophy as metaphysics, as laid down by Hegel, then Hegel is in advance of Marx? In the *Letter on Humanism* Heidegger says that Hegel first brings to language the essence of history as absolute metaphysics. He adds, "the absolute metaphysics belongs with its inversions through Marx and Nietzsche in the history of the truth of being."[46] We should not miss how Heidegger, in understanding Marx, understands Marx in relation to Nietzsche, and as we shall see more and more, understands Marx and Nietzsche to be speaking out of the same region of thought.

How is Marx to be compared to Nietzsche? How is Marx even to be understood in so strong a relation to Hegel? Nietzsche is, surely, the thinker of the *Niedergang*, the decline, as the "going down" of Zarathustra, the thinker of European nihilism, of the history of thinking as the abandonment of every "aim," of the essential *lack* of the human essence, except in its taking over the essence of the will to power by driving in to the power to will, the will to will itself (although this latter phrase, as we shall see later, is a definition, not of Nietzsche's, but of Heidegger's)? In the *Letter on Humanism* we find Heidegger saying "what Marx recognised in an essential and significant sense from out of Hegel as the estrangement of human beings . . ."[47] Earlier

43. Martin Heidegger, "Hegel und die Griechen" (*GA*9), 444. "Ἀλήθεια ist der Geschichte der Philosophie zuvorgekommen."

44. Ibid., 443. "Bereich der Unverborgenheit."

45. Ibid., 443. "Nur wo diese schon waltet, kann etwas sagbar, sichtbar, zeigbar, vernehmbar werden."

46. Martin Heidegger, *Brief über den Humanismus* (*GA*9), 336. "Die absolute Metaphysik gehört mit ihren Umkehrungen durch Marx und Nietzsche in die Geschichte der Wahrheit des Seins."

47. Ibid., 339. "Was Marx in einem wesentlichen und bedeutenden Sinne von Hegel her als die Entfremdung des Menschen erkannt hat . . ."

I noted that we have yet adequately to determine the meaning of alienation and estrangement, *Entfremdung* and *Entäußerung*, but both derive from the *Economic and Philosophical Manuscripts.* Marx's identification of the positive moment of Hegel is *Aufhebung*, which I translated as "negation." This negation is to be understood *within* estrangement as the possibility of its overcoming, so that the attainment of the task of negation—the revolutionary process as the attainment to communism—is "in the real appropriation of [man's] objective being [*Wesen*—essence] through the annihilating [*Vernichtung*] of the *estranged* determination of the objective world, through its negating [*Aufhebung*]."[48] What Marx describes here is the *positive* movement of history. This is how history *is* historical for Marx: it is how the passage of time is identified with the destiny of the being of being human. This positivity is, however, based essentially and fundamentally on a *negating* which is at the same time an annihilating (*Vernichtung*). Marx and Marxism resist every attempt to identify him and it as a nihilism, and yet at its very center is a constant annihilating (it is from out of this constancy that Trotsky's and Mao's understanding of the revolution as "permanent" has to be understood). Marx appears in every sense to proceed in the *opposite* direction to Nietzsche's will to power and triumph of the subjectivity of the subject as that one who attains to the highest through a self-identification with the will to power.

There is in Hegel an ambiguity in the activity of sublation, *Aufhebung*, negating. The synthesizing structures of *aufheben* appear to *pro*ceed, but, as we shall come to see, actually operate in the manner of *re*ceipt, that is, they operate backward. The essential character of the motion of negativity is, therefore, circular. This means that the structures of sublation can be interpreted in either direction, or even in both. Marx and Nietzsche, as the inversions of Hegel, each takes up and predominates in one of these directions, while never losing the connection with the other. Nietzsche prevails as the *descending*, the *Niedergang*,[49] Marx, the straining forth, the *production* of history, the *ascending*. Elsewhere, I have argued: "At the very beginning of Nietzsche's text, Zarathustra goes under—the verb is *Untergehen* which means not simply to go down, but to sink, to de-cline, to come to an end, to disappear: 'Thus began Zarathustra's going-under.'"[50] This *Untergang* opposes the *trans-scendens*. Zarathustra begins by moving to an end.

48. Karl Marx *Ökonomisch-philosophische Manuskripte* (*MEW*40), 583. "Die wirkliche Aneignung seines gegenständlichen Wesens durch die Vernichtung der *entfremdeten* Bestimmung der gegenständlichen Welt, durch ihre Aufhebung . . ." (Marx's emphasis).

49. Friedrich Nietzsche, vol. 6, *Also Sprach Zarathustra*, 12. "Also begann Zarathustra's Untergang."

50. Laurence Paul Hemming, *Heidegger's Atheism*, 241–42.

Heidegger says, "For Zarathustra begins by going under. Zarathustra's commencement is his downgoing. Nietzsche thought no other essence for Zarathustra."[51] This discussion comes in the context of a lecture entitled "Third Communication of the Doctrine of Eternal Return," a section entirely concerned with God, and with Zarathustra as the "god-less one." So for Heidegger, Zarathustra is the one whose going-under, *de*-cline is in consequence of his godlessness and it is to communicate this godlessness in its character that the downgoing occurs. The communication of godlessness is the devaluation of the uppermost values, it is the speaking out *of* and *as* the will to power. It is what Zarathustra has to say.

Marx criticizes Hegel's understanding of "*absolute negativity,*"[52] the dialectical movement of "the negation of the negation" as the attainment of an abstract movement, of absolute self-consciousness. Marx argues that what is required is to grasp the positive significance of the negation such that "in short [Hegel] grasps—within the abstraction—work as the *self-producing act* of the human being";[53] however, this is a structure already fully intended and implicit in Hegel himself, as I shall argue in the next chapter. For Marx, the materialist understanding of negating, of negativity as such, is the transition from self-consciousness to historical consciousness of the self-producing subject: history *as* work, *as* the producing *of* the subject (again, the objective and subjective genitives are in play). Here, we gain a glimpse for the first time of how history is, for Hegel and Marx, *worked* by humanity itself. We will return to this understanding as we proceed, to find out how production, producing itself, is the essence of Marx's metaphysics.

One word leaps out for us here: *negativity,* the subtitle of Heidegger's collection of essays and remarks on Hegel that he himself placed in the very middle of the volumes that collectively run under the title of *Das Ereignis.*[54] We have already begun to examine this "negating" in increasing detail, and see how all the positivity of Hegel, of Marx (and, in a different way, which we do not have time to examine, of Nietzsche) springs from this very negating. This situating of the volume in the very middle of the notebooks of *Das Ereignis,* as what must be got *around,* cannot be accidental. In this volume on Hegel there is hardly a word about Marx, except to note the extent to which inasmuch as the age in which Nietzsche is rooted is unthinkable with-

51. Martin Heidegger, *Die ewige Wiederkehr des Gleichen* (*Nietzsche* [*GA*6.1]), 323. "Zarathustras Anfang ist sein Untergang, ein anderes Wesen Zarathustras hat Nietzsche niemals gedacht."

52. Karl Marx, *Ökonomisch-philosophische Manuskripte* (*MEW*40), 585. "*absolute [ ] Negativität*" (Marx's emphasis).

53. Ibid., 584. "Kurz, er faßt—innerhalb der Abstraktion—die Arbeit als den *Selbsterzeugungsakt* des Menschen."

54. Martin Heidegger, *Hegel* (*GA*68).

out Hegel, so indeed socialism, of which Marx and Marxism is only a more determined formula, is by implication *also* unthinkable without Hegel.[55] To my knowledge Nietzsche never mentions Marx by name in any of his texts, although there is a strenuous thread of critique of socialism throughout Nietzsche's works. It is this silence over Marx, and savage critique of socialism, that Heidegger may well be alluding to: Nietzsche, speaking only in consequence of Hegel, fails to see the extent to which socialism (and so Marx's thought as its most determined form) is, as a countermovement to the will to power, also a movement from out of the same ground as Nietzsche's own metaphysical "standpoint." What the volume represents is Heidegger's tracing of the connections between Hegel's understanding of negativity and Nietzsche's metaphysics of nihilism, in their connections with *das Seyn als Ereignis,* be-ing as such, as *Ereignis.* The same connections pertain between Hegel and Marx, through the very same word. This is Heidegger's understanding of the superiority of the Marxist understanding of history: that it is necessarily marked by the same experience of the *nothing* that means that, even in the forgetfulness of being, as an event (*Ereignis*), this superiority paves the way for the speaking of be-ing as such. In a section entitled "Metaphysics" in this volume, Heidegger concludes by saying "the first beginning and its end. Hegel—Nietzsche,"[56] to which we must add "Marx," as the next chapters will seek to show.

55. Martin Heidegger, *Die Negativität* (*GA*68), 8. "Das Zeitalter in dem Nietzsche verwurzelt und verfangen war, ist ohne Hegel nicht denkbar; ganz zu schweigen von Marx und dem Marxismus, der ja mehr ist als eine bestimmte Formulierung des Sozialismus."

56. Martin Heidegger, *Hegel* (*GA*68), 55. "Der erste Anfang und sein Ende. Hegel—Nietzsche."

*Chapter 4*

# Logic and Dialectic

MARX'S RELENTLESS ANTIPATHY to religion represents his antipathy to every thought of the supersensible, one that marks his every work, from the very earliest: in the preface of his doctoral thesis, Marx made his own the words Aeschylus gives to Prometheus: " 'with a single word, I hate all gods!,' is [Prometheus's] personal confession, his personal statement against all heavenly and earthly gods."[1] Marx's use of the phrase betrays his relation to history and antiquity. For Prometheus, one punished by the gods, does not doubt whom he hates: his hate is testimony to the power of Zeus and the Olympians who seal his fate, however much Prometheus is portrayed in later ages as having set humanity on its way. Prometheus's cry of hatred of the gods is addressed *to* a god, at least in Aeschylus's play, from the text Marx quotes.[2] In contrast, Marx's hatred of the gods is not that of the victim, but the victor punishing, by setting into flight, the Olympians and their Abrahamic successor. From Prometheus's and Marx's mouth, the word is not commensurate.

Marx's antipathy to religion sets itself as a historical task: "it is thus the *task of history,* once the *beyond-character of truth* has vanished, to establish the *truth of the here-and-now.*"[3] This is the means by which the task of philosophy is put into the service of history—"in this manner the critique of heaven transforms itself into the critique of the earth, the *critique of religion* into the *critique of right,* the *critique of theology* into the *critique of poli-*

1. Karl Marx, "Vorrede" in "Differenz der demokritischen und epikurischen Naturphilosophie" (*MEW*40), 262. "Das Bekenntnis des Prometheus: ἁπλῷ λόγῳ, τοὺς πάντας ἐχθαίρω θεούς ist ihr eigenes Bekenntnis, ihr eigener Spruch gegen alle himmlischen und irdischen Götter."

2. The line Marx quotes is addressed to Hermes, messenger of the gods. See also Aeschylus, *Prometheus Bound,* l.975.

3. Karl Marx, "Zur Kritik der Hegelschen Rechtsphilosophie" (*MEW*1), 379. "Es ist also die *Aufgabe der Geschichte,* nachdem das *Jenseits der Wahrheit* verschwunden ist, die *Wahrheit des Diesseits* zu etablieren" (Marx's emphases).

*tics*."[4] The sentence itself contains a transformation, for inasmuch as religion, subjected to "criticism," becomes the way in which we subject "right" (meaning here, as we shall see in the next chapter, law, and the state) to criticism, *what was once theology itself* is transformed into and becomes the *practice* of politics. Nothing is said whatsoever about religion itself in this statement: rather all of this is already secured on the way in which thinking *thinks*—its "from whence"—concerning the totality of being, "being as a whole." For inasmuch as Nietzsche had condemned Christianity as "Platonism for the masses,"[5] so also Marx means that religion is the pretext for a certain kind of thinking about being—the thinking that thinks from beyond to here, that takes for granted the *epekeina* of the "over there" as the more real world than the "here and now," the "real," the *da* of Heidegger's *Dasein*. Marx's statements concern the emphatic rejection of every claim made for a "supersensible." In all of this, however, Marx only drives to an extreme a position already present in Hegel, while at the same time eliminating from Hegel the synthesis of the material with the religious that is the triumph of Hegel's *Phenomenology*. This synthesis is the crowning moment of ontotheology, of the sublation of Christian faith into philosophy, as a philosophy of human being.

The discussion of ontotheology in Heidegger has tended to emphasize the *ego*, the "single-subject" character of the "onto-ego-theo-logy" of Heidegger's invention of the term (while the "ego" qualification is rarely alluded to), but what is brought sharply in view here (from Heidegger's point of view) is the intensely political character of ontotheology, where the subjectivity of the subject in question is not the "individual," but the way in which what we call "society" is itself taken for granted as the concrete manifestation of a certain understanding of subjectivity as absolute subject. The absolute subject is not "somewhere else" ("over there") for Hegel any more than it is for Marx, but is always realized as "society as a whole" or as "the state," most of all as the state or society *should* come to be. The absolute subject, as what *I* am to be, is also how I produce the possibility of all other social relations that I encounter. This means that every social relation I encounter is measured up to how it *should* be: I become the judge of the social relations in which I am immersed for the sake of my own becoming. This means in every social relation I am

4. Ibid., 379. "Die Kritik des Himmels verwandelt sich damit in die Kritik der Erde, die *Kritik der Religion* in die *Kritik des Rechts*, die *Kritik der Theologie* in die *Kritik der Politik*" (Marx's emphases).

5. Friedrich Nietzsche: vol. 5, *Jenseits von Gut und Böse*, 12. "denn Christenthum ist Platonismus für's 'Volk'"; see also vol. 11, *Nachlaß 1884–1885*, 79. "Ohne Platonismus und Aristotelismus keine christliche Philosophie." ("Without Platonism and Aristotelianism, no Christian philosophy.")

able to take up a standpoint with respect to it: this relation is "progressive" (toward how society should be), that relation "regressive" (only functions with respect to an understanding of how society *has been,* an understanding that has *already* been sublated). The understanding of being-with-one-another, so central to *Being and Time,* and which Heidegger had argued there is always the "already," the "condition" of *my* being at all, becomes the locus of my judgments. This is the connection between ontotheology and society, or in more abstract terms, it is how sociology is itself ontotheological.

In the period during and immediately after Heidegger's accession to the rectorate of the University of Freiburg, he began the confrontation with Hegel which, I will later argue, formed the basis of his later political thought and made a central contribution to the fundamental transition into the thinking contained in the manuscripts of *Das Ereignis.* The historical significance of this confrontation for Heidegger's own development of his thought and his commitment to, and rejection of, Nazism will be considered in later chapters. Marx's later thought—the thought of *Das Kapital* and the *Grundrisse*—also arise on the basis of a confrontation with Hegel, or rather (in both Heidegger's and Marx's cases) the confrontation with the situation which Hegel himself attempts to bring to description. Marx's confrontation is carried out in the period of the early 1840s, the years of the so-called *Parisian Manuscripts,* the *Critique of Hegel's Doctrine of the State,* the essay *On the Jewish Question* and the *Critique of Hegel's Philosophy of Right.* In many ways these writings represent a single corpus of writing, although only some were published when they were written, others appearing (as we have seen) in the early twentieth century.

What is the fundamental insight that Hegel has, with which both Heidegger and Marx grapple, and which effects such a vigorous transformation in the thought of both of them? Marx's primary criticism of Hegel is that he inverts the true relationship between the idea (which Hegel represents as the state) and the empirical constituents of the state (civil society and the family). So Marx says "the idea comes to be subjectivised and the *real* relationship of family and civil society to the state comes to be constituted as their *inner imaginary* activity. Family and civil society are the prerequisites of the state, they are the real agents; however, in speculative philosophy this is reversed."[6] Marx

6. Karl Marx, "Kritik des Hegelschen Staatsrechts" (*MEW*1), 206. "Die Idee wird versubjektiviert, und das *wirkliche* Verhältnis von Familie und bürgerlicher Gesellschaft zum Staat wird als ihre *innere imaginäre* Tätigkeit gefaßt. Familie und bürgerliche Gesellschaft sind die Voraussetzungen des Staats; sie sind die eigentlich Tätigen; aber in der Spekulation wird es umgekehrt" (Marx's emphases). Heidegger was clearly familiar with these passages of Marx, and the means by which Marx effects a reversal in Hegel: he notes (in reference to other passages on the family and civil society) that Marx "thereby stands Hegel on his head." (Martin Heidegger, *Seminare: Hegel—Schelling* [*GA*86], 79. "Stellt dabei Hegel auf den Kopf.")

does not, however, deny the fundamental distinction between the empirical forms of social life and their object (the state), he simply raises the question of *how* the relation is constituted—the direction in which it proceeds. We have already seen that this direction is, in Hegel, ambiguous. However, Marx's criticism represents a fundamental insight into the requirement to radicalize Hegel's thought which the thought of "the state" alone cannot capture.

Heidegger also identifies the question of the relation of the state to its empirical forms as that unity toward which Hegel's thought is directed to resolving. Immediately after the rectorate, in the winter semester of 1934–35, Heidegger held a seminar with Erik Wolf on Hegel's *Philosophy of Right.* We have not only the protocols of this seminar (in two versions), but also, perhaps more importantly, Heidegger's preparatory notes for it. In these notes, Heidegger sets as the headline for the whole discussion "the speculative definition of the state: reality of the moral idea."[7] Both Marx and Heidegger draw attention to the "realization," literally "realness" (*Wirklichkeit*), of the idea, *as* the idea of the state. The idea of the state is (as we shall examine much more closely in the next chapter) *Geist* itself, realizing itself. We are apt to fall back into considering the state as a fixed or limited entity, but this is because Marx's fundamental insight into Hegel's thought already takes us beyond the connection between the realization of the state and the idea of the state itself. For Hegel the state, as *Geist,* is at the same time the absolute, and the infinite: it is what is constantly *becoming.* Hegel's fundamental insight is that the state, as a constant "becoming," is itself also a constant increase and development, as the motion of time and the unfolding of development in the "reality" of the real. Heidegger's notes understand that the idea of the state is not only the "counter-concept" to nature, but, in realizing itself *through* the natural sphere (the family, civil society, the empirical factuality of moral and social life), it is the way the counter-concept is the realization of "the all-concept: the absolute."[8] The state is the objectification, the realization, of the synthesis of "nature" and *Geist.*

The state is thus the highest concept of subjectivity—absolute subjectivity—taken for itself. One of the most enigmatic of Hegel's phrases—so enigmatic that some commentators have denied Hegel to be its author—is one that Heidegger draws attention to in his notes,[9] but seems not to have addressed in the actual seminar itself (neither of the protocols of the seminar mention it). The remark is in the additional notes provided by Eduard Gans to the *Philosophy of Right,* and so inasmuch as we argue that it is properly

7. Martin Heidegger, *Seminare: Hegel—Schelling* (GA86), 79. "Spekulative Definition des Staates—Wirklichkeit der sittlichen Idee."

8. Ibid., 79. "Gegenbegriff . . . All-begriff: das Absolute."

9. See ibid., 136. The quotation is underlined in the text.

Hegel's voice, it was, nevertheless, omitted from the first edition of the *Philosophy of Right.* The remark is prefaced by Hegel's statement that "the state is *Geist* itself," and then adds "it is the passage of God through the world, this [is what] the state is."[10]

The remark is so extraordinary that it is almost certainly Hegel's authentic voice (it is difficult to see how Gans could have fabricated such a daring claim): moreover it is entirely consistent with the opening sections of Hegel's discussion of the state in the *Philosophy of Right.* In the opening section Hegel distinguishes the domestic gods from the *Geist* of the nation or people (*Volksgeist*), citing the example of Athene, whose place as the mother-goddess of Athens means she was understood by the Greeks to be "the self *knowing* and *willing* divine" and the means by which ethical, moral life and political life are "the willing of the in and for itself purpose in its being thought."[11] The goddess, God itself, is the willing, the very *being and thinking,* the *purpose* of the inner *and* exterior unity of the people or nation as a whole—of humanity itself. The question, which remains open for Hegel, and which Marx will close decisively in the direction of humanity, is: is this unity something human (and so results in the "totality" of humanity, "humanism" as such) or other than human? Heidegger's understanding of the "Last God" is opened up by an answer that stands in opposition to Marx: the unity of the being of being-human is itself nothing human. This answer, however, never says "what," or even quite "who," the god is. However, we jump ahead of ourselves, for here, in his preparatory notes, Heidegger is preoccupied with the terms that Hegel employs in naming the unity of being itself. These terms—the will, the absolute, the infinite, the state, *Geist,* and God—are, in a sense, interchangeable, and summed up in the *idea* itself. In the state, as idea and as its realization, is achieved the inner unity of the most singularly human (absolute subjectivity) as the most general (the *all*).

What both Marx and Heidegger draw attention to in their respective confrontations with Hegel is the realization of the idea. Heidegger's headline note for his seminar mentions the *idea* as such and says "this realizing: reality is *unitedness* of the general and the particulars."[12] Marx's whole thrust is to concentrate on the "working-out" of the "realization" (what Heidegger

10. G. W. F. Hegel, *Grundlinien der Philosophie des Rechts,* 403. "Der Staat ist der Geist . . . [er] ist der Gang Gottes in der Welt, daß der Staat ist." Knox simply omits this remark from his translation: Allen Wood (*Hegel: Elements of the Philosophy of Right,* 279) translates it far too strongly as the "march of God in the world."

11. G. W. F. Hegel, *Grundlinien der Philosophie des Rechts,* 403. "(Athene) das sich *wissende* und *wollende* Göttliche . . . das Wollen des an und für sich seienden gedachten Zweckes" (Hegel's emphasis).

12. Martin Heidegger, *Seminare: Hegel—Schelling* (GA86), 79. "Idee . . . Diese Erwirkung: Wirklichkeit ist *Einheit* des Allgemeinen und Einzelnen."

names in the German as *Erwirkung*): thus realization is the goal and purpose realized *through* labor, work, itself. Work here, is the goal and purpose that the concrete realities (civil society, the family) ever strive toward and *produce.* Hence the working-out produces and reproduces social relations overall—what Marx understands Hegel's naming of the state (as the infinite and the absolute, not as the material institutions) to be striving to achieve. Labor, *work itself,* is the "through which" ontotheology "realizes" itself after Hegel, after Marx. It is only if we understand this that we are able to understand the force of Marx's critique of religion, and his forceful replacement of God as "the creative" with man as the one, individually and collectively, who creates and so himself reproduces the *all.*

It is in this sense that ontotheology (as a name for metaphysics) is a "social" or "political" understanding of being in totality, overall. For Hegel, the idea of the state is only mediately realized in the constitution or interior right of particular states: the relations between states reveal the exterior *Staatsrecht,* the right or constitutional law of the state "as such." This, however, is "the universal idea as *genus* and absolute power over against individual states, the *Geist* which occurs in the reality of the process of *world-history.*"[13]

Marx's understanding of the world-historical transformation of the human essence, even as it progressively rejects the specificity of the preservation of individual states in the realization of the idea of the power of the state, nevertheless proceeds from within this thought. In this the *actual* state, as much as the party, is an intermediate stage of the relationship between the "social" in its particular realizations in specific places or lands (the materialization of the social in places), and the development and realization of world history overall: it is for this reason that the state is only a provisional concept, the consequence of production as such, but not its final end. Marx embodies the understanding of power that exists "over against" bourgeois states in the proletariat itself, and so not in an abstract form but its concretization as a historical force. In this he simply drives to an extreme a possibility latent in Hegel. This embodiment takes material, historical forms, the instances of which Marx analyzes in their specificity. Speaking of the events leading up to Napoleon's coup of 1799 (the "June days"), Marx argues that "all classes and parties had united themselves during the 'June Days' as the party of order against the proletarian class."[14]

13. G. W. F. Hegel, *Grundlinien der Philosophie des Rechts,* 404. "Die allgemeine Idee als *Gattung* und absolute Macht gegen die individuellen Staaten, der Geist, der sich im Prozesse der *Weltgeschichte* seine Wirklichkeit gibt" (Hegel's emphases).

14. Karl Marx, *Der achtzehnte Brumaire des Louis Bonaparte* (*MEW*8), 123. "Alle Klassen und Parteien hatten sich während der Junitage zur *Partei der Ordnung* vereint gegenüber der proletarischen Klasse" (Marx's emphasis).

So pervasive has the material understanding of the world become in the way in which we already take for granted that the world is to be seen (and the very capacity to take up the notion of "the world" at all and know in advance what is indicated by it), that it has resulted in even the fundamental connections within Hegel's own philosophy (as the grounding description of this very materialism, the conversion of the entire surrounding world as so much "stuff" that lets itself be manipulated by "human history" as "world history") becoming difficult to see.[15] It is essential to understand that this priority of the material, of the "real," is the very ground from out of which Hegel's philosophy itself sets out. It is this ground that Marx also occupies and from within which he develops his thought. It is Marx's natural voice, the attitude in which he so often speaks, to assume an oppositional and polemical relation even to those from whom he derives most and to whom he is most indebted. In taking up and intensifying Hegel's innermost tendencies of thinking, he consistently presents himself as arguing against Hegel: an *against* which is at the very same time a coming closest *to.* Whilst Marx's radicalization of Hegel makes far more tangible an essential understanding of what it is that Hegel attempts to name with his discussion of the State as idea, namely the infinite and the absolute, Heidegger rejects Marx's reversal of Hegel through his privileging of the "empirical facts" of the state (civil society, the family) because he understands Marx's materialism to be *less materialistic* than Hegel's own. Heidegger notes that Marx's reversal of Hegel leads him to understand "that *Geist* is only the ideological *superstructure,*"[16] and so Marx, along with "the whole [last] hundred years" fails to understand how what Hegel names as *Geist* makes possible and sets itself in sway over the whole of the end of metaphysics—a rulership that allows Marx's understanding of (human) work and labor to be the force that carries out what Nietzsche had called the devaluation of the uppermost values. In this, Heidegger argues, "Marx has understood Hegel *un*speculatively."[17]

This "unspeculative" understanding of Hegel has, for Heidegger, a fundamental effect on Marx. Marx's relentless materialism leads him to a more limited understanding of work than Hegel provides. Hegel's speculative thought preserves the fundamental orientation toward the *un*human that all this talk of divinity attempts to name: "the occurring of the world-

15. See Thom Brooks, *Hegel's Political Philosophy: A Systematic Reading of the Philosophy of Right,* for an analysis of the troubled history of the relation of Hegel's *Philosophy of Right* to Hegel's *Logic* and, to a lesser extent, his *Phenomenology.*

16. Martin Heidegger, *Seminare: Hegel—Schelling* (GA86), 610 (protocol of Wilhelm Hallwachs). "Der Geist ist nur der ideologische Überbau."

17. Ibid., 610 (protocol of Wilhelm Hallwachs). "Marx hat Hegel *un*spekulativ genommen" (Heidegger's reported emphasis).

spirit, wherein it brings itself *to* itself, is *properly* work itself."[18] This is in accord with Hegel's reference to Athene, and to the attempt to name where the god *stands* in relation to the nation. It is out of this that we can begin to understand what Heidegger will come to mean by "the Last God," as that which, being nothing human, holds sway and passes through the occurring of the people, the nation. In contrast, Heidegger argues, through his relentless drive for an absolutely *unspeculative* materialism Marx denatures the character of work such that "the worker becomes only the *mere* worker (the industrial worker)."[19] Nevertheless, this denaturing and devaluation is a consequence of Hegel's speculative thought, and is the drive into the end and completion of metaphysics.

The drive for the priority of the material is *itself* an event in the history of thinking, which means, in the prevailing way in which thinking *thinks*. In a 1957 lecture course under the title "Basic Laws of Thinking," Heidegger drew attention to how Marx develops the manner of Hegel's thinking: the thinking itself whose appearance Hegel brings to description and which comes to prevail. Heidegger means not only the "content" of Hegel's thought, but also even more primarily *how* Hegel's thought is able to think what it then thinks, and so makes possible for thinking to think at all. All of this, Heidegger says, "brings Marx truly into an extreme opposition to Hegel, but through this opposition Marx remains within the metaphysics of Hegel."[20]

It is necessary to understand Hegel's thinking as already in confrontation with the "supersensible" of Kant's thought, and with Kant's failure to reconcile the question of freedom and necessity through the separation of the phenomenal and the noumenal worlds. The connection of Hegel's thought with the understanding of reason as Kant presents it is unshakeable: "reason is a priori the prescribing of law for freedom and for its peculiar causality, as the supersensible in the subject, for the sake of an unconditioned practical knowledge."[21] The movement of history, and its vicissitudes, and the pressing demand of "reality" itself, shatter the certainties of this claim. Philosophy as historical, as primordially worked out from the "real" and "actual," is not so

18. Ibid., 611 (protocol of Wilhelm Hallwachs). "Das Geschehen des Weltgeistes, worin er sich zu sich selbst bringt, ist die *eigentliche* Arbeit" (Heidegger's reported emphasis).

19. Ibid., 611 (protocol of Wilhelm Hallwachs). "Der Arbeiter [ist] nur noch der *bloße* Arbeiter ist (der Industriearbeiter)" (Heidegger's reported emphasis).

20. Martin Heidegger, *Grundsätze des Denkens* (GA79), 95. ". . . bringt Marx zwar in einen äußersten Gegensatz zu Hegel, aber durch diesen Gegensatz bleibt Marx innerhalb der Metaphysik Hegels."

21. Immanuel Kant, *Kritik der Urteilskraft*, 106. "Die Vernunft ist a priori gesetzgebend für die Freiheit und ihre eigene Kausalität, als das Übersinnliche in dem Subjekte, zu einem unbedingt-praktischen Erkenntnis."

much Hegel's "achievement" as Hegel's own response to a collapse in reason, a crisis concerning the supersensible that marked the thought of the nineteenth century after Kant, and so to a situation that itself had arisen historically. It is in this respect that we have to attend to, so that we can understand, the "speculative Good Friday,"[22] an idea which Hegel introduces with his essay "Faith and Knowledge" of 1802–03, and developed further in the final sentence of the *Phenomenology* as the "Calvary of absolute Spirit."[23]

Taking up a sentence of Pascal's *Pensées,* that "nature is such that it *indicates* everywhere a God *lost* as much within man as outside man,"[24] Hegel speaks of the "godlessness" (*Gottlosigkeit*—literally, God-losing-ness, not just the prior absence, but the very departing of God) of the *once* historical, *now* speculative, Good Friday. "Speculative" is the term Hegel uses for the transition of a *single* concept into the performance of philosophy, as a constant attribute of thinking. What Good Friday *once* revealed as a historical event or singularity (that God can die, that God has died) is now visible and so repeated for those who can see (from Latin *specula,* a "watching-place," *specto,* "I watch or observe"). In all seeing, all *stand*point (from which to set myself up and watch), I "see" that God is dead. It is in this sense that Hegel (rather than Nietzsche) is the first in German philosophy to proclaim the death of God, even if he is the one who announces the "overcoming" of this death, that through human life, through the living human being, God *can* be resurrected. This repetitive "Good Friday" is that through which "the highest totality, in its entire earnestness and out of its deepest ground, at the same time can and must rise from the dead in the all-embracing and happiest freedom of its form."[25] We should note that this "godlessness" is repeated by Heidegger in several significant places in his own thought,[26] and so is given a preparatory history as the effect and consequence of the "Christianization of philosophy" over many centuries.

The singularity of finite subjectivity is what it means to be *living* through the godlessness of "nature" as it passes over dialectically to become absolute spirit, absolute (infinite) *Geist,* subjectivity as such. What

22. G. W. F. Hegel, *Glauben und Wissen,* 124. "spekulative(r) Charfreitag"

23. G. W. F. Hegel, *Phänomenologie des Geistes,* 531. "Schädelstätte des absoluten Geistes."

24. G. W. F. Hegel, *Glauben und Wissen,* 123–24, citing B. Pascal, *Pensées.* "La nature est telle qu'elle *marque* partout un Dieu *perdu* et dans l'homme et hors de l'homme."

25. G. W. F. Hegel, *Glauben und Wissen,* 124. "Die höchste Totalität (kann and muß) in ihrem ganzen Ernst und aus ihrem tiefsten Grunde, zugleich allumfassend und in die heiterste Freiheit ihrer Gestalt auferstehen."

26. See especially Martin Heidegger, *Geschichte der Philosophie von Thomas von Aquin bis Kant* (*GA*23), 77. It is in this text that Heidegger makes the daring claim, never fully developed here or in later work, that the origins of modern subjectivity are to be located in medieval metaphysics rather than in Descartes and later speculative idealism.

this means is that all thought is related to the actions brought about in and through the human person. In this sense Hegel's is every bit as much a philosophy of "becoming" as Nietzsche's, and on the same metaphysical basis. Hegel argues elsewhere that "God . . . can only be grasped through living"[27] (which means *brought back to life in the life that I am,* the very basis of the "aestheticization" of all sensory experience in its relation to *Geist*), the very activity of coming in to the full happiness of *form* (*Gestalt*). The "form" in question is what "I" am to become in realizing what "I" have thought and making it manifest. No longer is this form to be located in the supersensible; *now* it merely exists in the future, a future which *looks back at me* and sets me in place as the person I must eventually "be" (whom I must become). Every action I take now is either with respect to, or against, this future becoming. We could be tempted to read these passages theologically, and indeed they are in a certain way guided by an understanding of God founded in and driven by the history of Christianity: however, they are above all else a description of a prevailing metaphysics, the same metaphysics that drives Nietzsche's thinking. Nor is Hegel's any less philosophical than Nietzsche's own proclamation of the death of God, and not less than Marx's own writings do Hegel and Nietzsche together announce the *end* of metaphysics. In this sense Hegel writes from out of a metaphysical situation and in consequence of a history of thinking, rather than (as he is more conventionally interpreted) writes a "theological" metaphysics.

Hegel radicalizes a possibility that opens up only with the distinct configuration of God to the self of Descartes's subjectivity, while at the same time explaining Pascal's own thought (of the absence of God in nature and in the subject). In Hegel the assimilation of the particularity of the subject into absolute spirit *as* the movement of time is the way in which particular, specified "times" (the countable moment, Aristotle's *to nun*) are *through the very activity of living* synthesized to absolute time which is at the same time the totality of time *as* infinity. Here the godlessness of nature is "sublated" by infinity itself. At the same time in the historical movement of sublation, infinity becomes visible and concretized in the real. As we saw in the last chapter, the relentless drive toward the material, the materialism of Hegel's own thought, is the absolutely ineluctable drive to make comprehensible how the infinite as a horizon becomes manifest in the real, or finitude.

This orientation to time is an essential feature of Hegel's thought. Hegel never makes thematic in his work, but shows in outline, how the orientation to time, as the horizon *toward which* the human being lives, is an

27. Cited by Martin Heidegger in *Hegels Phänomenologie des Geistes* (GA32), 142, citing G. W. F. Hegel, *Hegels theologische Jugendschriften*. "Gott . . . kann nur mit Leben erfaßt werden."

essential aspect of human life. The horizon appears through what the human being, the subject, "does," how he or she "experiences." Every experience, because it carries within it an intrinsic relation to infinity, at the same time is revealed as an actual temporal moment. Heidegger understood that the becoming-visible of this horizon in human being was itself a historical occurrence, a genuine development in the history of being, even if it pointed toward (and drew upon) the way in which Aristotle especially had developed his understanding of human experience, *aisthesis,* in Aristotle's *De anima* and *Rhetoric.* Hegel is a step on the path of thinking as the history of being, toward the overcoming of the forgottenness of the *question* of being. Heidegger notes in this respect that for Hegel "being is the essence of time, being that is, qua infinity."[28] For Heidegger the problematic of *Being and Time* is related to Hegel's thought inasmuch as "the thesis *the essence of being is time* is the direct opposite of that, which Hegel in his entire philosophy sought to demonstrate . . . being is the essence of time."[29] Heidegger does not understand himself merely to be "reversing" Hegel, turning him upside-down to posit an "alternative." Heidegger believes himself to be dismantling the way in which the infinite announces itself in every moment of human experience. His question, therefore, is "if Hegel understood the infinite (being) to be made visible and present in every (finite) moment, on what more originary basis was this possible?" The answer is twofold: *first* on the basis that the infinite as "being" is coextensive with the concept of "God," and second (but in a way precisely masked by the history of being itself, the history of the *forgottenness* of being), because more originarily, the essence of being is time. In this sense Heidegger understands his own thought to be an even more radical, more originary, understanding of the death of God: the "concept" of God is not to be brought back to life by human beings "realizing" and so understanding for themselves the making visible of the infinite *in* the finite, but in understanding that the infinite is only a *mask* for the concept of God. The way through to this (the "essence" of the book *Being and Time*) is to show how time is the essence of being (and human time is finite because human beings are mortal). It is in this sense that Heidegger had declared in 1925 that "philosophical research is and remains atheism."[30] Not every inversion is a mere reversal.

Both Heidegger and Marx secure their thinking on the basis of an un-

28. Martin Heidegger, *Hegels Phänomenologie des Geistes* (*GA*32), 209. "Das Sein ist das Wesen der Zeit, nämlich qua Unendlichkeit."

29. Martin Heidegger, *Hegels Phänomenologie des Geistes* (*GA*32), 209. "Denn die These: *Das Wesen des Seins ist die Zeit*—ist das gerade Gegenteil von dem, was Hegel in seiner ganzen Philosophie zu erweisen suchte. . . . das Sein ist das Wesen der Zeit" (Heidegger's emphasis).

30. Martin Heidegger, *Prolegomena zur Geschichte des Zeitbegriffs* (*GA*20), 109–10. "Philosophische Forschung ist und bleibt Atheismus."

derstanding of a temporal horizon, and on the basis of their own determinative relation to the death of God. We can only allude to Marx's understanding at this stage, because so much else needs to be said before it will become clear how Marx's relation to Hegel is a relation to the way time enters philosophical thinking with Hegel. As we shall come to see, Marx secures the being of humanity on the basis of species-being—the concrete, material, exemplary being of human being that is his own understanding of absolute subjectivity. The temporal horizon that Marx secures is that of the infinite as the *end* of history, history in the fulfillment of its entirety, as a whole. It is from out of who "man" will be in this "end" that every individual human existence *now* is taken off and measured against (all fall short, all are estranged from who they—we—are *to* become). The "end" in question is not God, but social relations in the end of history: society as it *should* be, "communism." Heidegger, on the other hand, secures the essence of the being of being human on the basis of temporalization, by abandoning the "infinite" or the realization of the being of the end (Hegel's absolute subject: "God") altogether, for the sake of being itself.[31]

In securing being as the essence of time, Hegel describes the very befalling of an absolute imperative: how history befalls the humanity whose history it is. For the movement of particular subjectivity into absolute *Geist* is at the same time the overcoming of the dread "earnest" of suffering, and so of the very interiorization of the effect of godlessness in a nature evacuated of God. This is the emergence in its very *self* of the pressing imperative of the method of doubt *as* an imperative. The method of doubt is methodologically necessitated by the present situation of the being of being human.

Descartes states at the very opening of his *Principles of Philosophy* that "it is necessary for the one seeking the truth, once in his life—insofar as he is able—to doubt all things."[32] Descartes says that it is not possible to know what *is needed to be known* without already once having doubted: doubt is the precursor of the securing of what is binding for man as binding. For Descartes, as indeed for the whole of the modern age, what is "binding" is not what is asserted to be the case, or even what can be argued or demonstrated, but strictly that which can in *no* way be refused. This is Descartes's concern with the mathematical: the assertion "one plus one is two" cannot be gainsaid: the proof of the structure of the triangle is certain because it could

31. This does not mean "being" replaces "God," but rather that the nexus between being and God, originating in Plato and developed in the highest degree by the history of philosophy's entanglement with theistic faith, is formally broken. Now God and being are formally set apart. This does not stop the believer from believing "in the beginning God created the heavens and the earth," but ceases to make of this scriptural revelation a canon of philosophical fact.

32. René Descartes, vol. 8, *Principiorum philosophiae,* 5. "Veritatem inquirenti, semel in vitâ de omnibus, quantum fieri potest, esse dubitandum."

never be other. The assertion *cogito, ergo sum* is not a demonstration or even the outcome of a syllogism, it is binding because it carries with it a force of necessity—there is no way to deny it. This is the purpose of the "method" of doubt: to establish what is binding as what can *never* be doubted or evaded, and so he adds, "indeed the doubtful should be considered false."[33] From the very outset, therefore, Descartes takes up a position which is not world-indicating, but world-denying—world-effacing—in order to establish what is "most certain and easy to know":[34] what is therefore binding. What is most certain and easy to know, however—even while supposing "that there be no God and that there are no bodies, and even that we ourselves not to have . . . indeed any body at all"[35]—is the cognition that "*ego cogito, ergo sum* is of all things the first and most certain."[36] This securing of the self, as then secured by God, makes possible the securing of (the) world. Only a self and a world made Godless could be secured on this ground, but the tragic aspect, the baleful misery (the speculative Good Friday of the place of the skull, this Calvary-in-general) is "made happy" by sublating the world *to* the infinite. Sublation means at one and the same time uplifting, fulfilling, and canceling—the *negation* of the particular and finite in its assimilation to the infinite: but understood to unfold from *within* the being of being human.

If we return to the notion of godlessness as it is raised by Pascal, inasmuch as we trace it to Cartesian philosophy, we would be better and more historically accurate to understand it arising from out of the same ground of which Descartes himself also argues. For the origins of Pascal's claim have more to do with the debates in and around the consequences of Suárez's metaphysics as foundational than with the present philosophical situation. Heidegger's own comparison of Aquinas and Suárez in a 1929 lecture notes that "for the development of modern metaphysics . . . direct influence was exercised by the Spanish Jesuit Franz Suárez."[37] A central argument of Suárez was the existence of a "pure nature" apart from God, on which God can choose to act.

The philosophical elucidation of a nature apart from God on the one hand, and a nature which can be reclaimed into God on the other, proceeds in not one, but two directions, which arise on the basis of the *same* metaphysical ground—the "godlessness" of philosophy. Again the issue here is

33. Ibid., 5. "Dubia etiam pro falsis habenda."

34. Ibid., 5. "Certissimum et cognitu facillimum sit."

35. Ibid., 7. "Nullum esse Deum, nullum cœlum, nulla corpora; nosque etiam ipsos non habere . . . nec denique ullum corpus."

36. Ibid., 7. "*Ego cogito, ergo sum*, est omnium prima et certissima."

37. Martin Heidegger, *Die Grundbegriffe der Metaphysik* (*GA*29/30), 77–78. "Für die Entwicklung der neuzeitlichen Metaphysik . . . hat . . . der spanische Jesuit *Franz Suárez* [ausgeübt]."

not who "thinks up" or "does" philosophy in a particular way, but rather what befalls philosophical thinking: what thought is given to think.

Marx (as does Nietzsche) inverts the "Christian" philosophy of Hegel, while taking up the godlessness of which Hegel speaks and first brings to a full metaphysical description: yet this inversion is only a carrying to its most extreme a possibility which Hegel has laid hold of and described. This inversion in Marx brings to the fore the "productive" character of the situation in which "man" is to be understood: "*man makes religion,* religion does not make man."[38] We should not overlook that the essential thought here is neither God nor man, but *making,* the "productive" and creative itself. In the absence of God (and God as creator, as "the creative"), "man" comes to the fore as the one who stands in the place of production and creation: this is his assumption of godlessness. What is brought to the fore here is production as the work of man: labor. Labor "determines the self-production of man as the entire reality of the real."[39]

It is the *same* godlessness, however, the same radical de-divinization of nature and man alike, that we can trace at least as far back as Suárez (and some have even to Socrates and Protagoras).[40] In the wake of godlessness something like "nature as a whole," "nature as such," and "human nature" are brought into being as regions of specification and inquiry: we would have to say: as objects. Brought into being does not simply mean "are": whatever is in being as a whole is also denoted here. With respect to being as a whole, the imperative demand that the object-character that the terms "nature" and "human nature" make, indeed press and force on us, has to be understood: something has to be resolved in a new way that was as yet unresolved, and out of a situation that both did not pertain before and at the same time can be widely seen now (and so to have emerged). Widely seen really means "experienced": this is what "befalls us," despite ourselves.

It is here that Hegel's metaphysics manifests itself as dialectical thinking—the thinking that he carries through in his *Logic,* the first part of the three volumes of Hegel's *Encyclopaedia of the Philosophical Sciences.* For the logic describes how the "natural" is both assumed and taken up through *Geist* and made self-conscious, as the "means by which" the actual character of the transition through which individual *Geist* becomes absolute *Geist.* However,

38. Karl Marx, "Zur Kritik der Hegelschen Rechtsphilosophie" (*MEW*1), 378. "Der *Mensch macht die Religion,* die Religion macht nicht den Menschen" (Marx's emphasis).

39. Martin Heidegger, *Grundsätze des Denkens* (*GA*79), 95. "[Die] Selbstproduktion des Menschen (bestimmt) alle Wirklichkeit des Wirklichen."

40. Although for a discussion of the accusation of atheism in the latter, see Laurence Paul Hemming, *Postmodernity's Transcending,* 210 and following.

absolute *Geist* remains concrete: that is, it continues to manifest itself in concrete, historical forms. Experience, as the fundamental condition of life itself, and at the same time the subject becoming conscious, comes into, and overcomes, these historical forms so that in this way subjectivity is *essentially* productive. It is here that Heidegger sees the connection between Hegel's and Marx's thinking. Heidegger says that although Marx appears to take up the meaning of work as labor in the sense of activity and performance, in fact "the word [work] speaks in the sense of Hegel's concept of work, which is thought as the basic character of the dialectical process, through which the becoming of the real in its reality unfolds and is completed."[41]

It is in the *Logic* that Hegel laid out what Heidegger calls "Hegel's dialectical interpretation of thought-laws."[42] Heidegger continues:

> However, one should note, that today as soon as there is talk of dialectic, it becomes talk of dialectical materialism. One takes it for a worldview, representing it as ideology . . . Dialectic is today, one, perhaps even the world-reality. Hegel's dialectic is one of those thoughts, which—from distant repercussions—"guides the world," as powerful in those places where dialectical materialism is believed, as those where it is supposed to be disproved, but is in only a slightly transformed sense the same thinking. Behind these, one might say, confrontations of worldviews, rages the struggle over domination of the earth.[43]

This phrase "worldview" Heidegger had also reserved for the political outlook and metaphysics of the Nazi regime and fascism more generally, and characterizes the completion of metaphysics. Heidegger understands what dialectic names—he calls it a "dimension" of thought, experienced as a lawfulness—to govern and regulate those forms of political life that have a "worldview." In 1957, when Heidegger made these remarks, these forms are communism and "world democracy," together with the still recently memorable forms of Nazism and fascism.

We have already examined the relation of sublation to the history of

41. Martin Heidegger, *Grundsätze des Denkens* (*GA*79), 95. "Das Wort spricht im Sinne von Hegel's Begriff der Arbeit, die als Grundzug des dialektischen Prozesses gedacht ist, durch den das Werden des Wirklichen dessen Wirklichkeit entfaltet und vollendet."

42. Ibid., 88. "Hegels dialektische Auslegung der Denkgesetze."

43. Ibid., 88. "Zwar vermerkt man, sobald heute von Dialektik die Rede ist, daß es einen dialektischen Materialismus gibt. Man hält ihn für eine Weltanschauung, gibt ihn als Ideologie aus. . . . Die Dialektik ist heute eine, vielleicht sogar die Weltwirklichkeit. Hegels Dialektik ist einer der Gedanken, die—von weither angestimmt—'die Welt lenken,' gleichmächtig dort, wo der dialektische Materialismus geglaubt, wie dort, wo er—nur in einem leicht abgewandelten Stil des selben Denkens—widerlegt wird. Hinter dieser, wie man sagt, weltanschaulichen Auseinandersetzung tobt der Kampf um die Erdherrschaft."

thinking as transcendence. At the center of dialectical reasoning, in all its forms—technological, historical, material—there stands a fundamental comportment which is determinative for thinking as such. This centrality is thinking's very law. Heidegger traces the origins of nihilism right back to Plato, such that the inception of metaphysics with Plato and Aristotle takes place with the setting in place of the *merely* apparent world *over-against* the "real" world which is at the same time *epekeina—jenseits,* "beyond" and "over there." The essence of transcendence is in this taking of the world as one of mere appearances. The "mere" appearances of things are the mere representations of things as they "really" are in the supersensible world. This position takes its most extreme form in the philosophy of subjectivity, in the thought of Kant, when Kant says in the third *Critique,* speaking of the sublime ("upliftment"), "the pleasurable in the upliftment of nature is therefore only negative."[44] Nature is "sublimated," which means not suppressed but uplifted, in the *experience* of the transcendence of the sublime, an experience which "befalls" me, and so over which I have no control. At the center of this is the subjectivity of the subject, for whom this is a psychological event. The motor-force of the "befalling character" of the subject is in Hegel, however, not an experience of a transcendental realm but of sublation, as etymologically related to "sublimation" as Kant's German term *das Erhabene* is to Hegel's sublation, *die Aufhebung.* This is how I argued that Hegel transfers what for Kant is a category of aesthetics—the sublime—to every human experience, or what I earlier called the "aestheticization" of experience. This "law" of thinking is the law of negation.

The "object" of experience here is not, however, an experience of *the* transcendent (as it had been in Kant), but of the very transition of the subject from particularity to absolute subjectivity in the transformation of "the natural" through consciousness to absolute subjectivity: the object is, therefore, the "infinite," as such. This movement is attained through negation. Thus negation (historically) accomplished by thinking is "the first negation—the abstract." This is succeeded in Hegel's dialectical *Logic* by "the absolute negation—the negation of the negation":[45] the negation of the negation does not abstract the different from the same, but overcomes the different and returns it to the identical. The full force of this will not become clear until we can discuss later how this same understanding of negativity (negation) is at work in Marx, but what Heidegger draws attention to is the transformation of the character of negativity in Hegel's dialectic. For negativity is necessarily connected to *the* nothing. Heidegger's concern is always to show how

44. Immanuel Kant, *Kritik der Urteilskraft,* 116. "Das Wohlgefallen am Erhabenen der Natur ist daher auch nur negativ."

45. Martin Heidegger, *Hegel: Die Negativität* (GA68), 18. "Die erste Negation—die abstrakte. Die absolute Negation—die Negation der Negation."

the nothing as such makes possible the *nihil* of nihilism. *The* nothing allows difference—"otherness"—to come into being. The nothing is the ground of the manifold, because—again in contradistinction to Hegel—it is not that every being makes the *infinite* visible, but rather that every being is marked by a kind of "not-ness" in virtue of its singularity. Finitude means that every finite thing is marked by having an end, a "not-ness."[46] However, the subjectivity of the subject always remains the same, even as an empty postulate. As such, the negativity within it explains how it undergoes change while remaining the same.[47] Difference, "otherness" explains who the one is other to, to the other—"this difference sets both apart from one another."[48] Absolute negation produces "*absolute otherness—the unconditioned self-within-itself-self-relating.*"[49] Such negativity, lying at the heart of the dialectical, explains the movement of time as the production of objects *through* the subjectivity of the subject: the concrete and historically manifest, not the abstract. It will be essential to keep this understanding in view throughout the rest of all that we discuss, especially in the interpretation of Marx.

This is how Hegel transforms transcendence from a projection forward into the unchanging, transcendental, region of thought, the "noumenal" toward a pure horizon of becoming, which nevertheless is not understood to be unchanging. As changeable, it has the power to effect change—indeed it is the conditioning possibility of change in material forms: it is what makes development possible.

All of this Heidegger understands as the connection between production and thinking: "each production is already in itself already re-flexion, is thinking."[50] This analysis is profoundly in accord with Heidegger's critique of

46. Heidegger notes how Aristotle had touched on this, and, in taking it for granted, not made it an explicit theme in his investigation of δύναμις in the *Metaphysics*. Thus in every "producing" there is the possibility of the force that produces sinking into an "un-force." See Martin Heidegger, *Metaphysics Θ 1–3* (GA33), 154. "Dieses Negativum steht nicht einfach als das Gegenteil neben dem Positiven der Kraft, sondern lauert dieser in ihr selbst auf und dies deshalb, weil jede derartige Kraft ihrem Wesen nach mit der Zwiespältigkeit und also mit einem 'Nicht' versehen ist." ("This *negativum* does not simply stand next to the positive of force as its contrary, but lurks within it and inside it, and this is because every force of this kind in its essence has within itself divisiveness and so a 'not.' ")

47. We should note here Aristotle's notion of that kind of change that takes place purely within the psyche—ἀλλοιώσις, "transformation." Compare Aristotle, *Metaphysics,* 1022b15; *De anima,* 416a33 and following.

48. Martin Heidegger, *Hegel: Die Negativität* (GA68), 18. "Dieser Unterschied setzt beide von einander weg."

49. Ibid., 19. "*Absolute Andersheit—das unbedingte Sich-auf-sich selbst-Beziehen*" (Heidegger's emphasis).

50. Martin Heidegger, *Grundsätze des Denkens* (GA79), 95. "Jede Produktion ist in sich schon Re-flexion, ist Denken."

Marx's eleventh of the "Theses on Feuerbach," and clarifies yet further how Heidegger understands what Marx says there. We are accustomed now to understand thinking itself as "production": all thought "projects," thinking creates new possibilities. It is in this that the modern separation between "experience" and "thinking"—a separation unthinkable in antiquity—resides. What is experienced by each one of us is marked by a kind of enforcement (it befalls us as "binding" on us, hence why experience has come to be so privileged a category of *proof*—you must attend to what I say because what I say is derived from what I *feel* and *have felt*), it is that in which I have no choice; experience is a befalling; it seems it could not be other. Even when I seek out certain kinds of experience, I seek out so that I come to know what "it is like to be befallen-to in that way." For Heidegger, however, the very fact that thinking thinks in certain ways means that even when I assume that I am "producing," and so am involved in a "project," I could not think other than thinking lets me think. Thinking—even dialectical thinking—follows certain "laws" of thought.

By "experience" is therefore meant what was discussed earlier as "what is binding in thinking." With Descartes and after him, the essence of rationalism has been a kind of ahistoricism, which manifests itself in claims like "one and one equals two in all possible worlds and at all possible times," or that the law of the excluded middle is a *necessary* truth of thinking. Arithmetical "truths" of this kind are easy to "prove" and so "experience" as binding. The sillier aspects of recent postmodern attempts to question this binding character even in arithmetic, however, do point to something deeper.[51] The formula "one plus one equals two" is only a formula: that it *is* recognizably binding does not explain *why* or *how* it is binding, and yet the Greeks, for instance, knew that there was a "why" and a "how" (and that there is a why and a how does not mean the "consensus is broken" or that the binding character is lessened, despite even Wittgenstein's claims on this point).[52] The law of the excluded middle is a metaphysical position which, as such, can at least be inquired into. This does not make arithmetical truths somehow contingent or relative, but it does show them to have a history, that they are part of the being-historical of man. It is precisely in this light that Hegel's *Logic* has to be understood. Moreover, Hegel's description of dialectical reasoning is illustrative of the extent to which arithmetic can be understood to have an ontological basis, in this case grounded in the transcendent structures of the subjectivity of the subject. The dialectical interpretation of the "principle

51. See, for instance, the chapter on Kristeva in Alan Sokal and Jean Bricmont, *Intellectual Impostures,* 37–47.

52. See Ludwig Wittgenstein, *Bemerkungen über die Grundlagen der Mathematik,* especially 37–38.

of identity" where A=A is negated to mean A= *not*-A because A overcomes A, and so A comes to be (be-comes) more than A, and yet remains in some sense determined *from out of* A is precisely the connection between the supposedly merely copulative "is" of A *is* A, but now thought as a *temporal* determination. A exceeds A means, in being A (in being *known* as A), inasmuch as A *is*, it *is*, with respect to (the) infinite.

Put another way, inasmuch as A, knowledge of A yields: *that there is infinity*. This is not mere postmodern trickery: precisely not. It is the binding character, the so-called experiential proof of life and being as becoming: as change. At the very end of Hegel's *Phenomenology*, we find Hegel asserting: "the nature, moments and movement of this knowing have thus resulted in this, that it is the pure being-for-itself of self-consciousness; it is I . . . this and no other I."[53] Therefore "it must on this basis be said, that nothing comes to be known as existing, which is not in *experience*, or as it might also be expressed, which is not *felt* to be true, as an inwardly revelatory eternity, as sacralities from the exercise of faith, or whatever other expressions are required."[54] This is what, after Hegel (the "after" being heard in the widest possible sense, thus, even through his inversions in Marx, Nietzsche, and so forth), makes all modern philosophies of becoming possible.

The inversions of the metaphysical situation that emerge from this comportment to the newly found *thingliness* and object-character of "nature" arise out of the *single* event of the absence and departure, the closure, of the divine. Why is it that Hegel calls his principal work a *phenomenology* of *Geist*? We see that the proper object of the inquiry is the self, but the self taken in a particular way. Thus what appears, the phenomenon, is not what actually *is* but rather what indicates the being of something else: the infinite. It is the *being* (living) "here" of the absolute concept ("there"), of absolute self-consciousness for itself. What appears does so for the sake of making manifest something that it itself is *not*, that is to say something that is other than itself, while at the same time manifesting what it is not in virtue of what lies already *in* what is not as what is *really* to be seen in what is manifest "here and now." Thus this is a phenomenology only insofar as it makes what the self in its self-appearing appear *for*, which is the immutable and permanently self-subsisting, the absolute concept as such, *being*. Hegel says that "being no

53. G. W. F. Hegel, *Phänomenologie des Geistes*, 523. "Die Natur, Momente und Bewegung dieses Wissens hat sich also ergeben, daß es das reine Fürsichsein des Selbstbewußtseins ist; es ist Ich, . . . dieses und kein anderes Ich."

54. Ibid., 525. "Es muß aus diesem Grunde gesagt werden, daß nichts gewußt wird, was nicht in der Erfahrung ist, oder wie dasselbe auch ausgedrückt wird, was nicht als gefühlte Wahrheit, als innerlich geoffenbartes Ewiges, als geglaubtes Heiliges, oder welche Ausdrücke sonst gebraucht werden—vorhanden ist."

longer has the significance of the abstraction of being,"[55] but as "rest [is] of itself as absolute-restless infinitude" where the "differentiation of movement is resolved . . . the simple essence of time which in its itself-self-sameness has the pure form of space."[56] The pure absolute strictly speaking has no time, but *as* time, or "temporalized," it gives time to the appearances. It is the condition for the differentiation that movement *is* itself (A=A to A=/A such that A overcomes the A that it is). Thus the movement in question turns out at the same time to be the movement of all phenomenal (i.e., appearing) things, and the movement in which the self actually knows *it*self and so in some sense also *is*.

We are accustomed to understand Hegel as an up-building, a constructive straining forward for an infinite horizon, even when the horizon will be realized in concrete, historical, forms. Here, however, we see that what in fact allows the straining-forth, the constructive activity of the dialectic to undertake the work of becoming, is the way that motion unfolds not as a forward-moving, but as it were, *backward* so that the phenomenal appearances disclose something which is already-there, already present, and so strictly speaking ("ideally") "already present," and as an "already" this "future" horizon is in fact already *past*. The striving forward that is the self proceeding from consciousness into self-consciousness is the proceeding forward down this passageway of the *transcendens*. In fact, however, the proceeding forward is toward, and in synthesis of, the making-apparent of what is already there, being *as* the absolute, and at the same time empty (inasmuch as it makes change and becoming actual) concept. As we saw in the last chapter, in this sense the synthesizing processes of sublation appear to *pro*ceed, but actually operate in the manner of *re*ceipt, that is, they operate backward. The essential structure of the motion is (as with negativity) circular—which is why it is possible for the direction of the motion to be mistaken: it only *appears* to be a forward motion in becoming; it *really is* a backward motion in making becoming, the appearability of what as appearance is only appearance *for*, appearance *of*, being as such.

This is fundamentally in accord with Hegel's understanding of philosophy as a science: "each of the parts of philosophy is a philosophical whole, a circle itself self-enclosed in itself, but the philosophical idea is established within a particular determination or element [of the whole]."[57] The whole

55. Ibid., 123. "Das Sein hat nicht mehr die Bedeutung der Abstraktion des Seins."

56. Ibid., 123–24. "Die Ruhe ihrer selbst als absolutunruhigen Unendlichkeit . . . das einfache Wesen der Zeit, das in dieser Sichselbstgleichheit die gediegene Gestalt des Raumes hat."

57. G. W. F. Hegel, *Enzyklopädie der philosophischen Wissenschaften I (Logik)*, 60. "Jeder der Teile der Philosophie ist ein philosophisches Ganzes, ein sich in sich selbst schließender Kreis, aber die philosophische Idee ist darin in einer besonderen Bestimmtheit oder Elemente."

nevertheless develops and moves—it *is* over time: "the singular circle breaks through the limitations of its elements inasmuch as it is in itself totality, and establishes a yet greater sphere."[58]

Although there is not the space to show why, in fact this circularity is properly and strictly in accord with the peculiar temporal structure of the cogito which Descartes develops in the *Meditations,* now transformed to indicate not the changelessness of form, but development and becoming. The cogito secures itself as finite substance *against* what it doubts, and then proceeds to secure itself upon what is already *infinitely* there, and so already lying present. Thought, for Descartes and for Hegel, stretches forward to discover and so disclose—which means give appearance to, allow to appear phenomenally—what is already *prior* in its presence: God; the infinite. It is for this reason that Heidegger is able to say with absolute correctness that "for Hegel the formerly, the *past,* constitutes the essence of time" and "for Hegel being (infinity) is also the essence of time."[59] In fact both Nietzsche's "will to power," as not the "willing of a subject" but rather the willing *from out of which subjectivity appears at all,* and Marx's "end" of history both operate from out of precisely the same temporal metaphysics, made possible only in the wake of the Cartesian subject, where inasmuch as time (as becoming) discloses the whole of being, "being is the essence of time." This is why in the deposition of God, of what God has been made to become, something is forced into the place that is identified and seized upon when God is declared to be dead. For Hegel this is the infinite, as particular subjectivity acceding to, and becoming, absolute subjectivity;[60] for Nietzsche this is the devaluation of the uppermost value (God) *for the sake of* a revaluation; for Marx this is the becoming-absolute of the *singular* and universal essence of the humanity of man. For Heidegger, in contrast, the "death of God," which is only the death of the metaphysical understanding of God, lets the nothing come forth once more as that most fundamental determination of being that lets difference *be.*

In tracing the genealogy of this understanding of the movement of subjectivity into (absolute) spirit as the annihilation of the particular for the sake of the *all* is itself a prevailing metaphysical condition. By this we mean an imperative that befalls present humanity, from Descartes to Hegel. Understood in this way, it becomes possible to move outside the voluntaristic language

58. G. W. F. Hegel, *Enzyklopädie der philosophischen Wissenschaften I (Logik),* 60. "Der einzelne Kreis durchbricht darum, weil er in sich Totalität ist, auch die Schranke seines Elements und begründet eine weitere Sphäre."

59. Martin Heidegger, *Hegels Phänomenologie des Geistes* (*GA*32), 211. "Daß für Hegel das Ehemals, d.h. die *Vergangenheit* das Wesen der Zeit ausmacht . . . [für] *Hegel*—das Sein (Unendlichkeit) ist auch das Wesen der Zeit."

60. See G. W. F. Hegel, *Logik,* 142, §59.

of "what Hegel did," to understand the extent to which Hegel himself provides us with a genuine *phenomenology,* a formal indication of being in its appearances, by showing how what Hegel describes prevails *even now,* such that what he describes performs and refigures—to use Hegel's own word, *lives*—the movement Hegel himself describes.

Hegel unfolds the province of dialectic, an unstable region of thinking that collapses difference into the humanity of man, and that establishes the ground for all future thinking. Dialectic becomes the logic of thinking. Marx never formally defines dialectical thinking, and yet his whole oeuvre unfolds from dialectical reasoning *as* a materialism. In this sense Marx never exceeds or surpasses Hegel. Engels's attempts to codify "dialectical materialism" in Marx's wake were imprecise and troublesome (as Sidney Hook was to suggest),[61] and yet in no sense did Engels falsify Marx or traduce the region of (dialectical) thinking that Hegel exposes to have set itself in place. It is this region, or dimension, of thinking that Heidegger has to bring himself into confrontation with to enter into the "productive dialogue" at its deepest level. It will be impossible for us to exhaust this confrontation in a small book like this. At most, we can hope to identify and bring to light the main outlines of the dialogue in the coming chapters in a way that has perhaps not fully been seen before. First, however, we must clarify in what way *theology* becomes *politics,* or rather in what way Hegel's understanding of the state, and Marx's and Nietzsche's understanding of the "human," are developed and remain entirely within the province of Hegel's metaphysics, at least from Heidegger's understanding.

61. See 26.

*Chapter 5*

# Metaphysics of the Human State

IN THE LAST TWO CHAPTERS we have examined Hegel's "speculative," abstract thought, a philosophy which Marx regarded as still too concerned with the supersensible. Already we have begun to see how this speculative thinking is connected with "the political" and with what Hegel understood by the word "state," at least in a preliminary way. Understood from Marx's standpoint, even if the concept of being has turned out to be an empty concept, the object of the articulation, the "goal" of the phenomenon of subjectivity as absolute subject still names a form of the Christian God. Anglophone interpretation of Hegel has often resisted the essential connections between Hegel's abstract, speculative, thought (exemplified in the *Logic* and the *Phenomenology*) and its concrete manifestations (foremost, in the *Philosophy of Right*, but also in the lectures on history and aesthetics), and yet neither Marx nor Heidegger ever interpreted Hegel in this way, and no interpretation which seeks to understand Hegel's speculative thought can fall prey to such a bifurcation. In turning our attention to the material and concrete conditions of life—life in the polis in civil society, and in the state—we must, I want to argue, keep Hegel's speculative thought constantly in view, especially if we are to understand what Marx and what Heidegger both draw from, and owe, to Hegel.

In the thought of both Marx and Heidegger something quite decisive is worked out in confrontation with Hegel's more "practical" philosophy. If Hegel's thinking is always phenomenological, that is, if he is ever innovating, it is always because he is *describing*, and his description goes in to the very heart of what is "there," here to be thought *of*, then we must also agree with Marx that the *Philosophy of Right*, inasmuch as it is "phenomenological" (descriptive of how things really are), is descriptive of a German world that is yet to come, that was in the early nineteenth century only just coming about. Understood in this way, we can see the extent to which Hegel's is a spiritual (*geistig*) struggle both to understand and to bring to an adequate word. To describe the "truth," a truth only yet being born, is the philosopher's highest vocation, and yet it is fraught with danger and error. Marx's most trenchant criticism of Hegel, as we shall see, is not that Hegel errs, so much as he has not seen far enough in practical terms, given the strength and length of the light cast by his speculative thought. In this sense, Marx sees further than Hegel (to the end of history), but in another sense, only because Hegel has brought the end in view, and brought the possibility of thinking it about. For Heidegger, the matter is more stark: not just in this chapter, but also later in the book, we will see—if only in outline—the extent to which Heidegger is forced by actual events (especially the Nazi catastrophe of Germany between 1933 and 1945) to think *right through* Hegel, but this leaves him at the far side with only darkness and a lack of light. At the far side of Hegel's thought, we might say *beyond* Hegel, there is little yet to be seen. Even now, even today, we live in the West, and so in a world which is still fulfilling Hegel's descriptive power: in this sense Hegel is still describing the future for who we are now. When the editors of the *Will to Power* took from Nietzsche's notebook of November 1887–March 1888 the words "what I recount is the history of the next two centuries," to open the *Preface,* they perhaps did not see that what Nietzsche says there could as much be said of Hegel as it could of Nietzsche himself.[1]

In Heidegger's question "what is society?" it is necessary to hear what is at issue in his answer that "contemporary society is only the absolutizing of modern subjectivity." The term "absolutizing" (*Verabsolutierung*) is already a reference to Hegel: it is through what Hegel brings to description that "social" philosophy attains to a certain, very specific, representation of the subjectivity of the subject. The text central to this description, as we have hinted, is Hegel's *Philosophy of Right.* If Anglophone commentators on this text have been apt to argue that it need not be read within Hegel's metaphysical and logical system, as if Hegel's metaphysics had nothing to do with his understanding of politics, because Hegel's metaphysics concerns the concepts of being, and God, and his politics concerns only material life and law, then this presupposes the very separation which Hegel himself is striving to overcome: the very presupposition blocks and obscures *how* to read Hegel's work at all.

We saw at the beginning of the last chapter that Marx establishes this question of the relation of the material to the "metaphysical" (taken in the broadest sense) as a task: the establishment of a genuinely material thinking is at the same time the way that the "critique of theology" (by which he means this broadest sense of metaphysics, in the form given it by Hegel) is to

1. Friedrich Nietzsche, Peter Gast, and Elizabeth Forster-Nietzsche, eds., *Der Wille zur Macht,* 3 (= *Friedrich Nietzsche,* vol. 13, *Nachlaß 1887–1889,* 189). "Was ich erzähle, ist die Geschichte der nächsten zwei Jahrhunderte."

be transformed into the "critique of politics."[2] Marx argues that "atheism as an overcoming of God [is] the coming to be of theoretical humanism."[3] The burden of the argument of the previous chapter was to show how in Hegel this transformation is already fully at work, and so to what extent Hegel prepares the way and establishes the very possibility of Marx providing an answer to Hegel at all. It is the unfortunate characteristic of so much of Marx's (and Engels's) thinking that what is in fact a development and expansion of (indeed, to some extent a retreat from) the possibilities laid out by those on whose shoulders he stands is figured as a retort and a contradiction of what has already been made possible. What does Hegel mean by the word "system"? Early on in the *Logic* he says "a philosophizing without system cannot be scientific," and concludes: "a limited philosophy separated in its principle from others [i.e., other philosophical principles] is falsely understood under the word *system;* a more truthful philosophy has the contrary principle of including every particular principle in itself."[4] This is because, Hegel stresses, truth can only be concrete when it holds and contains in itself the unity and totality of the "freedom of the whole."[5] What this means is that in any genuine system any one part of the system—any principle derived from the unity of the freedom of the whole—will manifest in itself the whole in its particularity. This *is* how Hegel resolves the problematic legacy of Kant's thought, of how freedom and determinacy are to be reconciled. Heidegger understands the whole history of metaphysics within the history of being to be expressed in Hegel's thinking through the question of freedom in its relation to absolute presence: "The understanding of being as constant presence and its particular problematic has not only continued since antiquity right up until Kant, but this interpretation of the understanding of being comes to a renewed interpretative expression where Occidental metaphysics has attained its proper fulfillment, that is, in that place where the thread of ancient philosophy, together with the essential motives of philosophical questioning ever since, reach a unified expression and are brought to full presentation, with Hegel."[6] Within the history of being, Heidegger

2. See 82–83.

3. Karl Marx, *Ökonomisch-philosophische Manuskripte aus dem Jahre 1844* (*MEW*40), 583. "Der Atheismus als Aufhebung Gottes [ist] das Werden des theoretischen Humanismus."

4. G. W. F. Hegel, *Enzyklopädie der philosophischen Wissenschaften I (Logik),* 20. "Unter einem *Systeme* wird fälschlich eine Philosophie von einem beschränkten, von anderen unterschiedenen *Prinzip* verstanden; es ist im Gegenteil Prinzip wahrhafter Philosophie, alle besonderen Prinzipien in sich zu enthalten" (Hegel's emphases).

5. G. W. F. Hegel, *Enzyklopädie der philosophischen Wissenschaften I (Logik),* 20. "Die Freiheit des Ganzen."

6. Martin Heidegger, *Vom Wesen der Menschlichen Freiheit* (*GA*31), 109. "Das Verständnis des Seins als beständige Anwesenheit hat sich nicht nur seit der antiken Philosophie bis zu Kant

suggests that in Hegel we see "the problem of freedom as the problem of metaphysics."[7]

The problem of freedom within metaphysics, materially understood, manifests itself in Hegel as the problem of the state. Hitherto the problem of freedom (especially with Kant, and what he inherits from the tradition that precedes him) is identified as a problem about free will and necessity in the mind and existence of God. But the state *takes over* the place of God in Hegel's speculative thought. Thus the state becomes the locus of the problem, not only of freedom, but also of the will. Reconciling the individual will with absolute will is the means by which the state comes to be realized in human history. The state stands in some fundamental material way (which we are yet to show) as the metaphysical expression of being as constant presence. Heidegger never formally developed his understanding of Hegel's political philosophy in this way, but carried it out practically both in his own political involvement and later in his critique of Hegel's understanding of the state. Moreover, it is only with this understanding of Hegel in the background that we can make sense of Heidegger's claim that contemporary society is the absolutizing of modern subjectivity. Freedom, conceived in this way, depends on two things: first, of the possibility of the finite subject to *develop*, infinitely (which overcomes the limitation of formal determinism that had dogged Kant); second, that the freedom of the individual is the freedom to make manifest the *idea* of the state as constant presence. This material basis is the life of the individual in its concrete forms, the structures and institutions in which he lives (be they legal, political, educational, and so forth). The individual lives in these structures which make manifest the idea as his (and her) possibilities for freedom.

The problem of freedom in its relation to the metaphysical understanding of being as constant presence, inherent to idealism (and a central concern of Hegel's contemporary, Schelling), was taken up by Heidegger repeatedly in his lectures on Schelling.[8] These problems do not directly affect the questions that arise in the "productive dialogue" with Marx, and

durchgehalten und die Problematik bestimmt, sondern diese Deutung des Seinsverständnisses kommt gerade da erneut zum deutlichen Ausdruck, wo die abendländische Metaphysik ihre eigentliche Vollendung erreicht hat, d. h. dort, wo der Ansatz der antiken Philosophie ebenso wie die seitdem erreichten wesentlichen Motive philosophischen Fragens zum einheitlichen Austrag und zur vollen Darstellung gebracht sind, bei *Hegel*" (Heidegger's emphasis in the German text).

7. Ibid., 112. "Das Freiheitsproblem als das Problem der Metaphysik."

8. See Heidegger's 1936 lecture course published as Martin Heidegger, *Schelling: Vom Wesen der menschlichen Freiheit* (GA42). The whole of the first section (23–106) is an extended discussion on the meaning of "system" and its consequences in overcoming the problems of free will and determinism raised by Kant, especially in Kant's *Opus Postumum*.

so they are well beyond the scope of this study, but Marx makes no higher contribution to the resolution of the question of freedom than Hegel does, and makes no higher contribution to their overcoming. It is only if we see that Marx's understanding of the fulfilled human being as that one in whom the entire species (the "species-being") emerges, that we can see the formal relation of the individual to "constant presence." "Constant presence," and "species being" (a term, central in Marx's writing, which we have not yet investigated), for Heidegger, name, and are, the same phenomenon. The question of freedom manifests itself both in Hegel and in Marx as the question of freedom for the whole, the freedom to realize and make manifest absolute presence, and so *not* as the question of the "freedom of the subject."[9] The only freedom the individual has is to be coordinated to absolute freedom, which is the freedom for absolute becoming, not individual "self-expression."

Thom Brooks notes the attempt by John Rawls and others to suggest an "ontological" reading of Hegel as a more "reasonable" account than any account which is "systematic" and so integral to Hegel's system of thought. It is already clear from what we have seen from Hegel's *Logic* that in every particular or regional aspect of philosophy the idea as such is capable of manifesting itself (and the idea, inasmuch as it is known, always has material consequences), and, in so doing, makes manifest the whole as a totality in its becoming (which is at the same time its freedom—precisely, the freedom of the idea to increase and so become). Brooks concludes: "oddly, an ontological (and allegedly 'not metaphysical') reading of Hegel remains a metaphysical reading."[10] Brooks, in a clear confrontation with the prevailing Anglophone reading of Hegel, demonstrates the extent to which this understanding consciously and deliberately misread Hegel when he cites Alan Woods's statement that a reading of Hegel's thought as a whole, and so as a system (a "systematic" reading), "would also dictate that you write a book not about Hegel's ethics but about his logic."[11] The peculiarly provincial viewpoint of so much English-speaking philosophy could not be more visible than at this point. At the opening of Hegel's *Philosophy of Right* stands an entirely metaphysical statement: "the philosophical science of right has the idea of right, the concept of right, and its realization, for its object."[12]

What, however, is meant by Hegel's term "right"? The word *Recht* in German means variously "right" and "law," and is essentially jurispruden-

9. It is for this reason that the question of justice (as justification) never arises either in Marx, or for that matter, in Hegel, and why it does arise in Nietzsche.

10. Thom Brooks, *Hegel's Political Philosophy,* 2.

11. Thom Brooks, *Hegel's Political Philosophy* (citing Allen Wood's "Reply," 35).

12. G. W. F. Hegel, *Grundlinien der Philosophie des Rechts,* 28. "Die philosophische Rechtswissenschaft hat die Idee des Rechts, den Begriff des Rechts und dessen Verwirklichung zum Gegenstande."

tial—a province of meaning which Hegel constantly indicates and references in his amplifications of the central theses of the text, especially in the introductory sections. The jurisprudential origin of the term, however, is derived from the Latin and Roman legal term *recte,* meaning that which is properly and rightly done: whatever flows from the rectitude of the whole of the law. It indicates, therefore, the law considered as regime and regimen, as an *ordering* to some greater whole. Heidegger comments on the connections between reason (Latin *ratio*), the *recta ratio* of proper thinking, and *verum,* Latin truth, in his lectures on Parmenides from the early 1940s. In a section entitled "Clarification of the Transformation of *Alētheia*" he speaks of how "*veritas* is *rectitudo,* we say 'correctness.' This originally Roman stamping of the essence of truth, which secures the all-pervading basic character of the Occidental essence of truth."[13] Truth as *verum* in this manner is the counter-development to *alētheia.* If *a-lētheia* is "dis-closing," then the introduction of the words *verum, veritas,* as constituting the "regime" and ordering of truth has, Heidegger argues, its origin in the Indo-European **wer,* meaning "to cover."[14] Heidegger traces this to the Greek word *eruma* (another word, like those we have seen already, that has dropped its digamma, ϝέρυμα), as a name for the defensive weapon, the covering, the enclosure; and concludes "*verum, eruma,* the encapsulated, covering; *al-etheia:* the un-covering, dis-closing."[15]

Heidegger argues that the Roman understanding of truth as the ordering of all things to the *imperium* is precisely what enabled the Romans to establish themselves and their conquests in the way they did: the *pax Romana* sprang from a fundamental orientation to a grounding meaning of truth: the ordering of the particular to the whole. At the same time that meaning of truth springs from the forgetfulness of being, the *Seinsvergessenheit,* which means that the essence of truth in its meaning has undergone a fundamental transformation. As *verum,* truth no longer discloses itself in the unfolding of the whole of being, but can now be worked out and calculated (ratiocinated), and so is given an essential meaning through *reason.* Reason is the means by which the "correct" ordering of the particular to the whole is uncovered. It is hardly accidental that in the early 1940s Heidegger can be found emphasizing how to read the question of truth in relation to the Roman imperial state (and at the same time expressing his resistance to what this implied), at a time when the politics most immediate to him was making the same

13. Martin Heidegger, *Parmenides* (*GA*54), 71. "Veritas ist rectitudo, wir sagen 'Richtigkeit.' Diese ursprünglich römische Prägung des Wesens der Wahrheit, die den alles durchherrschenden Grundzug in das Wesensgezüge des abendländischen Wahrheitswesens festmacht."

14. From which the *Wehr,* "defense" and shelter, of *Wahrheit,* "truth."

15. Martin Heidegger, *Parmenides* (GA54), 70. "*Verum,* ἔρυμα, die Verschließung, Bedeckung; ἀλήθεια; die Ent-deckung, Entbergung."

identification, especially in Italy, but also not infrequently in the propaganda of Nazi Germany.

The most decisive point that Heidegger makes in this transformation of truth is to draw attention to how "the *ratio* is a *facultas animi,* a power of the human spirit, whose *actus* plays itself out in the inner man."[16] The consequence of this is that every human being is to be conceived as having the same power for ratiocination, and so the same basic possibility for ordering itself successfully to the whole. It is in this fundamental shift in the essence of truth, from truth as disclosure to truth as *rightness* (Roman *verum, recta ratio*) in which, Heidegger argues, the way is prepared for truth to become so decisively a psychological faculty of the "human spirit," an entirely humanistic understanding. Tracing the intensification of this understanding in the history of the Christian development of truth as *iustitia,* justice, Heidegger (citing Thomas Aquinas) argues that truth becomes *rectitudo rationis et voluntatis*—correctness of the reason and the will, concluding that "the striving after correctness is the basic form of the will to will."[17] The will to will, thought of in this way, will always (correctly ordered, through reason) will the *right* thing.

Marx never addresses the question of "right" as such: it is left to Heidegger to explain why the question of the meaning of "right" represents in Hegel the resolution of the impasse of individual and absolute subjectivity. Heidegger says, "we must clarify for ourselves *how* right arises metaphysically."[18] After Descartes, and above all in Hegel "willing is knowing in its *actuality*":[19] a claim that exactly relates to Heidegger's understanding of Descartes's employment of the verb "cogito" as always a *co-ago*—not just "I think" and "I deliberate," but "I act," "alongside and together *with,*" and so contains within itself the extension over both thinking and action that Marx attempts to secure a renewed understanding of through the eleventh of the "Theses on Feuerbach." However, Heidegger observes, "*thus* freedom belongs to willing . . . where there is willing, freedom *is.*"[20] We understand willing, however, to be the willing of some one—the individual. In

16. Ibid., 74. "Die ratio ist eine facultas animi, ein Vermögen des menschlichen Geistes, dessen actus sich innerhalb des Menschen abspielt."

17. Ibid., 75. "Das Streben nach der Richtigkeit ist die Grundform des Willens zum Willen." See also Thomas Aquinas, *Commentary on the Sentences,* vol. 1, Dist. II, Q. 1, art. 5, exp.

18. Martin Heidegger, *Seminare: Hegel—Schelling* (*GA*86), 575 (protocol of Wilhelm Hallwachs). "Wir müssen uns klar machen, *wie* Recht metaphysisch entsteht" (Heidegger's reported emphasis).

19. Ibid., 577 (protocol of Wilhelm Hallwachs). "Wollen ist das *eigentliche* Wissen" (Heidegger's reported emphasis).

20. Ibid., 577 (protocol of Wilhelm Hallwachs). "*So* gehört die *Freiheit* zum *Willen* . . . Wo Wille ist, *ist* Freiheit" (Heidegger's reported emphases).

this sense, Heidegger argues, "freedom *is* will. The '*is*' is to be understood dialectically."[21] What this means is that "I cannot first act from the will, and then ask: is the will free? But to determine the essence of willing, I must at the same time have determined the essence of freedom, and vice versa."[22] The question of right is resolved through the meaning of the essence of freedom: but, at the same time, the ambiguity in all metaphysics concerning the meaning of subjectivity reappears *as* the question of right. Heidegger argues that "right is *existence* [*Dasein*] of freedom." As such it appears as something at the disposal of the will. But precisely because it is *right,* that is to say, it is ordered as the attainment to a particular kind of value (the right or "correct" value), "the complete reality of the recognition [i.e., of right] is the *state.*"[23] It is here that Hegel overcomes the essentially negative opposition of the individual will to the general will posited by Rousseau: the individual (subject) is *himself* sublated through the attainment to "right" to absolute subjectivity. This is the "existence" (*Dasein*), the inner experience, of right, experienced as will, or rather, *through* the will to will.

The "philosophy of right" therefore arises on a very specific basis, a specific and metaphysical shift in the understanding of truth, as a restriction of the securing of the being of beings to the activity of the psyche of man. Here is the fundamental ambiguity of Hegel's metaphysics, an ambiguity repeated and deepened in both Marx and Nietzsche. For on the one hand this restriction is to the psyche of the particular subject: on the other, to subjectivity as a whole, the "absolute subject" as such (for Hegel, realized through the state): the identical essence of human subjectivity that makes itself manifest in every particular subject. The resolution of this ambiguity can be found only in the absolutization of every subject in the infinite horizon of its *becoming,* as absolute subjectivity. Totality is not, therefore, that *wherein* the subject arises (the state), but is rather to be understood as already contained within the productive becoming of the subjectivity of the subject. It is in this sense that "right" has to be understood. Right is the willed coordination of the (individual) human spirit (*Geist*) to a fundamental ordering, to final (and rational) absolute "correctness." This "coordination" becomes (in Hegel at least) the basis of the ethical, as the human essence's life in the "ought" of the ethical imperative to universalize itself. Hegel speaks of how "the con-

21. Ibid., 577 (protocol of Wilhelm Hallwachs). "Freiheit *ist* Wille. Das '*ist*' ist dialektisch zu verstehen" (Heidegger's reported emphases).

22. Ibid., 577 (protocol of Wilhelm Hallwachs). "Ich kann nicht zuerst vom Willen handeln, und dann fragen: ist der Wille frei? Sondern um das Wesen des Willens zu bestimmen, muß ich zugleich das Wesen der Freiheit bestimmt haben und umgekehrt" (Heidegger's reported emphases).

23. Ibid., 578 (protocol of Wilhelm Hallwachs). "Recht ist *Dasein* der Freiheit. Die vollendete Wirklichkeit der Anerkennung ist der *Staat*" (Heidegger's reported emphases).

sequent *concrete* identity of the good and of subjective willing, their very truth, is *ethics as such.*"[24] Hegel prefaces the definition of the ethical with the heading "transition from morality into ethics as such,"[25] since ethics in this form is counterposed to mere morality.

Both Marx and Nietzsche identify in different ways the sense in which this formulation falls short of the metaphysical ground from out of which it speaks. If, on the one hand, Nietzsche announces the way in which the subjective will of the subject constitutes the "moral life" of the will to power by destroying all previous morality (to establish the will to power as a genuine becoming) and so by opposing the morality of the hitherto as what stands against what is most to become, on the other hand Marx also understands the "ethical" as even more demanding than a mere imperative, because the transformation of the material life that constitutes itself as "the ethical" is not a requirement but an ineluctable inevitability. Marx, as much as Nietzsche, has no "morals" because he drives to an inevitable conclusion the distinction Hegel himself makes between the moral and the ethical: the ethical is the *condition,* and therefore horizon (the "becoming"), of future social life. In *The Communist Manifesto* Marx insists that religion and morality alike are to be abolished, not established anew. Communism "thus contradicts all historical developments hitherto."[26]

There is a direct connection between the *eruma* as "the encapsulated" and so rationally, correctly, ordered, and Heidegger's later notion of the epoch of technology as the epoch of the "frame," *das Ge-Stell.*[27] The "frame" is that which sets in place: it is the condition within which subjectivity occurs. The enclosure, or "enframement," as the psychological condition of the creativity of the subject as the basis for the way truth manifests itself in the epoch of technology, is for Heidegger grounded in the relation to truth established as correctness or "right."

It is not the title, but the subtitle of Hegel's *Philosophy of Right* which gives it its essential orientation. The subtitle says: *Natural Right (Law) and Science of the State in Outline;* the *Philosophy of Right* first appeared in 1821, where what became the subtitle was in fact the first part of the full title.[28] What became the subtitle therefore explains the eventual title, but

24. G. W. F. Hegel, *Grundlinien der Philosophie des Rechts,* 286. "Die somit *konkrete* Identität des Guten und des subjektiven Willens, die Wahrheit derselben, ist die *Sittlichkeit*" (Hegel's emphasis).

25. Ibid., 286. "Übergang von der Moralität in Sittlichkeit."

26. Karl Marx and Friedrich Engels, *Manifest der Kommunistischen Partei* (*MEW*4), 480. "[Der Kommunismus] widerspricht also allen bisherigen geschichtlichen Entwicklungen."

27. See also Martin Heidegger, "Das Ge-Stell" (*GA*79).

28. G. W. F. Hegel, *Grundlinien der Philosophie des Rechts oder Naturrecht und Staatswissenschaft im Grundrisse.*

in what way? Hegel had dealt with the question of natural right in a series of earlier articles published in 1802 and 1803.[29] These handle the question of natural right in an entirely formal and abstract manner. At the center of them lies a critique of (Kant's and Fichte's) separation of reason into "pure" and "practical" forms, which at the same time is a struggle to find the formal identity of the "real" and the "ideal."

The *Philosophy of Right* develops the understanding of the material forms of human life in their concrete expression under various headings: abstract right (of property, its use and alienation, contract, and wrongdoing); morality; ethical life (in terms of marriage, family, and civil society); and the state and its constitution. The *Philosophy of Right,* while dealing with the same divisions known to Aristotle of the individual, the family and the polis,[30] introduces a further distinction in the manifold of humanity, "civil society," a term frequently picked up by Marx in his confrontation with Hegel. Civil society is a general term, and has a primary reference to the particularities of human social life taken overall.[31] As a term it covers economic activity; the ordinary forms of social interchange; and what Hegel identifies as the various classes of society. These are the "functions" of civil society.

In sections of *Concerning the Scientific Manners of Handling Natural Right* Hegel had drawn attention to a distinction which he does not appear adequately to resolve there, on which the "natural" scientific understanding of right, and the positive science of right, both rest. Both are ideas: in other words, both have concrete historical forms from which their ideas may be understood. Thus the movement that Hegel seeks to describe is not from the concretion of "natural" right to the abstract ideal of right, but a "double movement" of the natural and ethical such that "this twofold relationship determines the doubled aspect of the necessity or the appearance of the absolute."[32] The absolute (the idea of ideas) *appears,* and it does so out of the necessity of its various concrete forms—of which the natural and the ethical are also the organizing possibilities, and as such, are also themselves, ideas.

29. See G. W. F. Hegel, *Über die wissenschaftlichen Behandlungsarten des Naturrechts, seine Stelle in der praktischen Philosophie und sein Verhältnis zu den positiven Rechtswissenschaften.* (*Concerning the Scientific Manners of Handling Natural Right, Its Place in Practical Philosophy and Its Relation to the Positive Science of Right.*)

30. Aristotle, *Politics,* 1252a7–15; 1252b9–1253a29. See especially 1252b19–20: καὶ πρότερον δὴ τῇ φύσει πόλις ἢ οἰκια καὶ ἕκαστος ἐστιν (thus by nature is the πόλις prior to the household) and 1252b25: ὅτι μὲν οὖν ἡ πόλις καὶ φύσει πρότερον ἢ ἕκαστος, δῆλον (it is clear therefore that the πόλις is prior by nature to each [individual]).

31. See G. W. F. Hegel, *Grundlinien der Philosophie des Rechts,* §§181–87.

32. G. W. F. Hegel, *Über die wissenschaftlichen Behandlungsarten des Naturrechts,* 456. "Dieses zweifache Verhältnis bestimmt die gedoppelte Seite der Notwendigkeit oder der Erscheinung des Absoluten."

In the *Philosophy of Right* the abstract unclarity of this movement is resolved and given concrete form in terms of the institutions of human life. Civil society therefore corresponds to the idea of natural right, while "the state is the reality of the ethical idea."[33] Thus both of these ideas, "natural right" and "the ethical," have material forms: civil society, and the state. The transition from natural right to ethical right is therefore civil society *realizing itself* as the state (the actual synthesizing of the two ideas), which occurs through the pursuit of individual interests in the particularity of subjective needs both natural and willed, so that unconscious civil society comes to (reasoned) consciousness, and is through this process "raised [*erheben*] to *formal freedom* and formal universality of knowing and willing, whereby their particularity is constructed as subjectivity."[34] The state is therefore *not itself* the absolute subjectivity of the subject, but the *formal condition* for the appearance of the absolutized subject, as a historical phenomenon. *Right* is then the necessary condition of "knowing and willing" (which for Hegel are identical)—we might say, "correct, proper reasoning"—that secures the possibility from out of which the absolutized subjectivity of the subject can come to be, and so *be manifest.* "Right" is the way the subjectivity of the subject is willed, in the concrete, political sphere. Here is why there is a distinction between civil society and the state, or why Hegel has to introduce a further distinction in accounting for what the Greeks would have known simply under the one "idea" of the polis. Civil society is the possibility of coming in to what is to be known. To come in to what is to be known (the idea) is to enter into the possibility of making the transition from the idea of the concrete forms as they initially present themselves, to their higher realization in the idea of the state. To come to know is to come into what is to be known: similarly to strive forward in willing is to come into what is (already, in a sense, lying present, as what is to be striven-for and so realized) *there* to be willed: the highest will, the realization of the formal possibility as a concrete actuality (the actualization of constant-presence). Every individual, *through* the prior forms of civil society, is coordinated to the higher form of the state.

Hegel concludes that "the state is the reality of concrete freedom; *concrete freedom,* however, consists in this, that personal individuality and its personal interests have for themselves their fully complete *development* and the *acknowledgment of their right* (within the system of the family and civil society), as they *make the transition* for the sake of themselves in the

33. G. W. F. Hegel, *Grundlinien der Philosophie des Rechts,* 398. "Der Staat ist die Wirklichkeit der sittlichen Idee."

34. Ibid., 343. "Der *Prozeß . . . zur formellen Freiheit* und formellen *Allgemeinheit des Wissens und Wollens* zu erheben, die Subjektivität in ihrer Besonderheit zu *bilden*" (Hegel's emphases).

interest of the universal, for the sake of knowing and willing themselves."[35] Hegel is at pains to point out that in the state living for one's own interests is, rightly known and thought, at the same time willing and knowing the universal and in the light of the universal. Freedom is always freedom *for* "the highest."

It is only in accomplishing this understanding of Hegel that Marx's radicalization of Hegel can properly be understood. The early Marx says, as he lays out his most explicit inception of the thinking of communism in the *Critique of Hegel's Philosophy of Right:* "but *man:* this is no abstract essence squatting beyond the world. Man—that is *the world of man,* state, society."[36] He adds that *man* as such appears in the overcoming of religion, something that is realized only when we uncover that it is man that makes religion, religion does not make man. Inasmuch as for Marx the achievement of a proper orientation on humanity is the attainment to a materialistic reduction of religion, so a fundamental trait of Hegel is overcome, namely the connection between philosophy and religion. Put another way, Marx, recognizing in Hegel the pinnacle of attainment of a philosophical orientation, must explain this orientation in the light of the absolute restriction of thought to the occurrence, and this means the activity, of the subjectivity of the subject: of *man* itself. Inasmuch as Hegel absolutizes the synthesis of religion and philosophy (as what Heidegger will call ontotheology), Marx attempts to overcome the synthesis by overcoming not only religion but also philosophy as well: however, Marx grasps and realizes this through a critique of Hegel's own account of political forms, but at the same time shakes them free of their abstract manifestations as mere "ideas" (religion, ethics, the state) in order to show with even more verve how they constitute (historically) different forms of the subjectivity of the subject. Whereas Hegel makes a defense of private property in the *Philosophy of Right,* in exactly the place where Marx speaks of the attainment to atheism as the ground of theoretical humanism, Marx next argues that "communism as the overcoming of private property is the vindication of real human life as man's property, thus is the advent of practical humanism."[37] Inasmuch as Heidegger names the whole of Hegel's

35. Ibid., 406. "Der Staat ist die Wirklichkeit der *konkreten Freiheit;* die konkrete Freiheit aber besteht darin, daß die persönliche Einzelheit und deren besondere Interessen sowohl ihre vollständige Entwicklung und die *Anerkennung ihres Rechts* für sich (im Systeme der Familie und der bürgerlichen Gesellschaft) haben, als sie durch sich selbst in das Interesse des Allgemeinen teils *übergehen,* teils mit Wissen und Willen dasselbe" (Hegel's emphases).

36. Karl Marx, "Zur Kritik der Hegelschen Rechtsphilosophie" (*MEW*1), 378. "Aber *der Mensch,* das ist kein abstraktes, außer der Welt hockendes Wesen. Der Mensch ist *die Welt des Menschen*" (Marx's emphases).

37. Karl Marx, *Ökonomisch-philosophische Manuskripte aus dem Jahre 1844* (*MEW*40), 583. "Der Kommunismus als Aufhebung des Privateigentums [ist] die Vindikation des wirklichen

thought not as ontotheology but as onto-ego-theo-logy, for Heidegger, what Marx attains to is the full restriction of the whole of metaphysics to the egoity, the I-ness of the subject, both in its particular and absolute form.

Marx carries over into his own thought the ambiguity I have already identified in Hegel of the drive and requirement to resolve the difference between the particular, individual, subject and absolute subjectivity. While Hegel attempts to resolve the ambiguity through the dialectical relationship and synthesis of the individual, who, situated in family life, is extended into civil society, and then finally realized and absolutized in the state, Marx collapses this sequence of differentiations as the drive of history itself to eliminate any real difference between the individual in his or her particularity, and the absolutized, final individual realized in communist society. It is on this basis that communism appears as the realization of the human historical process, and why communism is itself a metaphysical concept, whenever communism is announced as the explicit goal. Communism, for Marx, is the final idea (and reality) from out of which every present (and contingent) reality takes off its meaning. The fully communist society is the metaphysical description of absolute presence. It is in this sense present *now* as determining what the present (and what present social relations) have yet to attain to.

In several early texts Marx adopts Feuerbach's term *Gattungswesen*, usually translated as "species being" or "genus-being," for man as he is in essence, a term we have already touched upon several times.[38] In addition to *Gattungswesen*, Marx employs a whole panoply of terms related to the word *Gattung*, literally "genus"—hence the translation "species": *Gattungsleben* (species-life), *Gattungsdasein* (species-existence), *Gattungstätigkeit* (species-factuality), *Gattungswillen* (species-will), and so forth. Each of these terms indicates the concrete expressedness of aspects of the species-life that man assumes in material, historical, situations. Although the term and its cognates does not really reappear with the same frequency in later texts, neither does it disappear, and the fundamental metaphysical position that it indicates continues to function in the same way (as we shall see) in the *Grundrisse* and *Das Kapital* as it does in the earlier texts where it is first worked out and explored. The term first makes its appearance not in Marx, but in Feuerbach's *The Essence of Christianity*, where Feuerbach speaks of "the essence of spe-

menschlichen Lebens als seines Eigentums, [ist] das Wenden des praktischen Humanismus." This sentence follows on from the sentence quoted in note 3 in this chapter.

38. The term appears in places in centrally important texts from the period of the fiercest confrontation with Hegel, 1843–44: the *Economic and Philosophical Manuscripts* (*MEW*40), "On the Jewish Question" (*MEW*1), "Critique of Hegel's Philosophy of Right. Introduction" (*MEW*1), and the "Critique of Hegel's Doctrine of the State."

cies, which is the absolute essence of the individual,"[39] leaving unclear how he thinks this essence is to be resolved. Marx's taking up of the term has much more to do with Feuerbach's explanation of it in the essay *Basic Principles of the Philosophy of the Future,* where he says "the singular man possesses for himself the essence of mankind neither in the sense of a moral nor a cogitative essence. The essence of man is only contained in society, in the unity of man with man as a oneness, which itself, however, is only underpinned by the reality of the difference between I and you."[40] We can see immediately the parallels between this and Hegel's reference to freedom and unity in his *Logic.* Marx concludes that "the individual and the species-being of man are not *different*":[41] in this Marx collapses all the differentiations that Hegel describes in material human existence in the *Philosophy of Right:* individuality, family life, civil society, even the state, into one: species-being. Marx repeats this direct and far-reaching formulation in the sixth of the "Theses on Feuerbach": "But the human essence is no abstraction inhering in each particular individual. In its reality it is the ensemble of social relations."[42] The individual life of man is not what he lives now, but what he is to become. Differentiations are the consequence of history, but history is ended in the accomplishment of the abolition of the formal condition of difference (private property) and, Marx asserts, the accomplishment of communism "is the resolution of the riddle of history and knows itself as this solution."[43]

In what sense is species-life a metaphysical principle? In the *Grundrisse* Marx argues that man "appears originally as a *species-being, tribal-being, herd-animal,* if, however, in no way as a *zōon politikon* in the political sense."[44] This is because "man individuates himself only in the historical

39. Ludwig Feuerbach, *Das Wesen des Christentums,* 9. "Das Wesen der Gattung, welches das absolute Wesen des Individuums ist."

40. Ludwig Feuerbach, "Grundsätze der Philosophie der Zukunft," 318. "Der einzelne Mensch für sich hat das Wesen des Menschen weder in sich als moralischem noch in sich als denkendem Wesen. Das Wesen des Menschen ist nur in der Gemeinschaft, in der Einheit des Menschen mit dem Menschen enthalten in einer Einheit, die sich aber nur auf die Realität des Unterschiedes von Ich und du stützt."

41. Karl Marx, *Ökonomisch-philosophische Manuskripte* (*MEW*40), 539. "Das Individuelle und das Gattungswesen des Menschen sind nicht *verschieden*" (Marx's emphasis).

42. Karl Marx, "Thesen über Feuerbach" (*MEW*3), 6. "Aber das menschliche Wesen ist kein dem einzelnen Individuum inwohnendes Abstraktum. In seiner Wirklichkeit ist es das ensemble der gesellschaftlichen Verhältnisse."

43. Karl Marx, *Ökonomisch-philosophische Manuskripte* (*MEW*40), 536. "Er ist das aufgelöste Rätsel der Geschichte und weiß sich als diese Lösung."

44. Karl Marx, *Grundrisse* (*MEW*42), 404. "[Der Mensch] erscheint ursprünglich als ein *Gattungswesen, Stammwesen, Herdentier*—wenn auch keineswegs als ein ζώον πολιτικόν im politischen Sinn" (Marx's emphasis).

process."[45] The recovery of humanity's original appearance as a species-being is the accomplishment of history: the end of history is the metaphysical realization of the finality of the species-being "man," having passed through and overcome every process along the way. This is how *man* attains to being as such, being as constant-presence, absolute being (man enters the place otherwise laid out by the metaphysical understanding of "God"). History does not proceed forward therefore, but, in exactly the way we have already encountered in Hegel's thought, history is the horizon of infinity from out of which the realization of humanity is let out, through its being fulfilled. The "political," or rather social, being of humanity is the overcoming of individuation through the historical actualities of every kind of individuation, which accomplishes the point where individuation no longer entails difference. This is the formal accomplishment of metaphysics because every prior appearance of individuation, of human individuality (prior to the accomplishment of the end of history) is less than, and merely the provisional occurrence, of what species-being itself is to become. It is exchange, and so the processes of production which make exchange possible, which is the basis of this history as such, which humanity hitherto and until now must experience as development. The real being—*Wesen,* essence—of humanity lies ahead of every particularity as something to be accomplished in the working-out of historical processes. This is what history is "for." Every *historical* appearance is an approximation of the absolute essence, the species-being (of) "man."

The appearance of Aristotle's phrase *zōon politikon* in Marx's text shows how Marx conceives of how the animality (as the life, *zōē*) of man is realized through its being-accomplished: "the animal is immediately one with its life activity . . . Man makes his life-activity itself as the object of his will and his consciousness. . . . It is conscious life-activity that divides man immediately from animal life-activity. Indeed it is only in this way that he is a species-being."[46] The animality of humanity is realized, however, in production: "they begin to distinguish themselves from the animals as soon as they begin to produce their means of subsistence."[47] What Hegel calls "absolute subjectivity" is for Marx the fulfillment of species-being as such, as an entirely human affair. The engine of this accomplishment is production, but here not production merely understood as the activity of self-alienation that is described in the *Economic*

45. Ibid., 404. "Der Mensch vereinzelt sich erst durch den historischen Prozeß."

46. Karl Marx, *Ökonomisch-philosophische Manuskripte* (*MEW*40), 516. "Das Tier ist unmittelbar eins mit seiner Lebenstätigkeit. . . . Der Mensch macht seine Lebenstätigkeit selbst zum Gegenstand seines Wollens und seines Bewußtseins. . . . Die bewußte Lebenstätigkeit unterscheidet den Menschen unmittelbar von der tierischen Lebenstätigkeit. Eben nur dadurch ist er ein Gattungswesen."

47. Karl Marx and Friedrich Engels, *Die deutsche Ideologie* (*MEW*3), 21. "Sie selbst fangen an, sich von den Tieren zu unterscheiden, sobald sie anfangen, ihre Lebensmittel zu produzieren."

*and Philosophical Manuscripts*, and that seems to fall into the background. Alienation, as the objectification of self through labor into commodities, is driven by an even more basic process, which itself is the basis of the overcoming (sublation) of alienation itself: self-production, or (in fact) reproduction.

Much has been written about the importance of the term "species-being" for the relation between humanity and "nature" as Marx conceives it.[48] It is true that Marx conceives man as the creative being, whose productivity therefore takes into itself and becomes the possibility for the existence of nature as a whole: man (as opposed to God) becomes "the creative" as such. The "essence" of man is not a fixed essence: we have seen already how in Hegel becoming overtakes any understanding of a "fixed" or perfected being, such that being, strictly speaking, remains an empty, negated, possibility, filled out and enlarged by the actuality of what is to become. Marx argues that "species-life, as much with man as with the animal, consists physically only in this, that man (like the animal) lives from inorganic nature, and the more universal the man or the animal, the more universal is the realm of inorganic nature from which he lives."[49] Man, however, as the species-being, is the most universal of beings, he is that being whose nature is not fixed, but whose it is to become, and so the intermediate, historical, forms of this becoming are dependent on man taking the whole of nature into his productivity: "[the animal] produces only itself, while man reproduces the whole of nature."[50]

It is clear from his discussion of man and species-being in the *Economic and Philosophical Manuscripts* how Marx understands the *geistige* character of human consciousness to be that means by which the whole of "inorganic nature," by which he means in fact the whole of what is not human (this is the very burden of the "while," *während*) is ordered *through its very being produced* by man, to the being, the species-being, of man. In *Das Kapital* this emerges on the basis of social relations themselves: "in his organized working together with others, the worker strips off the limits of his individuality and develops his species-capability."[51]

48. For three contrasting views, see Michael Gagern, "The Puzzling Pattern of the Marxist Critique of Feuerbach"; Hans-Martin Sass, "The 'Transition' from Feuerbach to Marx: A Re-Interpretation"; and Paul Santilli, "Marx on Species-Being and Social Essence."

49. Karl Marx, *Ökonomisch-philosophische Manuskripte* (*MEW*40), 515. "Das Gattungsleben, sowohl beim Menschen als beim Tier, besteht physisch einmal darin, daß der Mensch (wie das Tier), von der unorganischen Natur lebt, und um so universeller der Mensch als das Tier, um so universeller ist der Bereich der unorganischen Natur, von der er lebt."

50. Ibid., 517. "[Das Tier] produziert nur sich selbst, während der Mensch die ganze Natur reproduziert."

51. Karl Marx, *Das Kapital*, vol. 1 (*MEW*23), 349. "Im planmäßigen Zusammenwirken mit andern streift der Arbeiter seine individuellen Schranken ab und entwickelt sein Gattungsvermögen."

This, however, is not the totality of the meaning of what Marx has in mind, and is why the term "species-being" falls to some extent into the background in later texts. For history is the arena of the alienation of man as the objectification of himself in nature. But the true simultaneity of the *species*-being of the animality of man with his finality as species-*being* is not through production but through self-production. Self-production is at one and the same time the reproduction of the individual *as* the totality. Here the "biological" character of the species "man" is realized in the way that the whole of being becomes the object and finality of humanity: biologism as such. At the center of Hegel's account of the *Philosophy of Right* is an essentially ahistorical account of reproduction which has the effect of functioning as the engine of the production and reproduction of civil society. Hegel argues that "the family completes itself in three steps,"[52] in the form of its immediate concept as union (*Ehe*), in its exterior existence through property and wealth, and in the upbringing of children and the dissolution of the family (which prompts the return to the possibility of further union and the recapitulation of the cycle all over again). The word I have translated as "step" is in German *Seit*—"side," normally indicating "one side or the other": but there are three. The third "side" is clearly the return to the first—the essential motion described is circular, over time. The family is in this sense a material microcosm of Hegel's dialectical logic. The production of children and dissolution of the family presupposes the immediate reproduction of the process: the movement from immediate concept, to material existence, and final resolution and (possibility of and condition for) repetition. This, Hegel argues, is the "liveliness in its totality, namely of the reality of the *species* [*Gattung*] and its process."[53] Marx's effective critique of this process of reproduction is further to show how liveliness is literally the living-character of humanity as species and has historical determinations which are only overcome in the accomplishment of the genuine species-life of man, once man takes into production the process of reproduction itself.

Human reproduction becomes the origin itself of exchange, as the need to fulfill history. The family "which in the beginning is the only social relationship,"[54] becomes at the same time the origin of the division of labor,[55] and in

52. G. W. F. Hegel, *Grundlinien der Philosophie des Rechts,* 309. "Die Familie vollendet sich in drei Seiten."

53. Ibid., 309. "Die Lebendigkeit in ihrer Totalität, nämlich als Wirklichkeit der *Gattung* und deren Prozeß" (Hegel's emphasis).

54. Karl Marx and Friedrich Engels, *Die deutsche Ideologie* (*MEW*3), 29. "Die im Anfange das einzige soziale Verhältnis ist."

55. Engels reports the source of this to be among Marx's contribution to *The German Ideology* (see Friedrich Engels, *Der Ursprung der Familie, des Privateigentums und des Staats* [*MEW*21], 68). In fact, the sentence Engels cites does not appear in the *MEW* edition of *The*

Engels's view, "the first class-antagonism to appear in history, occurs together with the development of the antagonism of man and wife in monogamy."[56] In *Das Kapital* Marx indicates how this is the fundamental determination of the end of history and the emergence of communism: "every social process of production is at the same time a process of reproduction."[57] Marx relativizes production *as* reproduction to the historical situation in which it occurs, saying "the conditions of production are at the same the conditions of reproduction."[58] This means that the historical and concrete conditions will determine the character and reality of production: "if production has a capitalist form, so then with reproduction."[59] However, this very historicality and dependency is only possible on the basis of the full attainment to full, conscious, species-life where the individual and the species are one and the same.

Marx's transforms Hegel's description of the state by fundamentally ordering the whole of being—"nature," "world," "the surrounding environment"—to the subjectivity of the subject: in this he accomplishes in act what Hegel laid out as a possibility: the absolute fusion of the material and theoretical possibilities of Hegel's *Logic* and dialectic. In this transformation every institution, every social form is made both a necessity (in its materiality, as the concrete factuality of human life) and contingent (in that it is dependent on the life of man, and subordinate to the historical period in which it occurs). What Hegel understands to be materialized and concretized in specific institutions as bodies, Marx drives to its most radical conclusion by arguing that "the universality of man manifests itself in practice in that universality which makes the whole of nature his inorganic body."[60] Once again

---

*German Ideology* (despite a footnote attributing Engels' citation to 31 of the *MEW* edition), and so Engels is almost certainly citing a different manuscript version than the published version. There is a closely related paragraph on 32 of the *MEW* edition which says something very similar to Engels's citation (see Karl Marx and Friedrich Engels, *Die deutsche Ideologie* [*MEW*3]).

56. Friedrich Engels, *Der Ursprung der Familie, des Privateigentums und des Staats* (*MEW*21), 68. "Der erste Klassengegensatz, der in der Geschichte auftritt, fällt zusammen mit der Entwicklung des Antagonismus von Mann und Weib in der Einzelehe." Although we appear to have swung suddenly from Marx to Engels in this discussion of the family, we should be clear that Engels very specifically notes that his understanding of the family is itself only derived from ideas laid out earlier by Marx in *The German Ideology*.

57. Karl Marx, *Das Kapital*, vol. 1 (*MEW*23), 591. "Jeder gesellschaftliche Produktionsprozeß [ist] daher zugleich Reproduktionsprozeß."

58. Ibid., 591. "Die Bedingungen der Produktion sind zugleich die Bedingungen der Reproduktion."

59. Ibid., 591. "Hat die Produktion kapitalistische Form, so die Reproduktion."

60. Karl Marx, *Ökonomisch-philosophische Manuskripte* (*MEW*40), 515–16. "Die Universalität des Menschen erscheint praktisch eben in der Universalität, die die ganze Natur zu seinem unorganischen Körper macht."

we see how species-being comes to name constant presence as Heidegger understands it.

Heidegger never comments explicitly on Marx's formulation of species-being, nor on Marx's surpassing of Hegel's understanding of the state through the restriction to an understanding of the whole of humanity as a *single* species-body, but he does raise the question of how the body appears in thought as a not merely biological, but fully metaphysical object. The "body" has become a well-rehearsed topic of "recovery" both in the various discourses of the politics of gender, but also in the sciences and social sciences. Hervé Juvin's *The Coming of the Body* traces the genealogy and development of the emergence of the body into the discourses of postmodernity in the pessimistic voice of one who both recognizes and repudiates the inevitability of the transformation of the body into a domain of total technological control: "a different 'end of history' is in play in the capacity to produce an emotional and sensory environment, immutable in its essential components and unceasingly renewed in the way these components are combined and arranged . . . through the genius of a technology which promises that generation that, for it, the hour will never be tolled."[61] Perry Anderson, in reviewing Juvin's account, while criticizing its cultural pessimism and a position that "sounds like a standard refrain of neo-liberal critiques," points to the fundamental connection between the Marxist regimes and the economies of "world democracy" in noting Juvin's success in detailing "a sinister paradox: what communism set out to do, and disastrously failed to achieve, capitalism is in the process of realising."[62]

It should be enough for us to understand that the total technological control of the body means that the body is *first* secured metaphysically (as what it *is to become* or against how bodies *actually are*) so that every present body is measured against, and up to, the emergent technological possibilities for it (regardless of who will have access to, or be able to afford them—these questions are always secondary when the possibility presents itself as the horizon against which those excluded appear). Heidegger himself drew attention to the fact of the metaphysical account of embodiment in the figure of Zarathustra. Heidegger's point is that Zarathustra, as that one who "goes down" and so revalues the sensory in the course of the "down-going" devaluation of the supersensible, the uppermost values, is *himself* not a "real" body,

61. Hervé Juvin, *L'avènement du corps,* 176–77. "Et c'est une autre fin de l'histoire qui se joue, dans la capacité à produire une environnent émotionnel et sensoriel immuable dans ses composants essentiels, sans cesse renouvelé dans la combinaison et la structure de ces composants . . . par le génie d'une technique qui lui promet que jamais, pour elle, ne sonnera l'heure."

62. Perry Anderson, "The World Made Flesh: Review of *L'avènement du corps,*" 135 (compare 137), 136.

but a type or literary trope who represents a philosophical type, the "overman" who transcends, and so "goes over" by means of *descent.* The same must be said of the body of Ernst Jünger's *typus* of "the worker," heavily dependent on Nietzsche's thought. Citing a sentence taken from a notebook of Nietzsche's of 1885 and inserted into the Gast edition of the *Will to Power* which says "essential, to set out from the body and employ it as guide,"[63] Heidegger comments: "if, however, the 'body' is to become the 'guide' for all world-interpretation, then this does not speak as if the whole of beings were transformed into the 'biological' and 'vital' and thought 'vitally,' but it indicates: the particular realm of the 'vital' is grasped metaphysically as the will to power."[64] Heidegger speaks in this context of how this understanding of the body, and its essential connection in the metaphysics of subjectivity with Nietzsche's understanding of the will to power, is the consequence of Hegel's completion of the metaphysics of subjectivity, and represents the essential production of the thought of the overman. It becomes clear now, not that Marx's thought of "species-being" somehow "is" the will to power, but rather that in the collapse of the individual life of men and women into the metaphysical thought of the species-being as such, Marx with his thought of species-being and its consequences attempts as much to think through the completion of the metaphysics of subjectivity through absolute presence as Nietzsche also does with the thought of the will to power, itself a figure of the metaphysics of absolute presence, and the notion of the *Übermensch.* In a way almost paralleling Marx's systematic transformation of the theological into the political, and his exclamation against the gods in celebration of Prometheus, Heidegger explains all this as the completion and fulfillment of metaphysics by citing the cry that Nietzsche makes in Zarathustra's voice: "dead are all gods, now we will that the overman live!"[65]

63. Friedrich Nietzsche, vol. 11, *Nachlaß 1884–1885,* 635 (= *Der Wille zur Macht,* §532, 366). "Wesentlich, vom Leibe ausgehen und ihn als Leitfaden zu benutzen." Heidegger also indicates, but does not cite, Friedrich Nietzsche, vol. 11, *Nachlaß 1884–1885,* 565–66 (= *Der Wille zur Macht,* §659, 440–41).

64. Martin Heidegger, *Nietzsches Metaphysik* (*GA*50), 48. "Wenn aber der 'Leib' zum 'Leitfaden' der Weltauslegung wird, dann sagt dies nicht, das 'Biologische' und 'Vitale' sei in das Ganze des Seienden hineinverlegt und dieses 'vital' gedacht, sondern es heißt: Der besondere Bereich des 'Vitalen' ist metaphysisch als Wille zur Macht begriffen."

65. Ibid., 52, citing Friedrich Nietzsche, *Also sprach Zarathustra,* 102. "'*Todt sind aller Götter: nun wollen wir, daß der Übermensch lebe*'" (Heidegger's emphasis).

*Chapter 6*

# The Situation of Germany

HEGEL DESCRIBES A POLITICS and a philosophy of becoming: even more than this, Hegel describes a metaphysics of becoming that is at the same time a material becoming. The metaphysics of becoming *is* the politics of becoming. Heidegger himself noted that in 1818 Hegel ceased to be a professor of philosophy in Heidelberg, and went to Berlin. Quoting a letter of Hegel's on the occasion of his departure, Heidegger notes that Hegel himself says "that he is not going to Berlin with philosophical purposes, but political ones: his state-philosophy was completed."[1] Heidegger concludes that "his philosophy achieved a most remarkable influence on the attitude of the state."[2] The centrality of Hegel, and of Germany for the description of an understanding of the state and a material, political, metaphysics that is yet to come, is a theme not only of Heidegger's but also of Marx's. Germany's emerging preeminence in the nineteenth century—politically, industrially, intellectually—is not simply a matter of Heidegger's nationalism or Marx's understanding of historical materialism. Throughout Europe there was a sense—for some a highest hope, for others a source of fear, either of competition (in trade and development), or worse—that something is to be decided. That Heidegger, or anyone else, could claim that "we [Germans] are a people that still has *a fate*" speaks not just from the "revolution" of 1933, but of the whole thrust of the events of the nineteenth century.[3] The reunification of Germany in 1989 raised again the specter of that fatedness,

1. Martin Heidegger, *Sein und Wahrheit* (*GA*36/37), 18. "Daß er nicht in philosophischen Absichten nach Berlin gehe, sondern in politischen: die Staatsphilosophie sei fertig." In drawing attention to this letter, Heidegger cannot have been unaware of parallels in his own situation—in September 1933 he was formally offered a chair in philosophy in Berlin (and, at the same time, in Munich). These lectures, when this remark will have been made, will have begun much earlier than that, but there is every likelihood negotiations had already opened, or at least overtures begun, by the opening of the summer semester of 1933.

2. Ibid., 18. "Seine Philosophie gewann einen höchst merkwürdigen Einfluß auf die Staatsgesinnung."

3. Ibid., 80. "Wir sind ein Volk, das noch *ein Schicksal* hat" (Heidegger's emphasis).

a ghost anxiously chased off in the statements and actions of Germany's leaders at the time.[4] Heidegger's privileging of Germany has normally been cited by his critics as evidence of his nationalism, radical "right" conservatism, and indeed, Nazism (and not without cause—the real question being whether they are themselves causes and motives that are "psychological" in character, or were symptoms of something else), but given that Marx (and, as we shall see, even Lenin) made similar statements about the place of Germany, more needs to be said in order for this question to be understood. Why does the materiality of place affect what is to be thought and said? This question deserves a fully thought-through answer, although it is far beyond the scope of this present book to attain to that. We have the space and time only to answer this question in terms of the "productive dialogue" whose meaning we are seeking to elucidate. It is to this question, and in this way, that we must now turn.

Both Marx and Heidegger present arguments for the centrality of Germany philosophy to European metaphysics and Occidental thought: one as evidence of German backwardness, the other as evidence of Germany's thoughtful destiny. If, for Marx, among other peoples "Germany was their *theoretical conscience,*" this was because "the Germans have, in their politics, *thought* what the other peoples have *achieved.*"[5] Marx's ironic, almost mocking, analysis of the German situation of the 1840s has for him a serious basis. His assessment of Germany's very backwardness in political and social development has, he argues, resulted in a philosophical outlook whose apogee is Hegel's thought: Marx argues that "the criticism of the *German philosophy of the state and of right* has attained through Hegel its most consistent, richest and final form,"[6] a philosophy which has developed in the absence of its concrete and material forms, and so whose very absence indicates the imperative of their coming presence. Germany, Marx argues, did not pass through the practical intermediate stages of political emancipation in step with other modern peoples, it only theorized them in Hegel's speculative thinking. The paradox of this absence of gradual transition is that the pressure for total revolutionary change is consequently all the more increased. This is because theory is the abstract form of concrete, material need: theory does not lead the way, it is abstracted from the path already trodden: except

4. For an analysis of the careful management of this issue by the then German chancellor, Helmut Kohl, see Frank Costigliola, "An 'Arm around the Shoulder': The United States, NATO and German Reunification, 1989–90."

5. Karl Marx, "Zur Kritik der Hegelschen Rechtsphilosophie" (*MEW*1), 384. "Die Deutschen haben in der Politik *gedacht,* was die andern Völker *getan* haben. Deutschland war ihr *theoretisches Gewissen*" (Marx's emphases).

6. Ibid., 384. "Die Kritik der *deutschen Staats- und Rechtsphilosophie,* welche durch Hegel ihre konsequenteste, reichste und letzte Fassung erhalten hat" (Marx's emphasis).

in Germany's case. Germany experiences the need for change in respect to the history of its more industrialized neighbors as a theoretical imperative.

The speculative philosophy of Germany arises only because of the hitherto absence of the development of an industrial proletariat, a proletariat only emerging as a social fact and political force as Marx himself writes (we are reminded of Engels's first letter to Marx of early 1844).[7] The sections of Marx's text in which he analyzes the situation in Germany contain the record of his earliest understanding of how class antagonism leads to revolutionary fervor: "In order that *one* class par excellence be the class of the liberation, then conversely another class must be the obvious class of the subjugation."[8] The class of liberation, as subjugated, takes on the role of emancipatory force for the whole of society: as oppressed it discovers not only its need for liberation for itself, but also its need to be the liberative force for the whole of society *as* the whole of humanity, proclaiming, Marx says, for itself and to all: "*I am nothing and I must be all.*"[9] The *I* in question is precisely the universalized, species-defining absolute subject, as that subjectivity which foresees and so attains to its absolute task.

However, neither the class of the liberation, nor the class of the subjugation, come from nowhere: the emergence of the proletariat is the sign and fact that it is formed "out of the dissolution of the middle class,"[10] and so out of the dissolution of a certain stage of development of society itself. The proletariat's experience of deprivation, that private property is denied to it, is the presupposition for a sublated advance and conscious discovery by the proletariat as a class that the negation of private property is itself the demand for the coming communism in concrete social form. Although Marx does not say so, the corollary of this is that the portion of the middle classes who are in this process being dissolved (and so reduced) into the proletariat carry also with them, almost like a subconscious effect, a schooling in the speculative philosophy of the state and of right that itself is the precursor to *action*, the action of the revolution. The philosophy of absolute subjectivity, speculatively derived as a phenomenological description of a state of affairs that is precipitately being prepared for in the actual creation of an industrial proletariat and the dissolution and reformation of society itself, is thereby the preparation for the revolutionary action that takes place as the realization of what was hitherto merely theoretical. This is the discovery that "the only

7. See 43.

8. Karl Marx, "Zur Kritik der Hegelschen Rechtsphilosophie" (MEW1), 388. "Damit *ein* Stand *par excellence* der Stand der Befreiung, dazu muß umgekehrt ein andrer Stand der offenbare Stand der Unterjochung sein" (Marx's emphasis).

9. Ibid., 389. "*Ich bin nichts, und ich müßte alles sein*" (Marx's emphasis).

10. Ibid., 391. "Aus der Auflösung des Mittelstandes."

*practically* possible liberation of Germany is liberation on the standpoint of *that* theory which explains that man is the highest essence for man," and so proves that "the *emancipation of the German* is the *emancipation of man*." This says nothing other than that Germany must assume the vanguard in the coming transformation of Europe, and thereby the world, in the advent of communism as the resolution of the very differentiations and contradictions that themselves produce "history" as a phenomenon. Marx concludes that "the *head* of this emancipation is philosophy, its *heart* is the *proletariat*."[11]

Marx's understanding of the central position of Germany in any coming revolution, precisely because of the presence of philosophy in its midst (thereby qualifying and throwing an entirely fresh light on the eleventh thesis on Feuerbach), comes remarkably close to Heidegger's own understanding—perhaps even, in the months of Heidegger's embrace of Hitlerism, coinciding with Heidegger's view (not least, as we shall see, in Heidegger's odd espousal for the brief period of the rectorate of Freiburg University in 1933–34 of a rhetoric resonating strongly with elements of Hegel's thought). Marx's privileging of the German situation in relation to the revolutionary transformation of society as a whole and in every land through the relationship of philosophy to revolutionary possibility has nowhere, nor ever, been interpreted as any kind of nationalism. Neither is this true for Marx, nor even of Lenin, who in 1918 had argued: "It is an absolute truth that without a German revolution we are doomed . . . if the German revolution does not come, we are doomed."[12] It is in this light that we must read Heidegger's own understanding of the centrality of Germany—not as a kind of German imperialism, nor as a negative "nationalism of the right," but as something with consequences for the planetary reach of European thinking and the destiny of the Occident.

Lenin saw the German revolution as more decisive for the future of communism, and more privileged in its importance, than the possibility of revolution in either Britain or America (although these too were never underestimated).[13] Marx's understanding of the concrete character of material conditions means that in the inevitable course toward the accomplishment of communism, neither history nor geography is uniform. This means that some historical periods (and the particular histories of some peoples), and some places, are inevitably to be understood as more decisive in the

11. Ibid., 391. "Die einzig *praktisch* mögliche Befreiung Deutschlands ist die Befreiung auf dem Standpunkt *der* Theorie, welche den Menschen für das höchste Wesen des Menschen erklärt. . . . Die *Emanzipation des Deutschen* ist die *Emanzipation des Menschen*. Der *Kopf* dieser Emanzipation ist die *Philosophie*, ihr *Herz* das *Proletariat*" (Marx's emphases).

12. Vladimir I. Lenin, "Political Report of the Central Committee, March 7, 1918," 98.

13. In particular, Lenin made repeated references and wrote addresses to the "American proletariat."

working out and resolution of the *whole* of history. Heidegger's own understanding of the unfolding of the history of being (*Seinsgeschichte*) is not different. Yet Heidegger's critics have routinely denounced his privileging of the place of German philosophy and thought, and so Germany's place in Heidegger's understanding of the destiny of European and global thinking itself, as nothing more than *mere* nationalism,[14] and evidence of his enduring commitment to Nazism.[15] While his understanding of the place of Germany cannot and should not be disengaged from his Nazi misadventure, something much greater and more significant is at stake in what he says, if we can only hear it through the polemical clamor (of his own, and that of others).

Evidence of Heidegger's "extreme nationalism" appears to come from his aside in the 1935 lecture course *Introduction to Metaphysics,* where he privileges the German language together with the Greek tongue, "for this [Greek] language (seen from the possibilities for thinking) beside German is at once the most powerful and most *geistig.*"[16] Heidegger repeats this point in his 1966 interview with *Spiegel* magazine, speaking of "the special inner relationship of the German language with the language of the Greeks and their thinking."[17]

Like Marx, Heidegger understands concrete, material circumstances to give rise to, and forge the reality of, the historical fate of a particular situation or nation. In a passage also from the lectures that became *Introduction to Metaphysics* and that has been singled out by several commentators for evidence of Heidegger's culpable nationalism, Heidegger comments on

14. Victor Farías speaks in this context of Heidegger's "extreme nationalism" and cites the critique of Heidegger by Robert Minder in *Hölderlin unter den Deutschen und andere Aufsätze zur deutschen Literatur,* 132 f. See Victor Farías, *Heidegger and Nazism,* 218 and n. 12. Richard Wolin repeats and amplifies many of these charges in his introduction to Richard Wolin, ed., *The Heidegger Controversy,* 1–22, especially 13 and following.

15. See Otto Pöggeler, *Der Denkweg Martin Heideggers,* 316. Pöggeler makes the point here that Heidegger may never really have departed from proximity to National Socialism ("in die Nähe des Nationalsozialismus geriet, ohne jemals wieder wirklich aus dieser Nähe herauszukommen"), a view also often attributed to Theodore Adorno, but for which I can find no cited incidence. It would certainly not be inconsistent with Adorno's view of Heidegger, which especially after the war, was extremely critical.

16. Martin Heidegger, *Einführung in die Metaphysik* (*GA*40), 61. "Denn diese Sprache ist (auf die Möglichkeiten des Denkens gesehen) neben der deutschen die mächtigste und geistigste zugleich." Heidegger insisted that these comments, together with those on 208 concerning the "inner truth and greatness of this movement [of National Socialism]" ("[die] innere Wahrheit und Größe dieser Bewegung") remain in the 1953 (first) and all subsequent editions of this text.

17. Martin Heidegger, "*Spiegel*-Gespräch mit Martin Heidegger" (*GA*16), 679. "Ich denke an die besondere innere Verwandtschaft der deutschen Sprache mit der Sprache der Griechen und deren Denken."

the situation of Germany.[18] Again the fact that this passage remains in the 1953 publication of these lectures, taken together with several other remarks he made after the war, suggests he did not think the postwar situation of Germany markedly different from the situation in 1935 when the lectures were delivered. If this at first seems shocking in its implications, it is at least consistent: both before and after the war, before and after his public commitment to Nazism, Heidegger equated the politics of communism, fascism, and "world democracy" as springing from the same metaphysical root. Heidegger speaks (in a passage we will consider again later)[19] of how "this Europe, in unholy blindness always on the verge of killing itself, lies today in the great pincers between Russia on the one hand and America on the other. Russia and America are both, metaphysically understood, the same hopeless frenzy of unchained technology and of the same displaced organization of the normal man."[20] It is this understanding of the "normal," sometimes translated as "average,"[21] in which Heidegger locates the metaphysical unity of Bolshevism and Americanism. He adds: "We lie in the pincers. Our people, as standing in the center, experiences the sharpest pincer-pressure, the people richest in neighbors and so the most endangered people, and in all that the metaphysical people."[22] Hegel had understood and described the

18. See Victor Farías, *Heidegger and Nazism,* 218; Richard Wolin, *The Heidegger Controversy,* 13. Many others—too numerous to list—have commented on this passage.

19. See 148, n. 27.

20. Martin Heidegger, *Einführung in die Metaphysik* (*GA*40), 40–41. "Dieses Europa, in heilloser Verblendung immer auf dem Sprunge, sich selbst zu erdolchen, liegt heute in der großen Zange zwischen Rußland auf der einen und Amerika auf der anderen Seite. Rußland und Amerika sind beide, metaphysisch gesehen, dasselbe; dieselbe trostlose Raserei der entfesselten Technik und der bodenlosen Organisation des Normalmenschen." This statement comes from the lectures given in the summer semester of 1935 and published originally by Niemeyer in 1953 in an edition edited by Heidegger himself, and from which he refused to remove the reference to the "inner truth and greatness" of the movement of National Socialism, which, Heidegger asserted, has nothing to do with a philosophy of values but rather "the encounter between global technology and modern humanity." See also Martin Heidegger, *Einführung in die Metaphysik* (*GA*40), 208. "Dies alles nennt sich Philosophie. Was heute vollends als Philosophie des Nationalsozialismus herumgeboten wird, aber mit der inneren Wahrheit und Größe dieser Bewegung (nämlich mit der Begegnung der planetarisch bestimmten Technik und des neuzeitlichen Menschen) nicht das Geringste zu tun hat."

21. See the two English translations of this lecture course: Martin Heidegger, *An Introduction to Metaphysics,* trans. Ralph Manheim, 37; Martin Heidegger, *Introduction to Metaphysics,* Gregory Fried and Richard Polt, trans., 40 (*GA*40). Both miss the references to "normality" a few pages later (44, "normal denkenden Menschen . . . Normalmenschen"), which both translations render as "normally thinking . . . normal").

22. Martin Heidegger, *Einführung in die Metaphysik* (*GA*40), 41. "Wir liegen in der Zange. Unser Volk erfährt als in der Mitte stehend den schärfsten Zangendruck, das nachbarreichste Volk und so das gefährdetste Volk und in all dem das metaphysische Volk."

relations between states as an essentially rational one.[23] Marx, conversely, understands the relationship between states in a way more fitted to Hegel's own metaphysical thinking, as able to make the *idea* of history visible through the material conditions within states and in uneven stages of development in relation to each other, hence why the situation of the proletariat in Germany, yet emerging from a still degenerating middle class and pressed in by the speed of the industrialization of Germany, takes on the role that it does. He singles out the German proletariat out for a sharper and so more immediate destiny in the making present and realization of the idea of a pan-European (certainly), and then finally planetary, communism. Yet again we hit upon why the Marxist understanding of history is, in Heidegger's view, superior: it is not a merely speculative description of what ought to pertain, it bases itself on the material conditions of physical life. Heidegger also understands the destiny of a nation and of a people to arise on the basis of the material conditions of lived experience. The relation between the German and the Greek languages, another of Heidegger's claims in the *Introduction to Metaphysics* that earned him huge notoriety,[24] is not an accident: it is materially accounted for by Germany's being both richest in neighbors and being most endangered by them. Not less rich nor less endangered, Heidegger might have argued, was Homeric (and later) Hellas: this richness and danger was, in his view, the way that Greek thinking was itself a consequence of the Greek experience of life. A language both forms a people and is marked by (and records) the "experience" of that people. Heidegger also understands the German language to have arisen in its particularity, and to speak, in part at least, as a result of the situation of the German people. The people richest in neighbors, and most endangered, is yet, he wanted to claim, the *destiny* of those who enrich *and* endanger it. This understanding, of the fate of a people determining the fate of the planet as a whole, is not so far from claims made by Marx (or Lenin and other revolutionaries).

In the *Spiegel* interview the interviewers challenged what they perceived as Heidegger's nationalistic claims, citing a passage from Heidegger's *Nietzsche* lectures which speaks of the conflict between the Dionysian and Apollonian, which Heidegger had said (in 1936–37) "is a hidden stylistic law of the historical destiny of the Germans," adding there, "Hölderlin and Nietzsche have with this conflict set a question mark up before the Germans, to find their essence historically."[25] Heidegger's mention of the Germans as

23. See 87.

24. See Martin Heidegger, *Einführung in die Metaphysik* (*GA*40), 61.

25. Martin Heidegger, "*Spiegel*-Gespräch mit Martin Heidegger" (*GA*16), 678, citing *Der Wille zur Macht als Kunst* (*GA*6.1), 105 (= *GA*43, 122). "Ein verborgenes Stilgesetz der geschichtlichen Bestimmung der Deutschen ist . . . Hölderlin und Nietzsche haben mit diesem

the "most endangered" is in itself an oblique reference to two of the opening lines of Friedrich Hölderlin's *Patmos,* and Heidegger's repeated return to these lines in various places: "Where therefore danger is, grows / from it the saving."[26] It is not accidental, therefore, that when the *Spiegel* interviewers pressed Heidegger on this understanding of the destiny of Germany, asking "Do you specifically allocate a task particular to the Germans?,"[27] Heidegger appeared to evade the question by replying "Yes, in this sense, in dialogue with Hölderlin."[28]

If the question hanging over Heidegger really is about his political nationalism and an undisclosed but still persisting commitment to Nazism, then Heidegger is indeed being devious by shifting the ground from the privileged place of the German language and the German people to the question of dialogue with a German poet. We take for granted in contemporary thinking that nationalism is in some sense "reprehensible." We also take for granted that in any interrogation, every response must be interpreted as masking devious intent (in this sense *we* become no better than interrogators, we place ourselves in the seat of the police). None of the commentators (Wolin, Farías, *Spiegel,* and so forth) need to explain *why:* we (the interrogators, the police, who are always on the side of right) are presumed instinctively to be ones who reject nationalism. *We* already know: the essence of nationalism is domination—in terms of race, class, gender, and so forth, and the essence of *German* nationalism (in National Socialism) is exemplified in the hideous crimes carried out in the name of that domination. The evidence is before us: "look what nationalism leads to!" Heidegger's evasions fall out easily in front of us, because we know this chain of reasoning so well.

That nationalism is a historical evil presents itself as a proven historical fact. Moreover, the domination inherent in nationalism, as the biological privileging of one human "people" over another, is arbitrary—it obliterates the *essential* sameness of every human organism (where differentiations of race, even of sex or gender, or physical or intellectual ability, are always merely incidental to the essence of the "same" of the human subject) for the sake of a theoretically, politically, morally, foundationless *choice* for one race

Widerstreit ein Fragezeichen vor der Aufgabe der Deutschen aufgerichtet, geschichtlich ihr Wesen zu finden."

26. Hölderlin, *Patmos,* 350. "Wo aber Gefahr ist, wächst / Das Rettende auch." See, for one of Heidegger's central discussions of these lines, the fourth of the Bremen lectures, entitled "The Turn" (Martin Heidegger, "Die Kehre" [*GA*79], 72 and following). Another, which concentrates on the whole meaning of 'the danger' is *Why Poets?* (Martin Heidegger, "Wozu Dichter?" [*GA*5], especially 296).

27. Martin Heidegger, "*Spiegel*-Gespräch mit Martin Heidegger" (*GA*16), 679. "*Spiegel:* Sie messen speziell den Deutschen eine besondere Aufgabe zu?"

28. Ibid., 679. "*Heidegger:* Ja, im Sinne, im Gespräch mit Hölderlin."

or people or gender, and so on, over against the other. This argument, stressing the essential identity of the human organism with the human essence (as we have already seen and shall come to see more) is itself the *essence* of Marx's communism. There is no differentiation of race, class, education, geography, history, identity, ability, that can justify or secure the privileging of one human being over another. The emergence of the proletariat, as that class whose task is the end of history and the accomplishment of communism and the establishment of the species-being of the life of the individual, is only a particular task assigned to a particular class of the species for the sake of the species as a whole and in its entirety: even this particularity will be abolished and sublated in the course of the accomplishment of the task itself. Inasmuch as every man or woman is on the way to becoming a "species being," no man or woman can attain to a formal or essential difference which is their specificity, except by accident. Our immediate rejection of nationalism is, however (and however much concealed from us), as metaphysical a *decision* as Marx's metaphysics of communism, even if the decision is not *mine* but one in which I already stand because it is so obvious to me, and has been made *for* me (elsewhere, I know not where, although I *know* what is right and wrong). What we take as self-evident—as Marx and Heidegger would both have asserted—occurs from out of what it is that thinking already lays out and makes possible for us to think.

Understood like this, we take it self-evidently that Heidegger's claim for the supposed superiority of the German language, alongside the Greek, is a claim that can be solved by merely technical analysis and means. We ask: how well does German "translate" the Greeks? How do German grammar and syntax demonstrate their superiority in the history and range of Indo-European languages (alongside the other families of languages), and what (if any) are the "technical" reasons for this language's superiority over, say, English, as the now most universal language, or (as Heidegger had suggested) over French (or any other)?[29] Heidegger does not, however, locate the superiority of German in the vocabulary, grammar, or syntax of the language, but in a person: Hölderlin. German attains to superiority because it is the language in which this poet says what he is given to say.[30] The language is

29. In the *Spiegel* interview Heidegger had said: "The French today have confirmed this to me again. If they begin to think, they speak German; they insist that they could not get through with their own language." Martin Heidegger, "*Spiegel*-Gespräch mit Martin Heidegger" (*GA*16), 679. "Das bestätigen mir heute immer wieder die Franzosen. Wenn sie zu denken anfangen, sprechen sie deutsch; sie versichern, sie kämen mit ihrer Sprache nicht durch."

30. Andrjez Warminksi has examined this reply in some detail in relation to questions of language and interpretation and how "a historical people is at home in its own language not of itself, that is, not without its contribution (its act in addition, *Zutun*). Hence it can happen that we indeed speak 'German' and yet talk in nothing but 'American.'" Andrjez Warminksi,

shaped by the poet, and so by what the poet brings to speech through what he *hears*.

What, then, is superior about the poet (rather than the language)? Hölderlin is not merely that one who, in the words of Paul de Man, was a "philo-Hellenist," and so attends with an exaggerated affection to the world of the Greeks. Rather, for Heidegger, is Hölderlin to be understood as that one who attends *to* what the Greeks attended *to*. The Greeks are the origin of the destiny of the Occident because what they thought and how they said it has been, and is yet still, decisive for the whole of history, and so, also, for European, metaphysical, thinking in its global reach. Yet the original thinking of the Greeks has undergone transformation after transformation in the history of thinking (and for Heidegger, these transformations are themselves the history of being). Hölderlin is that one who, Heidegger claims, makes this decisiveness live yet again in pristine form (as what *let* the Greeks think what they thought) from out of its origin, even in the present age. The special destiny of Germany, if there is one, is not to dominate every other European nation and thereby thrust forward into a global subjugation of all other peoples to the triumphal Germans. It is to be that place, and the Germans those ones, who let their neighbors *in* to the meaning of their "whither" and "whence" (*wozu*) from out of their origination in the experience of being and thinking from out of which the Greeks also took off their beginning: the Occident. For Heidegger, this means the Greeks as they think before the advent of philosophy: before the inception of metaphysics (and nihilism) in the thought of Plato and Aristotle. This thinking lives in its highest form in the pre-Socratic poetry of the Greece of antiquity.

Hölderlin is that one who attends poetically (and therefore not philosophically, i.e., as he attends to the voices that speak *before* philosophy, *before* the inception of metaphysics, before Plato and Aristotle) to what the Greeks attended to: the poem. The poet is, for Heidegger, that one who, returning to the source of Occidental thought, speaks from out of the whole history of Europe: either *in* its source (as with Homer and the lyric poets) or recapitulates its whole history by returning *to* the source. Heidegger's elucidation of Hölderlin is an elucidation of the whole history of thinking, and so of *the* whole history of being, all at once. The Marxist view of history is superior for Heidegger because it is that understanding of history which stands at the gate of the elucidation of the history of the Occident, and opens it. It opens it because it has the power to attain to the gateway: it cannot enter in to what lies within, at the very origin, because Marx and Marxism can speak only of man's experience of man. The poet is the one who can speak *more*, can speak

---

"Monstrous History: Heidegger Reading Hölderlin," 197–98, citing Martin Heidegger, *Hölderlins Hymne "Der Ister"* (*GA*53), 79–80.

more of the origin *again,* and yet his words are not his own. He speaks, not of Europe, but of the destiny of the Occident itself. The poet speaks "the distance of the nearing god."[31] This phrase is parallel to the thought of "the Last God" of the texts of the notebooks of *Das Ereignis,* and indicates the real province that Heidegger believes Germany, or rather Hölderlin, to open up, as a destiny. Heidegger is concerned, not with nationalism, but with the end of the flight of the gods, and the dawn ahead to which the Occident (as the Evening-Land) points.[32]

Heidegger says of Hölderlin that he has "his own": "as soon as Hölderlin has 'his own,' he persists in the destiny allotted him, he is the poet of his poem . . . what is 'his own' for the poet? What is proper, that is allotted to him?"[33] Heidegger uses two words for "own": the possessive pronoun (*das seine*), and the word from which he derives *das Er-eignis,* the word that means what is "proper" in the sense of "property" as what is "owned": *eigene.* The poem is able to do what philosophy is never able to do: to name the nearness of the gods. The first two lines of Hölderlin's *Patmos,* immediately preceding the lines concerning the danger and the saving, say: "near is / and hard to take hold of, the god."[34] What is proper to the poet (which was Socrates's actual complaint against the poets)[35] are the words given him (or her) by the god. This is why the poet has to come *in* to his own, to *make* (*poiein*), and so produce, as his own a word given him from elsewhere. The poet, says Heidegger, is a poet only because he is one "suffering compulsion by the holy."[36]

In private notes from 1939 Heidegger challenged the "brute 'political' misrepresentation of Hölderlin"[37] in the (Nazi) taking-up and abuse of the idiom of "the fatherland" in Hölderlin's work, citing the concluding line of Hölderlin's dedication of his translation of Sophocles, which speaks of "the angel of the holy fatherland." The issue, Heidegger stresses, is not the "fa-

31. Martin Heidegger, "Das Gedicht" (*GA*4), 190. "Die Ferne des nahenden Gottes."

32. See Heidegger's discussion of the relation of the evening to the night and the morning in Martin Heidegger, *Das Ereignis* (*GA*71), 94–100.

33. Martin Heidegger, "Das Gedicht" (*GA*4), 185–86. "Sobald Hölderlin 'das seine' hat, ist er inständig in der ihm beschiedenen Bestimmung, ist er der Dichter seines Gedichtes. . . . Was ist 'das seine' für den Dichter? Welches Eigene ist ihm beschieden?"

34. Hölderlin, *Patmos,* 350. "Nah ist / Und schwer zu fassen der Gott."

35. Compare Plato, *Protagoras,* 347e. Socrates complains that the poets may not be asked what the meaning of their words is, because their words, they claim, are *not* their "own," they are the words of the gods.

36. Martin Heidegger, "Das Gedicht" (*GA*4), 186, quoting line 89 of Hölderlin's "At the Source of the Danube" (Friedrich Hölderlin, "Am Quell der Donau" in *Gedichte,* 323). "Heiliggenot[h]iget."

37. Martin Heidegger, "Zur politischen Mißdeutung des 'Vaterlands' bei Hölderlin" (*GA*75), 277. "Die rohe 'politische' Mißdeutung Hölderlins."

therland," but the relation to the holy, to the gods, that is to be understood, and concludes by asking "if it will be possible to find a German hearing of the word of this poet?"[38] The question is not one about the superiority or otherwise of the German language, but whether modern German ears will ever be equal to what has been said by the angel (Hölderlin himself) who bears to them what they must hear.

In the 1936–37 lectures (lectures which coincide with the beginning of the notebooks of *Das Ereignis*) which the *Spiegel* interviewer cited in questioning Heidegger, the thinker several times emphasizes that even before Nietzsche's typology of the opposition of the Dionysian and Apollonian, "Hölderlin already had seen and grasped this opposition in a yet deeper and more noble manner."[39] The *Speigel* interviewer never inquires into why the conflict between Apollo and Dionysus lives in Nietzsche, and more primordially in Hölderlin (especially since Hölderlin never names it directly; or rather, never names it as Nietzsche names it, in the names of these two Greek gods). Or rather, the interviewer never inquires into why a question about the destiny of the Germans turns out to be resolved through an understanding of the more primordial Hölderlin: that one who is for Heidegger *the* poet: the poet of "the danger" and of "that which saves."

In the lecture course *The Will to Power as Art* Heidegger never fully resolves how either Nietzsche or Hölderlin grasps this opposition between Apollo and Dionysus. Heidegger emphasizes two things. First, that in Nietzsche the opposition is grasped through the understanding of art and experience as "rapture" (*Rausch*), that is, as the compelling—as what in human experience cannot be evaded and so what overcomes man—the self-evident as the experience he cannot evade. Nietzsche, unsurprisingly, emphasizes, from his writing of *The Birth of Tragedy* onward, what he refers to as the Dionysian. Dionysus is the god who lets man into death and rebirth: as the god in whose honor the Greek tragedies of Aeschylus, Sophocles, Euripides (and others) were written, celebrated, and contested, he lets man into his fate as mortal. Dionysus, through Nietzsche, lets man into the death of God and the flight of the gods, into the essence of nihilism and the philosophy of becoming, *more* than Nietzsche is able to name the Apollonian, as the fixed, and as permanence (the metaphysical experiences of being as *aei*, "ever," "the same": permanent presence). Second, Heidegger emphasizes that Nietzsche is the thinker of the death of God and of how this is the pre-

38. Ibid., 278. "Wenn [soll] das Wort dieses Dichters ein deutsches Hören finden können?"

39. Martin Heidegger, *Der Wille zur Macht als Kunst* (*GA*43), 122 (= *GA*6.1, 104). "Hölderlin [hatte] diesen Gegensatz bereits in einer noch tieferen und edleren Weise gesehen und begriffen." See the discussion of "Dionysus as witness for divine and human be-ing" in Martin Heidegger, *Hölderlins Hymnen: "Germanien" und "Der Rhein"* (*GA*39), 187–91.

vailing experience of being (and so in Nietzsche, "Dionysus" as the celebration of *life*), and names how "this danger is *the* danger."[40] Nietzsche is that one who names how, in the destiny of Germany, the Germans are the most endangered, as *those ones* who will let Europe into its experience of the dangerous, as what will befall it and overcome it and bring it to annihilation (not for nothing does Nietzsche speak of "daybreak"). In Heidegger's understanding, Marx speaks from the same province as Nietzsche: Marx speaks of, and from out of, the basic experience (the compelling, enrapturing experience, the experience that befalls European thinking and that it cannot evade, and at most, must embrace and live through to the full and the end, enraptured with this thought) of the death of God. As one of the speakers of the death of God, of humanity as "the creative" and "the productive," as the "dionysiac" *life* that flows inexorably from the proclamation of the death of God, Marx leads humanity into the greatest danger. Marx leads Europe, and the globe, *in*—to the place from out of which a saving might *also* emerge: Marx is the falling light of the evening and the preparation for night: the Occidental *voice.* Marx has the power to lead man up to that place from out of which the god might pass by: from whence the word the god might utter could be heard.

The rites of Dionysus were invariably celebrated at temples of Apollo: the opposition between Apollo and Dionysus of which Nietzsche speaks is itself a metaphysically constituted opposition. Dionysus, as the "strange" god, is often said to have arrived "from the east." Many recent commentators take this literally, speaking of how Dionysus is added later to the Greek pantheon; borrowed, perhaps from the Persians, or from elsewhere, once the Olympians had themselves been settled. None of this is true: Dionysus, most Greek of all gods, is, rather, the Greek experience *of* the strange, as the uncanny.[41] Dionysus is named as a stranger because he *is* "the strange." At the center of Heidegger's interpretation of Hölderlin is an interpretation of man himself as the uncanny: "man the uncanniest of the uncanny."[42] In the uncanny, man experiences the meaning of life and death, and the fateful. This is the bond between humanity and Dionysus: man learns to speak of his strangeness and uncanniness through the enrapturing advent of Dionysus.

It is in giving an account of the uncanniness of man in 1942 that Hei-

40. Martin Heidegger, "Wozu Dichter?" (*GA*5), 295. "Diese Gefahr ist *die* Gefahr." (Heidegger's emphasis)

41. See, for a discussion of this, Walter F. Otto, *Dionysos: Mythos und Kultus,* especially 51–62.

42. Martin Heidegger, *Hölderlins Hymne "Der Ister"* (*GA*53), 65. "Der Mensch das Unheimlichste des Unheimlichen." There is a second, not less important, discussion of the uncanny (*das Ungeheure*) in the lecture course of the following semester from this, published as *Parmenides* (*GA*54), 148–56.

degger has the most severe things to say of the "pincers" in which Europe is caught, in the sharp unfolding of the situation of the war. Whereas in 1935 Heidegger had spoken of how Germany was gripped by Russia on the one side and America on the other, now he adds: "Bolshevism is only a variety of Americanism,"[43] and "so we know today that the Anglo-Saxon world of Americanism" (and so by implication Bolshevism as well) "is resolved to annihilate Europe, that is, the homeland, and that means the origination of the Occidental."[44]

We can hear this either as a statement of Heidegger's support for the Nazi regime in the storm-eye of the drama of the Second World War, or we can hear it in the poetic voice that attempts to explicate the speaking of the destiny of Germany, of the Occident, and the planetary reach of European thinking: a voice that will not change even after the war is done, because the destiny itself has not changed, even if its materiality takes a new form. Already by 1942, as we know from Heidegger's private notebooks, he had become a fierce critic of the Nazi regime and its political program. This statement cannot, therefore, be heard as mere propaganda, although, without doubt, the statement is somewhat coded, accommodated to the moment in which it is spoken. Heidegger is, though lecturing on Hölderlin at the moment in which the Americans enter the war, attempting to grasp the meaning of the present situation (of the greatest historical danger, when the pincers really threaten to close) in its full historical essence and reach.

The Apollonian is set in *opposition* to the Dionysiac only by Nietzsche, in the metaphysical opposition he proclaims pertains between being and becoming, an opposition we have seen prepared to be understood in this way in the thought of Hegel. Becoming is the future of humanity: being is nothing more than (in Hegel's words) an empty thought—equated to the nothing; in Nietzsche's, a mere "empty fiction."[45] The Apollonian is not, however, metaphysically opposed to the Dionysiac in the poetry of the Greeks: rather here, for the Greeks, they belong together: they are to be understood as "the same" and through the same. The Apollonian is not the permanence of presence, of the metaphysical understanding of being as the philosophical thought of God, or absolute reason, or absolute subjectivity, or its overcoming. Rather is the Apollonian to be understood poetically, as what it is to attend to the nearing god. "Poetically attending" means fastening upon, holding in place, delaying and detaining (in the oldest senses of these two latter

43. Martin Heidegger, *Hölderlins Hymne "Der Ister"* (*GA*53), 86. "Der Bolschewismus ist nur eine Abart des Amerikanismus."

44. Ibid., 68. "Wir wissen heute, daß die angelsächsische Welt des Amerikanismus entschlossen ist, Europa, und d. h. die Heimat, und d. h. den Anfang des Abendländischen, zu vernichten."

45. Friedrich Nietzsche, vol. 6, *Götzen-Dämmerung*, 75. "Das Sein [ist] eine leere Fiktion."

words—to "be possessed of," and to cause to "tarry"). No god can be held fast by a mortal: but the poet may, in stillness, bring to a stand the passing-by of the god, by speaking what the god has given him to speak. The poet in stillness, stills the nearing god. Only in metaphysics, in the rage to secure and hold fast by means of the will does such holding-fast and holding still become transformed into the metaphysical drive for permanence: the securing of eternity, "eternal truth," in a "word" that compels and enforces what it says. Such a permanentizing and securing is the very drive that puts the gods to flight: such a word can never be poetically uttered. Rather, then, should such "stilling" be a holding of something in place. Heidegger says of it: "the *stilling* of the passing-by of the Last God."[46]

The Dionysian, then, is the fatedness that this delaying and stilling also comes to an end, it also passes away. The passing-by of the nearing god. The Dionysian is the fatedness that even the stilling of the god is *itself* fated to end: it can never be held "forever," *aei,* the same. The fate of permanence is held by arising and decay: dwelling in impermanence is also what lets the understanding *in* to a knowledge of the unchanging and ever-same. The poet knows that the flight of the gods indicates only that the *present* gods withdraw, and are yet to make their presence felt. Heidegger argues that the gods who are near, yet stay back, are not "the returning gods of the flight from ancient Greece,"[47] they are the arriving (advent), the present gods, who, yet once more truthful, are already present, and will let their presence be felt again *for man.* Noting that this is how the gods have need of the poet, and have need of man, Heidegger concludes "the poet himself names 'the present gods' 'stilly.' 'Still' indicates: stilled, come to rest."[48] In attempting to unfold the meaning of the poem, and of the poet's allotted task as his "own," Heidegger cites a line of Hölderlin's from the poem "The Archipelago" which speaks of the glory or fame of the gods needing the hearts of feeling men.[49] Heidegger adds "fame and glorying are thought here in the Pindaric, Greek, sense as letting-appear."[50] The destiny of the poet, the destiny of Ger-

46. Martin Heidegger, *Beiträge zur Philosophie* (*GA*65), 17. "Die *Stille* des Vorbeiganges des letzten Gottes" (Heidegger's emphasis).

47. Martin Heidegger, "Das Gedicht" (*GA*4), 184. "Die wiederkehrenden entflohenen Götter des alten Griechenlands."

48. Ibid., 189. "Der Dichter nennt sich 'die gegenwärtigen Götter' 'stille.' 'Still' bedeutet: gestillt, zur Ruhe gekommen."

49. Friedrich Hölderlin, "Der Archipelagus," in *Gedichte,* 255, v. 60. "Immer bedürfen ja, wie Heroën den Kranz, die geweihten / Elemente zum Ruhme das Herz der fühlenden Menschen." ("Always, as heroes need their wreaths, the hallowed elements likewise / Need for fame the heart of feeling men.")

50. Martin Heidegger, "Das Gedicht" (*GA*4), 191. "Ruhm und rühmen sind hier im pindarschen, griechischen Sinne zu denken als Erscheinenlassen."

many, is not domination, but a certain "letting-appear." To let-appear is to let beings *be* as they are. The Occidental destiny of Germany is, for Heidegger, to let it happen that beings *be,* in which letting, man also appears as one of the beings that *is* and has a proper letting-be-seen. Man does not restrict the whole of being to himself (Marx's claim that "man reproduces the whole of nature"),[51] but inasmuch as "nature" is a metaphysical name for *phusis,* the being of beings, man stands out as *one* among beings, in being, and lets this standing-out appear, and be seen for itself.

For Heidegger, the moment of Germany's greatest danger is not its being engulfed in the maelstrom of the criminal Nazi regime and its attempt at domination of the planet: rather the destiny of the Germans is, for him, to attend to what Hölderlin had attended to in the very opposite of domination, in stillness: to the whole reach of Occidental thinking from its inception, and to speak of that attending, for the sake of its neighbors and from out of, and in the saving of, the greatest danger of its existence. The whole reach of European thinking *is* the history of being, it is how the history of being comes to appear, both as a history, as metaphysics, and as a destiny for those who *are,* under its sway: to understand this reach is the destiny of the Occident. The headline under which the *Spiegel* interview was published, taken from the central statement of the interview: "Now Only a God Can Save Us,"[52] can only be read as a reference to the destiny of Germany, of the Occident, and of the planetary reach of European thinking. It can only be read like this because what Heidegger says is a reference to that one who attends to the stilling of the passing-by of the Last God: Hölderlin. In his claim that now we can be saved only by a god, Heidegger was referring to Hölderlin.

51. See 119.

52. Martin Heidegger, "*Spiegel*-Gespräch mit Martin Heidegger" (GA16), 671. "Nur noch ein Gott kann uns retten."

*Chapter 7*

# The Ideology of Germany

THE PUBLIC AND SCHOLARLY evaluation of Martin Heidegger's decision to become a Nazi began in 1946, as we have already seen, with the publication of Karl Löwith's denunciation of Heidegger's political engagement in the French journal *Les Temps Modernes,* under the title "The Political Implications of Heidegger's Existentialism." Since then there have been two other major "waves" of discussion, one based around the publication of Victor Farías's *Heidegger and Nazism* in 1989 (in various languages), and the latest, in 2005, beginning with the French publication of Emmanuel Faye's work, translated into English in 2009 as *Heidegger: The Introduction of Nazism into Philosophy.* The second of these discussions is likely to prove by far the most ferocious—that initiated by Faye being so overstated as to be unlikely to provoke the avalanche of books and commentary that lasted into the mid-1990s, after Farías had sought to make a connection between Heidegger's Nazism and his philosophy. Concerning this attempt to generate a third discussion, Taylor Carman and Peter Gordon have noted, "Faye's lame arguments and manipulations of evidence are wholly unnecessary, since the only conclusion they pretend to support is what we already know of Heidegger from the abundant record of his offensive remarks and deeds."[1] The actual deeds and remarks are well documented by (best among many others) Hugo Ott, Hans Sluga, and Rüdiger Safranski.[2]

What is it, however, that we think we know? Too often in engaging with Heidegger's politics we are tempted to "take up a stance," to identify where we stand with regard to the whole of the evil of National Socialism

1. Taylor Carman, "In and With: Flawed Efforts to Discredit Martin Heidegger's Philosophy," 27, citing Peter Gordon, review of Emmanuel Faye, *Heidegger: The Introduction of Nazism into Philosophy.*

2. See Hugo Ott, *Martin Heidegger: Unterwegs zu seiner Biographie;* Hans Sluga, *Heidegger's Crisis: Philosophy and Politics in Nazi Germany;* Rüdiger Safranksi, *Ein Meister aus Deutschland: Heidegger und seine Zeit.*

in "deciding" how we relate to Heidegger's political engagement. Yet the productive dialogue with Marx will itself put "taking up a standpoint" into question, as we shall see in the final chapter. To "take up a position" in this way is not, therefore, merely to enact our refusal of Nazism, it is itself evidence of a way of thinking in which we are already stood, as if all politics were merely a matter of "personal decision," or "commitment." I want to suggest, on the contrary, that it is the very factical and material character of the extraordinary historical situation in which Heidegger found himself that enabled him to think through to its end the question of the "political." Without such a thinking-through, even his own engagement with Marx would have remained at the level of a "standpoint" and "counter-position," the inherent opposition between, say, fascism and Bolshevism that before 1933 Ernst Jünger had claimed indicated the intrinsic unity of both, a claim that Heidegger was to repeat in 1935 and later.

This chapter represents a necessary detour, to try to provide no more than an outline which traces the effect of Heidegger's material, political, engagement on his thinking, and to show how that detour, in transforming his understanding of Hegel, brought Heidegger into a renewed and deeper engagement with Marx. In doing this I will seek to show that there is a transformation in his thinking, which is worked out through his confrontation with Hegel. It was only during the period of Heidegger's publicly avowed Hitlerism, a period that largely coincides with his tenure as rector of Freiburg University (the period of "the rectorate"), that Heidegger asserted the identity of the German state with "being" itself. It is only in this period that Heidegger speaks of being as if being possessed a kind of agency in itself. In a lecture course from the winter semester of 1933 he speaks of "the *superior power of being*," which roots man in language.[3] The word Heidegger employs—*Übermacht*—has the suggestion of what is superior by means of what "overpowers." The section from which it comes is headed "The Binding-Together of Man in the Superior Power of Being and the Necessity of Language."[4] The importance of the relation of the human being to language is something which will be essential for us to explore in relation both to the Greek definition of man as *zōon logon echon* (the living being having, and held, in language) and in relation to Marx's own understanding of language.[5]

Heidegger made a marginal note next to the phrase "the superior

3. Martin Heidegger, *Sein und Wahrheit* (GA36/37), 101. "Die *Übermacht des Seins!*" (Heidegger's emphasis).

4. Ibid., 100. "Die Gebundenheit des Menschen in die Übermacht des Seins und die Notwendigkeit der Sprache."

5. See chapter 10.

power of being," which the editor of the text thinks was added "presumably later," and which simply says "the other way around!"[6] What does "the other way around" mean? Does it mean the text should have spoken of "the superior being of power"? How is this different from "the superior power of being"—in the context of the overpowering force of the state which Nazism unleashed first onto Germany and then on to the world, how would this reversal have said anything different? The manuscripts of *Das Ereignis* return not once, but over and over again to the question of power—to asking "what" is power in its essence and how power manifests itself. At the same time, the "power" of power has—even more so since Foucault's indebtedness to Nietzsche—become the way in which we interpret the modern subject and the present age. Posed within the question of the essence of language, the binding of power and language suggests something like Lacan's "law of the father," the possession of the power of the whole symbolic order: whoever can lay claim to possess *this* power has the means to overpower all.

Heidegger's understanding of power is quite other. Especially the manuscripts of *Das Ereignis* explore the essence of *Machenschaft*—often translated as "machination" (not incorrectly, with all the connotations of manipulation that seem concealed in the exercise of power),[7] but which could also be transliterated as "powerhood." Reversals, as Heidegger himself often argued (especially, for instance, in relation to Nietzsche's reversal of Platonism, and as I have argued with Marx's seeming overturning of Hegel) do not depart from the originary ground which they at the same time appear to overturn. To indicate a genuine transformation in Heidegger's thought we would seek, not a mere overturning ("the superior power of being": "the superior being of power") but a stepping away, which allows us to understand how it is that the overpowering claim—the claim that had us in its grip—could have been made at all. We have already seen how that stepping-away is carried through, for instance, in the "stilling" that Heidegger opens out in his reading of Hölderlin. Overturning the superiority of being means stepping back into the "still": not the power, but the power*lessness* of being. Be-ing, for itself, Heidegger came later to unfold in his thinking, is without power.

What then is the binding of being to language? The powerful, overpowering "word" is the shout, the utterance which overlays and drowns out all else that is said or heard. The "powerless" in relation to the word is en-

6. Martin Heidegger, *Sein und Wahrheit* (*GA*36/37), 101. "Anmerkung des Herausgebers: Vermutlich späterer Zusatz Heideggers: umgekehrt!" ("Editor's remark: Heidegger's presumably later addition: "the other way around!")

7. See especially Martin Heidegger, *Die Geschichte des Seyns* (*GA*69), §§40–43, which deal with "the concept of machination," "machination and devastation," and "'total war.'" Almost the entire fourth section of this work is a consideration of "power" (*Macht*).

countered in learning to hear. In German to hear (*hören*) and to belong (*gehören*) have the same root. To understand man as the *zōon logon echon* is to understand, not that man has language, and so has the power of the word in his possession and at his disposal, but rather that he only enters the essence of language and expresses how he is bound to it, in belonging. To belong to language is to know how to hear what is spoken: to be still. To be still is to lay aside one's own power for the sake of being taken up into the power the word has for itself. Later, as we shall see, Heidegger repeatedly says in many diverse texts that it is not man who speaks, but language. Heidegger argues: "Language speaks, not man. Man speaks [*spricht*], only inasmuch as he fatefully corresponds [*entspricht*] to language."[8] To correspond in this way is to belong, and so to hear, as much as to say. The "fatedness" in question, which could also be thought of as a "sending," is man's belonging to be-ing. We will not be able to understand fully what Heidegger is seeking to say here until chapter 10. It is only through Heidegger's political engagement, his embracing of what, and whoever, seeks and strives to overpower all, and then his stepping away from that overpowering, that enabled him to name and explain the essence of language. Without that, the productive dialogue with Marx would never have moved beyond mere standpoints, the mere taking up of political "positions," to attempt, at least, to reach a more original understanding. How did that stepping-away become possible, and what was manifest in it? This chapter is an attempt to answer that question.

Heidegger became a member of the Nazi Party, the NSDAP, on the first day of May—May Day—1933.[9] Just ten days before he had been elected rector of Freiburg University. On May 27 he gave his notorious rectorial address: the formal speech of accession to this public, indeed national, position in German life as rector of one of its leading universities: the so-called *Rektoratsrede.* The Nazis had finally attained a majority in the German parliament only in March 1933, after the Reichstag fire of February 27, 1933, the pretext itself for both the banning of the German Communist Party (KPD), and the arrest of its leaders and silencing of its organs, and the unleashing of a terror on all the parties and organizations across the spectrum of the Left, and Hitler's assumption of emergency powers through persuading President von Hindenburg to sign the "Reichstag Fire Decree."

The facts of Heidegger's involvement with Nazism are well known and straightforward: having joined the NSDAP in 1933 he never actually left it, to the point where the occupation of the Allied forces brought its activities

8. Martin Heidegger, *Der Satz vom Grund* (*GA*10), 143. "Die Sprache spricht, nicht der Mensch. Der Mensch spricht nur, indem er geschicklich der Sprache *entspricht.*"

9. NSDAP: Nationalsozialistische Deutsche Arbeiterpartei, or National Socialist German Workers Party.

to a close: on the other hand, to have attempted to leave the party without leaving the country would have been dangerous—possibly mortally—for him and his family. Heidegger appears to have been, even in the period immediately prior to 1933, a supporter of Hitler in some degree, and after 1933 enthusiastically so, at least until around the point of his resignation as rector of Freiburg University, ceasing to hold this office on May 2, 1934. From then on he privately became increasingly critical of the regime, and in public in ways that were only (and necessarily, given his desire to stay alive) coded. In commenting on Heidegger's situation, and indeed on the situation of the German nation generally, in the period 1933–45, it is all too often overlooked that what the Nazis instituted in the wake of the increasing political turbulence following the end of war in 1918 and the humiliation of the peace in 1919, was nothing short of a terror unleashed on the whole of German life. Some welcomed this terror; a multitude found ways to coexist with it; many fell foul of it—wittingly or unwittingly; few, if any, could possibly have doubted it for what it was. Its violence, its disappearances, the form (if not the horrific facts) of its death-dealing machinery were visible, and were intended to be visible, to all. If, after the ceaseless turbulence of revolution, the disintegration of the currency, mass unemployment on a scale unknown anywhere else in Europe, and international humiliation, the terror brought in its wake stability, employment, and the restoration of social and national self-confidence (provided you were not a leftist, Jew, homosexual, or any of the many other categories of enmity of the new state), it did so at horrific price, even before the engines of systematic mass extermination began to grind.

An essential element of the Nazi assumption of power was, even before the enactment of racial laws and the systematic and criminal persecution of anyone designated to be "racially Jewish," the crushing of all left-wing, socialist, communist, and trades-union opposition. Richard Evans notes that "with the communists already effectively out of the way . . . the regime now turned its attention to the Social Democrats."[10] The German socialist party, the SPD, was banned on June 22, 1933.

This was in many ways only the culmination of the sequence of events and political turmoil that followed on from the cease-fire of 1918, the armistice, and Germany's final admission of defeat in 1919. Between then and 1933 there had been repeated attempts at a socialist revolution in Germany, beginning with the declaration of a short-lived Soviet Republic of Bavaria (the "Munich Republic") on April 7, 1919. In 1945 Heidegger commented: "I saw at the time in the movement that had come to power the possibility

10. Richard J. Evans, *The Coming of the Third Reich,* 355.

for an inner marshaling and renewal of the people and a path toward discovering its historical-Occidental destiny. I believed that the university, in its self-renewal might also be called authoritatively to work together with the inner marshaling of the people."[11]

It is almost impossible for us to measure the distance between contemporary political turmoils and the turbulence of the European situation after the First World War. We have almost nothing to hand from Heidegger himself about his personal estimation of the situation facing Germany in advance of his actual political engagement. A letter from his wife, Elfride, to Elfriede Lieber, in 1932, conveys, however, important elements of the situation and outlook of the period. Elfride Heidegger writes of the disastrous situation following the Versailles treaty, of Germany's impoverishment, and of all the ills that had been warned and prophesied by the political right for "a nation [*Volk*] threatened and economically *absolutely* ruined from all sides."[12] Elfride Heidegger is careful to stress that she is uninterested in the aspects of the trappings of nationalism, of pretty blue dresses, dirndls, and the like. The real issue is the Left, and the fear of communism following the Russian Revolution and its effects throughout Europe: she hopes for the down-throwing of Bolshevism by National Socialism. Once again, the fate of Europe is what is here to be decided. Bolshevism is nothing with which one may do business, as at the time of the French Revolution. It is as enormous a transformation as Christianity itself was for Germanic pre-Christianity, though for the opposite reasons: "I am now of the opinion that the Bolshevik danger has already become so enormous—together with the Jewish-Marxist groundwork of the SPD."[13]

However offensive antisemitism is, notwithstanding our absolute rejection of it in all its forms, and however we trace the roots and origins of the Holocaust in the trajectory of antisemitism, we must understand that antisemitism takes a qualitatively different form now than it did in the prewar period. In prewar Germany, both Right and Left appropriated antisemitism

11. Heidegger, Martin, "Das Rektorat 1933/34" (*GA*16), 374. "Ich sah damals in der zur Macht gekommenen Bewegung die Möglichkeit zu einer inneren Sammlung und Erneuerung des Volkes und einen Weg, zu einer geschichtlich-abendländischen Bestimmung zu finden. Ich glaubte, die sich selbst erneuernde Universität könnte mitberufen sein, bei der inneren Sammlung des Volkes maß-gebend mitzuwirken."

12. Elfride Heidegger, letter to Elfriede Lieber of January 12, 1932, *Heidegger-Jahrbuch*, 4: 268. "Von allen Seiten bedrohtes und wirtschaftlich *absolut* ruiniertes Volk" (Elfride Heidegger's emphasis).

13. Elfride Heidegger, letter to Elfriede Lieber, *Heidegger-Jahrbuch*, 4:269. "Ich bin nun der Meinung, dass die bolschewistische Gefahr schon so riesengroß geworden ist—auch der jüdisch-marxistischen Vorarbeit der SPD."

in their propaganda. Evans gives an example of the identification of communism with Jews in his *The Coming of the Third Reich,* citing a propaganda cartoon of the May 14, 1933, where a communist activist receives a clean-up, "a 'cut (hair and beard)'—the German word is the same as that for circumcision,"[14] and gets "exercised" in a concentration camp, resulting in his effective "arianisation" and so the "normalisation" of the "malcontent," trading on middle-class fears of the communist threat that associated "criminality, poverty, and extreme left-wing commitment."[15]

Hitler routinely refers in *Mein Kampf* to Marxism as a threat arising from "the contents and striving of the Jew Karl Marx's life's work,"[16] and the rancid antisemitism of the entire text prompts the appropriate scholarly question, "Why was Nazism's murderous threat to Jews not visible from the beginning?" The answer is that antisemitism was not the peculiar property of the political right, as the historian Michael Burleigh points out through the words of the Marxist, half-Jewish, German KPD activist Ruth Fischer, when he quotes her saying "whoever cries out against Jewish capital is already a class warrior, even when he does not know it . . . Kick down the Jewish capitalists, hang them from the lampposts, and stamp on them!"[17] Walter Dorn notes that Fischer "supplies a full and precise report on the Comintern and Stalin's conquest of the German Communist Party at a time when she herself played a leading part."[18] Fischer was hardly unrepresentative. Why she argued what she did we will return to later.[19]

None of this mollifies the evil of antisemitism either at the time or that was wrought in the Holocaust: it does, however, show the extent to which antisemitism was part of the backdrop of political rhetoric (to left and right), more than many Heidegger commentators—those seeking to exonerate or condemn—have bothered to explain.

Heidegger was not above a certain antisemitism himself, speaking in 1929 in a letter of the "Jewification of the German intellectual life,"[20] al-

14. Richard J. Evans, *The Coming of the Third Reich,* 382 and following, plate 26.

15. See Ibid., 206 and following, caption on plate 16.

16. Adolf Hitler, *Mein Kampf,* 234. "Ich begann wieder zu lernen und kam nun erst recht zum Verständnis des Inhaltes und Wollens der Lebensarbeit des Juden Karl Marx."

17. Michael Burleigh, *The Third Reich,* 55, citing Ossip K. Flechtheim, *Die KPD in der Weimarer Republik,* 178. "Wer gegen das Juden-Kapital aufruft . . . ist schon Klassenkämpfer, auch wenn er es nicht weiß . . . Tretet die Juden-Kapitalisten nieder, hängt sie an die Laterne, zertrampelt sie!" (modified from Burleigh's translation).

18. Walter L. Dorn, review of *Die Kommunistische Partei Deutschlands* in *American Historical Review,* 901.

19. See 194 and following.

20. Martin Heidegger, letter of 1929, reproduced by Ulrich Sieg in *Die Zeit,* December 22, 1989, 50. "Die Verjudung des deutschen Geistes."

though now we have a context for this nevertheless shocking statement, as one as much about the political as the racial character of those Heidegger seeks to describe. There are other similar statements.[21] We raise this question of antisemitism, both of the times and in Heidegger, for two reasons. First, because it is impossible to confront Nazism today without also confronting the question of the Holocaust, the primary effect of the biological racism of the Nazi regime and its defining crime; second, because the interpretation of Marxism, an interpretation in which Heidegger himself was implicated, although only indirectly and in a way that has so far been impossible to prove with any precision (which is why I cite the letter of Heidegger's wife, as opposed to anything of Heidegger himself) is the association of Marxism with "Jewish thinking," worse, the "Jewification of thought."

Whether Marx was a Jew or not, whether "Jewification" is to be taken synonymously with "Bolshevization," I hope we have seen already that Marxism itself is intrinsic to the history of Occidental thought in its metaphysical forgetfulness—intrinsic to the Greek understanding of being as Heidegger himself understood it, intrinsic as much in the German Lutherans Hegel and Nietzsche, as the Jew Marx and the Catholic Heidegger. There is no psychological explanation, no racial explanation, nothing biological, that I want to bring to bear here on Heidegger's Nazism, on Marx's communism, on Nietzsche's nihilism. I cannot explain the Jew (or even the Muslim) then or now as the "outsider" precisely because the historical Jew, the historical Muslim, the historical Christian are nothing of the kind, as Heidegger himself well knew: the metaphysical determinations of Jewish, Muslim, and Christian theism are, for good or for ill, like it or not, European in their ground and Occidental in their origin whenever they are a metaphysics.[22] We are interested only in an account of the forgottenness of being (*Seinsvergessenheit*) and in bringing to an adequate description Marx's humanism.

To unfold the productive dialogue it is necessary neither to evade nor to overcome Heidegger's engagement with National Socialism. It is also necessary to interpret this engagement historically, as the event that it is, and so not as evidence of an already existing "mind-set" or predispositions or some such. Ernst Jünger's essay *Total Mobilisation* had spoken in 1930 of the political movements of fascism, Bolshevism, Americanism, Zionism,

21. For a full, scholarly, catalogue of Heidegger's antisemitic statements that have come to light so far, see Thomas Sheehan, "A Normal Nazi," in *New York Review of Books*, January 14, 1993, 30–35.

22. It is only as faith that each can come into its own, as unfolding the God of Israel, of Jesus, of Mohammed. Here we depart utterly from the province of philosophy and enter the realm of a revelation which is *not* Occidental in its root: insofar as the Abrahamic God speaks, God reveals God for himself.

and others, a language Heidegger also takes up in the prewar period.[23] The question is always Europe and (for Heidegger) its destiny as the Occident. After the war Heidegger modified the language of "Americanism" to "world democracy," such that everything is "the universal rule of the will to power within planetary history. Today everything is part of this reality, whether it is called communism, or fascism, or world democracy."[24] The development and existence of America and Russia, as events in history, however, originate in Europe. Heidegger speaks of an *Entmachtigung des Geistes,* which, characterizing both America and Russia, nevertheless originates in nineteenth-century Europe as a "collapsing of German idealism."[25] How are we to translate *Entmachtigung des Geistes*? Perhaps the most demanding word is *Geist,* which we have already encountered as spirit, intellection, life, religion, piety. *Geist* names the being of being human: it as much names the *being* of being human as the *humanity* of being human. *Geist* is what is proper to man and yet never owned by him: in this sense the *Phenomenology* as a phenomenology of absolute subjectivity was both a pinnacle, the *Vollendung,* the fulfillment of metaphysics, and its *Zusammenbruch,* its collapse. What Heidegger names here, as the specter of Europe's "collapse," is an *Entmachtigung,* a vitiation of the powers, of the end of metaphysics: a "disempowering" that is not a mere slide into decline, but the very naming of the continual declining, of the continual falling-away while always having the pinnacle in sight. Marxism is the latest and last of these, which is why its understanding of history is superior, it is the preparation for the history that is to come.

If Russia and America are thoroughgoingly events of European metaphysics, they are this because the whole world is at issue. Heidegger asks, "What does world mean, when we speak of a world-darkening? World is always *geistige* World."[26] The question before Europe is the question of being: " 'Is 'being' a mere word and its meaning a vapor, or the *geistige* destiny of the Occident?' "[27] Whatever can be called *geistig* is counterposed—precisely—to the material. We have therefore to understand that Heidegger's own support for, and passing through, Hitler, National Socialism, and the darkness of

23. Ernst Jünger, "Die Totale Mobilmachung," 27; Martin Heidegger, *Grundfragen der Philosophie: Ausgewählte "Probleme" der "Logik"* (*GA*45), 54.

24. Martin Heidegger, "Das Rektorat" (*GA*16), 375. "Die universale Herrschaft des Willens zur Macht innerhalb der planetarisch gesehenen Geschichte. In dieser Wirklichkeit steht heute Alles, mag es Kommunismus heißen oder Faschismus oder Weltdemokratie."

25. Martin Heidegger, *Einführung in die Metaphysik* (*GA*40), 49. "Zusammenbruch des deutschen Idealismus."

26. Ibid., 48. "Was heißt Welt, wenn wir von der Weltverdüsterung sprechen? Welt ist immer *geistige* Welt" (Heidegger's emphasis).

27. Ibid., 40. "Ist das 'Sein' ein bloßes Wort und seine Bedeutung ein Dunst, oder das geistige Schicksal des Abendlandes?"

Germany between 1933 and 1945 is, and retained after, the search for the adequate questioning that counterposed all that is *geistig* to the materialism of metaphysics—be it fascist, communist, or "world democratic" ("American"). In his rectorial address Heidegger had understood the situation of 1933 to be that very danger, that would nevertheless be the calling forward and placing of Germany such that "in the outermost questionableness of their ownmost existence [*Dasein*], will this people be a *geistiges* people."[28] Heidegger's Nazism originated, and is overcome, precisely here.

Jacques Derrida, in an essay translated as "Heidegger: The Philosopher's Hell" that was penned as a response to Victor Farías's *Heidegger and Nazism,*[29] raises questions central to our inquiry when he draws attention to the necessity of how, in Heidegger, there is no break with "other European discourses," but precisely "between 1919 and 1940, everyone was wondering (but are we not still wondering the same thing today?): 'what is Europe to become?' "[30] In this Derrida is (justifiably, as the texts were unavailable to him) unaware of Heidegger's increasing distinction between "Europe" and "Occidental thinking," and the emergence of the second Heidegger contained in the notebooks of *Das Ereignis.* Derrida interprets the period of the rectorate as the limitation of "the deconstructive movement that he had begun earlier. He maintains a voluntarist and metaphysical discourse upon which he will later cast suspicion. To this extent at least, the elevation of spirit, through the celebration of its freedom, resembles other European discourses (spiritualist, religious, humanist) which are generally opposed to Nazism. This is a complex and unstable knowledge which I try to untangle by recognizing the threads common to Nazism and anti-Nazism."[31] Tom Sheehan pushes this much further, annihilating the subtlety of the instability which Derrida attempts to name, by naming what he sees as the more pedestrian version, current in much Heidegger commentary: "Derrida attributes Heidegger's support for Hitler to a misguided 'metaphysical humanism' and subjectivism that blinded Heidegger for a while to the true mystery of Being. In 1933 this

28. Martin Heidegger, "Die Selbstbehauptung der deutschen Universität" (*GA*16), 113. "So ausgesetzt in die äußere Fragwürdigkeit des eigenen Daseins, will dies Volk ein geistiges Volk sein."

29. Jacques Derrida, "La réponse de Jacques Derrida à V. Farías."

30. Ibid. "Entre 1919 et 1940 (mais ne le fait-on pas encore aujourd'hui?) tout le monde se demande: 'Que va devenir l'Europe?' " See 185 of the English translation.

31. Ibid. "Le mouvement déconstructeur qu'il avait auparavant engagé. Il tient un discours volontariste et métaphysique qu'il suspectera par la suite. Dans cette mesure au moins, en célébrant la liberté de l'esprit, son élévation ressemble à d'autres discours européens (spiritualistes, religieux, humanistes) qu'en général on oppose au nazisme. Écheveau complexe et instable que j'essaie de démêler en y reconnaissant les fils communs au nazisme et à l'antinazisme." See 185 of the English translation.

metaphysical myopia misled Heidegger into viewing Nietzsche as a philosophical antidote—and Nazism as a socio-political one—to the rampant nihilism and technology that Heidegger saw as devastating the globe."[32]

Should we concur? Are we pressed to find here an "answer" to Heidegger's own humanism, which Derrida conjures and Sheehan names, or is something altogether more fundamentally *historical* at work? In considering Heidegger's relation to politics, and especially the politics of National Socialism, without doubt, Heidegger (as he himself noted after the war) had hoped to be a reforming influence on the movement that he perceived to be underway in National Socialism. He understood himself as one able to lead "all capable forces" toward "the possibility of an inner marshaling and renewal of the people." This was in virtue of "the movement that had come to power."[33] Heidegger's political involvement is not, therefore, driven by the plan to conform the polis to an already existing understanding of laws, but rather the sense of attending to, and being constrained to, a demand, namely that of "the entire situation of our people."[34] We could, as we proceed, take the direction sought by not a few others, seeking to establish, against Lévinas and Löwith, among others, the "fundamental connection" between the Nazi Heidegger and Heidegger's thinking—above all his thinking from the 1930s and the book *Being and Time.*

A suggestion of this kind also comes from Löwith, who, at a meeting with Heidegger in Rome in 1936 (Löwith, racially Jewish, there in exile), reports that he put to Heidegger "that his partisanship for national socialism lay in his philosophy. Heidegger agreed with me without reservation, and added that his concept of 'historicity' formed the basis of his political 'engagement.'"[35] What Löwith heard on that occasion, and what Heidegger actually said, are of the essence of the matter at hand. *Being and Time,* this thesis runs, although published in 1927 and so a full six years before Hitler took power, nevertheless pressed Heidegger toward an engagement for which he was already fatally committed. This has been the view of Victor Farías,[36] and most recently Emmanuel Faye, for whom Heidegger "conse-

32. Thomas Sheehan, "A Normal Nazi," 31.

33. Heidegger, Martin, "Das Rektorat" (*GA*16), 374. "Alle vermögenden Kräfte . . . zu einer inneren Sammlung und Erneuerung des Volkes maß-gebend mitzuwirken," "in der zur Macht gekommenen Bewegung."

34. Ibid., 375. "Die Gesamtlage unseres Volkes."

35. Karl Löwith, *Mein Leben in Deutschland vor und nach 1933,* 57. "Daß seine Parteinahme für den Nationalsozialismus im Wesen seiner Philosophie läge. Heidegger stimmte mir ohne Vorbehalt zu und führte mir aus, daß sein Begriff von der 'Geschichtlichkeit' die Grundlage für seinen politischen 'Einsatz' sei."

36. See also: Philippe Lacoue-Labarthe, *La fiction du politique;* Victor Farías, *Heidegger et la nazisme,* translated into German as *Heidegger und der Nationalsozialismus*—the German edi-

crated himself to placing philosophy as such in the service of the legitimation and diffusion of the very foundations of Nazism and Hitlerism."[37]

Even more serious attempts to trace the link between *Being and Time* and Heidegger's understanding of the political than that of either Fariás's or Faye's all too often fail precisely because in trying to explain how the writer of so remarkable a work could have fallen for the Nazi claptrap, they end up resorting to arguments that are all too often tendentious, or excessively psychologizing, or that simply twist the facts. Too much has been made by not a few of the only (and single) occurrence of a word with a Nazi resonance, the reference to *Volk* in §74 of *Being and Time* that I have already drawn attention to,[38] when we have already seen that not only Hegel but also Marx freely uses this word. Faye, for whom anyone who rejects the Cartesian account of subjectivity is suspect, extrapolates from this single mention that the whole of *Being and Time* encompasses the "destruction of the individual and the human self to give place to the community of the destiny of the people . . . with the doctrine of *Volksgemeinschaft*."[39] The demand and the perplexity with Heidegger is not so much that we should find either the place or the voice with which to judge, such that we can declare ourselves free of any contamination with Nazism because we now know how much or little, where, and on what terms, Heidegger the Nazi is to be found, but rather that we should understand the place from out of which Heidegger sought to speak. Understanding requires us to step back from judgment, to withhold from every claim that we already *know*. It requires that we allow ourselves to be addressed by what addressed Heidegger, and what he believed demanded to be said.

If we can agree with James Phillips that "Heidegger's engagement with National Socialism is clearly inextricable from his ontology,"[40] the inverse does not follow—that Heidegger's ontology *necessarily* entailed his engagement with National Socialism. The most we can say—something which Heidegger himself *did* say—is that *historically* Heidegger's National Socialist engagement arose on the basis of his interpretation of being. In 1966, in the *Spiegel* interview, Heidegger said "at that time [*damals*] I saw no other

---

tion is an expanded and corrected version of the French text. The English edition *Heidegger and Nazism* appears to be a version of the French edition.

37. Emmanuel Faye, *Heidegger: L'introduction du nazisme dans la philosophie*, 8. "Heidegger s'est consacré à mettre la philosophie au service de la légitimation et la diffusion des fondements mêmes du nazisme et l'hitlérisme."

38. Martin Heidegger, *Sein und Zeit* (*GA*2), 508.

39. Emmanuel Faye, *Heidegger: L'introduction du nazisme dans la philosophie*, 33. "La destruction de l'individu et du *moi* humain pour laisser place à la communauté de destin du peuple . . . avec sa doctrine de la *Volksgemeinschaft*."

40. James Phillips, *Heidegger's Volk: Between National Socialism and Poetry*, 41.

alternative."[41] We seek an understanding that does not exculpate Heidegger from his engagement with Nazism, and so that does not, as some commentators might seem to have done, simply say "it does not matter," thereby separating his politics from his philosophy precisely at the point where we want to ask about Heidegger's political engagement. Heidegger did not himself seek any exculpation, saying (reportedly) of his accession to the rectorate of Freiburg University in May 1933 that it "had been the greatest stupidity of his life"—this, we are led to believe, shortly after resigning in April 1934.[42] The deliberation that arises about Heidegger's engagement with National Socialism itself arises historically—which is to say who we are *now* is also as much in question in this deliberation as who Heidegger was and is. To do less than attempt to hold open this place in order to understand means we will never actually enter the essential character of what it is to deliberate historically.

In 1945 Heidegger wrote to Constantin von Dietze, who had been appointed by the French to assess the political situation of the university's faculty members in the Nazi period,[43] making the case that even in 1933–34 he had opposed the Nazi worldview, in the hope that the movement of which it was the head might take a quite different passage, one that would have identified with the social and general political tendency of the revolution that had begun. He added:

> I believed that Hitler would, after he assumed responsibility for the whole people in 1933, rise above the party and its doctrine, and that all would come together from a ground of renewal and marshaling in an assumption of responsibility for the Occident. This belief was an error, which I recognized from the events of June 30th 1934.[44] It brought me, however, into the intermediate position, that I affirmed the social and national (not nationalistic) and denied the intellectual and metaphysical foundations of the biologism of the party doctrine, because the social and national, as I saw it, were not essentially bound up in a biological-racial worldview.[45]

41. Martin Heidegger, "*Spiegel*-Gespräch mit Martin Heidegger" (*GA*16), 655. "Ich sah damals keine andere Alternative." Published the day after Heidegger's death on May 31, 1976.

42. Reported in Heinrich Wiegand Petzet, *Auf einen Stern zugehen*, 43. "Es sei die größte Dummheit seines Lebens gewesen."

43. For a discussion of this process and the role of von Dietze and his colleagues Gerhard Ritter and Adolf Lampe, see Rüdiger Safranski, *Ein Meister aus Deutschland*, 374–75.

44. The events of the "Night of the Long Knives" or Röhm Putsch, June 30—July 2, 1934.

45. Martin Heidegger, "Erläuterungen und grundsätzliches," letter to Professor Constantin von Dietze of December 15, 1945 (*GA*16), 414. "Ich glaubte, Hitler werde, nachdem er 1933 in der Verantwortung für das ganze Volk stand, über die Partei und ihre Doktrin hinauswachsen und alles würde sich auf den Boden einer Erneuerung und Sammlung zu einer abendländischen Verantwortung zusammenfinden. Dieser Glaube war ein Irrtum, den ich aus den Vorgängen des 30. Juni 1934 erkannte. Er hatte mich aber 1933/34 in die Zwischenstellung gebracht,

If my interpretation of Heidegger so far is correct, it confirms the outlines of this statement.

Once again, the issue here is Europe, entangled in a metaphysics that also cannot avoid biologism, in contrast to the destiny of the Occident in which biologism has no part. It is simply not possible for us in the space allotted to examine this question further: nevertheless Heidegger's opposition to biologism is in its very ground an opposition to metaphysics, which itself is for him only possible because of the history of the forgottenness of being.

If we begin by accepting the conventional narrative of Heidegger's life and work, taking the narrative suggested by, let us say, Emmanuel Lévinas as a (not entirely innocently) chosen example, then we will read Heidegger's central work *Being and Time* and the structural analytic of *Dasein* it contains as a recapitulation of subjectivity of the human subject.[46] We will, in turn, announce our fastidiously unimpeachable horror at Heidegger's disastrous political adventure of 1933 and his subsequent collaboration with Nazism. If we pursue this reading, we end up, perhaps with Lévinas and Karl Löwith, bracketing *Being and Time* out of the rest of Heidegger, thereby "rescuing" it from the rest of Heidegger's works which are otherwise *all* polluted with National Socialism. In this we follow the suggestion, often made (and that we have seen already from Otto Pöggeler), that the postwar Heidegger, as much as the Heidegger of up to 1945, never morally or intellectually left the Nazi Party.

There is in Heidegger's notebooks that collectively run under the title *Das Ereignis* an at times quite explicit criticism of the regime and what it represented which has yet to be fully examined, partly because so much of it is so newly published, partly because there is now such an industry (even among Heidegger's supporters) of ritual denunciation of Heidegger's Nazism without any serious inquiry into what form it took, or how Heidegger's thought developed in relation to the events through which he lived, and so what it all meant. Fred Dallmayr has examined much of this material and

---

daß ich das Soziale und Nationale (nicht nationalistische) bejahte und die geistige und metaphysische Grundlegung durch den Biologismus der Parteidoktrin verneinte, weil das Soziale und Nationale, wie ich es sah, nicht wesensmäßig an die biologisch-rassische Weltanschauungslehre geknüpft war." This passage has been cited by various authors—see Jacques Derrida, "La main de Heidegger" in *Psyché: Inventions de l'autre II*, 39–40; Maurice Blanchot and Paula Wissing (translated by Paula Wissing), "Thinking the Apocalypse: A Letter from Maurice Blanchot to Catherine David," 478; Michael Allen Gillespie, "Martin Heidegger's Aristotelian National Socialism," 142–43. (See note 10, 162.) Gillespie traces the citation only back to Blanchot, without locating it, either in Derrida or in Heidegger, presumably because Blanchot and Wissing provide no page or volume number to the reference in *Psyché*.

46. See, for instance, Emmanuel Lévinas, *Autrement qu'être: ou au-delà de l'essence*, 34. "L'effort heideggerien consiste à penser la subjectivité en fonction de l'être." ("The Heideggerian effort consists in thinking subjectivity as a function of being.")

notes that Heidegger "critiques National Socialism directly by ridiculing its chosen terminology,"[47] pointing to Heidegger's relating of Nazi slogans to an unconditioned subjectivity (a clear reference to Hegel). Heidegger pillories Nazism, saying "the essential consequence of this *subjectivity* is the nationalism of peoples and the socialism of the people."[48] Heidegger comments on the consequences of the Nazi terror unleashed within the nation, and its inevitable result in spilling over national borders to consume all, when he stresses that "the essential consequence of this history of subjectivity is the unlimited struggle for the sake of securing power, and the *limitless wars* which legitimize this power."[49] Dallmayr points to the way the text speaks of how the mighty rulers who seized power "are never 'possessors of power' but rather puppets in the grip of *Macht* and *Machenschaft;* they cannot 'seize' or 'possess' power because they are 'possessed by it' (in the manner of an obsession)."[50] Had this private ridicule become public knowledge, it alone would have been enough to earn him a death sentence. In fact, it is possible to show that what Heidegger makes explicit in his private notebooks is what he does, covertly, but with increasing frequency and boldness in the public lecture courses that are now in the public domain. This is why so much Nazi terminology is to be found, openly being discussed, in them—and so not, therefore, because of his support for the regime. Dallmayr remarks at the beginning of his study that "curiously and uncannily, Heidegger's work is deeply tainted by his complicity with totalitarian (fascist) oppression—despite the fact that his work, in its basic tenor, was always dedicated to 'freedom' and resistance to totalising uniformity."[51]

Too many commentators on Heidegger seek to uncover evidence of indications of an antecedent "predisposition" toward Nazism in his work before 1933. This essentially psychological approach to the man and his work has the effect of dehistoricizing the significance of Heidegger's work before, and during, the Nazi engagement itself. It provides no assistance in bringing us into a closer understanding of Heidegger. If National Socialism, or the turbulent history of the Germany of 1919–33, had never existed, Heidegger's

47. Fred Dallmayr, "Heidegger on *Macht* and *Machenschaft,*" 257, commenting in particular on one of the notebooks that constitutes the series *Das Ereignis, Die Geschichte des Seyns* (*GA*69).

48. Martin Heidegger, *Die Geschichte des Seyns* (*GA*69), 44. "Die Wesenfolge der *Subjektivität* ist der Nationalismus der Völker und der Sozialismus des Volkes." (Heidegger's emphasis: I have slightly modified Dallmayr's translation.)

49. Martin Heidegger, *Die Geschichte des Seyns* (*GA*69), 44. "Die Wesenfolge dieser Geschichte der Subjektivität ist der uneingeschränkte Kampf um die Sicherung der Macht und deshalb die *grenzlosen Kriege,* die die Machtermächtingung übernehmen" (Heidegger's emphasis).

50. Fred Dallmayr, "Heidegger on *Macht* and *Machenschaft,*" 257, commenting on 63–64 of Martin Heidegger, *Die Geschichte des Seyns* (*GA*69).

51. Fred Dallmayr, "Heidegger on *Macht* and *Machenschaft,*" 247.

National Socialist engagement would never have become clear in the way it did. This does not mean his National Socialism is irrelevant: quite the contrary. Material and historical conditions are an inescapable part of the very ground of who we are. Both Marx and Heidegger need to be understood from out of the historical situations in which they lived, and thought, and wrote. Both emphasize the facticity of life itself, as the only basis from out of which thinking can think. "Facticity" is a fundamental term of Heidegger's right from the beginning of his public lectures, from the very first lecture courses we have. He repeats frequently a phrase that is also central to the "father" of phenomenology, Edmund Husserl, and that originates with that first phenomenologist, Hegel—"all thinking is thinking of *something.*" Both Marx and Heidegger must be interpreted historically, and we in interpreting, must interpret them while bringing into view and keeping ahead of us the historical situation, our own facticity and materiality, in which we now read them.

Heidegger consistently distinguished between the Nazi Party and the "movement" that had brought it to power, in a way that has been too rarely acknowledged. In this Heidegger stands perhaps at his closest to Marx's own understanding of revolutionary change, in understanding there to be a historical mission and destiny of a people (the proletariat, the German nation) which is fulfilled by a revolutionary event, where that event is transformative of the "essence of man" and the "people" on a mass scale. In a lecture course given during the period of the rectorate, Heidegger argued: "When today the Führer speaks again and again of the reeducation for the national socialist worldview, this does not mean: spouting a few catchphrases, but bringing about an *entire transformation,* a *world-design* from out of whose ground he brings the whole people up."[52] In stark contrast to the interpretation of Hölderlin we saw Heidegger develop in the previous chapter, he argues in this same course, "philosophy arises from the *ownmost needfulness and strength of humanity* and *not* from *God.*"[53] This is probably one of the last times that Heidegger asserts the pure atheism of philosophy, and this claim stands in contrast to the understanding of the "Last God" that is discussed in the texts of *Das Ereignis,* developed from 1936 onward. From this period onward Heidegger increasingly separates speaking of "philosophy" from "thinking." The atheistic language of philosophy—which is at the same time the language of metaphysics—is *that* language he employs consciously,

52. Martin Heidegger, *Sein und Wahrheit* (GA36/37), 225. "Wenn heute der Führer immer wieder spricht von der Umerziehung zur national-sozialistischen Weltanschauung, heißt das nicht: irgendwelche Schlagworte beibringen, sondern einen *Gesamtwandel* hervorbringen, einen *Weltentwurf,* aus dessen Grund heraus er das ganze Volk erzieht."

53. Ibid., 10. "Philosophie entspringt der *eigensten Not und Kraft des Menschen* und *nicht* des *Gottes*" (Heidegger's emphases).

and directs to academic audiences unfamiliar with his work. We recall the phrase "the other language lies in the background." The language of thinking *is* able to speak of God, the "Last God," but only as a questioning.

In this period, if in no other, Heidegger must be understood as a *politically* revolutionary thinker, no matter how much we might be revolted by the revolution he celebrates. If Heidegger adopted a revolutionary attitude in the political sphere in the period 1933–34, we should understand this as the fundamental connection between his political understanding and his thinking. In his lectures in 1935, in the context of providing students access to the thought of Parmenides and Heraclitus and their relation to Nietzsche, there is again a detectable shift in emphasis away from the Hitlerism of the rectorate and toward the themes of the notebooks of *Das Ereignis*. Here Heidegger argues: "Ever and always must we impress on ourselves: exactly because we dare to take up the great and lengthy task of dismantling a world grown old, and truly, that is, historically, building it anew, we must know the tradition."[54] Heidegger stresses the need for the most radical historical knowledge, to avoid the repetition of "mere restoration and uncreative imitation." Text after text of Heidegger's that deals with the Nazi period speaks of the "movement," a movement that, we assume, Heidegger believed had arisen to be equal to this task, essentially a movement of and from, the people themselves, and which he increasingly understands to be quite distinct from the party apparatus.

When in 1956, in his *Festschrift* piece for Ernst Jünger, Heidegger employs the phrase "movement of nihilism" (*Bewegung des Nihilismus*), although clearly a reference to the ferment of the Germany of 1933–45 and specifically to the Nazi Party itself, it is not so clear that this does not also refer to the movement that brought Nazism to power.[55] Heidegger also uses the phrase in his *Nietzsche* lectures of 1937 onward, where nihilism itself is referred to as a "movement."[56] Heidegger argues "if European nihilism is not simply *one* historical movement among others, but *the* fundamental ground-movement [*Grundbewegung*] of our history, then the interpretation of nihilism and our viewpoint with respect to it from our relation to history in general, depends on whether and how the history of our humanity and being-human determines itself."[57] The 1961 edition of these lectures alters

54. Martin Heidegger, *Einführung in die Metaphysik* (*GA*40), 134. "Immer wieder muß eingeschärft werden: Gerade weil wir uns an die große und lange Aufgabe wagen, eine altgewordene Welt abzutragen und wahrhaft neu, d. h. geschichtlich zu bauen, müssen wir die Überlieferung wissen. . . . bloßer Wiederherstellung und unschöpferischer Nachahmung."

55. See *Zur Seinsfrage* (*GA*9), 386, 391–93, and 395.

56. Martin Heidegger, *Der europäische Nihilismus* (*GA*48), 61 (= *Nietzsche* [*GA*6.2], 101).

57. Ibid., 61 (*GA*6.2, 101). "Wenn nun aber der europäische Nihilismus nicht nur *eine* geschichtliche Bewegung unter anderen ist, sondern *die* Grundbewegung unserer Geschichte,

these words to intensify their significance within Heidegger's own thought. The last sentence changed the original phrase "humanity and being-human" for "human *Dasein,*" so that the whole reads "then the interpretation of nihilism and our stance with respect to it depend on how and whence the historicity of human existence determines itself for us."[58]

This shift represents the real transformation in Heidegger's thinking from taking over the will to will to abandoning the will to will for the sake of how human existence determines itself "for" us, and so falls to us. It is clear that for a brief moment (the period of the rectorate) he understood the Nazi accession to power as the moment for, not only Germany, but also Europe, to lay claim to an overcoming of the ferment that was itself reflected in the legacy of the culmination of metaphysics in Hegel. To understand how Heidegger was himself transformed in his thinking such that he was able to bring to an adequate description the events of the Nazi period, it is necessary to hear *how* Heidegger himself undergoes a change in his description of history itself.

In the summer of 1933, and so immediately following his accession to the rectorate and the Nazi accession to power, Heidegger lectured under the title "The Basic Question of Philosophy." The opening section is entitled "The *Geistig*-Political Mission as Decisive for the Basic Question."[59] The lectures begin in speaking of the situation in 1933 as the greatest of historical moments, through which the German people are going: "What then is happening? The German people as a whole is coming to itself, which means, finding its leadership. In this leadership the people, having come to itself, creates for itself its state."[60] Knowledge of this mission, Heidegger adds, is rooted from the outset in the heart and will of the people, and its uniqueness.[61]

Against these historical events, Heidegger places the task of philosophy, as the relentlessly questioning struggle concerning the essence (*Wesen*) and being (*Sein*) of beings. He asks whether we have come to understand through this situation the basic question of philosophy (by implication, the question of being, or *Seinsfrage*), and replies: "No—but we know the *direc-*

---

dann hängt die Deutung des Nihilismus und die Stellungnahme zu ihm von unserem Verhältnis zur Geschichte überhaupt ab und d.h. davon, ob und wie die Geschichte unser Menschentum und Menschsein selbst bestimmt."

58. Ibid. (*GA*6.2, 101). "Wie und von woher sich uns die Geschichtlichkeit des menschlichen Daseins bestimmt."

59. Martin Heidegger, *Sein und Wahrheit* (*GA*36/37), 3. "Der geistig-politische Auftrag als Entscheidung zur Grundfrage."

60. Ibid., 3. "Was geschieht denn? Das deutsche Volk im Ganzen kommt zu sich selbst, d.h. findet seine Führung. In dieser Führung schafft das zu sich selbst gekommene Volk seinen Staat."

61. Ibid., 3. "Einzuwurzeln in Herz und Willen des Volkes und seiner Einzelnen."

*tion and the path,* where we are to *arrive in the questioning of this question.*"[62] We therefore know that history must speak, because this questioning is the basic occurrence of our history; that history is not the past, but is what is arriving and in the future; and "that history only speaks if we press it toward confrontation."[63] This confrontation must at the same time spring out of a necessity of our existence (*Dasein*), and must address the pinnacle-position of the whole of history, whose conquest is decisive. This confrontation is, Heidegger says, aimed at one particular philosophical understanding: "in the *confrontation with Hegel* the whole Occidental history of *Geist* before him and after him up to the present speaks to us."[64] To address the basic question of philosophy is to enter into the beginning of philosophy, into the poetically thoughtful questioning of the Greeks. In this historical moment "*the essence of the beginning turns itself around,* it is no longer the *greatly anticipated origin,* but only now the as yet unreached tentative beginning of the coming development."[65] To address the basic question of philosophy is to enter into a historical confrontation with Hegel.[66]

James Philips argues that Heidegger's appropriation of Hegel in the period of the rectorate had the consequence that "without ever elaborating a philosophy of the state, Heidegger became a state thinker."[67] In fact Heidegger did elaborate a philosophical understanding of the state at this time, one in which Hegel receives no mention. Philips is not mistaken in his claim; it is simply that the protocols of this seminar were unavailable to him at the time he made his statement.

In the winter semester of 1933–34, Heidegger held a seminar entitled "On the Essence and Concept of Nature, History, and State." The connection between the three is not at all obvious, but gives us an insight into Heidegger's resistance of the Nazi biologism, even during the period of his greatest support for Hitler. Having established the sense in which, as timely, the human being is at the same time historical, Heidegger then draws attention to Aristotle's understanding of man as *zōon politikon* (a phrase we have already seen

62. Ibid., 12. "Nein—aber wir wissen *Richtung und Weg,* um *in das Fragen dieser Frage hineinzukommen*" (Heidegger's emphases).

63. Ibid., 12. "Daß die Geschichte nur spricht, wenn wir sie zur Auseinandersetzung zwingen."

64. Ibid., 13. "In der *Auseinandersetzung mit Hegel* spricht die ganze abendländische Geistesgeschichte vor ihm und nach ihm bis in die Gegenwart zu uns" (Heidegger's emphasis).

65. Ibid., 11. "*Das Wesen des Anfangs selbst kehrt sich um,* er ist nicht mehr *der große vorgreifende Ursprung,* sondern nur erst der unzureichende tastende Beginn der kommenden Entwicklung" (Heidegger's emphases).

66. James Philips devotes the first chapter of his study of Heidegger's Nazi engagement to Heidegger's "confrontation" with Hegel precisely because this is where Heidegger also begins. See James Philips, "The Death of Hegel," in *Heidegger's Volk,* 55–94.

67. James Philips, *Heidegger's Volk,* 56.

cited by Marx). In Greek there are two words for life: *zōon,* meaning that which is alive, the "animal," and *bios,* meaning the "whole" of a life, its "lived" character. Heidegger argues that this term *zōon politikon* is not to be taken in any biological sense, but rather indicates that "man is thus proper to the polis, *politikos,* as the living being therefore, who has the possibility and necessity for existence in the polis."[68] Drawing attention to a passage in Aristotle's *Nicomachean Ethics* where Aristotle speaks of a *bios politikos* rather than the *zōon politikon,* (and so makes a connection as well as a contrast between the two understandings of "life," and "living being"), Heidegger argues that as *zōon politikon* man in this way can have a life which is a *bios politikos,*[69] because "*bios* means here the history and existence of men."[70] Heidegger's concern is that the word *bios* does not indicate the racial determinations of a specified individual (even in the grisly racial pseudo-science of the Nazis), but rather *bios* names the life that is to be had in its being-lived, both individually and for the polis, that is, the nation or people (*Volk*), as a whole.

The genuine history and existence (nature) and history of humanity, however, is in understanding what it means to belong to a people (*Volk*). This is why, Heidegger says, the question of the state cannot be isolated from other questions, nor can the state be understood through a "theory" of the state, but the state can only be understood as "a manner of being and way of being of the people. The people is the particular being [*Seiende*], whose being [*Sein*] is the state."[71] The question we really need to pursue, Heidegger argues, is the question, not of nature, or history, or even the state, but that of the people (*Volk*). Heidegger proceeds to ask what the meaning of the "will" is, and replies that it is a problem for all democracies, and can only be fruitfully answered if the "leader-will and will of the people can be recognized in its essentiality."[72] It is here that Heidegger's support for Hitler is to be lo-

68. Martin Heidegger, protocols taken by Ital Gelzer of the seminar "Über Wesen und Begriff von Natur, Geschichte und Staat" in *Heidegger-Jahrbuch,* 4:71. "Der Mensch dann freilich zur Polis gehörig, πολιτικός, als das Lebewesen nämlich das Möglichkeit und Notwendigkeit hat zur Existenz in der Polis."

69. Compare Aristotle, *Nicomachean Ethics,* 1095b17–19: the discussion in question really begins at line 15.

70. Martin Heidegger, protocols taken by Ingeborg Schroth of the seminar "Über Wesen und Begriff von Natur, Geschichte und Staat," 78. "βίος heißt hier Geschichte und Existenz des Menschen."

71. Martin Heidegger, protocols taken by Ingeborg Schroth of the seminar "Über Wesen und Begriff von Natur, Geschichte und Staat," 79. "[Der Staat] eine Seinsweise und Seinsart des Volkes ist. Das Volk ist das Seiende, dessen Sein der Staat ist."

72. Martin Heidegger, protocols taken by Emil Schill of the seminar "Über Wesen und Begriff von Natur, Geschichte und Staat in Heidegger-Jahrbuch," 4:84. "Die Frage nach dem Willensbewußtsein der Gemeinschaft ist ein Problem in allen Demokratien, das freilich aber erst dann fruchtbar werden kann, wenn Führerwille und Volkswille in ihrer Wesenheit erkannt sind."

cated. It is only "the leader-state [*Führerstaat*]—as we have it—[that] indicates the fulfillment of historical development: the realization of the people in the leader."[73]

Emmanuel Faye, one of the most virulent critics of Heidegger the Nazi, reports from the protocols of a seminar from the period immediately after the rectorate that have a central bearing on the developments in Heidegger's thought concerning politics and the state from the period around the rectorate. Faye's somewhat forced polemic, derived from what he finds in these seminars, arises because he assigns an entirely uniform outlook to Heidegger's thinking, and so Faye's writing actually has the opposite effect to what he intends, namely of obscuring Heidegger's real relation to, and the extent of his complicity in, the regime.[74] If we set Faye's conclusions aside and concentrate on what he actually describes, it is possible to detect a marked shift in Heidegger's view immediately following the period of the rectorate. Here we are not interested in tracing to the month, or week, or hour, the moment of Heidegger's rejection of Hitlerism, or trying to elaborate the means by which he psychologically may have clung to a belief in the "movement" all his life even if he may have repudiated the Nazi Party as the means. None of this is of interest: quite the reverse: we are, or should be, interested in the gap between the movement of nihilism *as* a movement and the manner of its moving (the concrete forms political movement can and does take): as "the masses," as "the Nazi Party," as "Bolshevism," as "fascism," and indeed (in our own day and in Heidegger's), in the political forms thrown up by the demand for "world democracy."

Faye provides a very polemical account of the protocols of a seminar course of the winter semester 1934–35 held together with Erik Wolf entitled *Hegel: On the State.*[75] Faye seizes upon the report of Heidegger's statement

73. Martin Heidegger, protocols taken by an unknown hand of the seminar "Über Wesen und Begriff von Natur, Geschichte und Staat" in *Heidegger-Jahrbuch,* 4:78. "Der Führerstaat—wie wir ihn haben—bedeutet die Vollendung der geschichtlichen Entwicklung: die Verwirklichung des Volkes im Führer."

74. See Taylor Carman, "In and With: Flawed Efforts to Discredit Martin Heidegger's Philosophy," 26–27.

75. Martin Heidegger, *Hegel: Über den Staat.* Since the publication of Faye's work, two further protocols of these seminars have appeared in Martin Heidegger, *Seminare: Hegel—Schelling* (*GA*86), together with Heidegger's preparatory notes. The notes (59–68) indicate that much that Heidegger considered was never commented upon in the actual seminars. The first set of protocols were recorded by Wilhelm Hallwachs (548–611), the second by an unnamed source (613–55). The protocols are in close agreement and do not contradict Faye's citations. The original source for Faye's citations appears to be Jeffrey Barash in two works. See Jeffrey Barash: "Martin Heidegger in the Perspective of the Twentieth Century: Reflections on the Heidegger *Gesamtausgabe,*" 52–78; and *Heidegger et son siècle: Temps de l'être, temps de l'histoire.* Barash reports ("Martin Heidegger in the Perspective of the Twentieth Century," 68,

in these seminars that "it was said Hegel died in 1933: on the contrary, he has only just begun to live" as evidence of his formal commitment to Nazism.[76] In saying this, Heidegger is citing Carl Schmitt (while not naming him), suggesting (absolutely contrary to Faye's suggestion) in the very citation a transformation in the way 1933 should be read. In 1933 Schmitt had noted: "Only when the Reichspresident, on the 30th January 1933, named the leader of the National Socialist movement, Adolf Hitler, as the German chancellor, did the German Reich recover a political leadership, and the German state find the strength to annihilate Marxism, as the enemy of the state. . . . On this day, one might thus say, 'Hegel died.'"[77] The regime and its epigones (of whom Schmitt was one) made a clear association between Hegel and Marx: the one was "responsible" for the other. In his statement to the effect that Hegel had not died, Heidegger rejects the narrowness of this view, and in doing so recognizes that Hegel is fundamentally *describing* the character of the state in its relation to subjectivity as a whole (and so not just as "Marxism" secures it), and that the metaphysical position which Hegel lays out remains at the basis of not just Marxism, or Americanism and "world democracy," but Nazism as well. Heidegger returns to his understanding of Hegel's thought not as a speculative source of "theory," a mere set of opinions, but a genuine phenomenology—even if a phenomenology of the "completion of metaphysics"—of "the" political. Heidegger's description of Hegel's thought as the completion of metaphysics significantly predates Heidegger's own commitment to Nazism, and so we can see how, in making this judgment, Heidegger is returning to a view that he had briefly abandoned when, in embracing Hitler, he embraced the notion of the "leader" and the state as the "being" of the nation—a view which *in itself* is entirely consistent with Hegel's theory of the state. Heidegger, in other words, in arguing that in Nazism Hegel had come fully alive, is acknowledging his own

n. 54) that: "On the basis of students' copies there exist two variants of this course in the Heidegger archive in Marbach am Neckar," which he appears to have been able to consult. Faye seems to rely entirely on Barash's reports, and we must rely on Faye. Faye believed that the seminar protocols were to be published in volume 80 of the Heidegger *Gesamtausgabe*, despite the Klostermann prospectus making no mention of their inclusion in this volume. See Emmanuel Faye, *Heidegger: L'introduction du nazisme dans la philosophie: Autour des séminaires inédits de 1933–1935*, 333–41, especially 340.

76. Emmanuel Faye, *Heidegger: L'introduction du nazisme dans la philosophie*, 334. See Martin Heidegger, *Seminare: Hegel—Schelling* (*GA*86), 606. "Man hat gesagt, 1933 ist Hegel gestorben; im Gegenteil: er hat erst angefangen zu leben."

77. See Carl Schmitt, *Staat, Bewegung, Volk*, 31–32. "Erst als der Reichspräsident am 30. Januar 1933, den Führer der Nationalsozialistischen Bewegung, Adolf Hitler, zum Reichskanzler ernannte, erhielt das Deutsche Reich wieder eine politische Führung und fand der deutsche Staat die Kraft, den staatsfeindlichen Marxismus zu vernichten. . . . An diesem Tage ist demnach, so kann man sagen, 'Hegel gestorben.'"

commitment to Hegel's metaphysics, during his Nazism, and for the period of the rectorate, at least. In understanding the extent to which Nazism and Hitlerism are a form of the fulfillment of Hegel's theory of the state, and in embracing once again his rejection of Hegel as an overcoming of metaphysics, Heidegger is, without doubt (and whatever else he is doing), repudiating Hitler's claim to be the embodiment of the particularity of the "destiny" for the German people enshrined in the Nazi "program."

Faye, as he ordinarily does, ignores the provenance and the context of the citations from which he often makes great capital, and so fails to see that Heidegger's very reference in 1934 to Schmitt represents a challenge to Schmitt's interpretation of the events of 1933, and therefore to his (Heidegger's) own support for the events of 1933, when he had effectively thrown in his lot with Schmitt as much as with Hitler. Schmitt counterposed the Nazi state to the organization of the state in liberal democracy (the "Hegelian State" of which he speaks) because the Nazi state alone had the power to meet and overcome the challenge of Marxism, itself *also* a consequence of Hegel's theory of the state: it is in this sense that Hegel was "dead." In Heidegger's preparatory notes for the seminar for which Faye has the protocols, Heidegger's notes explicitly rejected Schmitt's interpretation, arguing "Carl Schmitt thinks as a liberal."[78] Indeed, this question of the character of the Hegelian interpretation of the state is where Marx himself had undertaken a central contribution to his own political departure, in 1843, with the "Critique of the Hegelian State Order."[79] In this text Marx had already foreseen that the state could itself be a mobilization of the whole of humanity, and not simply an objective manifestation of the phenomenon of absolute subjectivity in the hands of one class or caste (the civil service). More importantly, the central question of this text of Marx's is the extent to which "state" and "people" have separated and are unable to be brought back together by the present political conditions. In commenting on a text of Hegel's concerned with the particular and the general,[80] Marx says "however, here Hegel mixes up the state as the entire existence of a people [*Dasein eines Volkes*] with the political state."[81] Marx's critique implies the total activation of the people such that "Hegel shrinks back constantly in order not to describe the 'political state' as the highest, actual and explicit reality of social existence

78. Martin Heidegger, *Seminare: Hegel—Schelling* (*GA*86), 174. "Karl Schmitt denkt liberal."

79. Karl Marx, "Kritik des Hegelschen Staatsrechts" (*MEW*1).

80. G. W. F. Hegel, *Grundlinien der Philosophie des Rechts,* 473. "Nur so knüpft sich in dieser Rücksicht wahrhaft das im Staate wirkliche Besondere an das Allgemeine an" ("Only thus in this regard can the particular which is really in the state truly bind itself up with the universal").

81. Karl Marx, "Kritik des Hegelschen Staatsrechts" (*MEW*1), 282. "Aber Hegel verwechselt hier den Staat als das Ganze des Daseins eines Volkes mit dem politischen Staat."

[*sozialen Daseins*]."[82] This sense of the political state is an understanding that Marx will develop as a possibility for the fulfillment of the social relation of the individual to society, taken as social existence as a whole. Marx's critique is that Hegel's understanding of the state is not total enough, it is insufficient to the *all:* Heidegger argues that this *all* is precisely what Hegel had been aiming at.

It is this central question, of the relation of the individual to the state, which Heidegger had believed himself to be addressing in the period of the rectorate, and which Schmitt had also addressed in 1933 when Schmitt had said that "the political unity of the [Nazi] state is a tripartite summation of state, movement, and people. It differs from the ground up from the liberal-democratic state schema that has come to us from the nineteenth century."[83]

From the protocols of the 1934–35 seminar on Hegel and Faye's reports of them, we see emerging the main lines of Heidegger's critique of the political situation that is subsequently laid out from 1936 in the notebooks of *Das Ereignis*. With Hegel, Heidegger says, philosophy is finally "closed up" (recalling his understanding of Hegel as the summation of the fulfillment [*Vollendung*] of metaphysics).[84] Far more significantly, and recalling the language of "confrontation" with Hegel of the lecture course of the summer semester of 1933, Heidegger says: "Even with the danger that not one stone of Hegel's state-thinking may be left standing on another, we must enter into confrontation with him, precisely because Hegel's philosophy is thus far the *only* philosophy of the state."[85] It applies, in other words, to *all* Western forms of the state. The question turns on the meaning of Heidegger's expression "thus far." We are forced to ask: does Heidegger wish to supply the doctrine of the state, as the unity of leader, state, and people, such that the state is the being (*Sein*) of the being (*Seiende*) of the people (*Volk*), as he had

82. Ibid., 320. "So sinkt Hegel überall dahin hinab, den 'politischen Staat' nicht als die höchste, an und für sich seiende Wirklichkeit des sozialen Daseins zu schildern."

83. Carl Schmitt, *Staat, Bewegung, Volk*, 11–12. "Die politische Einheit des gegenwärtigen Staates ist eine dreigliedrige Zusammenhang von Staat, Bewegung, Volk. Sie unterschiedet sich von dem aus dem 19. Jahrhundert übernommenen liberal-demokratischen Staatsschema von Grund auf."

84. Martin Heidegger, protocols of *Hegel: Über den Staat* in Emmanuel Faye, *Heidegger: L'introduction du nazisme dans la philosophie*, 348, n. 17 (compare Martin Heidegger, *Seminare: Hegel—Schelling*, 550). "Abschließt."

85. Martin Heidegger, protocols of *Hegel: Über den Staat* in Emmanuel Faye, *Heidegger: L'introduction du nazisme dans la philosophie*, 362, n. 34, slightly corrected from Martin Heidegger, *Seminare: Hegel—Schelling*, 565. "Selbst auf die Gefahr hin daß von Hegels Staatsdenken kein Stein auf dem anderen bleiben sollte, müssen wir uns mit ihm auseinandersetzen, weil eben Hegels Philosophie die *einzige* bisherige Philosophie über den Staat ist" (Heidegger's emphasis, recorded by Faye). .

argued in 1933, or as Schmitt (in different terms) had asserted? Or given that we find Heidegger saying "*Where* now is the state today? . . . Is it *our* state? What does *being* mean here (the state *is*)? We have come upon a total lack of concepts, all is confused,"[86] is it that Heidegger has begun to test and inquire into the confusion of Nazi ideology and decide that the Nazi state is itself a malevolent and fractured expression of the possibilities that Hegel's theory of the state lays open?

The reappearance of the inquiry into Hegel as the means by which the state is to be understood marks the abandonment of Heidegger's assertion of the identity of being (*das Sein*) and the state as the triumph of the movement that brought Nazism to power in Germany. During his embrace of Hitlerism Heidegger had (especially in the rectorial address, but in other places as well) endorsed a language of "consciousness" and "will," asserting the primacy "the will to will" as something into the midst of which we are, and should be, inserted, a language which is aberrant to his thought both before and after this embrace; a language which even prior to 1933 and subsequent to 1934 with a slowly but steadily growing firmness he subjected to relentless critique. When after 1936 Heidegger mentions the "will to will" (especially in the notebooks of *Das Ereignis*) it is always to describe the will to will as the final form of the metaphysical will to power. In particular the "will to will" as what makes possible even the will to power is entirely rejected as the last expression of the fulfillment of metaphysics in the later notebooks of *Das Ereignis*.[87]

In the same way, the elevated language of "history" (*die Geschichte*) that we encounter in the Hitlerist lectures and seminars of the period of the rectorate gives way by 1936 to language of "the event" (*das Ereignis*) as a counter-position to "history." Heidegger's abandonment of the agent identity of the state as the expression of a "movement" of a people gives way to an understanding of the destiny, and so the fate, that befalls humanity, into which humanity enters and with which it must find its accommodation, but over which no organ like the state or the party, no apparatus, no conscious means of control, nothing determined by what every politics contemporary to him (and even now, contemporary to us) conceives of as the human *will* can be brought to bear. It is in this context that we have to understand Heidegger's confrontation with Nazism as *in itself* a development of his own

86. Martin Heidegger, *Seminare: Hegel—Schelling*, 566, cited in Emmanuel Faye, *Heidegger: L'introduction du nazisme dans la philosophie*, 362, n. 34. "*Wo* ist nun der Staat heute? . . . Ist es *unser* Staat? . . . Was aber heißt hier *Sein* (der Staat *ist*)? Uns fehlen vollkommen die Begriffe, alles ist wirr" (Heidegger's emphases, recorded by Faye).

87. See Martin Heidegger, *Das Ereignis* (*GA*71), §127, "Der Wille zum Willen," 127 and §146, "Die Verendung der Metaphysik im Willen zum Willen," 105–6.

understanding of being. The step into the thought of Hölderlin is a step out of and away from the humanism of Hegel's phenomenology, as the basis of *all* subjectival politics—fascist (Nazi), communist, and "world democratic." In the winter semester of 1934–35, and so immediately after the period of the rectorate, Heidegger lectured on Hölderlin and began to speak of the connection between thinking (as opposed to philosophy or philosophizing) and poetry. With this distinction comes the discussion of the archaism *das Seyn,* the understanding of be-ing for and in itself, in contrast to *das Sein,* being as manifest in the history of being and the history of the forgottenness of being. If *das Sein* is the province of philosophy, *das Seyn* is the concern of the more original language of poetry. It is not accidental that the first recorded mention of *das Seyn* occurs immediately after the Hitlerist adventure, nor that it occurs through a discussion of what an understanding of Hölderlin might bring—and this explicitly not because he "was 'also a philosopher' and thus one of those whom we might place next to Schelling and Hegel."[88] Heidegger's introduction to the Hölderlin lectures begins with the words: "Hölderlin is one of our greatest, that means our most futural *thinker* because he is our greatest poet. This poetical turning in the direction of his poetry is only possible as the *thoughtful* confrontation with the *revelation of be-ing* which is achieved in this poetry."[89] Hölderlin, not Hitler, is Germany's greatest thinker and its future: an inflammatory enough statement in 1934, hardly lessened by the qualification "one of" when Hölderlin, not Hitler is superlatively the "most futural." The word "revelation" is normally reserved for the doctrine of—especially Christian—theology, but not here. There is a revelation of be-ing to be encountered in Hölderlin's poetry, and so not through the state apparatus (nor, even, Christianity). From here on out, and especially from 1936 onward in the private manuscripts of *Das Ereignis,* Heidegger begins to elaborate with increasing depth and urgency the distinction and relation between *das Sein* and *das Seyn: das Sein* as the forgetfulness of being in its metaphysical manifestations; and *das Seyn* as

88. Martin Heidegger, *Hölderlins Hymnen: "Germanien" und "Der Rhein"* (GA39), 6. "[Hölderlin] 'auch Philosoph' war und sogar einer, den wir ruhig neben Schelling und Hegel rücken dürfen." Heidegger's point is that Hölderlin, Schelling, and Hegel had all been in close proximity and knew each other as students in Tübingen. Their biographical proximity has often suggested an intellectual proximity, something Heidegger had commented on in many places elsewhere. See, in the same volume, the discussion "Hölderlin und Hegel" 129–34, where the connection with Schelling is also discussed.

89. Martin Heidegger, *Hölderlins Hymnen: "Germanien" und "Der Rhein"* (GA39), 6. "Hölderlin ist einer unserer größten, d.h. unser zukünftiger *Denker* weil er unser größter *Dichter* ist. Die dichterische Zuwendung zu seiner Dichtung ist nur möglich als *denkerische* Auseinandersetzung mit der in dieser Dichtung errungenen *Offenbarung des Seyns*" (Heidegger's emphases).

how be-ing "is" in itself. In several places when the word *das Sein* appeared in the published texts, *das Seyn* was indicated in the original manuscript, something which has not become clear until the more recent publication of the manuscript versions of these texts in the volumes of the *Gesamtausgabe:* once again the "other" language of thinking lies in the background. What this distinction really entails for factical, material, life, and how being "is" in itself, we are not yet ready to clarify.

*Chapter 8*

# Nazism, Liberalism, Humanism

KARL MARX'S DEFINITION of the finality of human existence as species-being conceals, as I have already suggested, a fundamental ambiguity, between the individual human existence—mine, and yours, and his, and hers—and species-existence *as such.* This ambiguity is the metaphysically construed difference between beings and what constitutes them as beings: their metaphysical being as such, what makes and lets them be, and so *produces* their beingness. This is to name the ambiguity in terms which Marx himself would have rejected, but which Heidegger would have recognized. The relation is resolved for Marx, as I have argued already (and as we shall continue to see), by an appeal to history: the very appearance of the *historical* is what orders the individual (beings) to what makes them beingful. In this sense a fundamental shift has occurred, from a causation construed in terms of "being" (as unchanging, eternal) to a relation construed through time, thought as "history." It is this transformation which allows Marx (and Hegel before him) to understand his thinking as a thinking not of *being* but of *becoming,* and to resolve the ambiguity in question by arguing for a thinking that claims becoming over being.

For Marx, in the attaining to communism the particularity of material conditions will be sublated, or "leveled up" to an equalization, where every particular individual (what in the *Grundrisse* Marx calls the *individuum*) will *come* to manifest in his or her real, material existence the condition of species-being as such: this "leveling-up" is what it means to *become* in the highest degree. If we accept Heidegger's understanding of metaphysics (rather than Marx's dismissal of the metaphysical as the *merely* supersensible), then we see that the prior condition of the individual is always the not-yet apparent *idea* of species-being. In this sense Marx's metaphysics is indeed essentially a metaphysics of becoming: it is on the basis of what the individual is to *become* that he or she attains to the status of an *individuum.* Although Marx repeatedly asserts that social relations are the material conditions of the actual existence of the *individuum,* in fact how this is to be is to a large extent left opaque and unresolved. It will simply unfold as a necessity, from the imperative that the species-being of the whole of humanity be *realized,* and so *made* and *produced* as "the" real.

All of this, as we have seen, is prepared for and made possible by Hegel's metaphysics of absolute subjectivity. Marx fulfills and amplifies—indeed, drives to the limit in its relentless conclusions—Hegel's thinking as a material, social, thinking. In this, Marx thinks through to the very end the death of God and the restriction of every thought of world to the subjectivity of the subject that Hegel prepares. Although Heidegger only rarely says so, Marx completes one aspect (of which Nietzsche is the other) of the fulfillment of metaphysics that Hegel brings about.

In this, and historically, Heidegger increasingly speaks of the "overcoming" of metaphysics that he believes to be uncovered in his own thinking. Much confusion reigns about what exactly is meant by Heidegger's term *Überwindung,* the "overcoming" of metaphysics that he names. Some commentators have simply declared that they (perhaps even in place of Heidegger) have themselves "overcome" metaphysics, as if, having done this and enacted it in their writing, everything is now resolved—at least if you follow whatever program, or "philosophy," or whatever it is that they are asserting. If only everyone else would but see it. Such final resolution—so easily achieved when we have only ourselves and what *we* think to worry about—is very far from Heidegger's own thought. He remarks on one occasion "metaphysics does not let itself be undone as if it were a choice."[1]

The overcoming of metaphysics is twofold: at one and the same time it befalls humanity, such that humanity, either in an individual, or collectively (perhaps through a democratic vote?), is unlikely to make this overcoming up or "choose" it, only later to toss it to one side when it ceases to "work" or be "useful" or "practicable." Heidegger suggests that "the ending *lasts* longer than the history of metaphysics so far."[2] This befalling is the way in which we are bound to the history that we are: a history is not chosen, even if it contains choices. And, second, this overcoming itself is an opening, not a resolution, to thinking: as such the overcoming of metaphysics is *not*—precisely not—a sublation of metaphysics (its cancellation and negation): rather the ending takes into account and lives from the whole history of metaphysics, because this *also* is the historicality of the historical, and without it the end could not have come about. In many texts Heidegger uses the word *Verwindung* interchangeably with *Überwindung.* Joan Stambaugh notes: "Al-

1. Martin Heidegger, "Überwindung der Metaphysik" (*GA*7), 69. "Die Metaphysik läßt sich nicht wie eine Absicht abtun."

2. Martin Heidegger, "Überwindung der Metaphysik" (*GA*7), 69. "Die Verendung *dauert* länger als die bisherige Geschichte der Metaphysik" (Heidegger's emphasis).

though Heidegger uses the familiar word *Überwindung* for overcoming he means it in the sense of the less familiar word *Verwindung*. . . . When something is overcome in the sense of being *verwunden* it is, so to speak, incorporated."[3] We have already witnessed how Heidegger believed this opening to thinking which incorporates what went before belongs essentially to the poet, who in stillness "thinks" the thought of the passing-by of the Last God.

In this chapter we need to make a detour into Heidegger's thinking, to show from what place he himself could have believed himself to be able to enter into dialogue with Marx (as he did with Nietzsche, and Hegel) and with Marxism as a political form. Here we see how this dialogue emerges not as the mere exchange of "opinion," Marx's thought *versus* the thought of Heidegger, so that we might "critically" decide and judge who came off best, and so plump for the winner. Heidegger believed the dialogue with Marx to be above all a historical dialogue, a dialogue made possible only by the emerging of the possibility of the overcoming of metaphysics, as a historical *event,* the event made possible by the death of God as it is thought through by Hegel and Nietzsche, and therefore also by Marx. To enter into this dialogue means to enter into Heidegger's own confrontation with the essential ambiguity that presents itself in the metaphysics of subjectivity in the way I have described, the agonistic *difference* between the individual subject and absolute subjectivity, between the individual and its historical imperative to become *individuum.*

This ambiguity is resolved in these thinkers who think the completion and fulfillment of metaphysics through a philosophy of becoming, but, as Heidegger asserts time and again, becoming is counterposed by each of them to the (for them) now vacuous, but once plenitudinous thought of *being* with which metaphysics had its inception, in Plato, in Aristotle, and which was developed in Aquinas, in Suárez, and in Leibniz. Moreover, as Heidegger repeatedly says, the beginning only comes into view in virtue of the appearance of the end. But the beginning that comes into view is not only the *first* beginning as it historically set out with the Greek metaphysicians. Seeing the beginning as it once *was* and for itself means seeing what set the beginning off, which is a beginning again.

Our own beginning, setting off from where Occidental thinking first set off, is also made possible by our being able to encounter the first beginning. We can see now why the overcoming of metaphysics does not sublate, in the sense of negate, destroy, and leave behind, the history of metaphysics (as the hitherto history of being) but rather incorporates it, because we can see for the first time what this history means and why and how it unfolds as it does. This is why Heidegger speaks not just of the "first beginning" and the

3. Joan Stambaugh, *Overcoming Metaphysics,* 84, n. 1.

"other beginning" but "the beginningly":[4] how *beginning* to think is a power that emerges in thinking and that gathers us *in* to the way thinking thinks and has been thinking hitherto. To think in this way is to *correspond* with and to the history of thinking.

The ambiguity that is concealed in all metaphysics, between the particular and the general, the idea and its manifestation, the concretion and the abstraction, is not accidental, nor a "mistake," nor a misunderstanding. It belongs to the very constitution of metaphysics, although in a manner which metaphysics cannot itself bring to light or make visible, and which metaphysics is forced to leave opaque. In one of the notebooks of *Das Ereignis* Heidegger says, "the ungrounded basis of metaphysics conceals itself in the unquestioned division between beings and being itself."[5] Beings—particulars, individuals, "subjects"—and what makes them possible, "being as such," "beingness," the idea, the absolute, the "species." To experience the question posed by what has hitherto been unquestioned *is* to enter in to the overcoming of metaphysics.

The ambiguity lies hidden and unquestioned. How then, is the question to arise? Heidegger believes it to have arisen in his own work as the question concerning being, the being-question, that he investigated most systematically in *Being and Time* in the inquiry into the being of the human being—the inquiry that is a *self*-inquiry, the self-interrogation of human existence (*Dasein*).[6]

The detour therefore raises the question of how, and so by what means, Heidegger enters into dialogue with Marx's metaphysical understanding of the primacy of human being as "species-being," by showing what is at issue in Heidegger's own understanding of human existence, in the inquiry into human *Dasein.* This will prepare us for the discussion of Marx's thought in the next two chapters, especially the discussion concerning language and essence in chapter 10.

The word *Dasein* never functions in any of Heidegger's texts, however, as a masked name for the philosophical subject, especially the subject as described and understood in the thought of Hegel. If *Dasein* means anything different from "existence," the sense in which it is frequently used by Marx from the beginning to the end of his works (and the usual English

4. Martin Heidegger, *Über den Anfang* (GA70), §2, 13. "Die Anfängnis des Anfangs."

5. Ibid., 100. "Der ungegründete Grund der Metaphysik verbirgt sich in der nicht erfragten Unterscheidung des Seienden und des Seins."

6. See Martin Heidegger, *Sein und Zeit* (GA2), 6–11, where Heidegger lays out "the formal structure of the question that goes out after being" ("Die formale Struktur der Frage nach dem Sein"). Here the very word "the *inquired-into*" ("das *Erfragte*") that he names as "the unquestioned" in the passage I have quoted from *Über den Anfang* appears as the central of the three kinds of inquiry into being that constitute the thematic of *Being and Time.*

translation of the term), with all the ambiguities in German the word "existence" possesses in English, it indicates, through Heidegger's own drawing attention to the hyphenation he often (especially later) added to the term, *Da-sein,* the primacy of world in the "here" of the German word *da.* Literally translated *Dasein* means "here-to-be" or "here-being." As "existence" *Dasein* has all the ambiguity in German the word has in English: it can mean a particular existence (mine, yours, that person's); or it can mean a kind of existence—Heidegger often speaks of "human *Dasein*" or on occasion particular kinds or regions of *Dasein;* or it can mean existence in general, the whole of being.[7] In each case, for Heidegger, attention is drawn to the "here" indicated by the *da. Da* can also mean "there," as in "here and there" but it cannot mean "over there," which in German would be *dort, drin, draußen,* and so it speaks against the "supersensible" and the "beyond" of Plato's *epekeina. Dasein* most certainly does not mean "being-there," a translation Heidegger detested in Sartre's formulation and translation of it as "être-là";[8] at most, translated in this way, it could mean "being-the-here" (*être-le-là*), a translation Heidegger himself proposes.[9]

The very primordiality of the *here* is indicated by Heidegger as something that persists through the entire stretch of his work. Heidegger's own passage beyond metaphysics is rooted in the more primordial understanding of the *placedness* of being, of the *da* of *Da-sein.*

If Heidegger understands *placedness* of being as what held out in advance the path upon which all three steps of his thinking were taken, can we suggest how the primordiality of placedness was first uncovered? Placedness is an ontological determination—it is the placedness of places, from out of which the being of any particular existence, mine, yours, *Dasein,* is taken. It is this ontological determinedness that points up a repeated error of emphasis in the Macquarrie-Robinson translation, of translating the word *das Seiende* as "entity." For the word *Seiende* can indeed indicate *this* entity *here,* but it can just as much indicate the activity of being, the activity of the participle in question. In this sense it means both "entityness" (which can be heard in the word "entity") and "(*an*) entity, as such." What is indicated

7. In a rare and important discussion, Heidegger gives a comprehensive treatment of the ambiguities implicit in the reading of the terms *Dasein* and "existence," *existentia, Existential,* and *Existentiell* in relation to the original discussion of the meaning of the term *Dasein* in *Being and Time* and his developing understanding of it, in lectures given in 1941. See Martin Heidegger, *Die Metaphysik des deutschen Idealismus (Schelling)* (GA49), 26–74.

8. See the discussion of this in Laurence Paul Hemming, *Heidegger's Atheism: The Refusal of a Theological Voice,* 5–7.

9. A remark by Heidegger in Heidelberg in 1969, reported by Jean Beaufret in "En chemin avec Heidegger," 212. "Le *Dasein* n'est pas *là* de l'être, mais *être-le-là,* le *soutenir,* y *ek-sister*" (Beaufret's emphases).

in each case with respect to *Dasein* is the be*ing*, not *a* thing, *a* being, *in* its being. *Dasein* names the manner, the *how*, in each case, of the being of beings, and so of the manner and relation to *das Seiende*, the being, both as such and as a whole.

In 1945 Heidegger wrote to Rudolf Stadelmann that "over and above mere interpretations my thinking has become a conversation with the poet, and bodily nearness is the element of my thinking."[10] Heidegger understood his relation to politics from out of the poets, not the philosophers. This constitutes his understanding of the relation he claimed he understood to be unfolding in the "movement" of the German people in relation to beings as a whole. If we are to take not just Heidegger's, but Marx's (and Lenin's) claim for the priority of the German situation seriously, what this means is that Marx and Heidegger were both led to inquire into a phenomenon which they could see unfolding before them: the German political situation. Heidegger expressly distinguished this "movement" of the German situation from the formal "movement" of the Nazi Party: he says of his realization of the difference between these two things that even in the heat of his political engagement, "in this way I had hoped to oppose the headway of improper persons and the threatening supremacy of Party apparatus and Party doctrine."[11]

In a seminar of 1941 Martin Heidegger commented on the connection between a fragment from one of Nietzsche's 1885 notebooks and Heraclitus's Fragment 7.[12] The fragment of Heraclitus with which Heidegger concerns himself in citing this fragment begins with the words *panta ta onta*—"all things."[13] In naming a connection between Heraclitus and Nietzsche, Heidegger is already naming the inception and the overcoming of metaphysics: already with respect to time, an "all," *pan*, is opened up before us. *Panta ta onta*—"all things"—at the same time names Heidegger's own much-used phrase, *das Seiende im Ganzen*, usually translated as "beings as a whole"; but this is not quite right—the being in question is being itself (singular), *to on*, of *panta ta onta.* Surely, however it is the usual English translation and not Heidegger's German rendering that is closer to the Greek, since *onta* is clearly plural? What Heidegger draws our attention to is the *being* of the

10. Martin Heidegger, "Nachsinn über das Geschichtliche Selbstbewußtsein," letter to Rudolf Stadelmann of July 20, 1945 (*GA*16), 370. "Mein Denken ist weit über bloße Interpretationen hinaus zu einem Gespräch mit dem Dichter geworden, und seine leibhafte Nähe ist das Element meines Denkens"

11. Martin Heidegger, "Das Rektorat" (*GA*16), 374. "Auf diese Weise hoffte ich, dem Vordringen ungeeigneter Personen und der drohenden Vormacht des Parteiapparates und der Parteidoktrin begegnen zu können."

12. Martin Heidegger, *Seminare (Übungen) 1937/38 und 1941/42* (*GA*88), 167, using Hermann Diels's numbering of the Heraclitus fragments.

13. Heraclitus, "Fragment 7" in Hermann Diels, *Die Fragmente der Vorsokratiker,* 1:78.

being(s). He argues that for the Greeks, every being is taken with respect to the being *of* its being: even in the plural, the singular is always actively present, although unthematized. In metaphysics, especially in the "christianisation of philosophy" (by which he indicates all theistic appropriations of metaphysics, Jewish, Islamic, and so forth), this is transformed into what is most beingful in every being: *das Seiendste.*[14] Heidegger notes that the "first beginning" of philosophy, with the Greeks, where being *is* (and therefore is *for itself*) is succeeded by "the beginning of metaphysics: the idea is 'the most beingful,' *ontōs on.*"[15] What is most beingful in being, construed metaphysically (though not as he interprets Heraclitus), is for Heidegger not less than: God. And inasmuch—with Heidegger—as we name the whole history of metaphysics in between Heraclitus and Nietzsche, with God, we name a certain kind of "all," *to pan.*

In the rectorial address, Heidegger had fatefully declared himself and those whom he addressed to be submitting to "the power of the *beginning* of our spiritual-historical existence [*Dasein*]."[16] This beginning, italicized for emphasis in the text, is at the same time the awakening of Greek philosophy: the moment "when Occidental man, out of a nationhood [*Volkstum*], by virtue of his tongue, for the first time rises up against *being in general* [*das Seiende im Ganzen*] and questions and grasps it as the being that it is."[17] Without doubt, and whatever else he thought he was doing, Heidegger understood what was posed before Germany in that disastrous year of 1933 to open the same possibility, the same *demand,* as he believed had befallen the Greeks *such that it made of them Greeks,* and so first awakened their thinking.

We return to 1933 in order, however, to raise the question of this engagement as a *historical* question. An approach of kind might yet confirm what Löwith claimed Heidegger had said (that his political engagement was grounded in the analysis of *historicality* of *Being and Time*), without necessarily confirming the causal inference that Löwith suggests but does not elaborate. This is to ask the very same question Heidegger himself asks—

14. See Martin Heidegger, *Beiträge zur Philosophie* (*GA*65), 110.

15. Martin Heidegger, *Über den Anfang* (*GA*70), 53.

"*Der erste Anfang:*
Das Sein *ist* [. . .]
Der Beginn der Metaphysik:
Die Idee ist das 'Seiendste'ὄντως ὄν."

16. Martin Heidegger, "Die Selbstbehauptung der deutschen Universität" (*GA*16), 108. "Die Macht des *Anfangs* unseres geistig-geschichtlichen Daseins" (Heidegger's emphasis).

17. Ibid., 108–9. "Darin steht der abendländische Mensch aus einem Volkstum kraft seiner Sprache erstmals auf gegen das *Seiende im Ganzen* und befragt und begreift es als das Seiende, das es ist" (Heidegger's emphasis).

"how does history arise?" The fifth chapter of *Being and Time* begins under the heading "Timeliness and Historicalness" (translating over-literally).[18] Heidegger elaborates the existential analytic of *Dasein* in the following way: "all efforts of the existential analytic serve the one aim, of finding a possibility for responding to the question concerning the *meaning of being* in general."[19] What does the "in general" indicate here? Are we seeking *the* answer to the meaning of being, so that we can say "here it is," or "it has been answered," as if *Being and Time* were, like some *philosophia perennis,* deducing the final and necessary structure of the meaning of being, so that once we had *this* understanding, no other would be necessary?

This is exactly the approach metaphysics takes to *being in general* as "highest being," what is "most beingful" in things, divine, unchanging, and deathless. It is also the goal that every philosophy of becoming—Hegel's, Nietzsche's, Marx's—cannot evade, even though it privileges becoming and evacuates the meaning of "being," and so why all these philosophies of becoming are understood by Heidegger to be "metaphysics." It is exactly this meaning of "being in general" as "highest being" (Marx will say, highest being as "species being") that Heidegger seeks to leave behind. In doing so he speaks of how we must seek a sufficiently originary interpretation to be able to overcome the requirement for "highest being" that marks all metaphysics. This originarity (the Macquarrie-Robinson translation has "primordial") is attained[20] not through logical analysis, nor through positing the absolute ground structure of every self-conscious being (which would have to appear as something like Descartes's *cogito ergo sum*), but through the "entirety" of a factical life, the whole of the experience of an existence (*Dasein*) as the "stretch" of time between birth and death such that, for each existent being, "it stretches *itself* thereby, such that its own being is constituted in advance as a stretching-along. *In the being* of *Dasein* already lies the 'between' which relates to birth and death."[21] The in-between that is at issue here is what the Greeks named as the *bios* of man, the absolutely nonbiological possibility and necessity of his belonging in the polis. Heidegger understands this in-between as fundamentally constitutive of the "here" (*Da*) in the texts that constitute the discussion of *Das Ereignis.* Heidegger later says, in a language that is quite difficult, but nevertheless remains firmly within the province of

18. Martin Heidegger, *Sein und Zeit* (*GA*2), 492. "Zeitlichkeit und Geschichtlichkeit."

19. Ibid., 492. "Alle Bemühungen der existentialen Analytik gelten dem einen Ziel, eine Möglichkeit der Beantwortung der Frage nach dem *Sinn von Sein* überhaupt zu finden" (Heidegger's emphasis).

20. See Martin Heidegger, *Being and Time* (*GA*2), 372.

21. Martin Heidegger, *Sein und Zeit* (*GA*2), 495. "[*Dasein*] erstreckt *sich selbst* dergestalt, daß im vorhinein sein eigenes Sein als Erstreckung konstituiert ist. *Im Sein* des Daseins liegt schon das 'Zwischen' mit Bezug auf Geburt und Tod" (Heidegger's emphasis).

the thinking of *Being and Time:* "The in-between of the here [*Da*] is taken in advance of the spatial and in advance of the temporal, if 'space' and 'time' mean the objective realm of the at-hand and its place-and time-point-like representing. And indeed 'in-between' bespeaks of the double intimacy of *in-midst-of* and *in-meantime* (moment of the ungrounded)."[22]

If temporality is disclosive of the "here" that any particular *Dasein* is, it is because temporality is *taken off* from the historical character of human *Dasein,* human existence, in some wider sense. Here Heidegger speaks of *Dasein*'s "here-having-been" (*da-gewesen*).[23] In every occurrence of discovering humanity to have already-been, not the question of the past is posited, but the question of the past as coming to light through an already futural projection: the "wider sense" turns out not to be one of mere "scope," but of the "widest" as such, the way in which the present and past are read off in my finding myself in a common already-having-been-opened-up to futurity. Heidegger suggests this through the posing of a question: "But does *Dasein come* to be historical only through this, that it is no longer 'here' [*da*]? Or *is* it not historical precisely as something factically existing? *Is this Dasein only 'having been' in the sense of the 'having been here,' or is it 'having been' as the present-making-futural, that is to say in the timing* [time-character] *of its timeliness?*"[24]

It is important to be clear about what Heidegger has said here: it is not that the already secured self (the "subject") then "enters" history, discovers history, learns about history, decides *on* history, has history before it as something "at hand." Rather, through the analysis of temporality which Heidegger believes that by this section of *Being and Time* has already been achieved, the very unity of existence (*Dasein*) discloses this temporality as its historicality: *"the analysis of the historicality of existence seeks to indicate that this being is not 'timely' because it 'stands in history,' but conversely that it only exists and can exist historically because in the ground of its being it is timely."*[25] Later he adds, "the thesis of the historicality does not say that the worldless

22. Martin Heidegger, *Besinnung* (*GA*66), 117. "Das Inzwischen des Da ist *vor*-räumlich und *vor*-zeitlich zu nehmen, wenn 'Raum' und 'Zeit' den gegenständlichen Bereich des Vorhandenen und seiner ort- und zeitpunkthaften Vor-stellung meinen. Und zwar besagt 'Inzwischen' das gedoppelt Innige von *Inmitten* und *Unterdessen* (Augenblick des Abgrundes)" (Heidegger's emphases).

23. Compare Martin Heidegger, *Sein und Zeit* (*GA*2), 503.

24. Ibid., 503. "Aber *wird* das Dasein erst geschichtlich dadurch, daß es nicht mehr da ist? Oder *ist* es nicht gerade geschichtlich als faktisch existierendes? *Ist das Dasein nur gewesenes im Sinne des da-gewesenen, oder ist es gewesen als gegewärtigendes-zukünftiges, das heißt in der Zeitigung seiner Zeitlichkeit*" (Heidegger's emphases).

25. Ibid., 498. "*Die Analyse der Geschichtlichkeit des Daseins versucht zu zeigen, daß dieses Seiende nicht 'zeitlich' ist, weil es 'in der Geschichte steht,' sondern daß es umgekehrt geschichtlich nur existiert und existieren kann, weil es im Grunde seines Seins zeitlich ist*" (Heidegger's emphases).

subject, but the being which exists as being-in-the-world, is historical. *The occurring of history is the occurring of being-in-the-world.*"[26] Why the emphasis on being-in-the-world *over against* the worldless (Cartesian) subject? Because being-in-the-world lives (exists) from *out of* the *da,* the "here" of *Dasein.* Existence is *bound* to world, and cannot be unbound, as Descartes had tried to effect through his exercise of the "method of doubt."

You will recall that we earlier considered Heidegger's phrase concerning all efforts of the existential analytic, that they seek to find a possibility for responding to the question concerning the meaning of being in general. The "in general" here (*überhaupt*) turns out to be not the absolute beingness of being as the "ground of all things" (the metaphysical conception of God), but rather ground as *timeliness* (*Zeitlichkeit*), the "stretching-along" of the "in-between" of birth and death that at the same time discloses that every particular existence is a unity, and that the whole of existence is constituted by unity.[27]

From where does the ambiguity in the meaning of *Dasein* stem? Which is to say, is it an arbitrary ambiguity, a mere "fact" or peculiarity of the term which, *as* existence, can mean either "my" existence, the existence of this existent *here,* or existence "in general"? This ambiguity, Heidegger had noted, is even contained in self-reflection, since I can take "my" existence in relation to my self-reflection on my self-existing, or my own understanding of my existing in relation to being as a whole.[28] The ambiguity inherent in both the terms *Dasein* as "existence" and *Seiende* as "being" is not accidental, and appears only as an ambiguity insofar as we are incapable of resolving the question of the inherent unity of "world." The Cartesian subject has already excluded the possibility of the resolution of this ambiguity because the thought *cogito, ergo sum* has already excluded every aspect of world from its attainment, as the very possibility of its attainment at all. In this sense every "subject" attains to self-representation, self-manifestation as identical to every other subject. However, the thought *cogito, ergo sum* is deprived of any content—*as* a self-representation it is at the same time *in*determinate: its content is yet to be attained to. For Descartes this was not a problem, although the whole problematic of intersubjectivity arises at exactly this point, since the subject, having attained to itself, must then establish constructively

26. Ibid., 513. "Die These von der Geschichtlichkeit des Daseins sagt nicht, das weltlose Subjekt sei geschichtlich, sondern das Seiende, das als In-der-Welt-sein existiert. *Geschehen der Geschichte ist Geschehen des In-der-Welt-seins*" (Heidegger's emphases).

27. We would have to note here, therefore, that this understanding of timeliness arises precisely and only in virtue of the death of God.

28. This is the distinction Heidegger had made between *Existentiell* and *Existential* in *Being and Time.* See the important clarification of this understanding in Martin Heidegger, *Die Metaphysik des deutschen Idealismus (Schelling)* (*GA*49), 39.

the possibility of its relating to any other subject (in analytic philosophy this manifests itself as the problem of other minds).

In subjectivity it is already decided in advance of every differentiation of any particular subject that every subject is *essentially* identical to every other: difference is purely epiphenomenal: differences are *added on,* insofar as they are accidents of history, location, class, ability, race, and so forth. Every difference between subjects has the same structure as a value. The structure of a value is "taking something *as* something": here taking some one *as* some thing. This has a direct political corollary. Any politics arising on the basis of the human subject, thought through on the basis of the Cartesian subject or what Heidegger called *Vor-stellung,* re-presentation, will set out from an enforcement of an identity and equality between all subjects. It is on this basis that subjectivity—re-representation—produces an essentially *communistic* (*koinon*) politics, that is to say, a politics predicated on the essential identity of subjects and for which every difference has to be accounted for and so *constructed* and produced (we have to show where the difference "came" from). This "communistic" character is present in all political and liberal humanisms from right to left, irrespective of the attitude they then take up with respect to the question of difference itself.

Heidegger opens up the connections between the self, subjectivity as itself a historical phenomenon which poses itself as a question, and the question of the setting of the character of what I have so far only named using the notion of "the widest" sense of the *da* of *Dasein* in 1927 as a connection with that of the polis, thought as the nation or people (*Volk*). Heidegger suggests that "however, with the thesis 'existence [*das Dasein*] is historical' means that not only the ontical fact, that man is a more or less significant 'atom' in the workings of world history is laid out, and that he remains the plaything of circumstances and events. The thesis also lays on us the problem *to what extent and from the ground of what ontological conditions does historicality belong to the subjectivity of the 'historical' subject as an essential constitution?*"[29] Heidegger raises the question in this way precisely to illustrate how *not* to ask the question: that is to say, in raising the question of the atom-character of *an* existence, either singular or by means of a "periodisation" ("antiquity," "Georgian London," and so forth) this arises as a question about the subjectivity of the subject (the "atom" of individuality in relation to the

29. Martin Heidegger, *Sein und Zeit* (GA2), 505. "Allein die These: 'Das Dasein ist geschichtlich' meint nicht nur das ontische Faktum, daß der Mensch ein mehr oder minder wichtiges 'Atom' im Getriebe der Weltgeschichte darstellt und der Spielball der Umstände und Ereignisse bleibt, sondern stellt das Problem: *inwiefern und auf Grund welcher ontologischen Bedingungen gehört zur Subjektivität des 'geschichtlichen' Subjekts die Geschichtlichkeit als Wesenverfassung?*" (Heidegger's emphasis).

whole), but cannot be answered there. There is *no* "essential constitution," no "formal condition" for answering the question about the historicality of existence even on the basis of historical conditions themselves. We can neither answer this as a question about the formal condition under which a subject is a subject (Descartes), nor *even* from out of the presentness of the present, that is, by taking the answer *off* from circumstances (which is where Heidegger would, to a large extent, have located the researches of Dilthey). The "condition of historical conditions," however, arises as a question about futurity, and therefore the *destiny* of every existence as it presents itself *here* (*da*) from out of my "whence." However, any "whence" has to be secured: it is not merely sent to me, it also has to be taken over *within* existence.

It is here that Heidegger raises the question of "resoluteness" as "*anticipatory* resoluteness."[30] Heidegger raises the question of "the widest" by asking "nevertheless it must be asked, from whence *in general* the possibilities can be drawn, on which existence [*Dasein*] factically projects itself."[31] These possibilities are *fated*, that is, they have a positive *from whence*, not a merely open or infinite field. Something befalls existence rather than is posited or striven-for or chosen by mankind. As fated, it is binding, it is a destiny. Moreover, it is not that *an individual* draws himself off from historicality in general to come about. Most crucially for what we have yet to consider, Heidegger says: "the fated is not something that puts itself together out of individual fates, any less that being-with-one-another [*Miteinandersein*] can be grasped as the occurring together of several subjects. In being-with-one-another in the same world and in resoluteness for determined possibilities have the fates already been guided in advance."[32] Heidegger comments "this is how we designate the occurring of the community, of the people [*Volk*]."[33] What I have so far designated by "the widest" turns out in 1927 to be the nation, the polis, the people, but *in* its destiny, in what is granted and befalls *to* it.

How are we to understand what Heidegger indicates again here with the *überhaupt*, which we are now well aware *cannot* be taken in a metaphysical sense, as an originary first cause, but is given in the "stretching-along" of the existence of the nation as a whole—of its making present here its *future* inner unity and destiny, its fate? Earlier I pointed out that *das Seiende überhaupt* functions ordinarily in Heidegger as a name for the meta-

30. Ibid., 506. "*Vorlaufende* Entschlossenheit" (Heidegger's emphasis).

31. Ibid., 506. "Trotzdem muß gefragt werden, woher *überhaupt* die Möglichkeiten geschöpft werden können, auf die sich das Dasein faktisch entwirft" (Heidegger's emphasis).

32. Ibid., 506. "Das Geschick setzt sich nicht aus einzelnen Schicksalen zusammen, sowenig als das Miteinandersein als ein Zusammenvorkommen mehrerer Subjekte begriffen werden kann. In Miteinandersein in derselben Welt und in der Entschlossenheit für bestimmte Möglichkeiten sind die Schicksale im vorhinein schon geleitet."

33. Ibid., 507. "Damit bezeichnen wir das Geschehen der Gemeinschaft, des Volkes."

physical understanding of God. On May 27, 1933, Heidegger gave his rectorial address. We can do no more than note, if only in passing, that the very notion of self-assertion (*Selbstbehauptung*) is itself a radical critique of the central Nazi term of *Gleichschaltung*, the "bringing into alignment" of all the institutions of the state.[34] In this and every other respect it is not a merely Nazi speech. It was widely criticized among Nazi commentators for refusing to deal with the "principle" or doctrine of race. It was withdrawn from publication almost immediately after Heidegger resigned from the rectorate a mere twelve months later, ostensibly after refusing to dismiss two Jewish directors of university departments.

The rectorial address opens with the question of "*who we ourselves are*,"[35] and proceeds to answer it by speaking of how "only then, if we again place ourselves under the power of the *beginning* of our historical-intellectual existence [*Dasein*]. This beginning is the point of departure of Greek philosophy. Herein [*Darin*] Occidental man rises up from a *Volkstum* in the strength of his language against *being in general* [*das Seiende überhaupt*] and questions and comprehends it as the being that it is."[36] *Volkstum* is a distinctly Nazi term—meaning nationhood, national character (in a positive, "Aryan," sense)—which Heidegger is reworking to indicate the polis, *in* the manner of its being polis (irrespective of race). The transformation named here is the transition *from* a metaphysical understanding of the foundation of the intellectual-historical *to* one founded in being itself, the being *of* being.

Otto Pöggeler notes that "the first decisive public reference to Nietzsche" in Heidegger's work is to be found in the rectorial address of 1933.[37] Pöggeler's identification in the rectorial address of the first public reference to Nietzsche is identical with the first decisive *philosophical* reference to Nietzsche in Heidegger's work, in a lecture of 1925. This reference is to the death of God,[38] without which the very writing of *Being and Time* could not

34. Heidegger had already clashed with Krieck on these issues, in his having joined in March 1933 the Kulturpolitische Arbeitsgemeinschaft Deutscher Hochschullehrer. See Rüdiger Safranski, *Ein Meister aus Deutschland*, 266–70.

35. Martin Heidegger, "Die Selbstbehauptung der deutschen Universität" (*GA*16), 107. "*Wer wir selbst sind*" (Heidegger's emphasis). See for a repetition of this question, and the effective commentary on the *Rektoratsrede* that it represents, Martin Heidegger, *Logik als die Frage nach dem Wesen der Sprache* (*GA*38), 48–70.

36. Martin Heidegger, "Die Selbstbehauptung der deutschen Universität" (*GA*16), 108 f. "Nur dann, wenn wir uns wieder unter die Macht des *Anfangs* unseres geistig-geschichtlichen Daseins stellen. Dieser Anfang ist der Aufbruch der griechischen Philosophie. Darin stellt der abendländische Mensch aus einem Volkstum kraft seiner Sprache erstmals auf gegen das *Seiende im Ganzen* und befragt und begreift es als das Seiende, das es ist" (Heidegger's emphases).

37. Otto Pöggeler, *Der Denkweg Martin Heideggers*, 108.

38. Martin Heidegger, "Die Selbstbehauptung der deutschen Universität" (*GA*16), 111. "Friedrich Nietzsche sagte: 'Gott ist tot'–." Compare *Prolegomena zur Geschichte des Zeit-*

have been possible. Heidegger drew specific attention to his reference to Nietzsche in his 1945 reflection on the rectorial address, noting that "on essential grounds with this precept I opened my rectorial address."[39]

The speech deals critically with the issue of the death of God and the flight of the gods, but states that not a *subject* or "subjects," but a *people* (*Volk*) rises up and asserts itself against being as a whole for the sake of the being that it is, as once, Heidegger says, the Greeks had done—in that the death of God renews the possibility of the questionableness with respect to beings. The identity of Nietzsche and Heidegger is always marked by an essential difference, literally, a difference of grounds. If Nietzsche's ground is Descartes's cogito, as Heidegger himself claimed, Heidegger gave existence, *Dasein,* a quite other basis, as we have seen.

The question Heidegger considers is that of the relationship of the *Volk,* the nation, to the state. Nevertheless, the *fate* of the nation is decided by *the "how," the manner of its coming to be a nation.* Heidegger claimed in a lecture in 1934 that "the rulership of this state is the responsible implementation of the will of the leader, to whom the supportive fidelity of the people authorises the leading."[40] The state, Heidegger, continues, is not a mere apparatus for laws (*Gesetzesapparat*) but indicates the fidelity and responsibility "in which and through which the people realizes its historical existence [*Dasein*]."[41] It is *the* people, the people of *this historical moment,* and not *any* people, "a" people, that is at issue in this destinal moment. This means that for Heidegger and in 1934 a historical destiny is, for Heidegger as he writes, being granted and fulfilled.

In a lecture course of 1942–43 Heidegger examines the explicit connections of subjectivity, metaphysics, and the politics of Nazism which suggest even within these few years a radical transformation of his understanding of National Socialism and the question of the nation as polis and *Volk.* If the mention of the word *Volk* in *Being and Time* can only by the most tendentious means be connected with National Socialism, and if in the early

---

*begriffs* (*GA*20), 110. "Und gerade in diesem Atheismus wird sie zu dem, was ein Großer einmal sagte, zur 'Fröhlichen Wissenschaft.'" The first actual mention of Nietzsche in Heidegger's public work appears in a lecture of 1920, in connection with Heidegger's discussion of a misreading of Nietzsche's understanding of the apostle St. Paul. Compare Martin Heidegger, *Phänomenologie des Religiösen Lebens* (*GA*60), 120.

39. Martin Heidegger, "Das Rektorat" (*GA*16), 376. "Diesen Satz habe ich aus wesentlichen Gründen in meiner Rektoratsrede angeführt."

40. Martin Heidegger, *Die Deutsche Universität* (*GA*16), 302. "Die Herrschaft dieses Staates ist die verantwortliche Durchsetzung jenes Führerwillens, zu dem das gefolgschaftliche Vertrauen des Volkes die Führung ermächtigt."

41. Martin Heidegger, "Die Deutsche Universität" (*GA*16), 302. "In der und durch die das Volk sein eigenes geschichtliches Dasein verwirklicht."

1930s the use of the term can be seen to have been taken up into his philosophy but at the same time transformed by it, by the early 1940s Heidegger shows the extent to which he is in a formal confrontation with the linguistic apparatus of Nazism.

The converse political form to intersubjectivity, which, as converse, is at the same time thought out of the same ground, is no less a constructed form than any attempted through intersubjectivity. So whereas in intersubjectivity we attempt to think *through* to the "other" to ourselves as "object" to our subject, Heidegger himself noted: "following Kant, to the essence of I-hood [*Ichheit,* i.e., subjectivity] exactly belongs the sway of consciousness in general as the essence of a self-representing humanity."[42] This converse way of construing subjectivity is itself the consequence of the very ambiguity I have named. For either the subjectivity of the subject can be posited in the individual, either as myself or as the (objectified) "other," or—exactly as the ambiguity to which I have drawn attention makes possible—the subjectivity of the subject is posited in the "ideal subject," consciousness as universal (Kant) or absolute realized in concrete forms (Hegel). Every particular subject realizes himself through the *positum* of the universal, as ideal or *idea.* In the political sphere this again has precise correlates, which Heidegger does not hesitate to draw attention to: "selfhood in the sense of subjectivity and egoity as a result unfolds itself in multifarious forms which historically become evident as nation and as people [*Volk*]."[43] We might add to this list those of party and class, inasmuch as they arise from Marx's developments of Hegel's thought, but Heidegger explicitly attacks the ideological apparatus of Nazism by adding immediately "*Volkheit* and the *Völkische* are grounded in the essence of subjectivity and egoity. Only after metaphysics, that means the truth of being in general, has been grounded on subjectivity and I-hood, has the 'national' and 'popular' [*Volkhafte*] the exact metaphysical ground from which they can be a general historically possibility."[44]

The ambiguity of the terms "being" and "existence," however, does not stem from any ambiguity in the subjectivity of the subject. Rather the other way round: inasmuch as existence and being are the possibility of the existence and being of *any* one, they are at the same time the being and existence of *all.* This does not mean that placedness is prior to being—precisely not: we have already seen, placedness is another *name* for being, the being *of*

42. Martin Heidegger, *Parmenides* (*GA*54), 204. "Zum Wesen der Ichheit nach Kant gerade das Walten des Bewußtseins überhaupt gehört als das Wesen des auf sich gestellten Menschentums."

43. Ibid., 204. "Das Selbstsein im Sinne der Subjektivität und Egoität entfaltet sich in der Folge zu mannigfachen Gestalten, die geschichtlich als Nation und als Volk hervortreten."

44. Ibid., 204. "Die Volkheit und das Völkische gründen im Wesen der Subjektivität und Egoität."

beings. Placedness is therefore not prior either to *a* specific being, *my* being. Placedness, inasmuch as it is the being of beings, is *at the same time* the placedness of any specific being. Placedness lets beings be *in being.*

It becomes possible to see very clearly how James Phillips can argue that Heidegger rejects National Socialism in its Hitlerist form. As Phillips puts it, "what Heidegger holds against National Socialism is its liberalism":[45] in this he cites Heidegger's own critique of liberalism that permeates the *Beiträge,*[46] such that, Phillips concludes, "National-Socialism unwittingly revealed itself to be liberalism's response to its critics."[47] It is in Heidegger's confrontation with Hegel that we learn how Heidegger understands the term "liberal" to function. From the protocols of the centrally important seminar on Hegel and the state from immediately after the rectorate (1934–35) that we have already discussed, and which took place just prior to his beginning writing the *Beiträge,* Heidegger speaks of how, through Rousseau, the common understanding of liberalism concerns the notion of freedom as the freedom of the individual. Heidegger is reported as saying "Rousseau determines freedom negatively-abstractly; his freedom is 'freedom from.'"[48] This understanding places the citizen and the state in a particular (i.e., negative) relation of freedom. As such, "this liberalism is an interpretation of freedom, in which freedom primarily is grasped as freedom of the individual as an individual. That is a misunderstanding of freedom!"[49]

To demonstrate what is at issue, Heidegger cites a sentence of the *Philosophy of Right:* "The principle of the modern state has this uncanny depth and strength: it permits the principle of subjectivity to fulfil itself in the *self-sufficient extreme* of personal particularity, and at the same time *draws it back to substantial unity* and so through this preserving it in itself."[50] The protocols of the seminar report Heidegger saying that "with this statement Hegel surmounts the whole of liberalism."[51] The word "surmounts" (*überwindet*) at one and the same time says: sums up, accounts for, and overcomes.

Liberalism only appears to guarantee the open freedom of the indi-

45. James Phillips, *Heidegger's Volk,* 44.

46. Compare Martin Heidegger, *Beiträge zur Philosophie* (*GA*65), 25, 53, 181.

47. James Phillips, *Heidegger's Volk,* 43.

48. Martin Heidegger, *Seminare: Hegel—Schelling* (*GA*86), 649. "Rousseau bestimmt Freiheit negativ-abstrakt; seine Freiheit ist Freiheit von."

49. Ibid., 649. "Der Liberalismus ist eine Deutung der Freiheit, in der die Freiheit primär gefaßt wird als Freiheit des Einzelnen als Einzelnen. Das ist eine Mißdeutung der Freiheit!"

50. Ibid., 649, citing G. W. F. Hegel, *Grundlinien der Philosophie des Rechts,* 407. "Das Prinzip der modernen Staaten hat diese ungeheure Stärke und Tiefe, das Prinzip der Subjektivität sich zum *selbständigen* Extreme der persönlichen Besonderheit vollenden zu lassen und zugleich es in die *substantielle Einheit zurückzuführen* und so in ihm selbst diese zu erhalten" (Hegel's emphases).

51. Ibid., 650. "Mit diesem Satz überwindet Hegel den ganzen Liberalismus."

vidual: this guarantee, however, is a merely negative possibility that masks the totalizing inner force of liberalism. Freedom is located not in the open "choices" of the individual, resolved merely contractually through a relationship with the state, but rather in the state itself, that state *to* which the individual is totally to be coordinated: this is the positive (metaphysical) character of the freedom in question: freedom to realize and fulfill the demand for the *concrete,* material, realization of, and attainment to, absolute subjectivity. Heidegger is reported as concluding that, in contrast to the "misunderstanding" of the sense of freedom normally given in liberalism, "Hegel on the contrary determines the essence of freedom out of the essence of *Geist,*"[52] so that rather than establishing the individual merely as an individual, this freedom establishes the individual through the relationship of the self-sufficiency of the individual to *Recht,* "right" itself.

It is in this understanding of Hegel that we can see already what Phillips means by claiming that National Socialism was liberalism's answer to its critics: because we know that Heidegger was strenuously opposed to the very understanding and definition of liberalism that he supplies, we can see that concealed in this explication of Hegel's totalitarian understanding of the state as that *to which* the individual is always positively coordinated for the sake of the realization of absolute subjectivity, there is a not entirely concealed critique of the Nazi insistence on the coordination of every facet of social life to the state—what the Nazis termed *Gleichschaltung* or "coordination." Nazism is *one of* the possible fulfillments of Hegel's account of liberalism: it is for this reason that on the day of the birth of the Nazi state Hegel first began to live. It is not accidental that Heidegger is reported as arguing that once this conception of freedom is clarified, the place for speaking of "the relationship between the state and religion" is opened up, as we shall see in the next chapter.[53]

Phillips is not the first to have reached this judgment concerning Nazism's liberalism, he reminds us: Phillipe Lacoue-Labarthe had himself commented that "'Nazism is a humanism.'"[54] We have been able to grasp the extent to which Heidegger works out the meaning of *Dasein* and the structural analytic of *Dasein* as both political and historical. In undertaking this it has been possible to see the extent to which Heidegger was not unjustified in claiming that in 1933 "I saw no other alternative." We perhaps leave the last word to Heidegger, again from the *Spiegel* interview. The interviewer

52. Ibid., 650. "Hegel dagegen bestimmt das Wesen der Freiheit aus dem Wesen des Geistes."

53. Ibid., 651. "Das Verhältnis von Staat und Religion."

54. James Phillips, *Heidegger's Volk,* 45, citing Lacoue-Labarthe, *Heidegger, Art and Politics,* 95.

confronted Heidegger with a statement of his, to the effect that "the Führer himself and alone is the present and future German reality and its law." Heidegger replied: "These sentences are not to be found in the rectorial address, but only in the local Freiburg student newspaper, at the beginning of the winter semester 1933–34. When I took over the rectorate, it was clear to me that I would not get through it without making compromises. Today I would no longer write the sentences you cited. Even in 1934, I no longer said anything of the kind."[55]

Here we encounter the disconcerting and uncanny—to some infuriating—feature of Heidegger's political engagement. For what is strange about Heidegger's critique of politics is that it is without any kind of resolution, any kind of "practical" reflection on how the onslaught of Nazism, Marxism, world democracy might be, and might have been, overcome. It fails to say the things we would want to hear said: it fails to comfort us with the thought that we can take charge of this destiny and direct it according to our will. Heidegger's thought of the political fails, in other words, as a humanism. As this failure, it fails to announce a plan. Every plan arises on the basis of *technē*, of the taking of the historical situation in hand and placing it under control. Here we see the inherent connection between humanism, metaphysics, *technē*, and the demand for an adequate "technology"—a demand precisely being repeated in the requirement to pump the carbon dioxide from power stations into fissures in the depths of the earth, or seed the air with darkening particles (or even surround the planet with mirrors turned back against the sun) as the technological requirement to "save" the planet and so "save" its human inhabitants. Heidegger abandons humanity to the *fatedness* of its fate: which is to say no more than its fate is the playing out and unfolding of the planetary history of being. This is both the history being has (its own history) and the history it *is* (the history we *are* in the being of being human).

Everything revolves around the critique announced by Heidegger's reading of the eleventh thesis of Feuerbach: Heidegger accuses Marx, not of setting philosophy aside for the sake of action, but, in issuing the call to action, of not *even* having been capable of sufficiently setting philosophy aside.

55. Martin Heidegger, "*Spiegel*-Gespräch mit Martin Heidegger" (*GA*16), 657. "Der Führer selbst und allein *ist* die heutige und künftige deutsche Wirklichkeit und ihr Gesetz. *Heidegger:* Diese Sätze stehen nicht in der Rektoratsrede, sondern nur in der lokalen Freiburger Studentenzeitung, zu Beginn des Wintersemesters 1933/34. Als ich das Rektorat übernahm, war ich mir darüber klar, daß ich ohne Kompromisse nicht durchkäme. Die angeführten Sätze würde ich heute nicht mehr schreiben. Dergleichen habe ich schon 1934 nicht mehr gesagt" (emphasis in original text).

*Chapter 9*

# The Jewish Question

WHY IS THE QUESTION of the biological a metaphysical question? Hegel's philosophy, as the completion of metaphysics, is the rational securing of every being in advance of its becoming manifest through an already-grasped idea of it. What this means is that every being that *is*, is secured in terms of what it *ought* to be, or rather, what it must become. The being above all that metaphysics takes in hand and seeks to exercise absolute control over is the human being: metaphysics, as we have seen, is a humanism. This "securing" and "taking control" is therefore, and above all, the self-securing and self-controlling of the subjectivity of the subject: as we shall see with increasing clarity, this is what "production" is for Marx. Humanity is a "self-production." Nowhere is this stated more clearly by Marx than in the *Theories of Surplus Value* when he says "production for the sake of production means no less than the development of the human productive forces, or *development of the richness of human nature as an end in itself*."[1] The completion of metaphysics is at the same time the proclamation of the death of God. This means that material history itself, in the concrete form of social relations, must make manifest the death of God, as a way of demonstrating the absolute culmination, the concentration into the human, of the summit of all productive forces. Marx's next sentence in the *Theories of Surplus Value* is perhaps most prescient as an at least potential justification for many of the most criminal acts undertaken by states in the twentieth century: "if one places . . . the welfare of the individual above this end [of the development of all human productive forces] then one asserts that the development of the species must be *arrested* in order to secure the welfare of the individual, so that, for instance, no war might be pursued if some individuals were to be destroyed."[2]

1. Karl Marx, *Theorien über den Mehrwert*, vol. 2 (*MEW*26), 111. "Produktion um der Produktion halber nichts heißt, als Entwicklung der menschlichen Produktivkräfte, also *Entwicklung des Reichtums der menschlichen Natur als Selbstzweck*" (Marx's emphasis).

2. Ibid., 111. "Stellt man . . . um das Wohl der einzelnen zu sichern, daß also z. B. kein Krieg geführt werden dürfe, worin einzelne jedenfalls kaputtgehn." The remark is specifically made

This sentence arises precisely and only on the basis of the ambiguity between the individual and the whole of being that we traced in the last chapter. We should add that what Marx says here can *also* only arise when being as a whole has both been grasped as a single entity (a single *future* possibility—"species-being," "absolute subjectivity") and when that single entity is only and entirely explained through the "human being" and so not being itself, which is nothing human. Marx's analysis precisely accords with Heidegger's in this, differing only in that Marx proclaims a *goal,* and the means to its achievement; for Heidegger what is at issue is an explanation of the phenomenon of metaphysics in its concrete forms as arising on the ground of the *forgottenness of being.* It would be folly to hold Marx to account for the crimes of Stalin, Mao, and the many other "Marxist" leaders whose policies and actions resulted in the deaths of not millions but tens of millions across the years of the twentieth century, in the name of progress to communism. The fact that this and other remarks were interpreted in a particular way nevertheless shows the extent to which the question of interpretation can be decisive for the lives and fates of millions, and not just in the "intellectual" sphere. Marx's statement stands on an entirely metaphysical basis: there is no essence of humanity; man *is* what he is to *become.* No man who has not yet become (who *is* less than he will be) may stand in the way of the becoming itself. Mao's terrifying statement during the Great Leap Forward that "it is better to let half of the people die so that the other half can eat their fill" springs from the same metaphysical place.[3]

This chapter examines the material basis of the metaphysical understanding of the state and of "humanity" that has been unfolded in the last four chapters. If Marx orients the fate of the individual on the need to produce and realize the species-being of humanity, Nazism (no less than do contemporary liberal democracies) orients the fate of the individual on the state. The extreme form to which this was driven in Nazism was given the specifically Nazi technical term *Gleichschaltung:* "alignment." Every individual is to be aligned to the absolute authority and control of the state, and to the leader of the state. The fate of religion in the hands of Marxist states is complex and varied, with ramifications even to this day. The Marxist understanding of history is again, however, "superior" in the sense that Marx took for granted an already operative materialism in the relegation of religion to a private sphere,

in response to the humanitarian theories of Jean de Sismondi. Marx adds that Sismondi is only right to assert the welfare of the individual over against the development of the species against those (economists) who conceal (*vertuschen*—literally "hush-up") this contradiction.

3. Reported by Frank Dikötter in *Mao's Great Famine: The History of China's Most Devastating Catastrophe, 1958–62,* 88 (see also n. 16), from minutes kept by the Communist Party of China of a speech by Mao at Gansu on March 25, 1959, in response to the earliest reports of the famine caused by the drive for industrialization and collectivization.

as we shall see from Marx's own writing: nevertheless, every actual form of Marxist state has taken the form of state-socialism, where religion, as the embodiment of the claim to the supersensible, has been at the most relegated to the private "individual" sphere. The Nazis actively persecuted all forms of religion except their own state-sponsored form of "German Christianity" in the name of "alignment." In this they actively sought to make the metaphysical reality of the death of God manifest through the positing of the absolute state, which if it permitted religion, at the same time defined what it would permit. This is almost the very form of religion that is permissible in the state as Hegel had presented it. The state assumes the place of God in every sense. Contemporary liberal democracy does not persecute religion, but arrogates to itself the right to limit and dispose the "freedom" of individual religious liberty in accordance with the interests of the state as a whole, through a complex of legislation, law, and practice—in other words through the day-to-day workings of the state—in the name of the state as a whole.

No one who writes after the events of the Nazi regime can give adequate voice to, or account of, the phenomenon of the Holocaust. Nor can it be accidental that Jews were selected as the focus and singular bearers of the horror that was unleashed, even as others were also singled out and suffered similar fates before and around them. Commentators have struggled to find the "reason" for the Jewishness of the Holocaust, and perhaps the time in which this crime can be comprehended in its fullness is far from arriving with us.[4] It cannot be accidental, however, that the Nazi terror took the form of the systematic and public destruction of a people marked as chosen by God. To say that what went on in the camps was not known until later may be true in the strictest sense, but the public evacuation of homes, the public confiscation of shops, businesses, and professional practices, the liquidation of otherwise publicly lived lives could not have gone, and surely did not go, unnoticed: quite the reverse, this aspect of the destruction was *intended* to be visible. Forcibly to choose ones already marked as outsiders, and to destroy them, and in their wake (and in like manner) all who spoke out against the state, was the most effective way of forcibly aligning everyone not so selected *to* the state, a state set up in the name of *one,* the leader, while at the

4. An attempt to provide an overarching "metaphysical" reason for the Jewishness of the Holocaust is Gunnar Heinsohn's *Warum Auschwitz? Hitlers Plan und die Ratlosigkeit der Nachwelt.* Heinsohn overemphasizes the planned aspect of the Holocaust, according disproportionate weight to much of the evidence, and so underplays the political role of the terror on the wider population. He also fails to account for the haphazard way in which the decision to liquidate the Jews was finally reached, and so resorts to a view which depends too much on a rational "thesis" rather than one that was shaped by the unfolding of concrete historical events and their consequences. See, for a more measured account, Christopher R. Browning, *The Origins of the Final Solution: The Evolution of Nazi Jewish Policy, September 1939–March 1942.*

same time enforcing the public, social, *end* of the supersensible. This *also* is a restriction of every form to a metaphysically posed humanity, supposedly embodied in a singular form.[5] It is not accidental that Heidegger again took up the question of God and the atheism of philosophy during his most vehement support for Hitler.[6]

Every humanistic, metaphysical form of the state attempts to determine in advance the place religion may occupy. This remains a central question in the contemporary situation, the (legal and state) answers to which could almost have been written by Marx himself, as we shall see. Contemporary liberal democracy has, in the name of universal freedom, posited an atheist state in which every form of religion is permitted as a private affair. It is important to understand the extent to which the contemporary liberal state *also* operates out of the same metaphysical, material basis that Hegel and Marx both describe. If we take one of the foremost exponents of the theory of the liberal state in relation to religion, Martha Nussbaum, we find her saying from the outset that "all modern democracies are currently in a state of fear, and growing religious diversity is one of the things that most keenly inspires fear."[7] Nussbaum's thesis is that "liberty of conscience is incompatible with any type of religious establishment."[8] Nussbaum develops a position of "equal respect" (for which we should read the abstract indeterminacy of the subjectivity of the subject, an indeterminacy which is always determined *after* the—otherwise contingent—fact) which she strongly recommends to a Europe that she sees as inherently less rational and less constitutional than the "tradition" established in the United States.[9] The state, acknowledging the existence of God as a principle (Nussbaum speaks of a "ceremonial Deism" which "simply expresses our historical tradition"),[10] guarantees equal respect to every private expression of religion, and reserves to itself the right either to guarantee or curb the limits of that equal respect. Nussbaum inter-

5. We should not overlook the fact that the same rhetoric of the "singularity" of the leader—Hitler—also appeared around figures like Mao, Stalin, and Kim Il-sung: the so-called "cult of personality" denounced by Khrushchev.

6. See chapter 7, 155.

7. Martha C. Nussbaum, "Liberty of Conscience: The Attack on Equal Respect," 339. The ideas Nussbaum advances here are essentially a summary of her book *Liberty of Conscience: In Defense of America's Tradition of Religious Equality.*

8. Martha C. Nussbaum, "Liberty of Conscience: The Attack on Equal Respect," 339.

9. In fact, the highly rational position she describes is one which is being pursued, albeit slightly more haphazardly and by negotiating the quirks and anomalies of historical situations, in the European Union. Her quibble, in other words, is that Europe's solutions are not as technically predictable or planned as those possible under the Constitution of the United States, even if they—broadly—end up in the same place.

10. Martha C. Nussbaum, *Liberty of Conscience: In Defense of America's Tradition of Religious Equality,* 311.

prets the commitment to God in the American Constitution and on the U.S. banknote by saying "most people don't think of it as religious at all, and we are able to use the currency without noticing it."[11] Nussbaum's point is that the references to God are nothing other than the state-sanctioned acknowledgment of the possibility of private commitment, and mean nothing to the *business* of the state itself.

This understanding of the role of the state, while it strains not to appear coercive in any way (in practice it can be, and Nussbaum does not shrink from baring her teeth—the teeth of the expositor of this state doctrine, when she perceives that limits are "unjustly" transgressed), is also not different in its metaphysical basis from that found in any other form of the modern state. The state is directed absolutely to human, productive ends. Every commitment to any supersensible is either the sole possession of the state, or is permitted only insofar as it does not transgress the power of the state to regulate and dispose human, productive, ends. Jefferson's principle of "building a wall of separation between Church and State,"[12] which Nussbaum establishes as the basis of the modern state authority in the United States concerning religion, exists because "it was not a way of belittling religion, it was a way of respecting human beings."[13] The state is restricted to material, human, concerns: the absolute subjectivity of the state guarantees the freedom of every particular subjectivity (and is flexible enough to accommodate new subjective concerns as they arise).

Toward the end of the 1958 lecture *Hegel and the Greeks,* Heidegger makes a remark which we have already in part examined and to which I want to return. He speaks here of *alētheia,* and remarks that "Hegel experienced the essence of history out of the essence of being in the sense of absolute subjectivity. To this very hour there has been no experience of history which, seen philosophically, is able to correspond to this experience of history."[14]

I argued that the phrase "to this hour" names the gulf between the subject as it is metaphysically posed:[15] the absolute subject, as it comes to be understood and represented in either Hegel, Nietzsche, or Marx, and the "condition" of the present. In this gulf an imperative manifests itself, as that place from out of which the imperative to make the *actual* experience of history correspond to the *wonted* experience of history appears as

11. Ibid., 314.

12. Ibid., 113, quoting Jefferson.

13. Ibid., 114.

14. Martin Heidegger, "Hegel und die Griechen" (*GA*9), 441. "Hegel [hat] das Wesen der Geschichte aus dem Wesen des Seins im Sinne der absoluten Subjektivität erfahren. Es gibt bis zur Stunde keine Erfahrung der Geschichte, die, philosophisch gesehen, dieser Geschichtserfahrung entsprechen könnte."

15. See 73.

the utmost drive. It is in this manner that for Hegel, as much for Nietzsche and for Marx, the philosophically (and here is meant "metaphysically") secured "experience"—what "ought" to be known—is fitted to the "is," the presence of the present: this is how the imperative of history *is manifesting* itself. Every metaphysics of becoming functions in this way. This "experience of history"—the experience of absolute subjectivity—is no experience anyone has ever had (in this sense it is ahistorical, or rather it illustrates and makes manifest what Heidegger understands is the gulf between the "historical" and "the event," *das Ereignis*) as precisely what is thrown back on to every actual experience of events, and against which each experience must be made to measure up.

Marx, even more than any other of the political formulations that arise after Hegel in each of the historical forms that they take, depends on a securing of the subjectivity of the subject as a political securing. In the *Grundrisse* this emerges as a constant discussion of the form the individual is to take (the form of species-being), but on the basis of historical development (the same argument is to be found in *Das Kapital,* albeit presented through more concrete and specific examples). Marx, for instance, contrasts the situation of individuals "fixed to one another in a determined relation, as feudal lord and vassal" as opposed to later developments where "individuals *seem* independent . . . free to collide with each other and to engage within this freedom; but they appear thus only for someone who abstracts from these *conditions,* the *conditions of existence* . . . within which these individuals enter into contact."[16] Marx's understanding of these abstractions is itself historical: even as ideas (in the same sense as Hegel employs the term "idea," as the concrete manifestation of a metaphysical abstraction) "individuals are now ruled by *abstractions,* whereas earlier they depended on one another. The abstraction or idea is, however, nothing other than the theoretical expression of those material relations which rule over them."[17] In this sense the state is one of those material relations. As an abstraction, it is at the same time something alienated, and (as we have seen) provisional. Every attempt to separate the essential metaphysical understanding that is present in the arguments given in the *Grundrisse* from, for instance, the *Economic and Philosophical Manuscripts* or the texts of the early Marx fails to understand that the fundamental

16. Karl Marx, *Grundrisse* (*MEW*42), 96, 97. "Individuen in einer Bestimmtheit in Beziehung zueinander treten, als Feudalherr und Vasall . . . die Individuen *scheinen* unabhängig. . . . frei aufeinander zu stoßen und in dieser Freiheit auszutauschen; sie scheinen so aber nur für den, der von den *Bedingungen,* den *Existenzbedingungen* . . . abstrahiert, unter denen diese Individuen in Berührung treten" (Marx's emphases).

17. Ibid., 97. "Die Individuen nun von *Abstraktionen* beherrscht werden, während sie früher voneinander abhingen. Die Abstraktion oder Idee ist aber nichts als das theoretische Ausdruck jener materiellen Verhältnisse, die Herr über sie sind" (Marx's emphasis).

structure of alienation is fully at work in all of Marx's later descriptions of historical development, exemplified in the *Grundrisse,* but also to be found in *Das Kapital.*

What concerns Marx in this description, however, is not the "individual" as the "particular and particularised self." The issue is, as we have seen, the subjectivity of the subject in his or her concrete conditions, taken as a whole, that is, in the mass. Concerning the externalized relations which are the conditions of existence, Marx says, "an individual may perhaps get finished with them [i.e., overcome them]: but not the mass who are ruled by them, since their mere existence expresses the subordination and necessary subordination of individuals under them."[18] It is here that Heidegger understands Marx's subject to be the same as the "normal man," Heidegger's phrase from the *Introduction to Metaphysics* that we discussed in chapter 6.[19] This is in contrast to what we find in Nietzsche's explanation, where the attainment to the absolute subjectivity of the subject is achieved through a *difference* between subjects such that the (highest) one explains the possibility of all others. This explains Nietzsche's sustained polemic against all forms of "socialism," the triumph of the outlook and viewpoint of the herd, "socialism—as the tyrannical final thought of the least and dumbest, the superficial, the envious and the three-quarters actor . . . the total mollification of the democratic herd-animal,"[20] a standard polemic that can be found peppered throughout his works. In Marx it is the reverse that pertains: the mass is the standard. The exception, who evades the conditions of subjection for whatever reason, does not thereby have in himself the possibility to attain to the state of absolute subjectivity (species-being), which is a historical (futural) high point, rather than a spatial (highest versus lowest) possibility, for man.

The attainment of the absolute subjectivity of the subject is in fact for Marx the resolution of the necessity of alienation. This attainment does not mean that alienation ceases, but rather something else more fundamental occurs. In the present situation of alienation (for the worker), *more* is always objectified of him than he receives back in the form of exchange for

18. Ibid., 97. "Der einzelne kann zufällig mit ihnen fertig werden; die Masse der von ihnen Beherrschten nicht, da ihr bloßes Bestehn die Unterordnung und die notwendige Unterordnung der Individuen unter sie ausdrückt."

19. See 129.

20. Friedrich Nietzsche, vol. 11, *Nachlaß 1884–1885,* 586, 587 (= *Wille zur Macht,* §125, 90, 91). "Der Socialismus—als die zu Ende gedachte Tyrannei der Geringsten und Dümmsten, der Oberflächlichen, der Neidischen und der Dreiviertels-Schauspieler . . . die gänzliche Vergutmüthigung des demokratischen Heerdenthieres." The word "tyranny" is emphasized in the text of Gast's *Will to Power.* Walter Kaufmann notes in the English translation (77, n. 106) that "the manuscript is not in Nietzsche's handwriting but was evidently dictated by him, and then corrected and amplified in his hand."

his labor. Indeed, labor, as the calculable value of exchange, is precisely the surplus of which the worker is robbed: accumulated labor, or, more fundamentally yet, capital, as such. Likewise the capitalist (and his class) receives back *more* than is proper to him: this is also an alienation: his very receipt of this "more," the surplus, than is proper is a dehumanization, a reduction of his being. We will examine this more fully when we enter the question of production as such. For now it suffices that we understand in Marx the relation of alienation to subjectivity.

The historical task for both labor and capital are their self-abolition—this occurs as the historical opposition of the one to the other. Marx argues that capital itself, and the drive of capital to increase itself and to realize its increase as exchange, money, and the commodity produces the conditions under which labor abolishes both itself and capital:

> As the ceaseless striving after the general form of riches, capital drives labor out beyond its limits of its natural neediness and thus creates the material elements for the development of that rich individuality, which is as balanced in its production as in its consumption, and whose labor is therefore labor no more, but appears as the full development of activity itself, in which natural necessity in its immediate form has disappeared; because in place of natural neediness something historically produced has arrived.[21]

Alienation is overcome *historically* by having arrived at the end form through the mediation of the sublation of capital *and labor*. The overcoming of alienation means that the end form in question, absolute subjectivity (species-being), produces as much as it consumes, *not* that it abandons and ceases to be part of the logic (the dialectic) of consumption and production. The mass becomes fully self-present to itself through a stabilized, balanced (*allseitig*—where every particular "side" is equivalent identical to the *all*) individuation. Once again, Marx's later work is visibly developed from the metaphysically secured understanding of subjectivity (as species-being) to be found in his earlier confrontation with Hegel, especially in the years 1843–44.

An antisemitic rhetoric has also been a feature of the political language of communism, not least in the Germany of the period before 1933. We must ask, how is it that, for instance, a half-Jewish, self-avowed communist, a

21. Karl Marx, *Grundrisse* (*MEW*42), 244. "Als das rastlose Streben nach der allgemeinen Form des Reichtums treibt aber das Kapital die Arbeit über die Grenzen seiner Naturbedürftigkeit hinaus und schafft so die materiellen Elemente für die Entwicklung der reichen Individualität, die ebenso allseitig in ihrer Produktion als Konsumtion ist und deren Arbeit daher auch nicht mehr als Arbeit, sondern als volle Entwicklung der Tätigkeit selbst erscheint, in der die Naturnotwendigkeit in ihrer unmittelbaren Form verschwunden ist; weil an die Stelle des Naturbedürfnisses ein geschichtlich erzeugtes getreten ist."

member of the Central Committee of the German Communist Party (KPD), could have taken up such language in the period before Hitler's rise to power, when the extreme right in most of its forms was publicly and avowedly antisemitic?[22] The answer, extraordinarily enough, to some large extent lies in Marx's own writings—or rather in the prevailing Marxist interpretation of them. In February 1844, Marx published in the *German-French Yearbook* a text that was in many ways a continuation and development of the questions of the *Critique of the Hegelian State Order*, the latter only having been published by Riazanov in 1927, "On the Jewish Question."[23] Here Marx takes up the question of the Jew as foreigner, indeed deadly enemy, within the state: "However, the Jew only comports himself to the state in a Jewish way, which means as outsider to the state."[24] Judaism "is the deadly enemy of the state religion."[25] Marx reserves his harshest words, however, for the Jew as financier: "The monotheism of the Jews is therefore in reality the polytheism of many needs . . . The god of *practical needs and self-interest* is *money*. The God of the Jews has made himself worldly, he has become the World-god. Exchange is the real god of the Jews. His god is merely illusory exchange. . . . The *chimerical* nationality of the Jews is the nationality of the merchant, of the money man in general."[26]

If we have now identified the originating authorization of the originally Jewish, now communist, Ruth Fischer's excoriation of the Jewish financier

22. The question of the fate of the Jewish communities in the Soviet bloc especially (which meant particularly Russia and the Ukraine, where the largest and longest-standing communities were to be found) has been widely discussed. Robert Lynd stated the "official" view when he argued in "Planned Social Solidarity in the Soviet Union" that (187) "there seems no question that the Soviet Union is actively bent on eradicating such practices as anti-Semitism." Just a few years later Alfred Skerpan, then a former official in the American State Department, documented widespread Soviet antisemitism. See Alfred A. Skerpan, "Aspects of Soviet Antisemitism." A more thorough survey of both the contemporary literature and the earlier history of Soviet antisemitism can be found in Robert Weinberg, "Demonising Judaism in the Soviet Union During the 1920s," 120–53. Most bizarre of all Soviet-era antisemitism, perhaps, was the Romanian policy of effectively exchanging Jews for money, which was used to pay off the Romanian national debt. See Radu Ioanid, *The Ransom of the Jews: The Story of the Extraordinary Secret Bargain Between Romania and Israel.*

23. Karl Marx, "Zur Judenfrage" (*MEW*1).

24. Ibid., 348. "Aber auch der Jude kann sich nur jüdisch zum Staat verhalten, das heißt zu dem Staat als einem Fremdling."

25. Ibid., 348. "[Sie] ist die Todfeindin der Staatsreligion."

26. Ibid., 374–75. "Der Monotheismus des Juden ist daher in der Wirklichkeit der Polytheismus der vielen Bedürfnisse . . . Der Gott des *praktischen Bedürfnisses und Eigennutzes* ist das *Geld*. . . . Der Gott der Juden hat sich verweltlicht, er ist zum Weltgott geworden der Wechsel ist der wirkliche Gott des Juden. Sein Gott ist nur der illusorische Wechsel. . . . Die *chimärische* Nationalität des Juden ist die Nationalität des Kaufmanns, überhaupt des Geldmenschen" (Marx's emphases).

in the writings of the originally Jewish Karl Marx, we are, perhaps, at a loss for how to read this text. If we were to read it psychologically, we would say that what we have here is an example of how the alienation of the outsider (*Fremdling*) manifests itself in the most extreme self-hatred, so that Marx turns in on himself and, like Fischer, reduces himself to the miserable spectacle of the Jewish antisemite. This is, however, to transfer the contemporary dialectic that explains and has the structure of homosexual panic (as a merely psychological phenomenon) to the politics of nineteenth- and earlier twentieth-century revolutionary practice, and to do so is to miss the point. The use of the word *Fremdling* here does not mean "outsider," but "object of alienation." It speaks from out of the same place as the terms *Entfremdung* and *Entäußerung* of the 1844 *Economic and Philosophical Manuscripts.* The central issue of "On the Jewish Question" is not the status of the Jew (or even Judaism in general), but the status of the theoretically conceived German, Hegelian, state in its making-possible of the determinations of the being of being-human. It is in this sense that the text "On the Jewish Question" is the continuation of what Marx writes in the *Critique of the Hegelian State Order.* The text discusses throughout the status of the "Christian" state (with all the overtones, not just of Hegel's own Christianity as the highest historical form of *Geist,* but of the memory of the so-called Holy Alliance of 1815–25, the nineteenth-century prototype of the League of Nations). Marx notes that the fulfilled or perfected Christian state is not Christian at all, but "the *atheistic* state, the *democratic* state . . . The state which is still theological, which still officially professes the Christian faith, which dares not yet proclaim itself to be a state, has not yet succeeded in expressing in *worldly, human* form its *reality* as state, the *human* basis of which Christianity is the exaggerated expression."[27] The state, to *become* the state, sheds its religious affiliations and entanglements. The state *comes to be as "state"* as an atheistic phenomenon.

It is here that we can see the essential identity of the modern democratic state with the metaphysical form of the National Socialist state and the state forms that were thrown up under communism: they are all presupposed by a development only made possible and thought through by the presupposition of the state as it is described by Hegel. The modern democratic state, as much as the Marxist state, the Nazi, or the fascist, presupposes the death of God. Because there is no thinker of the democratic state on the level of a Karl Marx, in whom we "personify" this form of the state as we

27. Ibid., 357. "Der *atheistische* Staat, der *demokratische* Staat, der Staat . . . Dem Staat, der noch Theologe ist, der noch das Glaubensbekenntnis des Christentums auf offizielle Weise ablegt, der sich noch nicht *als Staat* zu proklamieren wagt, ihm ist es noch nicht gelungen, in *weltlicher, menschlicher* Form, in seiner *Wirklichkeit* als Staat die *menschliche* Grundlage auszudrücken, deren überschwenglicher Ausdruck das Christentum ist" (Marx's emphases).

personify Marxist states in Marx or as we personify the Nazi state in Hitler, does not mean that the state, in its modern democratic form, is not itself the consequence of what is *there* to be thought. The question is always, not what we *think,* as in think to be possible, but what we think *of,* think through and think out, and bring to description.

Marx continues:

> The most rigid form of opposition between the Jew and the Christian is the *religious* opposition. How does one solve an opposition? Manifestly, by making it impossible. How does one make a *religious* opposition impossible? Manifestly, inasmuch as one *sublates* [*aufhebt*] *religion.* Once Jew and Christian recognize their appositional religions as nothing more than *respective developmental stages of the human spirit* [*Geist*], as snake-skins cast off by history, with men as the snakes who wore them, they will no longer stand in a religious relation, but a critical, *scientific,* indeed human, relation.[28]

The name "Jew" here functions entirely metaphysically. The Jew, like the Christian, is that which is to be overcome, *sublated,* such that Marx (as much as Fischer might have been doing to herself) addressing himself says "we must emancipate ourselves before we can emancipate others."[29] Marx argues that "the *political* emancipation of the Jews, of the Christians, generally of the *religious* man, is the *emancipation of the state* from Judaism, from Christianity, generally from *religion.*"[30] In each case the historical conditions of the appearing of the individual are what is to be overcome, for the sake of what the individual is himself to become. In the securing of the individual as a species-being, a particular determination of the state is at the same time secured. Marx understands that the state itself is a provisional medium of the self-securing of the subjectivity of the subject, but even here, this is only for the sake of a certain determination of subjectivity: the state attains only the species-life (*Gattungsleben*) of the subjectivity of the subject. It is

28. Ibid., 348–49. "Die starrste Form des Gegensatzes zwischen dem Juden und dem Christen ist der *religiöse* Gegensatz. Wie löst man einen Gegensatz? Dadurch, daß man ihn unmöglich macht. Wie macht man einen *religiösen* Gegensatz unmöglich? Dadurch, daß man die *Religion aufhebt.* Sobald Jude und Christ ihre gegenseitigen Religionen nur mehr als verschiedene *Entwicklungsstufen des menschlichen Geistes,* als verschiedene von der *Geschichte* abgelegte Schlangenhäute und den Menschen als die Schlange erkennen, die sich in ihnen gehäutet, stehn sie nicht mehr in einem religiösen, sondern nur noch in einem kritischen, *wissenschaftlichen,* in einem menschlichen Verhältnisse" (Marx's emphases).

29. Ibid., 348. "Wir müssen uns selbst emanzipieren, ehe wir andere emanzipieren können."

30. Ibid., 353. "Die *politische* Emanzipation des Juden, des Christen, überhaupt des *religiösen* Menschen, ist die *Emanzipation des Staats* vom Judentum, vom Christentum, überhaupt von der *Religion*" (Marx's emphases).

worth considering at length how Marx understands the power of the state to function:

> Nevertheless, the political annulment of private property not only fails to abolish private property but even presupposes it. The state abolishes, in its own way, distinctions of birth, social rank, education, occupation, when it declares that *birth, social rank, education, occupation,* are *nonpolitical* distinctions, when it proclaims, without regard to these distinctions, that every member of the nation is an equal participant in national sovereignty, when it treats all elements of the real life of the nation from the standpoint of the state. Nevertheless, the state allows private property, education, occupation, to *act* in *their* way—i.e., as private property, as education, as occupation, and to exert the influence of their special nature. Far from abolishing these real distinctions, the state only exists on the presupposition of their existence; it feels itself to be a political state and asserts its universality only in opposition to these elements of its being. *Hegel,* therefore, defines the relation of the political state to religion quite correctly when he says: "In order . . . that the state should come into existence as the *self-knowing,* moral reality of the mind, its distinction from the form of authority and faith is essential. But this distinction emerges only insofar as the ecclesiastical aspect arrives at a separation within itself. It is only in this way that the state, above the *particular* churches, has achieved and brought into existence universality of thought, which is the principle of its form."
>
> Of course! Only in this way, *above* the *particular elements,* does the state constitute itself as universality.[31]

31. See ibid., 354. "Dennoch ist mit der politischen Annullation des Privateigentums das Privateigentum nicht nur nicht aufgehoben, sondern sogar vorausgesetzt. Der Staat hebt den Unterschied der *Geburt,* des *Standes,* der *Bildung,* der *Beschäftigung* in seiner Weise auf, wenn er Geburt, Stand, Bildung, Beschäftigung für *unpolitische* Unterschiede erklärt, wenn er ohne Rücksicht auf diese Unterschiede jedes Glied des Volkes zum *gleichmäßigen* Teilnehmer der Volkssouveränität ausruft, wenn er alle Elemente des wirklichen Volkslebens von dem Staatsgesichtspunkt aus behandelt. Nichtsdestoweniger läßt der Staat das Privateigentum, die Bildung, die Beschäftigung auf ihre Weise, d.h. als Privateigentum, als Bildung, als Beschäftigung *wirken* und ihr *besondres* Wesen geltend machen. Weit entfernt, diese *faktischen* Unterschiede aufzuheben, existiert er vielmehr nur unter ihrer Voraussetzung, empfindet er sich als *politischer Staat* und macht er seine *Allgemeinheit* geltend nur im Gegensatz zu diesen seinen Elementen. *Hegel* bestimmt das Verhältnis des *politischen Staats* zur Religion daher ganz richtig, wenn er sagt: 'Damit . . . der Staat als die sich wissende sittliche Wirklichkeit des Geistes zum Dasein komme, ist seine Unterscheidung von der Form der Autorität und des Glaubens notwendig; diese Unterscheidung tritt aber nur hervor, insofern die kirchliche Seite in sich selbst zur Trennung kommt; nur so über die *besondern* Kirchen hat der Staat die *Allgemeinheit* des Gedankens, das Prinzip seiner Form gewonnen und bringt sie zur Existenz.'

"Allerdings! Nur so *über* den *besondern* Elementen konstituiert sich der Staat als Allgemeinheit" (Marx's emphases).

Nothing could be clearer as an elucidation of the state's assumption of absolute subjectivity *in relation to* the particular subject. However, Marx does not seek to unravel this relation, but to radicalize it still further in arguing that the state is only a transitional form to the full achievement of species-being.

In this sense, Marx, as much as Heidegger, understood that the liberal state was itself totalitarian. If on the one hand Heidegger's political engagement represents an attempt to distinguish the nationalist state (rather than the Nazi state, recalling his letter to von Dietze and the Denazification Committee of 1946)[32] from the Nazi Party in identifying the mission of the people with the being of the state, a distinction which Heidegger came increasingly to repudiate, on the other hand Marx also sees the state as a totalitarian means on the way to the attainment of communism: Marxist theorists developed this even further into the use of the state in the dictatorship of the proletariat.[33] Indeed, Marx, even more than Heidegger in his Hitler period, forges for the (historical) task at hand an extreme identity of the nation with the party. If on the one hand "the communists are not a particular party over against the other worker parties" and "[the communists] have no interests separate from those of the entirety of the proletariat,"[34] on the other hand "the workers have no fatherland . . . Inasmuch as the proletariat must first of all acquire political rulership, must sublate themselves as the national class, must constitute themselves as nation, as itself a nation, if, however, in no bourgeois sense."[35]

Nationhood involves the fusion of the organ of the party with the state and constituting it as the nation: inasmuch as this is of the essence of Nazism and communism, it is the same only because this is the *only* possibility for the fulfillment of the liberal democratic state as "sufficient," completed, fulfilled. It is for this reason that Heidegger finally came to repudiate the notion of the nation in the modern, democratic sense as anything other than

32. Martin Heidegger, "Erläuterungen und grundsätzliches," letter to Professor Constantin von Dietze of December 15, 1945 (*GA*16), 414.

33. It is only on this basis that Lenin could establish a Soviet state in Russia in 1918. Lenin, writing against Kautsky in 1918, argues that precisely because the state is an apparatus established by one class for the oppression of another, the proletariat must seize the state apparatus and take over its machinery to eliminate the capitalist class as an oppressor. See Vladimir I. Lenin, "The Soviets Dare Not Become State Organizations" in "The Proletarian Revolution and the Renegade Kautsky," 257–63.

34. Karl Marx and Friedrich Engels, *Manifest der Kommunistischen Partei* (*MEW*4), 474. "Die Kommunisten sind keine besondere Partei gegenüber den andern Arbeiterparteien. Sie haben keine von den Interessen des ganzen Proletariats getrennten Interessen."

35. Ibid., 479. "Die Arbeiter haben kein Vaterland. Man kann ihnen nicht nehmen, was sie nicht haben. Indem das Proletariat zunächst sich die politische Herrschaft erobern, sich zur nationalen Klasse erheben, sich selbst als Nation konstituieren muß, ist es selbst noch national, wenn auch keineswegs im Sinne der Bourgeoisie."

the securing of the subjectivity of the subject, and he did this on the basis of his rejection of Hitlerism.

That Heidegger came to reject the Nazi totalitarianism is now beyond doubt. In the *Beiträge,* the first of the texts of *Das Ereignis,* early on, Heidegger associates the totalizing impulse with the organization of *Weltanschauung,* "worldview," a term central for the Nazis: the drive for totalization springs as well from *business.*[36] Fred Dallmayr detects in this discussion a distinct critique of managerialism, extending its significance from the political, or rather, showing the extent to which the political in its twentieth-century forms (and beyond) and the managerial have the same metaphysical roots.[37] Heidegger adds to this a critique of both "total political faith" which is just like "total Christian faith," both of whose struggles are all " 'propaganda' and 'apologetic,' " and we might now say, political "spin."[38] Heidegger asks: "Now, however, has not philosophy, and it above all, fully laid claim to 'the total,' inasmuch as we determine it as knowledge of being [*das Seiende*] as such *as a whole*? Indeed, as long as we think of it in the form of philosophy hitherto (metaphysics)."[39]

However, the totalitarianism at issue is a totalitarianism which is yet fully to be realized, but lies anything but dormant in the contemporary situation of the nation-state itself. This is irrespective of the endless contemporary talk of "states of emergency" and "states of exception" which are nothing but the working out of the franchises of individuality over against the necessities of the state as guarantor of the subjectivity of the subject, and nothing like final or formal determinations, since the state will always hold within itself the capacity to ground and secure, and therefore *lay out and at the same time restrict and define,* every possibility of the political existence of the specificity of subjects. In this the state understands itself as *itself* the permanentized and absolutized guarantor of the subjectivity of the subject. Indeed, the very seeming provisionality of the state, that it is plastic, and malleable, and subject to pressure, manipulation, or modification in the specific interests of individuals or nodes of power is the means by which it stands permanently, and this means metaphysically, able to lay claim to guarantee

36. Compare Martin Heidegger, *Beiträge zur Philosophie* (*GA*65), 40.

37. Fred Dallmayr, "Adorno and Heidegger on Modernity," 176. Dallmayr almost certainly has in mind that this passage needs to be taken together with the discussion of "total mobilisation" at 143 of the *Beiträge.*

38. Martin Heidegger, *Beiträge zur Philosophie* (*GA*65), 41. "Der totale politische Glaube und der ebenso totale Christliche Glaube [ist] . . . 'Propaganda' und 'Apologetik.' "

39. Ibid., 41. "Hat nun aber nicht auch die Philosophie und sie allen voran den Anspruch auf 'das Totale,' vollends, wenn wir sie bestimmen als das Wissen vom Seienden als solchen *im Ganzen*? In der Tat, solange wir in der Form der bisherigen Philosophie (der Metaphysik) denken" (Heidegger's emphasis).

the subjectivity of the subject as "freedom." Every restriction of the subject (every *subjection*) carries within it the capacity to be described as an emancipation (which is the exact basis of the politics of security, at every level, from the extension of health and safety regulations into every sphere of life to the ownership of nuclear weaponry).

What this reveals is that for Heidegger, humanism, of which the Marxist is only one form, is in its very essence totalitarian. Why this is so is yet to be explained. In the *Beiträge,* Heidegger lays out in dense form the critique of the metaphysical of the political subjectivity of the subject as nothing other than "biological-liberalism."[40] It is biological inasmuch as it secures the humanity of man on the basis of specificed conditions: "Jew," "Christian," and so forth: it is "liberal" on the basis that every particularity is to be annulled for the sake of the most generalized (and at the same time, ontologically indeterminate, because always *posited*) understanding of the ideal-being of the subjectivity of the subject (what man in his humanity "really" is, what he is to become, what he *really ought to be, to be at his "best" and "highest"*).

Heidegger concludes from this that what is at issue in the liberal and biological is "the final form of Marxism, which essentially has nothing to do with Judaism or Russia; if anywhere an unoutfolded spiritualism still lies dormant, then in the Russian people; Bolshevism is an originally western, European possibility: the emergence of the masses, of industry, technology, the dying away of Christianity; insofar, however, the rulership of reason as equalization of all is the consequence of Christendom, and this in its basis is of Jewish origin (see, for instance, Nietzsche's thought of the slave-rebellion of the moral), Bolshevism is in fact Jewish, however, then also Christianity is in its basis Bolshevist!"[41]

As "western" and "European" it is counterposed to and distinguished from Heidegger's understanding of the Occidental: this is emphasized in the text by the use of the unusual adjective *westlich.* We would think, in reading this passage, that Heidegger had written it in response to Marx's "On the Jewish Question." Perhaps he did, although we have no evidence for that. Certainly what is written here is intended as a riposte to the Nazi antisemitic polemic. Perhaps, more seriously, we would understand that Heidegger is

40. Ibid., 53. "biologische Liberalismus"

41. Ibid., 55. "Die Endform des Marxismus, die wesentlich weder mit Judentum noch gar mit dem Russentum etwas zu tun hat; wenn irgendwo noch ein unentfalteter Spiritualismus schlummert, dann im russischen Volk; der Bolschewismus ist ursprünglich westlich, europäische Möglichkeit: das Heraufkommen der Massen, die Industrie, Technik, das Absterben des Christentums; sofern aber die Vernunftherrschaft als Gleichsetzung aller nur die Folge des Christentums ist und dieses im Grunde jüdischen Ursprungs (vgl. Nietzsches Gedanke vom Sklavenaufstand der Moral), ist der Bolschewismus in der Tat jüdisch; aber dann ist auch das Christentum im Grunde bolschewistisch!"

thinking out of the same province from out of which Marx was also thinking in order to think what is written here: it is not what Heidegger thinks of Marx that is at issue, but rather what Marx and Heidegger are thinking *of* that leads them to speak of the same and within the same. This alone would prepare us to understand that Heidegger enters the same region of thought that Marx entered (but which Marx enters only as something to be overcome, to be resolved) only as a question to be entered *into.* For Heidegger precedes this passage with the question: "Here in fact the questioning of the question: 'who we are,' concerning humanity is more *dangerous* than any other opposition which we might indeed encounter from the selfsame region as a certainty."[42]

42. Ibid., 55. "Hier ist in der Tat das Fragen der Frage: wer wir sind, *gefährlicher* als jede andere Gegnerschaft, die einem je auf derselben Ebene einer Gewißheit über den Menschen begegnet" (Heidegger's emphasis).

*Chapter 10*

# Speaking of the Essence of Man

WE HAVE ALREADY SEEN how Marx, in the sixth thesis on Feuerbach, had asserted that "the human essence is no abstraction inhering in each particular individual,"[1] in a way entirely consistent with Hegel's essential metaphysical thought of becoming and Nietzsche's will to power. In arguing that species-essence is determined *from out of* the social relations in which it appears, although Marxism represents a "straining forth" *toward* what man is to become, and privileges the advance into the horizon of what is yet to come, nevertheless, the essentially circular movement implicit in Hegel's metaphysics is reproduced in Marx's thought in full, and manifests itself through the way in which every individual subject is derived from, and taken off, species-being as a whole, insofar as he or she appears at all. The "essence" of man is contained in his becoming, but becoming both *through* and *in* the social relations that he at the same time produces and makes concrete and "real." It is in this way that "man" is socially constructive (and can understand himself as having been socially constructed), but individual men and women are always on the way to realizing what and who "man" really "is" as what is to become (species-being). It is in this sense that species-being is an entirely metaphysical figuration of absolute subjectivity.

Heidegger also rejects an "essence" to man, but in a way that he believed spoke from the overcoming of metaphysics. To speak of essence in this way speaks simultaneously of the history of the speech about essences, and the end of that speech in Nietzsche and Marx, and allows us to understand the fundamental relation of "essence" to being. This speaking of the whole of history all at once, and at the same time overcoming the history of being as a history of metaphysics (the "Platonism" which is also a "materialism"), Heidegger called "the turning." The language that speaks of this "turning" is the language that lies in the background of the *Letter on Humanism,* and at the same time is the language that was found, and Hei-

1. See 117.

degger found a way to speak, through the manuscripts of *Das Ereignis.* It is this language, this language of thinking, and this alone, that allows Heidegger to enter with Marx into the productive dialogue: it is at the same time a language that Heidegger only found his way into after the rectorate. This language of thinking was first named as an ambitious possibility that was unable to be attained to, intended for the unwritten sections of *Being and Time.* In the *Letter on Humanism,* as we have already seen Heidegger explain, "the division in question was held back, because thinking failed in the adequate saying of this turn."[2] This chapter traces the long history of Heidegger's attempt to bring this turning to speech. This history is not merely Heidegger's history, but also his confrontation with the historical events through which he lived. In this sense, no less than the death of God and the industrialization of Europe as actual occurrences, which shaped and gave voice to Nietzsche's and Marx's thought, was Heidegger's voice also a voice of, and from out of, his age.

At issue, for Heidegger, is language itself. In the *Letter on Humanism* Heidegger describes language—speech—as follows: "language is clearing-concealing advent of being itself."[3] We translate in this rough and awkward way because the missing definite article ("the clearing-concealing") is even more conspicuous and jarring to the ear in German than it is in English: Heidegger intended it to be heard in this way, with the entire emphasis on what occurs as an active, verbal, happening. Because only man is the being who speaks, it is in language that Heidegger finds the particular belonging to being of man. Part of the "productive dialogue" therefore, is to inquire into the particularity of man, in relation to Marx's claim that the whole of nature is in a very direct way here "for" man. What belongs to humanity, and what humanity belongs to, poses the question of the locatedness of man. In this sense the phrase "man is the being who explains all other beings" can be understood either as the one who takes control and has mastery and disposal over all other beings, or the one who alone can speak *of,* and *for,* other beings. To provide a full account of the development of Heidegger's understanding of language would require a book in its own right. Here we can do no more than provide a fragmentary account for the sake of allowing us to enter into the productive dialogue, in itself a concern of how to speak and how the conversation is able to take place, not as an abstract "exchange of views," but as a genuinely historical event, in which our own locatedness is also brought to the fore.

2. See 36.

3. Martin Heidegger, *Brief über den Humanismus* (*GA*9), 326. "Sprache ist lichtend-verbergende Ankunft des Seins selbst."

If Heidegger asks the question "who we are"[4] concerning humanity, a question which, he says, is "more *dangerous*" than any certainty in any of those *answers*—liberal, National Socialist, Marxist—that spring from the same region of thinking,[5] this question is above all a historical question. Who we are asks our "whence": our "wherefrom" and our "whereto." The *Beiträge zur Philosophie* is first in the seven volumes that collect together all the manuscripts of the series *Das Ereignis.* The *Beiträge* lays out the difference between *seynsgeschichtliche Denken,* be-ing historical thinking, and the forgetfulness of being, *Seinsvergessenheit.* In the *Beiträge* and in the notebooks of *Das Ereignis,* forgetfulness of being is clarified as *Seinsverlassenheit,* taking leave of, or abandonment of, being. Here again the ambiguity of the objective and subjective genitives are in play and must be heard.[6] To think this difference *in* its difference, is to think *how* what Marx thinks *of* and what Heidegger thinks *of* differ, and yet how they each persist in thinking "from the selfsame region."[7]

Abandonment of being is grounded in what Heidegger calls the "guiding question" that grounds all metaphysics: "what is the being?,"[8] that appears from the inception of metaphysics with the Greeks (Aristotle and Plato) onward: *ti to on?*[9] Be-ing historical thinking, however, occurring after the death of God, after and following on from, the fulfillment of metaphysics asks, not "what is the being" but "wie west das Seyn?"[10] There is no easy translation of this sentence. *Ein Wesen* in German is another way of saying "a being," a presence, an "essence." There is no verb *wesen* in modern German. At the same time Heidegger contrasts *das Seyn* to *das Sein.* Speaking of *das Seyn* arises specifically in consequence, and out of, his political engagement—indeed, the whole burden of this book, as should by now have become clear, is that Heidegger understands the thinking of *das Seyn* only on the basis of this engagement. *Das Seyn* is not, however, what we think, as in "think up," "think for ourselves and myself," "think creatively and productively." The

4. A question Heidegger repeats immediately after the Hitlerist adventure of the rectorate, in the lectures on Hölderlin of the autumn of 1934. See Martin Heidegger, *Hölderlins Hymnen: "Germanien" und "Der Rhein"* (*GA*39), 48 and following.

5. Martin Heidegger, *Beiträge zur Philosophie* (*GA*65), 55. "Der Frage: wer wir sind, *gefährlicher*" (Heidegger's emphasis).

6. See ibid., 68. "Abandonment of being (at first the decay of the understanding of being and forgetfulness of being)." ("Seinsverlassenheit [zunächst Verfall des Seinsverständnisses und Seinsvergessenheit].")

7. Ibid., 55. "Auf derselben Ebene."

8. Ibid., 12. "Alle Metaphysik (gegründet auf die Leitfrage: was ist das Seiende?)."

9. Ibid., 38.

10. Ibid., 54.

thought of *das Seyn* is the most originary thought, what *lets itself be thought,* what addresses me and befalls me, inasmuch as *I* am ready to be addressed, by how being unfolds. Being-ready is itself not an act of genius, of personal worth, of cleverness, or creativity: absolutely the reverse. It is a bestowal, it is how I think most originarily: how I am given to think. "Wie west das Seyn" asks "how is it that be-ing is, being as 'be-ing originarily' *is, happens*?"

We could, if we were to mishear this question, think that what is at issue is an attempt to recover the *philosophia perennis* of Leibniz, the thinking that is always and everywhere and at all times the same thinking (the metaphysical thought of God—subjectively and objectively). Nothing could be less possible for Heidegger. *Wie west das Seyn* is never the most general, most universal thought: quite the reverse, it is the most particular, most historically given, and most factical and concrete thought. The *how* always presupposes the *for whom* this is thought, the thinking that can only ever have a particular locale, and time (not hour, or moment of the clock, but the *event* in its eventuality). It is the question that arises in the *da,* the here, from out of which *Da-sein* occurs for itself (*sich-ereignet*). It is a question that can only ever be "mine."

The question concerning the subjectivity of the subject, the "humanity" of humanism, is always a "what-question," a question that asks about the being of an essence. The what-question asks about universals: above all, the universal of the human-being. Heidegger argues that the "who-question" arose with Nietzsche: thus, he asks in the very title of an essay of 1953, *Wer ist Nietzsches Zarathustra?: Who Is Nietzsche's Zarathustra?*[11] Early on in this text Heidegger speaks of how, through securing an understanding of Zarathustra's self-definition "with this assertion we have brought the essence [*Wesen*] of Zarathustra to a definition."[12] To bring an essence to definition, metaphysically thought, is to know what "it" "is." The essence of Zarathustra is that he is the advocate of what stands before us, "that all being is will to power."[13] Later Heidegger argues that, following Leibniz, Kant, and Fichte, and in Hegel and Schelling, "Schopenhauer indicated the same, inasmuch as he gives his principal work the title '*The World* (not Man) *as Will and Representation.*' Nietzsche thinks the same, inasmuch as he recognizes the originary-being of beings as Will to Power."[14]

To think an essence metaphysically, as we have already seen with

11. Martin Heidegger, "Wer ist Nietzsches Zarathustra" (*GA*7), 99–124.

12. Ibid., 103. "Mit dieser Aussage haben wir das Wesen Zarathustras auf eine Definition gebracht."

13. Ibid., 103. "Daß alles Seiende Wille zur Macht ist."

14. Ibid., 113. "Das Selbe meint Schopenhauer, wenn er seinem Hauptwerk den Titel gibt: 'Die Welt (nicht der Mensch) als Wille und Vorstellung.' Das Selbe denkt Nietzsche, wenn er das Ursein des Seienden als Wille zur Macht erkennt."

Marx's thought of the *individuum* in the *Grundrisse,* is to think the particular man out of the general thought of the future possibility of man as species-being. Except, as Heidegger points out, Zarathustra is not a human voice, but the *form* of a voice. Heidegger argues that "nowhere else in the history of Occidental metaphysics has the form of the essence of its respective thinker in this way been as properly related," with the possible, veiled, exception of Parmenides.[15]

The "who" of Nietzsche shows up the "who" of Marx: each is respectively a form that does not exist,[16] but that can only be thought from out of the way being-as-a-whole is secured. How that being as a whole is secured in Marx is to where we must now turn. But to ask "who," *not* in the figure of a form, is to enter into that question which places us in "be-ing historical thinking." Heidegger indicates this, and the difficulty—the "danger" named in the earlier quotation from the *Beiträge* and in many other places—when he says, in a statement as true of Marx's thought of the *individuum* as it is of Nietzsche's Zarathustra, "therefore something comes to light which this thinking itself was no longer able to think. . . . Where indeed a thinking brings metaphysics to fulfillment, it indicates in an exceptional sense the unthought, meaningfully and confusedly at the same time." Heidegger adds, mischievously, "but where are the eyes to see this?"[17] We understand this question only insofar as we understand the following: "*Dasein* as always *mine.*"[18]

The *form,* the "form of the essence" is that which is visible in each case: that which is "common," the "whatness" or "quiddity" of the being of the being *in* its being. How this being is let into being by the understanding at work of being-as-a-whole we are not yet ready to see. But how do we see what is common to every form? Writing on Ernst Jünger in 1940, Heidegger observed that Jünger himself had understood how communism and nationalism had "modified and become fused" into a singular phenomenon.[19] What

15. Ibid., 112–13. "Nirgends sonst in der Geschichte der abendländischen Metaphysik wird die Wesensgestalt ihres jeweiligen Denkers in dieser Weise eigens gedichtet."

16. It becomes clear now how and on what basis the form, *Typus* or *Gestalt,* of the worker in Jünger's *Der Arbeiter* is also secured.

17. Martin Heidegger, "Wer ist Nietzsches Zarathustra" (*GA*7), 120. "Dadurch kommt in Nietzsches Denken etwas zum Vorschein, was dieses Denken selber nicht mehr zu denken vermag. . . . Wo gar ein Denken die Metaphysik zur Vollendung bringt, zeigt es in einem ausnehmenden Sinne auf Ungedachtes, deutlich und verworren zugleich. Aber wo sind die Augen dies zu sehen.

18. Martin Heidegger, *Beiträge zur Philosophie* (*GA*65), 68. "Das Dasein als je *meines*" (Heidegger's emphasis).

19. Martin Heidegger, *Zu Ernst Jünger* (*GA*90), 237. "Abgewandelt und verschmolzen werden." Jünger in this sense makes a claim identical to that of many of Stalin's most severe (communist) critics: that the claim to be advancing toward the goal of "socialism in one state" was tantamount to nationalism.

underlies this, however, is something more fundamental: "Nietzsche recognized, furthermore, that the western democracies and the manner of their preeminence in modernity stand at the decisive beginning of what we today beyond Nietzsche and with an entirely wider, but perhaps essential conception, must today define as 'communism,' by which is meant neither 'party' nor 'worldview,' but the ultimate metaphysical position of modernity."[20] Here we identify another way in which the Marxist understanding of history is superior: beyond even Nietzsche, the fundamental metaphysical position of modernity is secured within it.

In the notebook of 1940 to which I drew attention much earlier,[21] Heidegger writes one Greek word next to the phrase "metaphysically understood communism": *koinon.*[22] *Koinon,* a central term for Plato and even for Aristotle, means that which is common in every occurrence, that which stabilizes and makes familiar the appearances—what is common to them all. The *koinon* is the *idea. Koinon,* a word Heidegger uses in his interpretation of Plato,[23] is also the title of the second subsection of the fourth notebook of the series *Das Ereignis, The History of Be-ing.*[24] This section is entitled: "Koinon. From Out of the History of Be-ing."[25] This text also is to be dated from the same period (1939–40) as the note in which the word *koinon* appears. The *koinon* is the "selfsame," what in every appearance appears to be common to all appearances.[26] As such, it is an orientation to being: to beings in their being. Elsewhere Heidegger notes that ever since Plato established *to koinon* as the essence (*Wesen*) of the common, "this characterization of the essence, as the 'in general' [universal] has since then remained the most usual, and at the same time is the most superficial."[27] This is because "the character of the *koinon* can not be the peculiar indication of the essence, because

20. Martin Heidegger, *Zu Ernst Jünger* (*GA*90), 238. "Nietzsche erkannte vielmehr, daß die westlichen Demokratien und die Art ihrer Vorrangstellung in der Neuzeit am maßgebenden Beginn dessen stehen, was wir heute über Nietzsche hinaus von einem ganz weiten, aber vielleicht dann wesentlichen Begriff her als 'Kommunismus' bezeichnen müssen, womit weder eine 'Partei," noch eine 'Weltanschauung,' sondern die metaphysische Endstellung der Neuzeit gemeint ist."

21. See 50.

22. Martin Heidegger, *Leitgedanken zur Entstehung der Metaphysik* (*GA*76), 299. "Metaphysisch verstandenen Kommunismus (κοινόν)."

23. Both Plato and Aristotle appeal to τὸ κοινόν. Compare Aristotle, *Metaphysics,* 1061a10f.

24. Martin Heidegger, *Die Geschichte des Seyns* (*GA*69).

25. "Κοινόν. Aus der Geschichte des Seyns."

26. Martin Heidegger, *Die Geschichte des Seyns* (*GA*69), 179: "das Seltsame."

27. Martin Heidegger, *Grundfragen der Philosophie* (*GA*45), 60. "Diese Kennzeichnung des Wesens, das Allgemeine zu sein, ist seitdem auch die geläufigste, freilich die oberflächlichste geblieben."

it is at most only the *consequence* of the essence."[28] Heidegger concludes: "We must say 'at most' because if we inquire after the essence of Plato or Frederick the Great, then we are certainly seeking the essence of these particular men, as the essence of something whose 'essence' is precisely singular and unique—that specific essence which is precisely of itself *excluded* from being valid for many."[29] The real "essence" of an individual is not what *identifies* him or her with every other human being, their "humanity," but rather, inasmuch as we already take them as ones among others (as beings who "are" with one another), what most individuates him and her, what makes this person the person that he or she most *is* in himself or herself.

What Heidegger indicates both in the lecture course of 1937–38 I have just been quoting, and in the text "Koinon. From Out of the History of Be-ing," is that what is at issue in the "most general" of the *koinon* of the Marxist understanding of the subjectivity of the subject, is what is also at issue in Plato's understanding of the *idea.* If the essence is always singular and unique, how can it be *an* essence? Except *an* essence *already* presupposes the metaphysical understanding of the "guiding question": "what is the being?" Inasmuch as there is *a* what, there *are* many "whats?" to be inquired into: essences. But there are no *essences,* there is only essence, that which is essenc*ing,* that which essenc*es, "west"*: the singular essenc*ing, "die Wesung."* The "what" question is succeeded by the "who" question. However, the only "who" question that can ever be asked without multiplying into multiple "whos" is that question which is a self-questioning: "*Dasein* as always *mine.*" Only the self-grounding of the questioning of the question concerning being opens up the possibility that world is essencing *for me.* Not *only* and *alone* for me (as if all the world were mine to possess), but that my self-inquiry with respect to myself is different in character—of a different order—to my inquiring into anything, or anyone, else.

That which lies as the "end-form," the "ultimate-position," both phrases which we have seen Heidegger use, of what Marx seeks to arrive at with his notion of the *individuum* which appears so decisively in the *Grundrisse,* are no less "fixed" forms, final "essences" than those given by the Platonic "ideas" or through Aristotle's notion of form (*morphē*). Heidegger's

28. Martin Heidegger, *Grundfragen der Philosophie* (*GA*45), 60. "Der Charakter des κοινόν kann nicht die eigentliche Auszeichnung des Wesens sein, sondern ist allenfalls nur die *Folge* des Wesens" (Heidegger's emphasis).

29. Martin Heidegger, *Grundfragen der Philosophie* (*GA*45), 61. "'Allenfalls' müssen wir sagen, denn wenn wir nach dem Wesen *Platons* oder *Friedrich des Großen* fragen, dann suchen wir zwar das Wesen dieser einzelnen Menschen, aber das Wesen von etwas, was seinem 'Wesen' nach gerade einmalig und einzig ist—nach jenem Wesen, das es gerade von sich *ausschließt,* für viele zu gelten" (Heidegger's emphases).

understanding of the self, that "who?" that is at the same time always "mine," can never be an idea as such, however, because it is always underway, always incomplete, always only given in that setting out underway which it is. In this sense the self is always historical, because always historicized, "with respect to" its time and place, the time in which it lives, the world in which it finds itself already to *be:* there can never be an "idea" of it that constitutes in advance and ahead of it what "it" "is" (there can therefore never be a formal *res cogitans*).

The danger at issue is always the danger of being abandoned, of losing and being unable to found itself, myself, within the world that *I* am, and that I *am.* By what means is this finding and losing? To answer this question, we turn to one of the texts of Karl Marx where these questions are most decisively worked out.

The *Grundrisse* has a fundamental structure whose significance must not be overlooked. It is divided into two sections, one preparatory (the section on money) for the other larger and more decisive (the section on capital). Inasmuch as one is preparatory for the other, they also follow a historical sequence: money appears (historically) before capital (for Marx). Inasmuch as Marx is fulfilling a metaphysical possibility laid out by Hegel, the second more decisive section, on capital, is the genuine precondition, even if one that only appears historically later, for the earlier.

What is accounted for in the earlier section is less important, because less decisive, than the latter. In the *Grundrisse* there is, parenthesized, what seems an almost throwaway thought that bears no direct relation to what is said either before or after it. After discounting the suggestion that money could be compared with blood, as a simile of circulation, Marx says: "(to compare money with language is not less erroneous)."[30] Although Marx does not reveal the source of this "erroneous" claim, the comparison of money and language (a thought also explored by Leibniz and Hobbes, but also set aside by both as false) seems to have originated with Francis Bacon.[31] Marx, who esteemed Bacon highly, is likely to have known either or both of the two texts where this comparison is to be found.[32]

In struggling to bring to an adequate description the position to which he had attained, Marx speaks in the *Grundrisse* of a question which must have emerged for him in the course of the need to work out the meaning

30. Karl Marx, *Grundrisse der Kritik der politischen Ökonomie* (*MEW*42), 96, 97. "(Das Geld mit der Sprache zu vergleichen ist nicht minder falsch)."

31. For a full discussion of the comparison in all three thinkers, see Marcelo Dascal, "Leibniz, Language, Signs and Thought" in A. Eschbach, *Foundations of Semiotics*, 1–29.

32. Francis Bacon, *Of the Proficiencie and Advancement of Learning, Human and Divine;* and *De dignitate et augmentis scientiarum*, ed. G. W. Kitchin.

not only of value, capital, and money, but also of how language speaks. Marx and Engels both speculate from time to time on questions which appear to be historical (we would now say "evolutionary"), questions like "what is the origin of language?" In the *German Ideology* Marx clearly associates the development of language with the historical development of the characteristics and means of production. Marx comments that in this process of development, "entirely in contrast to German philosophy, which steps down from heaven on to the earth, here it is a matter of ascending from earth to heaven."[33] Language is merely an indicator of the historical situation, and a consequence of development: "language is as old as consciousness, language *is* the practically existing real consciousness, also for other men, thus also for me myself as alone, and language exists, as consciousness, only from the requirement, the urgency, of exchange with other men."[34] The text indicates that Marx struck out the phrase "my relation to my surroundings is my consciousness" from the manuscript,[35] which suggests, not that Marx does not think that consciousness is consciousness of surroundings, but rather that he is precisely unable to relate the question of *language* to consciousness as consciousness of the surrounding environment. The suggestion is that consciousness here *precedes* the development of language. As society develops, language develops with it as an effect of that higher development. Language is a social consequence of the organization and development of production: language has, for Marx, not even the power of money as exchange, let alone the sheer productive power of capital.

In this sense language is for Marx subsequent to what is already "here." Every advance in social organization requires a heightening of language, but only in consequence of that advance: language is simply an instrument of technique. By contrast, and even in the *Letter on Humanism,* Heidegger refers to language as "the house of being," thereby attributing, far from a merely instrumental significance to language, in fact a fundamental one.[36]

Heidegger's lecture course of 1937–38 carried out the undertaking in

33. Karl Marx and Friedrich Engels, *Die deutsche Ideologie* (*MEW*3), 26. "Ganz im Gegensatz zur deutschen Philosophie, welche vom Himmel auf die Erde herabsteigt, wird hier von der Erde zum Himmel gestiegen."

34. Karl Marx and Friedrich Engels, *Die deutsche Ideologie* (*MEW*3), 30. "Die Sprache ist so alt wie das Bewußtsein—die Sprache *ist* das praktische, auch für andre Menschen existierende wirkliche Bewußtsein, und die Sprache entsteht, wie das Bewußtsein, erst auf dem Bedürfnis, der Notdurft des Verkehrs mit andern Menschen" (Marx's emphasis).

35. Ibid., see second note on 30. "Mein Verhältnis zu meiner Umgebung ist mein Bewußtsein."

36. Martin Heidegger, *Brief über den Humanismus* (*GA*9), 313. "Die Sprache ist das Haus des Seins." Heidegger appears to have made this assertion for the first time in public in the 1936 edition of the lecture "Wozu Dichter?" See Martin Heidegger, "Wozu Dichter?" (*GA*5), 310. "Die Sprache ist der Bezirk (templum), d. h. das Haus des Seins."

thinking that was planned as the second half of *Being and Time,* the half that, it was explained in the *Letter on Humanism,* had been "held back." Here Heidegger said, "the question of the *essence of truth* is *at once and in itself* the question of the *truth of essence.*"[37] This formulation Heidegger referred to elsewhere as "the saying of a turning within the history of be-ing."[38] Heidegger's understanding of the fulfillment of metaphysics made possible this saying of the turning, the "reversal" that *Being and Time* itself was to have been, but that was unable to be worked out until a full ten years later.[39] This understanding arises, however, on the basis of his political engagement: it is itself a historical event.

How are we to understand this saying that "the essence of truth is the truth of essence"? The essence of truth is an old metaphysical position. It appears as a "whatness," the "what truth is" in various guises, so that even when Nietzsche claims to have overcome the essence of truth by describing truth as a kind of error, he merely supplants one "whatness," "what it is" for another, such that the "essence of truth" becomes the "quiddity" of error—that is, understood through the character, the "it-ness" of error.[40] In the turning, however, the metaphysical proposition "there is an essence of truth" comes to be understood as an event: truth *essences.* Heidegger repeatedly describes his attempt to unfold the meaning of this understanding as the "truth of being." Truth here is understood as dis-closing: bringing from out of *lēthē,* hiddenness. Here we are no longer seeking a multitude of examples of essences—this "it," and this "it," and this "it," such that each being, each "it," in turn yields an understanding of the *koinon,* what is common to them all (their supporting "it-ness"). This, metaphysically thought, is the "essence" that is represented (*vor-gestellt,* re-presented, and at the same time conceived, "thinkable": *her-gestellt,* brought forth by each) and indicated by every appearance as its "what."

Inasmuch as (for Heidegger) essence "essences" (*das Wesen west*), the

37. Martin Heidegger, *Grundfragen der Philosophie* (*GA*45), 47. "Die Frage nach dem *Wesen der Wahrheit* ist *zugleich und in sich* die Frage nach der *Wahrheit des Wesens*" (Heidegger's emphases).

38. Martin Heidegger, "Anmerkung" (1949) to "Vom Wesen der Wahrheit" (*GA*9), 201. "Die Sage einer Kehre innerhalb die Geschichte des Seyns."

39. There is a full discussion of the "turning" and its significance, especially in these lectures and in the other "sayings of the turning" in Laurence Paul Hemming, *Heidegger's Atheism: The Refusal of a Theological Voice,* especially 75–133.

40. Friedrich Nietzsche, *Der Wille zur Macht,* ed. Peter Gast, §493, 343 (= Friedrich Nietzsche, vol. 11, *Nachlaß 1884–1885,* 506). "Wahrheit ist die Art von Irrthum, ohne welche eine bestimmte Art von lebendigen Wesen nicht leben könnte. Der Werth für das Leben entscheidet zuletzt" (emphasis added by Peter Gast in the *Wille zur Macht*). ("*Truth is the kind of error,* without which a certain kind of living being could not live. The value for life decides at the last.")

word "essence" needs to be translated as "being" (of whose verb it is, in any case, only a part).[41] The being in its be-ing, heard in the full sense of the verb. Essence essences *singularly:* that is, from out of the concealed, lēthē, in being, things come out into unconcealment and "are." How, in their be-ing in this way, are things recognized as not just "a book," but *this* book and *that* book, "many" books, if there is no common "it" (the "book-essence") in which they all share? Indeed, as philosophers have long known, it is far harder to recognize and bring to description something of which there is only "one," than when there are many. To know this is the only one, we have first to know what it is only "one" of—the recognizing of this "one" presupposes another (even if "visible" only in the "mind's eye") from whose recognition this one *here* is already taken off. Hence the *idea,* the *eidos* of the thing is *prior* to the thing itself: the "idea" is the necessary preexisting possibility of the thing, the reference point, against which we measure the thing before us to check that it corresponds to the idea that we already have. At this point it becomes recognizable: re-cognized (against the original cognition of the "idea").

There is another, equally significant, "saying of a turning" that Heidegger described in the three lectures given between December 1957 and February 1958, and later published as "The Nature of Language" ("Das Wesen der Sprache"). This saying says: "The essence of language: the language of essence."[42] The language of essence lets things into being. The language of being lets things be uncovered for what they are. This was a singular insight of *Being and Time,* that saying something "is," is nothing other than letting the thing be seen in its uncoveredness.[43] This "letting-be-seen" is, however, the essencing of essence, the being of being, itself. Heidegger suggests at one time that he did not even attempt to describe the character of this letting-be-seen as the essence of language in itself, *logos,* until the summer semester of 1934, and "meanwhile it took near another decade until I was able to say what I thought—even today the fitting word is lacking."[44]

Language is, for Heidegger, in a certain way, the house of being—

41. Derived as a participle from Latin *esse,* present infinitive of the verb "to be" (see *Oxford English Dictionary*).

42. Martin Heidegger, "Das Wesen der Sprache" (*GA*12), 189. "Das Wesen der Sprache: Die Sprache des Wesens."

43. Martin Heidegger, *Sein und Zeit* (*GA*2), 282–305, especially 289. "Die Aussage *ist wahr,* bedeutet: sie entdeckt das Seiende an ihm selbst. Sie sagt aus, sie zeigt auf, sie 'läßt sehen' (ἀπόφανσις) das Seiende in seiner Entdecktheit. *Wahrsein* (*Wahrheit*) der Aussage muß verstanden werden als *entdeckend-sein.*" ("The assertion *is true,* means: it uncovers the being in its self. It asserts, it points out, it 'lets be seen' (ἀπόφανσις) the being in its uncoveredness. *Being true* (*truth*) of the assertion must be understood as *being-uncovered*" (Heidegger's emphases).

44. Martin Heidegger, "Aus einem Gespräch von der Sprache" (*GA*12), 89. "Indes dauerte es noch einmal beinahe ein Jahrzehnt, bis ich zu sagen vermochte, was ich dachte—das gemäße Wort fehlt auch heute noch."

within which beings speak. But they speak within the house, which means, language, the capacity for uncovering things (beings) as they are, is always in advance of what is said. Language lets (human) beings speak of beings. In this, language is never an "instrument" because the uncovering is not separate from the being itself—it appears only in and through being-spoken. Language's being-in-advance cancels the possibility that words "correspond" to essences (or ideas). In speaking of the book I have to learn what a book is—I have to learn the language of books—before I can denote, uncover, this book *here* as a book. If I encounter something never before encountered, I have to work out and learn how to speak of it.

In the same place as Heidegger speaks of his struggle to bring to speech the essence of speaking, he also names the danger that lies in all language. For if language does not "represent" essences, then the sheer fragility of speaking and saying becomes visible for the first time. The fixedness and permanence of the essence was for a long time protected, first by the thought of the eternity of essences (in different ways) in Plato and Aristotle, and then as philosophy and Christianity (and Abrahamic monotheism) became fused together, in locating the ideas of things in the (singular, and so unifying) mind of God.[45] But Heidegger, no less than Marx, lives after the death of God—there is no universal "divine mind" in which the idea, the representation, of every thing—however singular—is preserved. Nor even, for Heidegger, is the meaning of every thing "socially constructed," an understanding which says no more than that society as a whole has displaced the place of God as the guarantor of essences, ideas, or "concepts" (values). The "social construction of reality," that most metaphysical of humanistic thoughts, is simply "being as a whole" in its final guise—the metaphysics that preserves itself in the very name of the death of God, the "beyond," the supersensible.

Heidegger's understanding of history is even more radically contingent, and so more absolutely radical, than Marx's. There is nothing which is not communicated historically, nor the understanding of which is not bound to the place and time in which it occurs. Language alone preserves meaning(s), the meanings of being(s). This being in advance of us when we speak, Heidegger captures when he says in various places that language speaks, a speaking to which man corresponds. He reflects more on this when he says "would we therefore also deny that man is the very essence, that speaks? In no way,"[46]

45. We can see how this is only possible if God is "one," which means if "God" takes over and supplants the unity of the ἕν, as thought by Heraclitus and Parmenides. This is why "being in the mind of Zeus" (or Apollo or Dionysus or Athena) and "being in the mind of the one true God" can never say the same.

46. Martin Heidegger, "Die Sprache" (*GA*12), 18. "Wollen wir auch noch leugnen, daß der Mensch dasjenige Wesen sei, das spricht? Keineswegs."

however, "how does language essence as language? We answer: *language speaks.*"[47] We must conclude: language is the very essencing of man. Heidegger makes this clearer elsewhere when he says "we would say: our languages speak historically. Given that there might be something true in the expression, language is the house of being, then the historical speaking of language is oriented and ordained by the particular sending of being. Thinking here about the essence of language, this means: language speaks, not man."[48]

After 1946 Heidegger is more ambiguous concerning his phrase "language is the house of being." In the text I have been quoting above he speaks again of the danger that arises in language, that is difficult to grasp or bring to a name or definition. This becomes especially clear when one language speaks of something for which another has no word. In this text, Heidegger speaks of his failure to understand the Japanese thought of *Iki,* adding, "some time ago I named it, awkwardly enough, language the house of being."[49] This is because "if man through his language dwells within the claim of being, then presumably we Europeans dwell in an entirely other house than the East Asian man."[50] Language does not constitute the earth, or world, in the sense of giving us a basis for the totalizing securing and grasping of the globe. Rather, language constitutes a people. It is only on this basis that we can understand Heidegger's claim to a French audience of 1955 that "the Greek language, and it alone, is *logos.*"[51]

This does not mean that *only* the Greek language has significance or "totalizes" every other language, but rather *logos,* how the Greeks were given to speak, was itself the setting of and setting out of the history, however constantly transformed across the centuries, of the Occident. The history of Europe, what Europe comes to think, is given in the Occidental *logos* given

47. Ibid., 18. "Wie west die Sprache als Sprache? Wir antworten: *Die Sprache spricht*" (Heidegger's emphasis).

48. Martin Heidegger, *Der Satz vom Grund* (*GA*10), 143. "Dürfen wir sagen: Unsere Sprachen sprechen geschichtlich. Gesetzt, daß an dem Hinweis, die Sprache sei das Haus des Seins, etwas Wahres sein sollte, dann ist das geschichtliche Sprechen der Sprache beschickt und gefügt durch das jeweilige Geschick des Seins. Vom Wesen der Sprache her gedacht, sagt dies: Die Sprache spricht, nicht der Mensch."

49. Martin Heidegger, "Aus einem Gespräch von der Sprache" (*GA*12), 85. "Vor einiger Zeit nannte ich, unbeholfen genug, die Sprache das Haus des Seins." Elsewhere, and about the same time, Heidegger said of language merely "which at one time was called the house of Being." (Martin Heidegger, "Der Satz der Identität" [*GA*11], 48. "Die einmal das Haus des Seins genannt wurde.")

50. Martin Heidegger, "Aus einem Gespräch von der Sprache" (*GA*12), 85. "Wenn der Mensch durch seine Sprache im Anspruch des Seins wohnt, dann wohnen wir Europäer vermutlich in einem ganz anderen Haus als der ostasiatische Mensch."

51. Martin Heidegger, *Was ist das—die Philosophie?* (*GA*11), 13. "Die griechische Sprache, und sie allein, ist λόγος."

to the Greeks. This is not as fanciful as it sounds: indeed, it is a very precise, factical (Marx might say, material) observation. The Greeks alone and first of all preserved their *logos* as a poetical *logos* and as a philosophical *logos*, in writing (this is the theme of Heidegger's address to French philosophers in *What Is That, Philosophy?*). In this preserved writing is the preservation of a thought even more historically original for the Occident than Christianity, although Christianity becomes intimately intertwined with it. This is why we are able to think, through thinking the essence of language, the whole of the Occident in its history, in its essence. Greek is the *first* Occidental language, both historically, and then, for thinking. The philosophical thinking that emerges in the languages first of Latin, then German, are constituted by attempting to put into these languages thoughts and words taken off from the Greek tongue, and from Greek poetry and Greek philosophy. Even that philosophical thinking which is counterposed to Greek is literally counter-posited, placed *against* what the Greeks first established. Even if in the early life of "Europe" there were others who thought in other tongues, we have no record of that thought because we have no writing in which the thought was preserved. Even if we accept that the Greeks took over some of their thinking from elsewhere (from Africa, especially Egypt, especially in the matter of mathematics), as is implied in myth, and in sections of Plato's *Timaeus* and other texts, we have no record of this taking-over except in the already for us entirely Greek manner of truth given in myth, and so given to us in an entirely Greek way.[52] Thus Heidegger prefaces his remarks about the "sending" of being with the remark: "if we restrict ourselves to Occidental languages and from the outset acknowledge this restriction, we would say, our languages think historically."[53]

From the very moment in *Being and Time* when Heidegger raises this question of the being of language, he begins to dissolve the subjectivity of the subject. It is in these sections, where the character of language is first discussed as "the question concerning the being of truth" that he assails the "idea of a 'pure I,'" an "'ideal subject.'"[54] We should not forget, however, that Heidegger names the departure point of the working out of the meaning of language as the essence of *logos* as the summer semester of 1934, the

52. Hence in the *Phaedrus* we find the myth of the discovery of arithmetic, astronomy, and above all writing as a gift from Thoth (Theuth), the Egyptian scribe to the gods. Compare Plato, *Phaedrus*, 274c–d.

53. Martin Heidegger, *Der Satz vom Grund* (*GA*10), 143. "Wenn wir uns auf die abendländischen Sprachen beschränken und diese Beschränkung zum voraus als eine Grenze anerkennen, dürfen wir sagen: Unsere Sprachen sprechen geschichtlich."

54. Martin Heidegger, *Sein und Zeit* (*GA*2), 303. "[die] Frage nach dem Sein der Wahrheit . . . 'idealen Subjekt' . . . die Idee[] eines 'reinen Ich.'"

first lecture course to be given after the disastrous adventure of the rectorate. This course, originally advertised under the title *The State and Knowledge,* was eventually given under the title *Logic as the Question Concerning the Essence of Language.* The editor of the lectures notes that "according to reports of several auditors, Heidegger—to the surprise and annoyance of a few Nazi functionaries, who had found their way to the lecture—announced the alteration categorically and demonstratively at the beginning of the first lecture with the words "I am teaching *Logic.*"[55]

It is in this lecture course that Heidegger raises the question of the being of the people (*Volk*), but for the first time (as far as I can discover) by raising the question of "who" over that of "what": "therefore the question of the being of being that we call man is not a what-question, but a who-question."[56] It is precisely by raising the question concerning "who" that we can enter the (being) question as a historical self, but it is also because "we posed the question concerning the essence of language."[57]

In these lectures Heidegger repeats, but in an importantly modified way, his claim that the state is the being of the people.[58] He modifies this claim with the adjective "historical": "the state as the historical being of the people."[59] However, and immediately, language itself is set up "as indeed historical, nothing other than as the occurrence of the exposedness of being as a whole [*das Seiende im Ganzen*] delivered to being [*das Sein*]."[60] The use of the word "occurrence" here is the nascent understanding of the event, *das Ereignis.* "Exposedness" indicates the uncovering, dis-closing, that was discussed in *Being and Time,* but now through the historicality of language as a whole, not just through the factical occurrence of individual *Dasein.* The "whole" in question concerns at one and the same time the whole of the "prevailing wholeness of the whole" which is "the *world,*" and, as language, it is "prevailing of the world-forming and preserving means of the his-

55. Günter Seubold, "Nachwort des Herausgebers," in Martin Heidegger, *Logik als die Frage nach dem Wesen der Sprache* (GA38), 172. "Nach Berichten einiger Hörer hat Heidegger—zur Überraschung und Verärgerung einiger NS-Funktionäre, die sich zu seiner Vorlesung eingefunden hatten—die Änderung zu Beginn der ersten Vorlesungsstunde kategorisch und demonstrativ mit den Worten 'Ich lese *Logik*' bekanntgegeben" (Seubold's emphasis).

56. Martin Heidegger, *Logik als die Frage nach dem Wesen der Sprache* (GA38), 164. "Deshalb ist die Frage nach dem Sein des Seienden, das wir Mensch nennen, nicht eine Wasfrage, sondern eine Werfrage."

57. Ibid., 164, 167. "Weil wir die Frage nach dem Wesen der Sprache stellten."

58. See 163.

59. Martin Heidegger, *Logik als die Frage nach dem Wesen der Sprache* (GA38), 164. "Der Staat als das geschichtliche Sein des Volkes."

60. Ibid., 168. "Die Sprache ist als je geschichtliche nichts anderes als das Geschehnis der an das Sein überantworteten Ausgesetztheit in das Seiende im Ganzen."

torical existence [*Dasein*] of the people."[61] All of this is at the same time to be understood in this way: "the power of time constitutes the timeliness of our essence."[62] This corresponds to a remark made by Heidegger in 1942–43: "In *Being and Time,* no matter how strange it must sound, 'time' is the given name of the originary *ground* of the word."[63]

Central in these lectures is the question of the subjectivity of the subject, as the dissolution of the subject—such that we seek constantly the self in its species.[64] Here surely is a point at which Heidegger enters into the "productive dialogue" without ever naming Marx: by raising the question of "species" in relation to the being of being human. At issue is always the overcoming of the ideal-individuality of the subjectivity of the subject for the concrete selfhood of the self, the self that belongs to a people. The question that Heidegger seeks to answer is "what is man? The answer to this question was already given in antiquity: *anthrōpos zōon logon echon.* Man is that live-essence [living being] that is ordered toward language":[65] as such, man can never be thought of as "species-being."

The "live-essence" named here is worked out over a full twenty-year period or more *not* as an *individuum,* who shares a common essence (*koinon*) with other *individua,* subjects, but rather that one *who* is spoken out of the essencing, the happening, the historical *eventing* of being. In this "world worlds," but for a people. For us, in the West (and so including every nation founded out of Europe—from North and Latin America to the southern antipodes), this means Europe. As Europe extends its grasp over the whole globe (for good or for ill) this means: Europe in its planetary, metaphysical, reach. At one and the same time the utmost fragility of our belonging within this *logos*-house of being coincides with the aggressive, unstoppable, totalizing securing of the planet that has been unfolding over centuries, since first the Greeks set out to conquer Troy. In 1934 these are laid side by side, as Heidegger takes leave of the dreadful, criminal, belief that the (Nazi) state is the being of the people, and comes over the next twenty years to reflect on

61. Ibid., 168. "Die waltende Ganzheit dieses Ganzen ist die *Welt*" . . . "Sprache als das Walten der weltbildenden und bewahrenden Mitte des geschichtlichen Daseins des Volkes" (Heidegger's emphasis).

62. Ibid., 168. "Die Macht der Zeit als Zeitlichkeit unser Wesen ausmacht."

63. Martin Heidegger, *Parmenides* (*GA*54), 113. "'Zeit' ist in 'Sein und Zeit,' so befremdlich das klingen muß, der Vorname für den Anfangs*grund* des Wortes" (Heidegger's emphasis).

64. Martin Heidegger, *Logik als die Frage nach dem Wesen der Sprache* (*GA*38), 43. "Ist das Selbst die Gattung zum Ich, Du, Wir, Ihr?" ("Is the self the species of the I, You, We, All of You?")

65. Ibid., 31. "Wer ist der Mensch? Die Antwort auf diese Frage wurde bereits in der Antike gegeben: ἄνθρωπος ζῷον λόγον ἔχον. Der Mensch ist dasjenige Lebewesen, das über die Sprache verfügt."

the essence of language, *as* the language of essence by elucidating not the "place" of Europe but the be-ing of the Occident. Uncovering the meaning of the essence of language is for Heidegger the only possible overcoming of the *abstracted* nihilism of metaphysics, where in each case, be it in the name of "the good" (Plato), *ousia,* or substance (Aristotle), God (Abrahamic theism), absolute subjectivity (Hegel), the will to power (Nietzsche) or human society (Marx), and finally in the "will to will" (*das Ge-Stell*), the unity of the being of beings is taken off from some other abstraction as the *idea,* the image, what humanity represents to itself as an abstracted origination of all beings, *other than* the essencing of essence as the being of beings: be-ing.

Heidegger says it took near twenty years for what was, nevertheless, already *thought* to be said—and even now the fitting word is lacking. What was there to be thought was no effort of will, no inner experience, but rather what *lay present to be thought.* It is in this way that language "speaks"—it is the wresting of the presencing of being from the unity of what lets world "world." In no sense is world's presencing in virtue of having been "caused" by a god, but world's presencing occurs from out of the presencing (Last) God. In this sense Heidegger and Marx both speak *after* the death of God, after the overcoming of the supersensible, that reopens the way to the passing by of the Last God.[66] The Last God must also not be thought "monotheistically" as the inner unity of world: rather it is out of the singular presencing of world *in itself* that the Last God can, indeed, pass by.

Why have we taken this long detour from a single, throwaway line in Marx's *Grundrisse*? Because Marx's setting aside of the meaning of language sets aside the uncovering of the being of beings in its forgottenness, as *not even* equal to the power and development of exchange, *let alone* equal to the power of capital itself, and therefore *not in the least* touching the power of history, as the history of the overcoming of the alienation of labor for the fulfillment of a humanism in which both labor and capital are sublated into the triumph of the *individuum,* absolute subjectivity, in its concrete, historical manifestation, as that one who receives back as much as is alienated from him in production. In language a gulf opens up between Marx and Heidegger, and yet precisely it is in language that the productive dialogue with Marx must begin. What is the essence of the gulf? In whom is it disclosed?

What it took Heidegger more than twenty years to bring to language he already knew, and first knew, in the extraordinary Greek word *alētheuein.* We translate this word as "speaking the truth." It literally means "letting lie present from out of the concealed." It is a word most often found in Aristotle. In 1934, and later, although in a modified, more nuanced, way, Heidegger understands that in the speaking, the saying, of man, beings are let

66. See 273.

out into the open. This is not another way of saying that reality is socially constructed. The social construction of reality, or the construction of social reality,[67] is precisely unable ever to let language let things *be,* nor to let essence *speak* in essencing, precisely because it functions in entirely the other direction: everything that is spoken of is *produced* and projected by speakers, even if society as a whole "speaks" (in notions of collective intentionality or the like). The speech of society as a whole and in its individuals in this understanding is always an artifice, a created product, a thing produced. It can never lie in advance of us, speaking from ahead of us and me, and prompting the thinker to the fitting word.

Yet Marx's place for language, for the *logos* itself, is in no sense a dismissal or diminishment of the *logos* as such: rather what is shown up here is the way in which language is *already* at work in his thought. If Heidegger's understanding of "the language of essence: the essence of language" is a genuine thinking into the be-ing of language and not the mere assertion of a "theory" or an "opinion," then Marx is himself shown up as a certain kind of "whom" in this understanding: that one for whom the speaking of language as the language of essence has become entirely hidden and concealed, in the *most* extreme way. Marx's understanding of language, as that which arises only on the basis of the history of production, in the way that production itself fulfills itself and seeks its own completion, yields that Marx himself is speaking from out of, which means is himself *spoken* from out of the *other side* of the "turning," *die Kehre* of which "the language of essence: the essence of language" is a "saying." It shows that Marx's own appropriation of the essence of language is *itself no mere theory or opinion,* but arises on the basis of the most fundamental appropriation to the fulfillment of a philosophical understanding: what Heidegger calls "metaphysics." We retain constantly our concern that we attend to what Heidegger speaks *of,* what Marx speaks *of.* For Marx, no less than Heidegger, is seeking to bring things to an adequate description: what Heidegger at one time called "phenomenology," and Marx refers to as the "real."[68] The real is at one and the same time, however, the descriptive, how things have been and *are,* and, as the "practical" and "revolutionary" how they should *become.* What is to become is as real as what already *is,* in fact it is more real, since what is to become is how things should be *even now.* In the "Theses on Feuerbach" Marx claims that

67. See John R. Searle, *The Construction of Social Reality.* Ingvar Johansson has noted that "[Searle's] ontology is a new kind of naturalism and materialism" (Ingvar Johansson, "Searle's Monadological Construction of Social Reality," 234). Whatever the truth of this claim, Searle's understanding is absolutely dependent on the notion of the ideal self as (monadological) subject. In fact this "monad" is far behind the breadth and universality of the monad as Leibniz describes it.

68. The German terms Marx uses, almost interchangeably, are "das Wirkliche," "reell."

in Feuerbach's very materialism (the binding to the "real" that Marx seeks) "he does not grasp from this the significance of 'revolutionary,' of 'practical-critical' activity."[69] It is for this reason that "the question, whether objective truth is attributable to human thinking—is not a question of theory, but a *practical* question. Man must prove through praxis truth, i.e., reality and power, the this-worldliness of his thinking."[70]

The language of essence: this can function as a name for the place from out of which Heidegger already thinks, and from which he strives to speak. The essence of language, as the taking and securing of a certain understanding of what an essence *is,* the essence of the human essence, "humanism," in its most extreme formulation, names the place from out of which Marx already thinks, and from which he strives to think. Yet we have only been able to open up this place in consequence of attempting to find our way into the place from out of which Heidegger believed himself to be speaking, because *this* place, the place which is itself the being of being, must also be able to speak of, and show up, the place from whence Marx utters his most fundamental words. The question is, how is the description accomplished, and through what thinking is it secured?

To understand the gulf of language that lies between Heidegger and Marx we have to turn to Aristotle, and through him, to an understanding of how the various modes, the possibilities, of *alētheuein* speak.

69. Karl Marx, "Thesen über Feuerbach" (*MEW*3), 5. "Er begreift daher nicht die Bedeutung der 'revolutionären,' der 'praktisch-kritischen' Tätigkeit."

70. Ibid., 5. "Die Frage, ob dem menschlichen Denken gegenständliche Wahrheit zukomme—ist keine Frage der Theorie, sondern eine *praktische* Frage. In der Praxis muß der Mensch die Wahrheit, i.e., Wirklichkeit und Macht, Diesseitigkeit seines Denkens beweisen."

*Chapter 11*

# Production—Previously This Was Called God

IN ORDER TO UNDERSTAND what Heidegger could have meant by a "productive dialogue" it is necessary that we understand Marx's own account of production. That account of production is in itself a confrontation with the whole history of thought, something of which Marx himself was acutely aware. Marx understood thought itself to be an effect of the history of production: that is to say, when we enter into an historical confrontation with the history of thought, we seek always and in each age what is *higher*—what thought *becomes* and leads up to, not what it thinks at the time. Marx's thought remains essentially ordered by Hegel's account of "sublation," of what is to be "let go" for the sake of what is to be attained *to.* This chapter therefore seeks to enter into Marx's understanding of production, and to show how Heidegger related himself to that understanding. What in each case we seek, with Marx, and with Heidegger, is their understanding of the *whole* as it presses in on us historically.

Karl Marx opens the *Grundrisse* with the heading "the object before us, at the outset, *material production.* Individuals producing in Society—hence the socially determined production of individuals is naturally the point of departure."[1] The participle—*produzierende* (producing)—introduces an emphasis in German that we could almost overlook in English: we could translate this as "socially producing individuals" to capture the ambiguity. At

1. Karl Marx, *Grundrisse* (*MEW*42), 19. "Der vorliegende Gegenstand zunächst die *materielle Produktion.* In Gesellschaft produzierende Individuen—daher gesellschaftlich bestimmte Produktion der Individuen ist natürlich der Ausgangspunkt" (Marx's emphasis). The introduction of the *Grundrisse,* written in 1857, was the first part of the manuscript to be published, in 1859, as an appendix to his "Zur Kritik der politischen Ökonomie" (*MEW*13). The *Grundrisse* first appeared in German in an edition of the Marxist-Leninist Institute, Moscow, in 1941, but because of wartime conditions the text, reaching a few libraries in America, remained largely unknown in the West. The first edition that became more widely known was the Berlin edition of Dietz Verlag in the German Democratic Republic in 1953, which formed the basis for the *MEW* volume, and for the English translation and with a foreword by Martin Nicolaus, *Grundrisse: Foundations of Political Economy (Rough Draft).*

one and the same time, individuals produce only in society (indeed, Marx follows this immediately with a critique of the naturalistic idea of the individual hunter as an example of the "unimaginative fantasies of the 18th-century Robinsonades," among whom he counts Smith and Ricardo),[2] and at the same time the object they produce is society itself.

It is essential to understand the sheer concreteness of Marx's thinking. The full force of his polemical writing had been addressed over and over again to those who understood communism as a mere "idea" that was to be striven toward, and realized on the basis of a mere "plan," the "plan" for a better "society." This is exactly Marx's critique of the idealistic communists, of, for instance, Bruno Bauer and others. In the *German Ideology* Marx draws attention to this understanding again, arguing that "communism is not a *situation* which is to be brought forth, an *ideal,* wherein reality (will) have to adjust itself. We name communism the *real* movement, which sublates the present situation. The conditions of this movement offers itself from the currently existing premise."[3]

This would appear to contradict the suggestion I have made that the metaphysical aspect of Marx's communism is precisely the fitting of the "ought" to the "is." This, however, would be to overlook the force of Marx's argument: that it is not *ideas* or arbitrarily conceived possibilities that drive the revolutionary thrust but concrete conditions. However, it is production itself as a force which establishes the necessity of revolutionary change in a specific and concrete form. Marx argues in the *German Ideology* that the history of communism shows that it is not "criticism" but concrete conditions that form the basis for the overthrow of social conditions. Marx continues: "this sum of forces of production, capital and social exchange, which every individual and every generation finds as something already given, is the real ground of that itself which philosophers have conceived as 'substance' and 'essence of man.'"[4]

Marx conceives of "substance" as the forces of production. This is at the same time the "essence of man." Substance, and essence, however, are simply other words for "being." The sum total of being, being as a whole, is at one and the same time nothing other than the sum of the forces of pro-

2. Karl Marx, *Grundrisse* (*MEW*42), 19. "Phantasielose[n] Einbildungen des 18. Jahrhunderts. Robinsonaden."

3. Karl Marx and Friedrich Engels, *Die deutsche Ideologie* (*MEW*3), 35. "Der Kommunismus ist für uns nicht ein Zustand, der hergestellt werden soll, ein Ideal, wonach die Wirklichkeit sich zu richten haben [wird]. Wir nennen Kommunismus die wirkliche Bewegung, welche den jetzigen Zustand aufhebt. Die Bedingungen dieser Bewegung ergeben sich aus der jetzt bestehenden Voraussetzung."

4. Ibid., 38. "Diese Summe von Produktionskräften, Kapitalien und sozialen Verkehrsformen, die jedes Individuum und jede Generation als etwas Gegebenes vorfindet, ist der reale Grund dessen, was sich die Philosophen als 'Substanz' und 'Wesen des Menschen' vorgestellt."

duction and at the same time the being of being human. This means that the being of being human is taken off from, derived from out of, the forces of production as they currently exist. At the same time the forces of production carry within themselves, and provide, the basis for the absolute process of development of human relations. The human being is at one and the same time the concrete relations within which he is situated (there is no such thing as the "isolated" individual), and he is the possibility, which means, necessity, of the development of those relations.

This possibility is in itself historical: "History is nothing but the succession of the separate generations, of which each exploits materials, capital funds, forces of production, handed down to it by all preceding generations, hence, on the one hand, continues the traditional activity in completely changed circumstances and, on the other, modifies the old circumstances with a completely changed activity."[5] When Marx says that only speculative history makes later history the goal of earlier history, he is again not so much disputing the goal of communism itself as something yet to be brought about, but disputing any attempt to suggest that communism is itself a speculative goal, a merely constructive "project" instead of the *necessity itself* of the fulfillment of where history is being driven, a force which is only understood in describing it as something already happening. Communism is not, therefore, produced as an idea, but rather the concrete drive toward communism's fulfillment is what lets the idea be seen (and so described).

Understanding of what? Marx notes that man is in the most literal sense the *zōon politikon*, directly employing Aristotle's phrase to explain the being of the human being in the polis that we have already encountered several times. As such the human being both produces and consumes; these are two halves of the same thing, although they are never equally distributed in all hitherto existing social relations. What Marx is moving toward, however, is the grounding relational understanding of the human being at all, which, he also points out, is itself a historically accomplished understanding, even if *what* is understood turns out thus: "It might seem that all that had been achieved was to discover the abstract expression for the simplest and most ancient relation in which men—in whatever form of society—play the role of producers."[6] This, however, is only one aspect of what was established: "for the most

5. Ibid., 45. "Die Geschichte ist nichts als die Aufeinanderfolge der einzelnen Generationen, von denen Jede die ihr von allen vorhergegangenen übermachten Materiale, Kapitalien, Produktionskräfte exploitiert, daher also einerseits unter ganz veränderten Umständen die überkommene Tätigkeit fortsetzt und andrerseits mit einer ganz veränderten Tätigkeit die alten Umstände modifiziert."

6. Karl Marx, *Grundrisse* (*MEW*42), 38. "Nun könnte es scheinen, als ob damit nur der abstrakte Ausdruck für die einfachste und urälteste Beziehung gefunden, worin die Menschen—sei es in welcher Gesellschaftsform immer—als produzierend auftreten."

general abstractions overall are established only within the richest concrete development, where one thing appears as common to many, common to all."[7]

The understanding of which Marx speaks is that of labor, of work itself, but his point is that although this is a thoroughgoingly historical abstraction—it does indeed explain all and every actual social relation in every case—nevertheless, its appearance as a universal possibility of exchange is precisely also historically determined. At the very point where the masses appear, where something "common to all" appears, the question of communism *also* appears, as that necessary social development which is an urgency (the very same word Marx had used of the phenomenon of language in the *German Ideology*) to be accomplished. Although Marx does not say so in the introduction to the *Grundrisse,* the precise reason for the urgency of the situation arises, not on the basis of any moral imperative, but rather on the basis of the sheer apparent freedom and exchangeability of labor. This freedom, which we have already discussed, is the freedom by which an individual may go to the market to sell his labor. It is only an *apparent* freedom, since the freedom is only freedom either to work or starve. In reality it is freedom for the capitalist *from* any responsibility he has toward the worker, except inasmuch as he can strike a bargain for the price of his labor (a price far below the true value, which the capitalist will extract as the surplus accruing to his own use). This argument is repeated in the *Grundrisse,* where Marx indicates this seeming freedom is an only apparent independence: "this independence, which overall is merely an illusion and is more correctly called a common determination in the sense of indifference."[8]

The appearance of the term "indifference," in German *Gleichgültigkeit,* literally means "sameness of value" as *in*difference is the concrete *possibility,* the *material basis,* of the accomplishment of a genuinely *conscious* production of universal difference. This sameness of value has a material condition: money. Marx really only defines the metaphysical conditions of money in the *Grundrisse* in the chapter on capital, which means he is only really able to think through the metaphysical meaning of money when it is superseded by the need to explain capital as such. Money is the means by which labor is conceived only as exchange value, and as such, this is the "equating" (*Gleichsetzung*) of "the individuals, the subjects, between whom this process [of exchange] carries on."[9] *Gleichsetzung* does not simply mean

7. Ibid., 38. "So entstehn die allgemeinsten Abstraktionen überhaupt nur bei der reichsten konkreten Entwicklung, wo eines vielen gemeinsam erscheint, alles gemein."

8. Ibid., 97. "Diese Unabhängigkeit, die überhaupt bloß eine Illusion ist und richtiger Gleichgültigkeit—in Sinn der Indifferenz—heiße."

9. Ibid., 166–67. "Die Beziehung . . . ihre Gleichsetzung, sind die Individuen, die Subjekte, zwischen denen dieser Prozeß vorgeht, nur einfach bestimmt als Austauschende."

equating as a judgment, but has an active sense of "positing the same." In the character of the money relation as a "rendering equal," "all immanent contradictions of bourgeois society appear to be extinguished" such that bourgeois democracy (i.e., concrete political forms and the means by which they are executed) even more than bourgeois economics "takes refuge in them."[10] The consequence of money relations is that "as subjects of exchange their relation is hence that of *identity*. It is impossible to find any trace of distinction, nor indeed of contradiction, within them, not even a difference."[11]

Indifference opens the question of "the universally developed individual, whose social relations, as their own communally developed relations, are therefore subordinated to their own communal control."[12] Social relations are, however, the product of labor: they both have to have reached a certain degree of historical development (they have to have been created *in the very form they take*) and at the same time the objective relation that is constituted by them, of the individual on society "is their product. It is a historical product."[13]

Here Marx concentrates on the absolute exchangeability of labor: as exchangeable, it is at one and the same time that which is most alienated from the laborer himself. It is not the alienation that concerns Marx, but rather that, at the point of the most extreme alienation, the extremity of the alienation finally becomes most visible. Hence, Marx's point is that Adam Smith's discovery of the general category of labor (as itself a break from the physiocrats, who believed that the relation to land was the basis of all economic explanation), which appears to explain labor in all its forms both present and historically, is at the same time an entirely novel, and therefore historically bound occurrence.[14]

10. Ibid., 166. "All immanenten Gegensätze der bürgerlichen Gesellschaft [erscheinen] ausgelöscht, und nach dieser Seite wird wieder zu [dem Geldverhältnis] geflüchtet."

11. Ibid., 166. "Als Subjekte des Austauschs ist ihre Beziehung daher die der *Gleichheit*. Es ist unmöglich irgendeinen Unterschied oder gar Gegensatz unter ihnen auszuspielen, nicht einmal eine Verschiedenheit" (Marx's emphasis).

12. Ibid., 95. "Die universal entwickelten Individuen, deren gesellschaftliche Verhältnisse als ihrer eignen, gemeinschaftlichen Beziehungen auch ihrer eignen gemeinschaflichen Kontrolle unterworfen sind."

13. Ibid., 95. "Er ist ihr Produkt. Er ist ein historisches Produkt."

14. Ibid., 39. "Dies Beispiel der Arbeit zeigt schlagend, wie selbst die abstraktesten Kategorien trotz ihrer Gültigkeit—eben wegen ihrer Abstraktion—für alle Epochen doch in der Bestimmtheit dieser Abstraktion selbst ebensosehr das Produkt historischer Verhältnisse sind und ihre Vollgültigkeit nur für und innerhalb dieser Verhältnisse besitzen." ("This example of labor shows strikingly how even the most abstract categories, despite their validity—for all epochs, are nevertheless, in the specific character of this abstraction, themselves likewise a product of historic relations, and possess their full validity only for and within these relations.")

The essence of man is labor, as both a historical production and a historical capability. This is not a merely free capability, but depends at each step on the concrete conditions that precede it, and itself produces *only* concrete conditions: "the abstraction or idea is however nothing other than the theoretical expression of those material relations, which are their lord."[15] The reference here to a "lord" (the same word that is often used for God as Lord of all—and in German the word is, as all nouns are, capitalized, so seems even more to be expressing the same thought) should not be missed: every theoretical idea, including that of God, is only a consequence of concrete conditions.

We should not overlook the relentless discipline that Marx imposes on ideas which is itself the fundamental, visceral, energy of his thinking, and represents its sheer power and superiority over every kind of merely speculative endeavor of thought. We are, Marx demands, to think from out of the material conditions of life, and we are to think nothing other than the material conditions of life. There is here, not less, a disciplining of the bane of the imagination as in some sense a "creative" force.

The essence of man is labor, but the essence of labor is production, as that capability for producing that manifests itself in all human activity. Production is at the same time the essence of history. However, society as such is the material condition for human history. This is Marx's mature understanding of alienation—"the labor of the individual, which is realized as his product, is not a product for him, but *becomes* such only in the social process, and since it *must* take on this general but nevertheless external form; and that the individual has an existence only as a producer of exchange value, hence the whole negation of his natural existence is already implied; that he is therefore entirely determined by society . . . That therefore this presupposition by no means arises either out of the individual's will or out of the immediate nature of the individual, but that it is, rather, *historical*, and posits the individual as already *determined* by society."[16]

The condition of money indicates the formal development, peculiar

15. Ibid., 97. "Die Abstraktion oder Idee ist aber nichts als der theoretische Ausdruck jener materiellen Verhältnisse, die Herr über sie sind."

16. Ibid., 173. "Daß sein unmittelbares Produkt kein Produkt für es ist, sondern ein solches erst *wird* im gesellschaftlichen Prozeß und diese allgemeine und doch äußerliche Form annehmen *muß;* daß das Individuum nur noch als Tauschwert produzierende Existenz hat, als schon die ganze Negation seiner natürlichen Existenz eingeschlossen ist; es also ganz durch die Gesellschaft bestimmt ist . . . Daß also nicht nur die Voraussetzung keineswegs weder eine aus dem Willen noch der unmittelbaren Natur des Individuums hervorgehende, sondern eine *geschichtliche* ist und das Individuum schon als durch die Gesellschaft *bestimmt* setzt" (Marx's emphases).

to bourgeois society, that subjectivity appears for the first time as an equalization, as the enforced making-identical of the appearance of every individual subject who is nevertheless determined out of the historical conditions which have themselves produced bourgeois society. The indeterminate subject, first posited by Descartes, as one who is without world, and so without differentiation, rank, or grade, as a pure thought of the *I*, is shown by Marx to remain undifferentiated (at least *potentially*) even in the midst of the factical conditions of material life. The enormous step that is attained here should not be missed. Descartes's cogito is indeterminate only as a pure abstraction *from* every material condition. Marx's individual in bourgeois society remains indeterminate even *in concreto*. It is here that Marx demonstrates the dynamic aspect of capital, and distinguishes capital precisely from the money relation, as the basis for this equalization. If the money-relation makes equalization manifest, capital is the means of overcoming the *indifferent* character of the equalization, precisely because it is the dynamic production of difference. Capital is itself a historic event. Capital, inasmuch as it is "objectified labour,"[17] must be understood "by setting out, not from labour, but from value."[18]

A thoroughgoing, systematic treatment of what is at issue for Marx here would want to demonstrate how it is that, inasmuch as value itself is the production of capital, it is at the same time the ground of the essence of labor: unfortunately, that is outside the immediate scope of this book. Value, as central a thought to Nietzsche as it is to Marx, must remain unexamined here, even though Heidegger investigated the meaning of value thoroughly and repeatedly in his *Nietzsche* lectures. At this stage the question is solely that of the "productive dialogue" of Heidegger with Marx—which means the dialogue over "the productive" as such.

Earlier I argued that the question of essence first manifests itself for Heidegger as a *who*-question. The appearance of the question "who?" enabled Heidegger to move beyond the guiding question of metaphysics, the question that asks "what is the being?" that appears from the inception of metaphysics with the Greeks (Aristotle and Plato) onward: *ti to on?* The transition from the guiding question to the grounding question, "how is (*west*, essences) being itself?" remains for Heidegger *the* question which sets itself up to be interrogated and investigated. Marx also secures the fundamental character of essence, of the being of being, through a delineation of the "who" in capital and labor. Thus Marx argues that "I can indeed separate capital from an individual capitalist, and pass it over to another. But inasmuch as he loses capital he loses the quality of being a capitalist. Hence capital is indeed sepa-

17. Ibid., 182. "*Vergegenständlichte* Arbeit" (Marx's emphasis).
18. Ibid., 183. "Nicht von der Arbeit, sondern vom Wert auszugehn."

rable from an individual capitalist, not from *the* capitalist, who as such stands over against *the* worker."[19]

What Marx lays out here is the binding character of the performative, as the necessary structure and contradiction of capitalism. In fact Marx raises, but does not pursue, his interest in the "who?" as a question, since in each case the "who!" appears not as an inquiry into the absolutely individuated one given essentially (hence why all inquiry begins as a self-inquiry, as an inquiry with respect to that *one* which each of us alone knows in an entirely ontologically individuated way, myself) but merely as a generalized subject-position, "the capitalist," "the worker," which is inhabited by an individual (some *one*), whose being, except as it appears in the contradiction or opposition of capitalist-worker is of no ontological self-interest to *me* (in the language of *Being and Time* it can never be *jemeinig*, "really mine," except as an accident: I *happen* to be a worker, or a capitalist). And yet the overarching structure of capital *produces* in each case subject-positions. What Marx is adamant we understand, is that both the capitalist and the worker are themselves *products* of the production process, indeed, they are the only products that matter. As products, they are at the same time what is to be overcome, for the subject-position in question is a preparatory, conditional, one: conditional on the contradictions in capitalism itself leading to the abolition of both subject-positions for the sake of *that* subject which the present concrete conditions have already prepared for: the *individuum* of the species-being, the concrete manifestation of the absolute subject.

It is here that Marx's understanding of value comes directly into play. For "what the worker exchanges against capital is his labor itself (in the exchange of his capacity for disposing it), he *alienates* it. What he obtains as the price is the *value* of this alienation. He exchanges the value-positing activity against a predetermined value, discounting the result of his activity."[20] Marx's central concern is that value is never *mere* value, just as capital is never constant, although it is constantly present. As the constantly present condition of the appearance of both capitalist and worker, it is the possibility of their production. We must hear this in the objective and subjective genitive senses: subjective in the sense that capital is what they produce, and one of them holds; and objective in the sense that they are themselves produced by the

19. Ibid., 225. "Ich kann das Kapital wohl von diesem einzelnen Kapitalisten scheiden, und es kann auf einen andern übergehn. Aber indem er das Kapital verliert, verliert er die Eigenschaft, Kapitalist zu sein. Das Kapital ist daher wohl vom einzelnen Kapitalisten trennbar, nicht von *dem* Kapitalist, der als solcher *dem* Arbeiter gegenübersteht" (Marx's emphases).

20. Ibid., 225. "Was der Arbeiter austauscht gegen das Kapital, ist seine Arbeit selbst (im Austausch die Dispositionsfähigkeit darüber); er *entäußert* sie. Was er als Preis erhält, ist der *Wert* dieser Entäußerung. Er tauscht die wertsetzende Tätigkeit gegen einen vorherbestimmten Wert aus, abgesehn von dem Resultat seiner Tätigkeit" (Marx's emphases).

existence of capital. Capital is not constant, it must, to be capital, produce a surplus. Here then is the problem of the increase of value—surplus value—which is both the object of labor (what it must always seek to do) and how labor overcomes the contradictions it at the same time produces.

Marx argues that "the self-preservation of capital is its self-application."[21] In Marx's German text, the term "self-application" is *Selbstverwerten,* a compound itself of the word "value" (*Wert*): once again we should not miss the sheer concreteness of Marx's language in this description. Value preserves itself *only* in engendering production—that is, in applying itself *to* production. We might say here that value is only realized and preserved in its absolute concretization, in its concrete application and recovery. Marx's point is that capital is neither labor in its activity, nor does capital itself work; it is constantly applied and dissolved into concrete conditions for the sake of its realization. Capital, and the capitalist's power and self-preservation, are the capacity to alienate the value of labor and appropriate (objectify) it: "not exchange, but rather a process wherein he obtains *objectified labor time,* i.e., *value,* without exchange can alone make of him a capitalist."[22] However, capital is of itself driven to multiply value. As multiplication, it is not value in general that is produced, but specific, objective, *values,* the objectifications of value: commodities, products. This is essential. The mere expanse of value cannot be realized: it is always realized in what lies *over against* value-production itself. That which lies over-against is the ob-ject, German *Gegen-stand,* that which is itself realizable *as* a value. This is the essential connection between the expansion of value as the expansion of realizable values. Always, Marx is driven into the concrete manifestations of whatever it is he is trying to show up and demonstrate.

Subjects, in subject-positions, produce: *what* they produce are the objectifications of products, "wares," salable commodities, objects *of value:* "the increase of values can therefore take place, only if a value over the equivalent is obtained, thus is *created.*"[23] Individuals are, as producing, creators (recalling Heidegger's description of the modern subject as "the creative," repeated in text after text). Because surplus value, *Mehrwert*—literally, increase in value—is an excess of values on the equivalent, surplus value can never arise on the basis either of the equivalent itself (the value applied to a particular process of production), nor out of circulation (money). It is here that we find

21. Ibid., 243. "Die Selbsterhaltung des Kapitals ist seine Selbstverwertung."

22. Ibid., 243. "Nicht der Austausch, sondern ein Prozeß, worin er ohne Austausch *vergegenständlichte Arbeitszeit,* d.h. *Wert,* erhält, kann ihn allein zum Kapitalisten machen" (Marx's emphasis).

23. Ibid., 243. "Und die Vermehrung der Werte kann nur dadurch stattfinden, daß ein Wert über das Äquivalent hinaus erhalten, also *geschaffen* wird" (Marx's emphasis).

both Marx's most fundamental determination as an economist, and his most fundamental brilliance as a metaphysician. The so-called fourth volume of *Das Kapital,* in fact three further dense volumes in their own right, deals with the failure of classical economics to be able to account for the increase of value in the application of capital. Marx has a fundamentally precise mind when it comes to questions of calculation—hence why his examples of the application and productive capacity of capital continually appeal to exact numerical examples. His fundamental insight into the character of surplus value, however, is that it is an extraction, not from within the process of the application of capital, but precisely it is the *beyond,* the self-transcending striving of value, not as an *increase* in present value, but as a *negation* of present value, which at the same time overcomes the present value and sets it aside, and converts "labor-time," the application of time itself, into a value *as an objectification*—something which itself can and must be negated in order to convert it into a value: the time that history *is,* is rendered through surplus values as objects. Surplus value in Marx is the objectification of labor time, or rather, it is the operation of history as such, in its realizable objectifications. Surplus value "has to arise from the production process of capital itself."[24]

Because the surplus value produced *must* be realized as something to be consumed, or its value as such cannot be realized *and so is not value,* value-production is both the spur (Marx uses the figure of a whip) to ever-greater value production, and it is the inevitable harbinger and tool of capital's demise, as the contradictions generated by the need endlessly to expand capital must themselves only be resolved as a drive to expand the labor capacity and consumption of labor—of *real workers who at the same time must constantly be converted into consumers for the value that is alienated from them to be realized.* This account does not concern us in its concrete description, but the general structure does: "the great historic one-sidedness of capital is to *create* this *surplus labor,* superfluous from the standpoint of mere use value, mere subsistence, and its historic determining is fulfilled,"[25] as soon as the very process of its own self-consumption and sublation (negation) is unleashed. Marx concludes: "Thence is *capital productive;* i.e., an *essential relation for the development of the socially productive forces.* It ceases to exist only as such, where the developing of these productive forces themselves discover a limitation in capital itself."[26] Marx is insistent that

24. Ibid., 243. "Er muß aus dem Produktionsprozeß des Kapitals selbst entspringen."

25. Ibid., 244. "Die große geschichtliche Seite des Kapitels ist diese *Surplusarbeit,* überflüssige Arbeit vom Standpunkt des bloßen Gebrauchswerts, der bloßen Subsistenz aus, zu *schaffen,* und seine historische Bestimmung ist erfüllt" (Marx's emphases).

26. Ibid., 244. "Daher ist *das Kapital produktiv;* d.h. ein *wesentliches Verhältnis für die Entwicklung der gesellschaftlichen Produktivkräfte.* Es hört erst auf, solches zu sein, wo die Entwicklung dieser Produktivkräfte selbst an dem Kapital selbst eine Schranke findet" (Marx's emphases).

capital is an advance in the development of the productive forces precisely because of its universalizing tendency. We are never interested simply in the working day, but rather the "indeterminate working day of an undetermined number of workers" such that "all relations of populations enter here."[27] Fundamentally, capital "is posited as a mere point of transition."[28] Transition toward what? "The universality of the *individuum* not as conceived or imagined, but as universality of his real and ideal relations."[29]

One word is consistently employed by Marx all the way through the *Grundrisse* to express that kind of possibility which is constantly to be fulfilled, concretely and historically, but nevertheless in this process which is nothing other than the highest metaphysics of the subjectivity of the subject. Marx says here, at the point where the working out of the meaning of capital is perhaps at its most electrically clear, "the result is: their tendency and *dunamei* for the general development of the forces of production—of wealth as such—as basis; likewise the universality of circulation, hence the world market as basis. The basis as possibility of the universal development of the *individuum* and the real development of individuals from this basis."[30] The *Marx Engels Werke* (*MEW*) edition of this text adds a note that the word *dunamei* means "the possibility."[31] The English translation, although leaving this (and other words) in Greek in the text in the two places where it occurs in the "Introduction," ignores the Greek entirely and simply reports "possibility."[32]

On page 91 of the English translation of the *Grundrisse* there is a reference to Aristotle's *Metaphysics,* where Aristotle connects two terms, *dunamis* and *energeia,* as both themselves *ousia,* "substance," and, he says, we now seek the *tis estin,* the "what is" of *dunamis* and *energeia.*[33] We should note that this inquiry into the "what" is singular. Aristotle takes for granted that we understand that in seeking out the "what," we are looking for a single entity. The entity in question is *ousia,* which we ordinarily translate as "substance," but which really means "being." We seek the entity of this being:

27. Ibid., 445. "Unbestimmter Arbeitstag einer unbestimmten Arbeitszahl . . . kommen hier alle *Populationsverhältnisse* herein" (Marx's emphasis).

28. Ibid., 445. "[Kapital] als bloßer Übergangspunkt gesetzt ist."

29. Ibid., 447. "Die Universalität des Individuums nicht als δυνάμει oder eingebildete, sondern als Universalität seiner realen und ideellen Beziehungen."

30. Ibid., 447. "Resultat ist: die ihrer Tendenz und δυνάμει nach allgemeine Entwicklung der Produktivkräfte—des Reichtums überhaupt—als Basis, ebenso die Universalität des Verkehrs, daher der Weltmarkt als Basis. Die Basis als Möglichkeit der universellen Entwicklung des Individuums und die wirkliche Entwicklung der Individuen von dieser Basis."

31. Ibid., 447, n. 46, "der Möglichkeit."

32. Karl Marx, *Grundrisse,* trans. Martin Nicolaus, 542. See also "Introduction," 91 and 106. On page 91 there is a reference to Aristotle, *Metaphysics,* "Bk. VIII, Ch. 6, 2."

33. Aristotle, *Metaphysics,* 1042b9–10. ἐπει δ' ἡ μὲν ὡς ὕλη οὐσία ὁμολογεῖται, αὕτη δ'ἐστὶν ἡ δυνάμει, λοιπὸν τὴν ὡς ἐνεργέιαν οὐσίαν τῶν αἰσθητῶν εἰπεῖν τίς ἐστιν.

the being *of* its being. There is no reference to Aristotle in either the 2005 edition of the *Grundrisse* in the *Marx Engels Werke* (*MEW*) nor in the 1953 Dietz Verlag edition published in Berlin.

What, then, do the English editors want to draw our attention to in this reference in a text of Marx's to Aristotle, and why? In this passage of Marx which mentions what is *en dunamei,* what this is at the same time is named as a "tendency." The editors and translators of the *Grundrisse* want to name this as "possibility," and this is not wrong. However, we think of possibility in a simply open sense, what is possible in terms of a choice or a free action. Marx, however, thinking in an absolutely Aristotelian way, thinks in terms of tendency as what is inevitably, inexorably, and forcibly directed toward its inmost and at the same time broadest possibility, what the Greeks called the *orexis,* that which it strives toward and strives utterly to fulfill. The possibility named here is *the* possibility as *the* drive to fulfill, to bring out into the open as an actuality, as we shall shortly see.

Marx speaks consistently of (in German) the *Basis,* the ground, but at the same time the platform and base from which we set off. Marx names himself to the core as a materialist. The "material" is therefore not the "basis" as the "lowest," but the basis as the *highest yet attained* of the possibilities open to us. We might, and we should hear, as I cited earlier, the *Basis* as the lord, the governing and ruling, as the possibility which demands to be fulfilled: "those material relations, which are their lord."[34] In this sense, Marx's materialism speaks out of the same drive for what Nietzsche named as the devaluation of the uppermost values, for the sake of a revaluation. This is the meaning of the revolutionary in Marx: not just the question of the transformative, as in a transformation of the social conditions, but at the same time, the inversion of all hitherto thinking, as its turning upside down. Marx does not, as Nietzsche does, endlessly rehearse this *Umwertung,* this "inversion" (and we should note the fundamental reference to "value" again in the word), but it is the constantly present condition of his thinking.

At the same time we must not lose sight of the fact that every single one of the major German figures who think through the question of Europe in the nineteenth and twentieth centuries, Hegel, Marx, Nietzsche, Heidegger, is each to the core a classical philologist. Two held professorial chairs in philosophy and classical philology (Hegel and Nietzsche). One held a chair in philosophy where he constantly taught Aristotle, Plato, and the pre-Socratic philosophers and even spoke from out of the texts of the lyric poets: Heidegger. And Marx: Marx is that one who wrote his doctoral thesis on Democritus and Empedocles, and, as I noted earlier, marked his thesis with a citation from Aeschylus's *Prometheus.* Each of these thinkers thinks the

34. See 225, n. 15.

destiny and question of Europe with respect to, and from out of, the beginning of European thought. If Heidegger is the thinker among these who most thematically and self-consciously seeks to connect the Occidental *first* beginning with the "other beginning" of the situation of Europe now, of the possibilities for thinking of, and in, and through, Europe *now,* Marx, no less than Heidegger is, almost without thinking, himself constantly meditating on the relation between antiquity and the present in which he writes.[35] Each of these thinkers thinks from out of the *whole* of European thought, and so by instinct as much as by the power of what it is they are trying to think *of,* think Europe from its dawn to its present. Heidegger understands Marx's confrontation with antiquity to have been determined from out of the transformations in thinking that the history of thinking itself have brought about. Marx, for Heidegger, is not seeking to enter into a confrontation with the whole history of Occidental thought, but is rather a final point *within* that history. Heidegger argues that "the humanism of Marx requires no return to antiquity," in contrast, Heidegger notes, to Hölderlin: "Hölderlin on the contrary does not belong to 'humanism,'" and so the return to antiquity found in Hölderlin's poetry is not humanistic.[36] It is for this reason that Marx's voice with respect to antiquity is quite different from Heidegger's. Marx, as one "further along" in the progress of history and the production of history, can never take up an originary voice with respect to antiquity because antiquity is always that which has been left behind, as sublated, and overcome. Heidegger understands Hölderlin to be that voice which, as addressed by an antiquity still entirely present and not even yet fulfilled in its original ground, is that which can never be exceeded or overcome. It is for this reason that Hölderlin's is the "poetic" voice of an antiquity *still present,* Marx's the polemical voice which favors the future (as becoming) over the past (as overcome). Even though Marx is addressed by antiquity through its transformations (its historical development), Marx always understands himself as that one who inaugurates his voice by judging the standpoint from out of which it speaks. The truly poetic voice is free from judgment because it speaks what *is to be spoken,* and so not the word it "judges" and "chooses" to be true.

There is in Hegel the most intimate connection between his thinking of absolute subjectivity and Aristotle. Early on, Heidegger makes a startling

35. There are frequent references to antiquity throughout Marx, but antiquity taken in its consequences, in what it means to have thought through what a fully developed *individuum* could possibly have been in antiquity as much as in his present. See Karl Marx, *Grundrisse* (*MEW*42), 446. "Bei den Alten, die das Bewußtsein hatten, wird des Reichtum daher direkt als Auflösung des Gemeinwesens denunziert." ("With those thinkers of antiquity who were possessed of consciousness, wealth came to be denounced as the dissolution of the commonweal.")

36. Martin Heidegger, *Brief über den Humanismus* (*GA*9), 321, 320. "Der Humanismus bedarf keines Rückgangs zur Antike" . . . "Hölderlin dagegen gehört nicht in den 'Humanismus.'"

observation: "*Hegel* took from Aristotle under the expression '*Aufhebung*' the phenomenon of *sōzein*."[37] Marx preserves that intimate connection above all in the thought of sublation, of *Aufhebung*. *Sōzein* means not to save, but to preserve and hold constantly in life, to preserve the living essence from one generation to the next, which means, in Marx's terms, from one social form to the next. Precisely, it is always the living form, life itself, which is to be developed to the highest degree. Every text of Marx's, but the *Grundrisse* above all, witnesses to this understanding of *sōzein* not once, but tirelessly. Heidegger says, for instance, of Hegel's Jena lecture of his philosophy of nature that it "is nothing other than a speculative paraphrase of Aristotelian physics."[38] The speculative aspect of this, however, is precisely the *subjective* aspect. Hegel recasts Aristotle through the metaphysics of subjectivity. Marx also preserves something of this, precisely in the sharp drive to deny the place of the idea, even as he unfolds an essentially metaphysical position. If there is in Hegel and Marx a most generous affinity to Aristotle, there is also in Heidegger. Heidegger's *Being and Time* would have been impossible without Heidegger's own sustained meditation on the texts of Aristotle throughout the 1920s. Even Heidegger's lectures on Plato's *Sophist* are in a full one-third taken up with a careful exposition of Aristotle.

Marx begins the *Grundrisse* not only with a reference to the central Aristotelian term *dunamis*, but also with a reference to the human being as the *zōon politikon*, a reference to Aristotle's *Politics*.[39] We do not need to demonstrate that Marx in some sense has Aristotle in view, therefore. Aristotle is constantly in view in Marx's thinking, inasmuch as his whole thought of *Kraft*, the *Produktionskraft* which we have so far translated as "forces of production," could also be translated as "powers," or even "possibilities of production." What Marx has in view at each stage is *dunamis*. The question is, *in what way* does Marx have *dunamis*, *Kraft*, power, possibility, and force in view? In some way that is genuinely Aristotelian? In some way that is genuinely metaphysical? Or has Marx been able to put these forces to work in a way that reaches beyond metaphysics, as he himself claimed? These questions represent the fundamental region of Heidegger's engagement with Marx. In the Le Thor seminars (at which both Jean Beaufret and Giorgio Agamben were present), the protocols show that Heidegger repeated his questioning of the eleventh of the "Theses on Feuerbach" and then said:

37. Martin Heidegger, *Grundbegriffe der aristotelischen Philosophie* (GA18), 196. "*Hegel* hat das Phänomen des σώζειν unter dem Ausdruck 'Aufhebung' von Aristoteles genommen" (italics in original).

38. Martin Heidegger, *Hegels Phänomenologie des Geistes* (GA32), 176. "Nichts anders ist als eine spekulative Paraphrase der Aristotelischen Physik."

39. See Aristotle, *Politics*, 1253a3. φύσει πολιτικόν ζῷον. ("In [the being of his] being, the political animal.")

> Concerning *which* transformation of the world do we have thus with Marx? Concerning a transformation in the relations of productions. Where, however, does production have its positing? In praxis. And how is praxis determined? Through a certain theory, which casts the concept of production as production of man through himself. Marx therefore has a theoretical representation of man, a very exact representation, which includes as its foundation the Hegelian philosophy.[40]

A note is added to the text which says "'without Hegel Marx would not have been able to alter the world,' said Heidegger emphatically."[41]

Heidegger acknowledges Marx's materialism by noting that, in reversing Hegel's idealism, Marx had required that "being be given precedence over consciousness." Heidegger then noted that, inasmuch as there was no understanding of consciousness in *Being and Time,* "one could think, there was something Heideggerian to be understood here! At the very least Marcuse had understood *Being and Time* in this way."[42] Heidegger concludes that "for Marx, being is production process."[43]

The question here is still *how,* and in what manner is being the production process, and in what way is this connected to Aristotle? We would be tempted to say "through technology": the plan is the means by which the production process is itself commandeered for the sake of the transformation of the world. While this may be an *effect* of Marxism, and in fact while it is no different from the *actual* effect of any other form of human organization, this does not touch either the fundamental connection with Aristotle, or, even more germanely for us, the fundamental connection between Heidegger and Marx. There is no understanding of consciousness in *Being and Time,* but there *is* consciousness in Marx, that of man laying hold of himself as subject becoming absolute subject: in Marx's terms, the very process of *realization* of

40. Martin Heidegger, *Vier Seminare* (*GA*15), 352–53. The seminars took place in Le Thor between 1968 and 1969, and were first published in 1977 together with protocols of a seminar that had taken place in Zähringen in 1973. "Um *welche* Veränderung der Welt geht es also bei Marx? Um eine Veränderung in den Produktionsverhältnissen. Wo aber hat die Produktion ihre Stelle? In der Praxis. Und wodurch ist die Praxis bestimmt? Durch eine gewisse Theorie, die den Begriff der Produktion als Produktion des Menschen durch ihn selbst prägt. Marx hat also eine theoretische Vorstellung vom Menschen—eine sehr genaue Vorstellung, die als ihre Grundlage die Hegelsche Philosophie enthält" (Heidegger's emphasis).

41. Ibid., 353. "'Ohne Hegel hätte Marx die Welt nicht verändern können' sagt Heidegger nachdrücklich."

42. Ibid., 353. "Indem Marx den Idealismus Hegels auf seine Weise umkehrt, fordert er, daß dem Sein der Vorrang vor dem Bewußtsein gegeben wird. Da es in *Sein und Zeit* kein Bewußtsein gibt, könnte man meinen, hier etwas Heideggersches zu lesen! Wenigstens hat Marcuse *Sein und Zeit* so verstanden."

43. Ibid., 353. "Für Marx ist das Sein Produktionsprozeß."

the demands of history are man's becoming-conscious of his historical task. In this the *party* is the means by which consciousness is both attained (as a subject position) and the same time corrected ("correct" consciousness is the way in which the revolutionary task of the proletariat attaining to nationhood is undertaken). In this, Marcuse's negatively liberal Marxism, "Marxism without the party," Marxism as an *individual belief,* is a falsification of Marx and a lesser understanding than Marx's own (an attempt to reconcile the negative understanding of freedom of the individual with Marx's higher, more Hegelian, understanding of freedom as freedom *for* what is to come).

In *The Communist Manifesto,* Marx speaks of the revolutionary role of the bourgeoisie. It is the bourgeoisie who "cannot exist without constantly revolutionizing the instruments of production, thus the relations of production, thus at the same the relations of society."[44] The attitude of every previous industrial class was unaltered conservation of the original modes of production: "The constant transformation of production, the uninterrupted disturbance of all social situations, the eternal insecurity and agitation marks the bourgeois epoch out from all before it."[45] In this constant revolutionary whirl "all that is solid melts into air."[46] The German has a direct social reference: more loosely, but more accurately, rendered for the contemporary ear, it says "all that is hierarchical and fixed floats off."

This uprootedness is also referred to, and captured by, Heidegger, but not in the fulfillment of metaphysics at its end, in Marx, but in its very inception, in Aristotle. Heidegger asks, in the drive to answer the question *ti to on?*—"what is the being?," the guiding question of metaphysics, "how can Aristotle equate *to on* and *to einai*? Why, therefore, if the inquiry to be pursued is into being (*einai*), can he say that the question would be concerning beings (*on*)?"[47]

The essential word of the *Grundrisse* is "equating" (*Gleichsetzung*), as we have seen.[48] This equating is either carried out in indifference, the indifference of the bourgeois pursuit and rulership of capital, as a transitional and

44. Karl Marx and Friedrich Engels, *Manifest der Kommunistischen Partei* (*MEW*4), 465. "Die Bourgeoisie kann nicht existieren, ohne die Produktionsinstrumente, also die Produktionsverhältnisse, also sämtliche gesellschaftlichen Verhältnisse fortwährend zu revolutionieren."

45. Ibid., 465. "Die fortwährende Umwälzung der Produktion, die ununterbrochene Erschütterung aller gesellschaftlichen Zustände, die ewige Unsicherheit und Bewegung zeichnet die Bourgeoisepoche vor allen anderen aus."

46. Ibid., 465. "Alles Ständische und Stehende verdampft." The German literally means "all that is corporeal and solid vaporizes."

47. Martin Heidegger, *Aristoteles, Metaphysik Q 1–3* (*GA*33), 18. "Wie kann Aristoteles τὸ ὄν und τὸ εἶναι einander gleichsetzen? Warum denn, wenn nach dem Sein (εἶναι) gefragt ist, sagen, nach dem Seienden (ὄν) sei die Frage?"

48. See 223.

provisional point, or in the full self-realization of the *individuum,* equalized from every difference, *self-consciously* as consuming as much as it produces. Even here the party, as much as the bourgeoisie and the state is a mere point of transition to this moment of equalization. Yet this essential word appears exactly here, for Heidegger, where being (*einai*) and beingness (*on*) are confused: "this equating [*Gleichsetzung*] is also today commonly made by us, although more with a sense of unenlightened confusion. Thus philosophy speaks often of being and means by that beingness. On the hand one uses the name beingness and means being." And yet, Heidegger says, we do understand something in this "even though everything dissolves into a fog" when we attempt to grasp it.[49]

For Heidegger, as we have seen, be-ing essentially unfolds in language, as the wresting of unconcealment from the concealed. Marx sets this aside for the sake of the production process: everything arises on the basis of production: society is self-producing as the concretization, the concrete manifestation of production. Society, is, however, as we have seen from the *Grundrisse, essentially* realized labor: "values" as "objectifications" which are then exchanged in sets of relations constituted as the "logic," the iron laws of the production process and *forces* of production as they have developed. The being-ness of these objectifications is the production process. The production process is, as we have seen Marx himself say, the force of creativity of these objectifications. The production process is at the same time society as a whole. The production process takes the place of being-as-a-whole, *das Seienden in ganzem,* metaphysically thought. This "taking the place" is the metaphysically named place of God: in a short article for the *New Zurich Times* in 1969, Heidegger confirms this interpretation, with specific reference to Marxist dialectic, when he says "industrial society, which today means the only and final reality—previously this was called God."[50] It is also what in Nietzsche is understood as the will to power (*Wille zur Macht*). It is in the next chapter that we will explore the connection with Aristotle.

49. Martin Heidegger, *Aristoteles, Metaphysik Θ 1–3* (*GA*33), 18. "Diese Gleichsetzung ist auch heute bei uns noch üblich, freilich mehr im Sinne einer heillosen Verwirrung. So spricht man oft in der Philosophie vom Sein und meint dabei das Seiende. Andererseits nennt man das Seiende und meint das Sein. Im Grunde begreift man weder das eine noch das andere. Und doch verstehen wir etwas dabei; wenngleich beim Versuch des Zufassens alles in einem Nebel verschwimmt."

50. Martin Heidegger, "Zeichen" (*GA*13), 212. "Die Industriegesellschaft, die heute als die erste und letze Wirklichkeit gilt—früher heißt sie Gott."

*Chapter 12*

# The End of Humanism

THE *LETTER ON HUMANISM* has been the guiding thread for this book: it is perhaps important, therefore, to recall once again Heidegger's caveat that "the letter still speaks in the language of metaphysics, and indeed knowingly. The other language lies in the background."[1] The letter opens with an enigmatic and difficult statement that could easily be overlooked as we rush forward for the more recognizable questions promised to come, and yet this statement functions as the headline for the entire letter. The opening says:

> We are still far from thinking about the essence of action decisively enough. We know action only as bringing about an effect. The reality [of the effect] is esteemed according to its profit. But the essence of action is fulfilment. Fulfilment means: to unfold something into the fullness of its essence, to bring it out to this fullness—*producere.* Being fully brought out is therefore only that which already is. But what before everything "is," is being. Thinking fulfils the relation of being to the essence of man. It does not make or bring the relation about. Thinking brings this relation to being solely as something given over to thought itself from being. This offering consists in the fact that in thinking being comes to language.[2]

1. See 39.

2. Martin Heidegger, *Brief über den Humanismus* (*GA*9), 313. "Wir bedenken das Wesen des Handelns noch lange nicht entschieden genug. Man kennt das Handeln nur als das Bewirken einer Wirkung. Deren Wirklichkeit wird nach ihrem Nutzen geschätzt. Aber das Wesen des Handelns ist das Vollbringen. Vollbringen heißt: etwas in die Fülle seines Wesens entfalten, in diese hervorgeleiten, producere. Vollbringbar ist deshalb eigentlich nur das, was schon ist. Was jedoch vor allem 'ist,' ist das Sein. Das Denken vollbringt den Bezug des Seins zum Wesen des Menschen. Es macht und bewirkt diesen Bezug nicht. Das Denken bringt ihn nur als das, was ihm selbst vom Sein übergeben ist, dem Sein dar. Dieses Darbringen besteht darin, daß im Denken das Sein zur Sprache kommt."

To hear this phrase "the essence of action," where I have repeated the translation of *Handeln* that both the published English translations of this text employ,[3] is, however, already to overinterpret. To our modern ears, attuned as they are to an only subjectival understanding of being, *Handeln*—"action"—is always in consequence of the intention of a subject. All action is conscious "doing." In this we are thoroughgoing Marxists even if we have never read a word of Marx. Action is better than words, better than any thinking: we abjure the "theoretical" in every case: we are a practical bunch. By *Handeln,* however, Heidegger means *praxis:* on more than one occasion this is how he translates each word into the other.[4] It need hardly be said that praxis is a central term both for Marx and for Marxism.

It becomes possible from this clarification of the text alone to see the extent to which the *Letter on Humanism* is, from the very outset, in dialogue with Marx. This chapter will seek to expand the understanding of action, and work, as the last of the expositions that open the way to the productive dialogue between Heidegger and Marx. This will require us entering into Heidegger's (and Marx's) interpretation of the Greeks one last time. Surely, however, praxis and action are the same thing? Except that, thought in a Greek way, *ta pragmata* are things, and so praxis is not action as such, but everything to do with things (*die Sachen*). In his reading of Plato's *Sophist,* Heidegger pointed out that the Greeks had "read off the meaning of being from the world as surrounding world."[5] This manner of reading-off results in a particular way of interpreting the world, and the beings encountered within the world: "the Greeks have also for this denoted field of being a very characteristic expression: *pragmata,* that with which one has to do, that which is here for *praxis.* Therefore the titles *on, einai, ousia, pragmata* are used identically."[6]

What this passage says, therefore, is that the way in which one interprets "praxis" will determine the relation both to beings and to the human being, the human essence. However, we have seen that the human essence is language: language speaks, a speaking to which man corresponds. Praxis

3. Compare Martin Heidegger, *Letter on Humanism,* trans. Frank Capuzzi and J. Glenn Gray, in *Basic Writings,* 217; revised in *Pathmarks,* 239 (*GA*9). The sentence in both translations reads: "We are still far from pondering the essence of action decisively enough."

4. Compare, among many examples: Martin Heidegger: "Phänomenologie und Theologie" (*GA*9), 58; *Platons Lehre von der Wahrheit* (*GA*9), 229; *Platon: Sophistes* (*GA*19), 38. (39, "πρᾶχις, Handeln").

5. Martin Heidegger, *Platon: Sophistes* (*GA*19), 270. "Sie (haben) den Sinn von Sein *an der Welt als Umwelt abgelesen*" (Heidegger's emphasis).

6. Ibid., 270–71. "Die Griechen haben auch für das genannte Feld des Seienden . . . einen sehr charakteristischen Ausdruck: pravgmata, womit man zu tun hat, und was fur die πρᾶχις da ist. Daher werden die Titel ὄν, εἶναι, οὖσία, πράγματα, gleich verwendet."

thought in this way cannot mean (intended, subjective) action. In fact, thought as Heidegger understands it (as the relation to the singular essencing of essence), the being of be-ing, praxis must in fact be a synonym for language itself. What this says is that all activity (rather than *intended,* "intentional," action) is a speaking. Activity lets things be seen, it uncovers beings as the beings that they are. Praxis understood in this way is never a *changing* of the beings *in itself,* even if, in praxis beings undergo a change. The praxis does not have their change, their transformation, as an inalienable intention *in* its activity.

Even more than this: all praxis is with respect to the fulfillment of the beings with which we have to do: all praxis already has in view their fulfillment, their completedness (Capuzzi's translation has "accomplishment"). The word that is surely barely able to conceal itself here is *entelecheia.* For Aristotle, every being that has come into the fulfillment of its being is an *entelecheia,* for which the English neologism "entelechy" was coined. The word *entelecheia* Heidegger interprets as "*en telei echei: entelecheia,* the having-itself-in-end,"[7] we must say, "full-fillment." Aristotle explicitly distinguishes *entelecheia* from *dunamis* in the work that has come down to us as the *Metaphysics,* where he also distinguishes *dunamis* from *energeia.*[8] Heidegger conducted a thoroughgoing inquiry into these three terms in a lecture course from the summer semester in Freiburg of 1931, which concentrated, not on book 8 (where these terms are also discussed), but book 9 of the *Metaphysics.*[9] In a later essay from 1939 (which I have already quoted) Heidegger says that "in place of the word he himself coined, *entelecheia,* Aristotle also employs the word *energeia.* Here, for *telos,* stands *ergon,* work, in the sense of the produced, and brought-forth."[10] *Energeia* means: the character of *en ere-gei,* "standing in the work," where the work involved has brought the thing about, has placed it in its end. Earlier I made clear that Marx has this understanding specifically in mind when he speaks of *energeia,* although in a way both connected to, and at the same time quite different from Heidegger's own understanding.

Heidegger connects *entelecheia* and *energeia* with *kinēsis,* movement, in a quite distinct interpretative way. Yet praxis, as we have seen, even in-

7. Martin Heidegger, "Vom Wesen und Begriff der *Φύσις*" (*GA*9), 284. "εν τέλει ἔχει: ἐντελέχεια, das Sich-im-Ende-Haben."

8. Aristotle, *Metaphysics,* 1045 b 32–35 and following.

9. See *Lecture 7,* note 33. Compare Martin Heidegger, *Aristoteles, Metaphysik Θ 1–3* (*GA*33), 18. The initial discussion of ἐντελέχεια, δύναμις ανδ ἐνέργεια is taken up in §1, 3–11, with the main discussion that concerns us to be found between 137–220.

10. Martin Heidegger, "Vom Wesen und Begriff der Φύσις" (*GA*9), 284. "Statt des von ihm selbst geprägten Wortes ἐντελέχεια gebraucht Aristoteles auch das Wort ἐνέργεια. Hier steht für τέλος ἔργον, das Werk im Sinne des Herzustellenden und Her-gestellten."

terpreted in the entirely conventional (metaphysical) way as "action," is also fundamentally a form of movement. In fact, freeing praxis from its connection with subjectivity (which Marx certainly does not do) shows up even more the character of praxis as a form of *kinēsis,* movement. The central interpretative insight that Heidegger has, which we can only touch on, is that what stands in its end, *entelecheia,* the thing "worked," "worked out," *as therefore being in a kind of rest, is also still in movement. Rest is, for Aristotle, a kind of movement.* Heidegger argues, and not for the first time, in this 1939 essay that "the purest enfolding of essence is there to be found, where rest does not mean stopping and breaking-off of movement, but where movedness collects into *holding-still,* and this holding-in, far from excluding movement, includes it, and not only includes it, but is the only unlocking of it."[11] Citing a line of Aristotle, Heidegger interprets this as the very *telos,* the end, where movement gathers itself up and essentially *is* movedness at all. The line Heidegger cites is *hora hama kai eōrake.*[12] Heidegger's translation is: "someone sees, and in seeing, he has at once already seen."[13] This is, once again, the term I have drawn attention to in Plato more than once: *eidenai,* ordinarily translated as "knowing" but which in fact means something more like "recognising now in virtue of having (already) once seen."[14]

If every being is *pragma,* a "moveable," then it *is* this even when at rest, and at the same time it is subject to movement, *kinēsis,* and subject to the relations which concern human beings with its movability. These latter relations we name: praxis. If you have been following this, at times quite difficult, argument—one which is very far even from being worked out yet—you should by now have noticed something quite strange. For so far, whenever we have discussed work, or labor, as it appears in Marx, or even in some of Heidegger, we have always discussed it not only as a fundamentally human concern, but even more than this, we have presumed without even questioning it, that all work is fundamentally *human* action and activity. Here, however, with Aristotle, *ergon,* work, and whatever is a reality (*entelecheia*) is not necessarily in consequence of human action. Most particularly, many of the things that are explained by *energeia,* as the things standing-in-work (hence the "real," as if that clarified anything at all) are exactly *not* in con-

11. Ibid., 284. "Deren reinste Wesensentfaltung ist dort zu suchen, wo die Ruhe nicht Aufhören und Abbruch der Bewegung bedeutet, sondern wo die Bewegtheit sich in das *Stillhalten* sammelt und dieses Innehalten die Bewegtheit nicht aus, sondern ein, ja nicht nur ein, sondern erst aufschließt" (Heidegger's emphasis).

12. Aristotle, *Metaphysics,* 1048b23. ὁρᾷ ἅμα καὶ ἑώρακε.

13. Martin Heidegger, "Vom Wesen und Begriff der Φύσις" (*GA*9), 284. "Einer sieht und sehend hat er (eben) zumal auch schon gesehen."

14. For a full discussion of this aorist infinitive, and its place in thinking, see Laurence Paul Hemming, *Postmodernity's Transcending,* 217–18.

sequence of human action and activity. Even things which arise and stand for themselves, the things capable of self-producing (the "phenomena" that arise on the basis of *phusis,* of what is capable of producing and brings itself about in and for itself, the things of "nature" and therefore quite apart from any human action), are "in work," *energeia.* In fact Heidegger understands *energeia* to be Aristotle's most fundamental determination of being. We have seen, however, that *energeia* and *pro-ducere,* that which is capable of leading itself forth and standing out for itself, are, historically at least, taken to be the same. How can there be a force of production which is not in human hands?

To ask the question in this way is, for Heidegger, to be confronted with the history of the transformation in the meaning of *energeia* itself. Heidegger examined this history in an essay of 1941, which was published with the publication of his *Nietzsche* lectures in 1961. It corresponds in date with the period of the working out of the manuscripts of *Das Ereignis,* and, it would seem, the period of Heidegger's fiercest confrontation with Marx and Marxism—even though Marx is never mentioned in the text by name. The history begins by understanding the original Greek thought of the "work" (*ergon*): "thought in Greek, the work is not work in the sense of the performance of a strenuous making, nor result and effect; it is work in the sense of that which is placed in the unconcealment of its appearance, and remains as the thing thus standing or lying. Remains means here: quietly present as work."[15] This means that *ergon* now distinguishes the manner of presencing. Presence, *ousia,* means therefore *energeia,* what in the work essences-as-work (conceiving essence verbally) or the workness. This does not mean reality as the result of a working."[16]

This understanding of work is absent in every sense from Marx. For Marx, all work is *intended,* the consequence of decision exercised through a kind of imperative. Work arises on the basis of reality and effects reality—as production it accounts for what already *is* and what is yet to come: constant production and creation. The imperative is the imperative of history itself, expressing itself in social relations. Yet the "quiet" in question in Heidegger's understanding of work here, that which has been brought to pass and brought into still presence, recalls the language of the Last God and indicates, in at least a preliminary way, the connection for the Greeks between

15. Martin Heidegger, "Die Metaphysik als Geschichte des Seins" (*GA*6.2), 368. "Griechisch gedacht, ist das Werk nicht Werk im Sinne der Leistung eines angestrengten Machens, auch nicht Ergebnis und Erfolg; es ist Werk im Sinne dessen, was in das Unverborgene seines Aussehens ausgestellt ist und so Stehendes oder Liegendes verweilt. Weilen heißt hier: ruhig anwesen als Werk."

16. Ibid., 368. "Das ἔργον kennzeichnet jetzt die Weise des Anwesens. Die Anwesenheit, οὐσία, heißt deshalb ἐνέργεια: das im Werk als Werk-Wesen (Wesen verbal begriffen) oder die Werkheit. Diese meint nicht die Wirklichkeit als Ergebnis eines Wirkens."

work and the gods, a connection which has nothing to do with intention or causation (a given "work" is not "caused" by a god). This connection is in no way an intention of the gods: rather the reverse: only in the stillness of the presence of the work can the presence of the god also come to pass. The work can let the god come to pass (we could almost say, in the most extreme understanding, the work has the power to let "be," and so "cause," the god's passing-by).

In his 1941 essay, Heidegger indicates a meaning for *energeia* that raises the question of how Aristotle took up the term, and so how it is that the history of being set off, not only from Plato's thinking, but also Aristotle's, as metaphysics. Heidegger traces how in each "work" as a thing lying present, "the *energeia* is the *ousia* (presence) of the *tode ti,* of the *prevailing* this and the *prevailing* that."[17]

Heidegger does not say so here, partly, perhaps, because in 1941 this question was not fully worked out even then. However, the question turns on the question of *essence* or rather not only of the presencing of the work, but the *naming* and *speaking of,* the presence of the work. You will recall that Heidegger had noted that when we seek the essence of a human being, we really seek what makes Plato or Frederick the Great in each case the unique man that he is, and yet essence has metaphysically been driven to speak not of the uniqueness of the human essence, but of the sameness—that Frederick the Great is one of the exemplars of the essence "man." The suggestion is that the *energeia* presented not only the workness of the work as a "what," but *in its manner of presencing,* and that *energeia* named what we distinguish as a duality, both the "what" and the "how" as a unity. In each case, speaking of this "work" lying present demanded that it be addressed for the being that it particularly *is.*

Heidegger argues that it is with Aristotle that "the distinction of a twofold *ousia* (presence) has become necessary."[18] From now on Aristotle will seek out *in each case* the "what" (*tode ti*) of the thing as a common "what." This is important because it is the essential connection between Aristotle and Plato: Heidegger says that what for Plato was the "common" (*koinon*) idea to every thing (this table and this table and this table: "tableness") is expressed for Aristotle in the finding out of the *tode ti,* the "particular whatness" of the table, what is common to the tables (the "essence," *ousia*). The matter of fundamental importance for Heidegger is that in connecting Plato and Aristotle's thought of essence the *manner* of presencing, which, he implies, *energeia* and *ergon* had *also* named, falls into the background and as-

17. Ibid., 369. "Die ἐνέργεια ist die οὐσία (Anwesenheit) des τόδε τι, des *jeweiligen* Diesen und *jeweiligen* Jenen" (Heidegger's emphases).

18. Ibid., 369. "Die Unterscheidung einer zwiefachen οὐσία (Anwesenheit) ist nötig geworden."

sumes merely secondary importance. From now on, the *tode ti* even as it is a being, an *on,* is a *mere* being, a mere example, a "not-really" being: "the *tode ti* is a *me on* and yet an *on.*"[19]

From now on, Heidegger argues, presencing, the *manner* of a being's being-present, disappears, and for both Plato and Aristotle means that particular beings are less than the "forms" and "energies" and "ideas," their "real being" that lets them be what they are, as exemplars of the "idea" or the "essence"—and this in itself is the birth of nihilism, of the slow disappearance and flight and forgetfulness of the being of beings. Heidegger allows that Aristotle preserves some of the original relation to presencing that Plato dissolves, but he adds "that Aristotle in this manner thinks in a more Greek way than Plato, does not mean to say that he again comes closer to the thinking of being of the beginning."[20] Aristotle, as much as Plato, sets off *from* the beginning. To think again the thinking of being will be to see how this setting-off took place, and how we may return to the original, "beginningly" thinking of being. It is only with the beginning of such a nihilism that the most fundamental transformation can occur in the meaning of the work, *ergon,* as *energeia.*

It now becomes possible to see why, for Heidegger, valuation is of the essence of nihilism. All valuing is taking something *as* something: estimating something *as:* we find ourselves saying in English, "setting a value upon" something. Such a way of addressing a thing only becomes possible out of the twofold that metaphysics initiates and lives out of, because, thought metaphysically, the thing is *never* really "for itself," and always an exemplar, a particular *one of* something "in general": the *idea,* the "whatness" (*ousia*), the species, the genus. Metaphysically thought, for Heidegger, no being is allowed to address us as the being that it is, both what it is and in the manner of its presencing, as a unity. As such, and in each case, we take the being over in its presence and assign it its essence (the place from which the meaning of the presencing of its presence "really" is to be found, the definition, the essence, the idea, the "value"). Marx, in recognizing the extreme to which this has been pushed in the ways not beings, but the values that can be extracted from them, are always produced, points not only inward, toward the innermost heart of the completion of metaphysics, but in calling for the overcoming of the alienation, of the estrangement (*Entfremdung*) of beings from themselves that valuation undertakes, points not only *within,* but in fact *beyond* metaphysics, to its overcoming. This is why Marx, as much as Hegel and Nietzsche, has the capacity to take us up to the threshold of the over-

19. Ibid., 372. "Das τόδε τι ist ein μὴ ὄν—und doch ein ὄν."

20. Ibid., 372. "Daß Aristoteles in der genannten Weise griechischer denkt als Platon, besagt jedoch nicht, er komme dem anfänglichen Denken des Seins wieder näher."

coming of metaphysics. However, thought from Heidegger's account, Marx is never able to attain to the overcoming of metaphysics because he is never able to step back in to the beginning of thinking sufficiently to see from what source valuation itself springs. Marx's only solution to the question of the essential differentiation implied in all value-thinking is not the *overcoming* of the thinking of value, but the *equalization* of every value with every other, as the accomplishment of the end of valuation as *difference,* and so the end of history. When everything means the same, and everything has a value posited for it and so potentially everything at one and the same time has the possibility to hold the highest or the lowest value, then everything means nothing. This is the point of the most extreme nihilism.[21]

Heidegger does not explain the relation to Marx of his thinking with Aristotle, nor of Marx's own relation to Aristotle, in the *Letter on Humanism,* let alone in his essay of 1939 on the essence of *phusis.* It should now be clear, however, why Heidegger thought that even though Marx was steeped in the classical and Greek sources, he was blocked—not by his own failing or some stupidity, but by the history of being itself—from being able to interpret them adequately, and so cannot break free from the way metaphysics thinks what the Greeks bequeath to it.

Marx's understanding of history is impossible without what itself makes history possible. If history is necessarily interpretation, nevertheless it is not what *I* interpret, but rather from out of what lets me into my own self-understanding am I able to interpret what unfolds historically. It is for this reason that history, which is nothing "historical," constantly degenerates into the historiographical, as how historical events are simply taken for granted as "facts," or as chains of "causes" and "effects." The history of being, as the history of the forgottenness of being, constantly both lays out and makes possible that history *is* at all, and how we take for granted its epochs as epochs of interpretation. It is on the basis of the forgottenness of being that history itself first stands and through which it must be brought to light. It is only because Heidegger is the thinker of the forgottenness of being that he can be an authentic interpreter of Marx's (superior) understanding of history. Yet the superiority of Marx's understanding of history lies in this—that only through Marx (which means only through the *experience* of what Marx writes of as the future history of humanity) can and does the forgottenness

21. Friedrich Nietzsche, vol. 12, *Nachlaß 1885–1887,* 213 (= *Der Wille zur Macht,* §55, 44). "Das ist die extremste Form des Nihilismus: das Nichts (das 'Sinnlose') ewig!" ("This is the most extreme form of nihilism: the nothing [the 'meaningless'], always!") See also Friedrich Nietzsche, vol. 12, *Nachlaß 1885–1887,* 350 (= *Der Wille zur Macht,* §§12–13, 12–16). See Heidegger's commentary on "the most extreme nihilism" and these sections in Martin Heidegger, *Nietzsche: Der europäische Nihilismus* (*GA*48), 91–96, especially 95 (= *GA*6.2, 72–77, especially 75).

of being again came out into the open and become capable of being remembered and disclosed all over again. Marx, as the outermost end of the beginning (who described what we are even now still experiencing), is at the same time the very possibility of the *other* beginning, the new beginning, in man's encounter with his own being-historical.

At a seminar in Zähringen in 1973, Heidegger quotes from Marx's "Contributions to the Critique of Hegel's Philosophy of Right": "to be radical is to grasp the root of the thing. The root for man is however man himself."[22] The protocols of the seminar say "from this thesis, Heidegger explained, rests the whole of Marxism. Indeed, Marxism thinks from out of production: social of society (society produces itself) and self-production of man as a social being."[23] To understand this in relation to Aristotle is to have to think Marx in terms of the whole history of philosophy: Marx, as himself the fulfillment and completion of metaphysics, is at the same time one pole, the very farthest pole, the end, of the beginning. The beginning in question is not Aristotle, although he is the *other* figure of the beginning, just as Nietzsche is the *other* figure of the end, but Plato. Heidegger makes exactly this point, and speaks of the relation between Marx and Plato, when he says:

> Through, and throughout, the whole of the history of philosophy, Plato's thinking in modified forms remains decisive. Metaphysics is Platonism. Nietzsche distinguishes his philosophy as inverted Platonism. With the inversion of metaphysics, which was already completed through Marx, the most extreme possibility of philosophy is attained. It has entered its final stage.[24]

Later in the seminar in Zähringen (in fact the following day) Heidegger expanded on this understanding of Marx as a fundamentally metaphysical, and therefore not political, understanding. Heidegger adds here, speaking of "my Marx interpretation," and saying that the same text emphasizes just

22. Martin Heidegger, "Seminar in Zähringen" (*GA*15), 387, citing Karl Marx, "Zur Kritik der Hegelschen Rechtsphilosophie" (*MEW*1), 385. "Radikal sein ist die Sache an der Wurzel fassen. Die Wurzel für den Menschen ist aber der Mensch selbst." Heidegger in fact cited not the *MEW*, but another edition of Marx's early works.

23. Martin Heidegger, "Seminar in Zähringen" (*GA*15), 387. "Auf dieser These, erläutert Heidegger, beruht der gesamte Marxismus. Der Marxismus denkt nämlich von der Produktion aus: gesellschaftliche Produktion der Gesellschaft (die Gesellschaft produziert sich selbst) und Selbstproduktion des Menschen als soziales Wesen."

24. Martin Heidegger, "Das Ende der Philosophie und die Aufgabe des Denkens" (*GA*14), 71. "Durch die ganze Geschichte der Philosophie hindurch bleibt Platons Denken in abgewandelten Gestalten maßgebend. Die Metaphysik ist Platonismus. Nietzsche kennzeichnet seine Philosophie als umgekehrten Platonismus. Mit der Umkehrung der Metaphysik, die bereits durch Karl Marx vollzogen wird, ist die äußerste Möglichkeit der Philosophie erreicht. Sie ist in ihr Ende eingegangen."

three lines later that "'*man is the highest being for man*' . . . With this vision and in this view I can say: with Marx the position of the most extreme nihilism is reached."[25]

In naming the position of extreme nihilism, Heidegger names not only his interpretation of Marx, but also his interpretation of Nietzsche: in this passage and the one quoted before it, it becomes clear that Marx had already carried out what Nietzsche was also carrying through. The outermost, or most extreme, nihilism, is explicitly a phrase of Nietzsche's, when he says: "That there is no given truth, no given absolute nature of things, no 'thing in itself'—this is itself a nihilism, and truly the most extreme. It places the value of things directly in this, that to these values no reality corresponds and corresponded, but only in their being a symptom of force on the part of the value-positers, a simplification for the goal of life."[26] What Nietzsche says here exactly connects his understanding of value with the understanding of value to be found in Marx. Value is always value-positing: Nietzsche, however, has no social "theory" of how value positing is to be undertaken. Or rather, we might say, value-positing is always understood through that one who, in order to posit values, stands out from the herd, stands apart from the mass, and constitutes social relations *through* corresponding in the utmost way to the will to power: *this* one makes *every* one. Marx's understanding is the inverse of this, and at the same time its mirror-image: the mass is shown always to be at a distance from its possibility of a unified, common, *koinon*, possibility of value-positing, such that the values posited by one would be the same as the values posited by all. *Any* one is *every* one.

In his lectures on Nietzsche of 1940, Heidegger says that Nietzsche indicates that "we experience the most extreme nihilism not as complete decline, but as the passage to new conditions of existence [*Daseinsbedingungen*]."[27] We need have no doubt that Heidegger interprets Marx in the same

25. Martin Heidegger, "Seminar in Zähringen" (*GA*15), 387, citing Karl Marx, "Zur Kritik der Hegelschen Rechtsphilosophie" (*MEW*1), 385. "'Der *Mensch das höchste Wesen für den Menschen sei* . . . .' Meine Marx-Auslegung . . . Mit diesem Ausblick und in dieser Sicht kann ich sagen: mit Marx ist die Position des äußersten Nihilismus erreicht" (Marx's emphasis).

26. Friedrich Nietzsche, *Der Wille zur Macht,* 16 (= vol. 12, *Nachlaß 1885–1887,* 351–52). "Daß es keine Wahrheit giebt; daß es keine absolute Beschaffenheit der Dinge, kein 'Ding an sich' giebt—dies ist selbst ein Nihilism, und zwar der extremste. Er legt den Werth der Dinge gerade dahinein, daß diesem Werthe keine Realität entspricht und entsprach, sondern nur ein Symptom von Kraft auf Seiten der Werth-Ansetzer, eine Simplification zum Zweck des Lebens." Nietzsche makes several other references to extreme nihilism in his *Nachlaß:* compare *Wille zur Macht:* §15, 17 (= vol. 12, *Nachlaß 1885–1887,* 354); §55, 44 (= vol. 12, *Nachlaß 1885–1887,* 213); §112, 82 (= vol. 12, *Nachlaß 1885–1887,* 468).

27. Martin Heidegger, *Nietzsche: Der europäische Nihilismus* (*GA*48), 96 (= *GA*6.2, 76). "Daß wir gerade den extremsten Nihilismus nicht als völligen Niedergang, sondern als den

way. What is central here is that this is an *experience* of the most extreme nihilism. It is not possible, as Heidegger explained in great detail in his elaboration of Nietzsche's figure of Zarathustra, to understand the experience of nihilism as a merely theoretical one: we cannot "think our way through" extreme nihilism, it must be lived. Does this arise precisely because of his own experience of the most extreme nihilism in Hitlerism? Are we therefore to understand that, in the way abandonment of being (*Seinsverlassenheit*) occurs for us and around us, we can abandon being, and be abandoned by being, but we cannot cease to be? This means that the experience of the abandonment of being seeks to speak, and in every genuine experience of being, even as abandonment, this speaking will press in on us, in the most concrete, factical ways.

What Nietzsche describes as value-positing is for Marx the action, not of some "one" but of history itself. History itself will produce and create the conditions for the unified positing of values. In this there is a divergence between Marx and Nietzsche, or so it would seem—in the proximity to what Marxism always calls "the real." Nietzsche says that the impossibility of the "thing in itself," a claim of Kant's, is in fact the appearance of the extreme of nihilism in that the thing is *never* in itself but *always* a value. Taking apart the obvious point that Marx says no less than this in making the thing in itself coincident with the value accorded it *as the end of history,* by which we mean exactly the "goal of life" as Nietzsche names it (*sōzein*), there is an important gap here. Marx and Marxist realism always claim to be coming close to the thing, laying claim to it by showing the extent to which we are already bound to whatever it is we lay claim to both produce and be produced by. In this we experience the visceral strength and concreteness both of Marx's capacity for thought and the way his thinking explains us to ourselves. For Marx pursues, especially in *Das Kapital* and in the *Grundrisse,* with an unflinching rigor and in pursuit of what cannot be evaded, what presses in on us and that to which we are bound. We could hope that anyone seeking to speak in Marx's name, or naming his thinking, would themselves endure and hold tightly to the fastenings of this truly dreadful rigor.

Why is Marx unable to touch or reach the "thing in itself," any more than Nietzsche (who in any case holds that any thought of doing so must be abandoned altogether)? Even more, why, if the determining thought for

---

Übergang zu neuen Daseinsbedingungen erfahren." See also Martin Heidegger, "Die seinsgeschichtliche Bestimmung des Nihilismus" (*GA*6.2), 306. "Nietzsche versteht seine Metaphysik als extremsten Nihilismus, so zwar, daß dieser zugleich kein Nihilismus mehr ist." ("Nietzsche understands his metaphysics as extreme nihilism, thus really, that at the same this is no longer a nihilism.")

Marx is that of "work," of labor, as *ergon* and the determining thought for Aristotle of being as a whole is *energeia,* why then do Marx and Aristotle not think the same?

The answer, for Heidegger above all, lies not in Marx but in Plato. As the most extreme form of nihilism, I have already said, Marx lies at one extreme of two poles. The other is the beginning, but precisely, the beginning in Plato. The answer is also to be found in Marx's understanding of humanism, and in Heidegger's reading of that understanding. It should be recalled that the *Letter on Humanism* was first published, not on its own, but together with a text that was written in 1940 and published finally in wartime conditions in 1942 (moreover, Heidegger always claimed, in difficult circumstances, such that the Nazis had tried to prevent its publication): *Plato's Doctrine of Truth.* In 1947 an edition was published of this text together with the *Letter on Humanism.* In *Plato's Doctrine of Truth* Heidegger essentially repeated and condensed a lecture course he had given in 1931–32; however, the relevant section, or any mention of the ideas within it, that occasioned the joining of these two texts, is not to be found in the original lectures.[28] The 1940 essay on Plato contains this passage, absolutely central to our concerns:

> The beginning of metaphysics in the thought of Plato is at the same time the beginning of "humanism." This word must be thought here essentially, and therefore in the broadest sense. Accordingly "humanism" means that which is wrapped up together in the beginning, in the unfolding, and in the end of metaphysics, whereby man, in quite differentiated respects but always deliberately, moves into the midst of beings, of course without thereby already being the highest being. "Man" sometimes means humanity or humankind, sometimes the individual or a community, and sometimes the people [*Volk*] or a group of peoples. It always means: in the realm of a fundamental, metaphysical basic structure of beings, from here onward "men" are defined as *animal rationale,* for the liberation of their possibilities, and bringing them to the certitude of their destiny, and the securing of their "life." This occurs as the shaping of their "moral" behavior, as the salvation of their immortal souls, as the unfolding of their creative powers, as the development of their reason, as the nourishing of their personalities, as the awakening of their civic sense, as the cultivation of the body, or as an appropriate combination of some or all of these "humanisms." What carries itself out in each instance is a metaphysically determined revolving around man, in narrower or wider paths. With the fulfillment of metaphysics, "humanism" (or said in "Greek,"

28. Martin Heidegger, *Vom Wesen der Wahrheit* (GA34).

anthropology) also presses on to the most extreme—and likewise unconditioned—"positions."[29]

Humanism turns out to be the whole history of metaphysics.

As this, humanism is, in its totality, both the history of metaphysics, and *Seinsverlassenheit,* "abandonment of being." Marx both brings to an end, and brings to the most extreme position, abandonment of being, and he does this *through* the most extreme orientation to history. This is because, as we have seen in Heidegger's quoting of the early Marx on Hegel's *Philosophy of Right,* at the end of metaphysics only man, and he alone, stands forth. This means that "work," *ergon,* considered as a merely and purely human affair, is only possible at the extreme end of metaphysics, when the surrounding world has decisively, and at the very last, been wiped off, exactly as had been prepared for in Descartes's "method of doubt," but which took a full two centuries further to attain. Having repeatedly examined Heidegger's statement concerning the superiority of the Marxist understanding of history, we can, in bringing into view this extreme abandonment of being, understand what Heidegger means when he says that this superiority is attained "because Marx, inasmuch as he experiences alienation, attains to an essential dimension of the historical."[30]

How does Heidegger describe the conversion of *energeia* into mere labor, as an affair not at all concerned with the surrounding world, and only concerned with the human being? The term we have so far failed entirely

29. Martin Heidegger, *Platons Lehre von der Wahrheit* (*GA*9), 236–37. "Der Beginn der Metaphysik im Denken Platons ist zugleich der Beginn des 'Humanismus.' Dieses Wort sei hier wesentlich und deshalb in der weitesten Bedeutung gedacht. Hiernach meint 'Humanismus' den mit dem Beginn, mit der Entfaltung und mit dem Ende der Metaphysik zusammengeschlossenen Vorgang, das der Mensch nach je verschiedenen Hinsichten, jedesmal aber wissentlich in eine Mitte des Seienden ruckt, ohne deshalb schon das höchste Seiende zu sein. 'Der Mensch,' das bedeutet hier bald ein Menschentum oder die Menschheit, bald den Einzelnen oder eine Gemeinschaft, bald das Volk oder eine Volkergruppe. Immer gilt es, im Bereich eines festgemachten metaphysischen Grundgefüges des Seienden den von hier aus bestimmten 'Menschen,' das animal rationale, zur Befreiung seiner Möglichkeiten und in die Gewißheit seiner Bestimmung und in die Sicherung seines 'Lebens' zu bringen. Das geschieht als Prägung der 'sittlichen' Haltung, als Erlösung der unsterblichen Seele, als Entfaltung der schöpferischen Kräfte, als Ausbildung der Vernunft, als Pflege der Persönlichkeit, als Weckung des Gemeinsinns, als Züchtung des Leibes oder als geeignete Verkoppelung einiger oder all dieser 'Humanismen.' Jedesmal vollzieht sich ein metaphysisch bestimmtes Kreisen um den Menschen in engeren oder weiteren Bahnen. Mit der Vollendung der Metaphysik drangt auch der 'Humanismus' (oder 'griechisch' gesagt: die Anthropologie) auf die äußersten und d. h. zugleich unbedingten 'Positionen.'"

30. Martin Heidegger, *Brief über den Humanismus* (*GA*9), 170. "Weil Marx, indem er die Entfremdung erfährt, in eine wesentliche Dimension der Geschichte hineinreicht."

to investigate in relation to Marx is not *energeia,* but *dunamis,* the "forces" or *Kräfte* of Marx's forces of production. For, as we saw in relation to the *Grundrisse,* as would be entirely possible to show from *Das Kapital,* Marx emphasizes not the *stability* of the substance of humanity but its dynamism.

In the *Metaphysics* Aristotle argues that *energeia* is prior (*proteron*) to *dunamis,*[31] and Heidegger interprets this both as asserting the priority of *entelecheia,* and that these two are prior with respect to *ousia.* He adds, interpreting this line of the *Metaphysics,* "one translates this sentence: 'manifestly standing-in-the-work is prior to appropriateness-for . . . ,' in which the Aristotelian, and that means at the same Greek, thinking reaches its pinnacle."[32] What this means is that *energeia* fulfills the essence of the stability of presencing—it "lets being be seen" more adequately than *dunamis* does. It is the letting-be-seen that is fundamental both to Aristotle and to what Heidegger calls Greek thinking. We have encountered this immediacy of the seen already. It is the mere *visibility* of the necessity of revolution that will bring it about, we can see *already* what needs to be seen and what spurs us to praxis, to the overthrow of the existing social relations for the sake of what *ought* to pertain. In *energeia* Aristotle "lets it be seen" that being "is." In *the present conditions* of work and labor, and through its alienation, Marx "lets it be seen" that the pure possibility of the forces of production must be fulfilled. These two are opposite ends of the same thing—recognition, "letting-be-seen," *eidenai* and *hora hama kai eōrake,* "someone sees, and in seeing, he has at once already seen."

How is it, however, that Marx can stand in so opposite a place to Aristotle, if both are speaking of the same, "letting-be-seen"? One of the most dramatic and impudent claims of *Being and Time* in 1927 had been: "Higher than actuality stands possibility. We can understand phenomenology only by seizing upon it as a possibility."[33] It is precisely this—*Dasein* as possibility *over* being as actuality, the basis on which Heidegger overcomes the necessity for "consciousness" in *Being and Time*—that Marcuse had perhaps also seen as an intrinsic connection between Marx and Heidegger, at least in the Heidegger of *Being and Time.* However, Marx does not rely for his rejection of Aristotle's understanding of *energeia* on the interpretation that Heidegger advances here (not least because it could not have been known to him—and,

31. See Aristotle, *Metaphysics,* 1049b5. Φανερὸν ὅτι πρότερον ἐνέργεια δθνάμις ἐστιν. ("It is evident that ἐνέργεια is prior to δυνάμις.")

32. Martin Heidegger, "Vom Wesen und Begriff der Φύσις" (*GA*9), 286. "'Offenbar ist früher das Im-Werk-Stehen als die Geeignetheit zu. . .' Übersetzt man diesen Satz, in dem das aristotelische und d. h. zugleich das griechische Denken seinen Gipfel erreicht."

33. Martin Heidegger, *Sein und Zeit* (*GA*2), 51–52. "Höher als die Wirklichkeit steht die *Möglichkeit.* Das Verständnis der Phänomenologie liegt einzig im Ergreifen ihrer als Möglichkeit" (Heidegger's emphasis).

we would want to go further, but have not the time to explain it here, Heidegger is only able to advance this interpretation *because* of the death of God, *because* of Marx, and because of Nietzsche). Marx is relying on an altogether more conventional—metaphysical—interpretation of *energeia* and *dunamis,* which Heidegger names when he says that if we translate the line of Aristotle I cited earlier in the usual way, "then it reads 'clearly actuality [*Wirklichkeit*] is prior to potentiality.' "[34]

The Romans translated *energeia* as *actus, actualitas,* and *dunamis* as *potentia,* which is exactly the sense in which Marx uses the phrase [*en*] *dunamei* in the preface and other places in the *Grundrisse.*[35] Heidegger concludes from this that the phrase "actuality is prior to potentiality" seems to be in error, since the opposite is both more obvious and more plausible. It is not, however, even in search of greater plausibility that led Marx to overturn the *taxis* of actuality and potentiality (nor, indeed, is this why Heidegger does so in *Being and Time*). The priority of actuality over potentiality becomes itself a metaphysical definition. The name *actus purus* became, in the Christian reception of Aristotle, above all by Saint Thomas Aquinas, the name for God. God is pure single act because he is the plenitude of presence as the totality of all actuality. Whatever "is," is in God first. It is this definition which Marx believes himself to be overturning in prioritizing *potentia, dunamis,* over the actual (in exactly the same way that Nietzsche seeks to prioritize becoming over being).

Heidegger makes explicit his tracing of the transformation of *energeia* into actuality in a section of the 1941 essay I have already drawn attention to that has exactly this title.[36] Fundamental for our discussion of Marx, Heidegger traces how "*energeia* comes to be *actualitas,* and this becomes reality [*Wirklichkeit*]."[37] This translation via Latin has consequence for other centrally Aristotelian terms: "Now *ergon* comes to be the worked of what is worked, the having been made of making, the act of doing."[38] To emphasize the transition, Heidegger in each case employs the Latin derivations of the terms in question (*operari, facere, agere*—I have translated them here, but in his German text they are left in the Latin). In discussing the transition from Greek to Latin and thence to German (and, by implication and for us, En-

34. Martin Heidegger, "Vom Wesen und Begriff der Φύσις" (*GA*9), 286. "Dann lautet er: 'Offenbar ist die Wirklichkeit früher als die Möglichkeit.' "

35. Compare chapter 11.

36. For a fuller discussion of this, see Martin Heidegger, "Der Wandel der ἐνέργεια zur actualitas" in "Die Metaphysik als Geschichte des Seins" (*GA*6.2), 374–83.

37. Martin Heidegger, "Die Metaphysik als Geschichte des Seins" (*GA*6.2), 374. "Die ἐνέργεια wird zur actualitas und diese zur Wirklichkeit."

38. Ibid., 375. "Jetzt wird das ἔργον zum opus des operari, zum factum des facere, zum actus des agere."

glish), Heidegger draws the astonishingly forceful conclusion that "the determining of being as *actualitas* extends itself therefore, if we reckon in epochs, through the whole of Occidental history from the Romans up to the latest time of modernity."[39] This has the consequence that "if being is transformed into *actualitas* (reality), then what is in being is the real, it is determined through working in the sense of causal making. From here on out the reality of human doing and divine creating come themselves to be explained thus."[40] It remains only for the death of God to fuse creating and making together and so to make of this an entirely human affair.

Marx's interpretation of, and decision *for*, work, as at root a human concern, and *only* a human concern, arises precisely on the basis of his interpretation of Hegel and Feuerbach, and their own metaphysical interpretation of Aristotle: it is the death of God, and the overcoming of religion, which complete the conversion of *ergon* and *energeia* into work as human labor. In this we are returned to Heidegger's consideration in the *Beiträge* that Marx and what he calls there "Bolshevism" are, strange as it may seem, a thoroughgoingly Christian, and theistic, affair.[41] We can see this precisely in the way in which, in the *Grundrisse,* Marx argues that the productive capacity of man takes over the role of creativity, of creation as such (from the way "Christian" metaphysics articulated it with respect to the divine): we recall that capital itself is the creative force for surplus value. However, capital is only the provisional or transitional point of absolute possibility as the highest creativity of man. At Zähringen, Heidegger asks: "For Marx, it is decided from the outset that man and only man (and nothing else) is what matters. From what is this decided? In what manner? With what right? By which authority?"[42]

To enter into a productive dialogue with Marx, means, therefore, to understand the relation to possibility of *Dasein,* and to show how Greek metaphysics as *energeia* comes to be understood as work. How is it that metaphysics, even for Aristotle, comes to enter into abandonment of being? Earlier I noted that there is in Hegel a fundamental *temporal* ambiguity: at one and the same time absolute subjectivity operates in the manner of a straining forth

39. Ibid., 376. "Die Bestimmung des Seins zur actualitas erstreckt sich daher, nach Zeitaltern gerechnet, durch die ganze abendländische Geschichte hindurch vom Römertum bis in die neueste Neuzeit."

40. Ibid., 377. "Wenn das Sein sich zur actualitas (Wirklichkeit) gewandelt hat, ist das Seiende das Wirkliche, ist es bestimmt durch das Wirken im Sinne des verursachenden Machens. Von hier aus läßt sich die Wirklichkeit des menschlichen Tuns und des göttlichen Schaffens erklären."

41. See 199.

42. Martin Heidegger, "Seminar in Zähringen" (*GA*15), 394. "Für Marx ist im vorhinein entschieden, daß der Mensch und einzig der Mensch (und nichts anderes) die Sache ist. Woher ist das entschieden? Auf welche Weise? Mit welchem Recht? Durch welche Autorität?"

for the highest horizon, and at the same time it operates in the manner of receipt. Marx attempts to capture this ambiguity when we saw him argue that in production, the present situation of the productive forces is at one and the same time both everything that has produced *us*, and our own relation to the forces of production such that we ourselves produce what is to come. Fundamental to this is sublation, *Aufhebung*, which is the very and continual activity of nihilation that is the actual operation of Hegelian and Marxist nihilism. Everything that was before is canceled for the sake of the higher situation that is constantly being brought about: the produced. This essential driving-forward of constant nihilation of all that went before is what Heidegger referred to at Zähringen as "the *imperative of progress*" such that "Marxism and sociology name the compelling of today's reality, 'imperatives.'"[43]

The "productive" is, thought in a Greek way, *technē*. We have held back examining this fundamental connection almost to the last. There is so much that needs to be said about Marx's relation to *technē* and technology (indeed, Axelos centered his whole discussion of Marx around this theme), but there has not been the opportunity to say it. In *technē* the orientation to time is quite different from any of the other modes of speaking that Aristotle names as *alētheuein*, "disclosive-uncovering." *Technē* is in its essence the "productive": Heidegger says "in *technē* the know-how is directed towards the *poiēton*, toward what is to be produced and hence is not yet."[44] Yet *technē*, as it dominates and holds sway over the whole history of metaphysics, ever-increasingly coming to the fore, contains a fundamental ambiguity, precisely the ambiguity that makes it the fundamental determinant for subjectivity and all subject-positions. For if we speak of *technē* as that which plans, and has in advance at each stage what is to be executed *next*, such that *technē* is the having of the blueprint in advance, and then the apportioning and taking-control over whatever is extant to realize the plan, nevertheless it is not at all clear *what*, and this means *who*, "plans" and has the plan in advance, or from out of which ground they conceive and prepare to execute the plan.

Marx's concern with technology arises precisely because through the technical control of the means of production the productive forces can be heightened and allowed to advance, such that communism itself can be ushered in—this communism which is above all a certain relatedness and production of the *individuum*, the subject as such (absolute subjectivity). Is it that man is planned by what lies ahead of him as already "there" (in Hegel) or lies prior to him as the "already having been produced" (as in Marx) such that

43. Ibid., 388. "Der *Progressionszwang*. . . . Marxismus und Soziologie nennen das, wozu die Wirklichkeit von heute nötigt, 'Zwänge.'"

44. Martin Heidegger, *Platon: Sophistes* (GA19), 40. "Bei der τέχνη ist das Sich-Auskennen auf das gerichtet, auf das ποιητόν, was erst herzustellen ist, also noch nicht ist."

at each stage man must take over and take control of *technē* in order to harness the forces of production? Or is it that these forces already master man, such that they lie beyond him and seemingly plan him with an iron necessity? In the Middle Ages this problem was solved by making God the origin and cause of all that is to be thought and planned, but with the death of God and the end of religion as the way being is to be thought this is no longer possible.

Here we can merely say that *technē* becomes the fundamental means of access to all knowledge, to the "real" in itself. "The productive," *technē* as such, becomes in Marx the means by which both past, present, and future are understood. The productive dialogue is the dialogue with, and out of, *technē*. As the completion of metaphysics, Marx represents the relentless, ceaseless drive to establish the basis (*Basis,* the word of the *Grundrisse*) from which the subjectivity of the subject appears equalized and leveled-off in what we would now call the political sphere. The essential metaphysical position of Marx is this equalization, that establishes by a reduction of transcendental force the absolute indeterminacy of the subjectivity of the subject. In Marx there is a rage to cancel and sublate every difference between subjects, to establish the common ground, the *mass* taken as the highest point of history and humanity hitherto, out of which alone difference can emerge. Difference here is utterly dynamic, provisional, and private: always confronted with the demand and imperious rule of the mass. From now on the subject, equalized, and flattened in every respect, is driven out, driven off to differentiate itself after the fact, after the equalization which it takes as its very origin and constitution. This appears, however, as something to be worked out and assumed by the assumption of subject-positions: what some commentators have called (very accurately) "subjection," without, however, being able to account fully for "what" subjects.[45] Subjection has the paradoxical effect that for the subject to appear at all, it must in each case appear in an already established subject-position, and so never "for itself," "as myself." Every subject-position is the attainment of a newly accomplished differentiation, never an authentic uncovering of myself from out of my own ground (every subject position is at the same time a valuation).

Marx, in his positing of the *individuum* and species-being, lays the basis for the metaphysics of subjectivity described by Nietzsche. Here is the explanation for why the word "justice" hardly ever appears in Marx, and yet becomes the driving idea for Nietzsche. For Marx, the accomplishment of the mass is inevitable, it is the proper goal of history. For Nietzsche every difference has to be justified, and it alone can only be secured, not in the exercise of violence and the claim of force (the foolish, cheapened, "fascist"

45. The central figures in the construction of this discourse are J. L. Austin, Ludwig Wittgenstein, and Judith Butler.

understanding of the will to power), but alone, secured in the claim of justice. Difference must be wrested from the same, which means you must be unable to deny me the justice of the difference that I am. You are the pretext of my self-justification. In this the essential understanding of Marx, of the individual as commanding relations, of existing only *in relation to* other individuals is preserved. What Nietzsche describes, however, is the metaphysics of *overcoming* the basis that is laid out by Marx, the accomplishment of the herd. Marx and Nietzsche: these two as first the achievement of the *koinon* of metaphysics, and then the unity of the self.

In attaining to this understanding we are no longer able to leave the "other language" of the overcoming of metaphysics hidden, or in the background, but must necessarily bring it to the fore, as Heidegger's overcoming of *technē*. For it becomes clear that what Heidegger attempts to think *of* is what first let metaphysics into being, and what therefore is completed in Marx's thinking out of it and thinking it out. I have argued that both Marx and Aristotle (and indeed Plato, with his thought of *eidos* and *idea*) think from out of what lets itself be seen. The seen is the (immediately) true. This is no less true for Aristotle's thought of being as *energeia* as it is in the eleventh of Marx's "Theses on Feuerbach." We see, immediately, that the world must be changed. And in each case we see, by first having seen. "Some*one* sees." This some*one* seeing, whether that *one* is man (as it usually is) or the presumption of an all-seeing divinity, is the essence of humanism: that in each case there is *one* seeing, by recognizing, and so already having seen.

If the essence of humanism is seeing, which abandons speaking because the seen is the self-evidently "true," at each stage the *Seinsvergessenheit* and *Seinsverlassenheit* has pointed to the unseen, the unsaid, that which on repeated occasions Heidegger calls the *un*essence. The *Unwesen* is what needs to be brought to language. In being brought to language, man speaks, but not from *his* essence, but *from out of essencing*, of *being as such*. This is the event, *das Ereignis*.

This explains the second half of that first enigmatic phrase of the *Letter on Humanism*, which immediately moves from talking of praxis to saying that "in thinking being comes to language." Heidegger says elsewhere, and with far more power, "the word is the treasure, which in itself rescues the beginning. Only from time to time does be-ing itself open itself. Then a pursuit of this commencing richness through human history begins; then in the word is be-ing eventual in the property of its truth."[46]

46. Martin Heidegger, *Das Ereignis* (*GA*71), 170. "Das Wort ist der Schatz, den der Anfang in sich birgt. Nur zuweilen lichtet sich das Seyn selbst. Dann geht ein Suchen nach diesem anfänglichen Reichtum durch die Menschengeschichte; denn im Wort ist das Seyn ereignishaft im Eigentum seiner Wahrheit."

We should say, rather, language, speaking, overcomes the preoccupation of metaphysics with the visible. But in the fragility of what is to be said, the original word is only ever occasionally uttered. When it is, being lets itself out into human history and is known, properly, and lights up world as available truly to be disclosed.

*Chapter 13*

# Between Men and Gods

THIS BOOK BEGAN by attempting to unfold Heidegger's talk of "that dimension within which a productive dialogue with Marxism becomes possible."[1] Our attempt to understand what is said here has aimed to keep constantly before us that both Heidegger and Marx are concerned with the historical, as a name for "that dimension" in which the being of man unfolds. For both Marx and Heidegger, it is not that "man is the historical being," and so has a "place," or takes place, in history; but rather, that the whole of history is always at issue in the unfolding of the life of man. If Heidegger's engagement with Marx takes as its public springboard the *Letter on Humanism* of 1946, I have argued that we must understand with far greater depth Heidegger's claim that "the *Letter* still speaks in the language of metaphysics, and indeed knowingly. The other language lies in the background."[2] I have wanted to show that this language remaining in the background, the language of "the new beginning," is a thinking which Heidegger only developed in its fullest form in a series of private notebooks which go under the general title of *Das Ereignis* (*The Event*), contained in seven volumes of his collected works (of which at the time of writing only six have appeared), across the period 1936–48, and which were written in the wake of his disastrous adventure with Nazism in 1933–34. The results of this preparation of a new beginning are only now becoming fully accessible, and during his lifetime were sporadically and minimally communicated in public places—really for the first time in the Bremen lectures of 1949, and then in isolated lectures, essays, and discussions up until Heidegger's death in 1976. Without understanding this "new beginning," without the necessary preparation that brings to the fore this language that otherwise hides, Heidegger's understanding of Marx itself remains hidden.

The language that lies in the background is not, however, merely "Heidegger's language," but rather, that language which becomes possible from

1. See 21.
2. See 39.

out of the unfolding of the history of being itself. If Marx's thinking is itself to be understood as that which comes to pass from out of the basic experience of the death of God, and the appropriation of that experience in the event (*das Ereignis*), which is the eventuality from out of which the language that hides in the background also comes to speak from out of, then the question arises—how is the death of God to be understood? In the period before *Being and Time* Heidegger had spoken of how philosophical research is and remains an atheism. We have seen how this atheism manifests itself in Marx both as the most resolute and determinate hatred of God and the gods, and as the most resolute and relentless "materialism" and denial of the supersensible. We also saw how in the course of Heidegger's own confrontation with Nazism and with Hegel, that Heidegger himself *passes through* the concreteness, the materiality, and resolutely binding character of historical events, an eventuality that marked him and scored itself into his speaking of being and everything of which he spoke thereafter (and from which thinking with him has not, and never can, separate itself), to begin to speak of a separation of "philosophical research" and thinking (the thinking of be-ing). If Hegel is marked by a most profound negativity, the "negation of the negation," there is a yet more profound negation in Heidegger—the negation of the death (as the negation and annihilation) of the divine, which returns Heidegger to being able to speak of the Last God and the advance of a coming god, but which opens him to await that coming. It is not the divine on whom Heidegger waits, but rather the coming itself, which is only a preparation for the coming divinity. We speak of divinity rather than any particular god or gods because what comes, comes for itself and not in a guise we might already determine in advance of its arrival.

In this Heidegger opens up a very different possibility in understanding Marx's hatred of the gods, and Nietzsche's announcement of the death of God. In the first of the Nietzsche lectures, from 1936–37, a section was left out of the version published in 1961, which was only recorded in the text of the expanded version from the edition published in 1985, an edition taken from the original transcripts and lecture plan. Here Heidegger says "the familiar interpretation of the word 'God is dead' says: Nietzsche speaks here unambiguously: the singular possible standpoint today is and will remain atheism. But indeed the contrary and nothing more is Nietzsche's true intention. The basic position from which he stood with respect to being [*zum Seienden*] was the knowledge that a historical existence without God as such and without the gods is not possible."[3]

3. Martin Heidegger, *Nietzsche: Die Wille zur Macht als Kunst* (*GA*43), 191. "Die gewöhnliche Auslegung des Wortes 'Gott ist todt' lautet: Nietzsche sagt hier ganz unzweideutig: Der einzig mögliche Standpunkt ist heute nur noch der Atheismus. Aber genau das Gegenteil und noch einiges mehr ist die wahre Meinung Nietzsches."

If historical existence is not possible without the gods, then we see how for Heidegger, and even in Marx, machination, technology, and the self-productive self-reproducing of humanity (humanity as absolute subjectivity) itself stands in the place of the divine—and so how for Heidegger Marx never reaches beyond Hegel's understanding of absolute subjectivity. However, the fulfillment of absolute subjectivity and its completion is—as a historical eventuality—itself the opening to a future historical existence. It is this futurity of which the language that hides in the background comes to speak, and of which it needs to speak. This speaking is no human speech—it is the language given by the coming god. Heidegger speaks of how this divinity arrives and must arrive: it arrives as a possibility and it fulfills the possibilities of historical existence only because everything that functions as the divine and in the place of the divine falls away and dies. Heidegger concludes that "the sentence 'God is dead' is no negation, but the innermost assent to the one arriving. In this knowledge and questioning Nietzsche wore out his existence [*Dasein*]."[4] There is a kind of "sublation" at work here, but quite other than that described by Hegel (as we shall discuss shortly). This sublation is not humanity's self-positing of itself as a whole and an absolute, and its self-overcoming as it assumes the place of that absolute ("species-being"), but rather our openness to that which befalls us, to that which is to come—which Heidegger persists in naming as "the Last God." This befalling is what befalls, not humanity as a whole, but a historical and historically realized people, while constituting it as the people that it is and making its destiny present for it. Hegel had said no less in naming the place of Athene as the *Volksgeist,* the spiritual presence of the people or nation.[5]

The language that hides in the background is, however, Heidegger's own and careful reference to the historical character of what we have come to understand of his speaking of the "forgottenness of being"—a forgetfulness both toward the question and the thinking of being, and a forgetfulness *of being* itself. If it is essential to any understanding of Marx to know how he understands history, and the development and unfolding of human presence in history, then the same can be said of Heidegger. That which hides is being itself, as Heidegger loved to illustrate in returning, not once, but often, to that sentence of Heraclitus's which says: *phusis kruptesthai philei,*[6] and which Heidegger translates in various ways, but most commonly "being loves (a) self-concealing."[7] If the fragment does not mention *being* (*on, einai*)

4. Ibid., 191. "Der Satz 'Gott ist todt' ist keine Verneinung, sondern das innerste Ja zum Kommenden. In diesem Wissen und Fragen hat Nietzsche sein Dasein aufgerieben."

5. See 86 and following.

6. Heraclitus, "Fragment 123," in Hermann Diels, *Fragmente der Vorsokratiker,* 1:101.

7. Martin Heidegger, *Der Satz vom Grund* (*GA*10), 95. "Sein liebt (ein) Sichverbergen." In his *Heraclitus* lectures of 1943–44, where there is an extended commentary on this fragment, Heidegger begins by offering the translation "the opening to self-concealing bestows favor."

but only that word that we ordinarily translate as nature (*phusis*), we see at once how Marx's entire and constant discussion of "nature" belongs with Heidegger's discussion of being. We have seen Marx say "man reproduces the whole of nature,"[8] such that Marx orders the whole of nature to human production and reproduction, and at the same time orders the production and reproduction of humans to history. In one of the notebooks of *Das Ereignis* we at the same time find, under the heading "The History of Be-ing," the following:

> The first beginning is *phusis* itself. "Being" is not divided against truth. Both "are" the same, which is why at the same the essential saying of Parmenides came to say: "for the same is for thinking as for being."
>
> "Being" is not set-apart from "becoming," that which was seen and differently said through Parmenides and Heraclitus out of the essence of *phusis*. For both is *phusis logos*.[9]

The thinking that Heidegger seeks to unfold aims to show up the essential connections between the ways in which the *same* has been named: as *phusis, logos*, gods, nature, man, being, becoming, language. If being and nature can be seen to belong together in this "same," out of which Heidegger and Marx even more essentially come to speak, then we can see how nature and language, being and speaking, belong together; and more essentially, how our understanding of the "wherein" of nature's and language's speaking of the *same* can open the way to see the belonging together in the *same* of what has otherwise been called *being* and *becoming*. As an understanding of the whole history of this *same*, Heidegger speaks of what I have translated as be-ing, *das Seyn*.

Had I even wished to, it would have been an impossible task to present all that is in the volumes of *Das Ereignis* through this book. It could be accounted a deficiency that there is no formal exposition in this book of

---

Martin Heidegger, *Heraklit* (*GA*55), 110 and following (see especially 110–23). "'Das Aufgehen dem Sichverbergen schenkt's die Gunst.'" See also Martin Heidegger, *Einführung in die Metaphysik* (*GA*40), 122.

8. See 139 and 157.

9. Martin Heidegger, *Die Geschichte des Seyns* (*GA*69), 132.

"Der erste Anfang ist die φύσις selbst.

"Das 'Sein' ist nicht unterschieden gegen die Wahrheit. Beide 'sind' das Selbe, weshalb auch alsbald der wesentliche Spruch von Parmenides gesagt wird: τὸ γὰρ αὐτὸ ἐστιν τε καὶ εἶναι.

"Das Sein ist nicht unter-schieden zum 'Werden,' das durch Parmenides und Heraklit aus dem Wesen der φύσις ersehen und verschieden gesagt wird. Für beide ist die φύσις λόγος."

what Heidegger meant by *das Ereignis,* "the event," of which he began to speak as early as 1919, in his first extant lecture course.[10] Marx has no immediately comparable thought of "the event" (unlike Nietzsche's "moment" or *Augenblick*) and so a discussion of this kind would have necessitated a long detour which at times might appear quite obscure. It is the matter for another book to unfold this thought. I have attempted only to prepare the sympathetic reader for what he or she might discover in opening these volumes of *Das Ereignis* and beginning to engage with them. Nevertheless, as I hope has become clear, whatever else they are, the volumes of Heidegger's notebooks *also* represent an engagement with Marx and the consequences of Marx's thought, especially when we understand Marx, as Heidegger did, to be one of the thinkers of the end and completion—indeed the overcoming—of metaphysics.

In reaching near the end of this book, have we now arrived at the place where the dialogue—or conversation—with Marx and Marxism can and should begin? In attempting to read the *Letter on Humanism* not through the language of metaphysics, but by allowing the language that otherwise hides in the background to speak the *same* of what the *Letter* speaks of, at least with respect to Marx, have we not discovered that the dialogue, perhaps now better understood as a conversation (*Gespräch*—the German word Heidegger actually employed) is not a "dialogue with," a chat between two neighbors on the bookshelf, but rather for Heidegger *the* very possibility of understanding the essence of man at all, an essence Marx also tried with the utmost verve to comprehend? The essence of man, however, turns out to be the essence of essence—taking "essence" to be part of the verb "to be," and so not treating "essence" as if it translated Aristotle's *ousia* or its later transition as *essentia,* the attempt to provide a dogmatic definition of the innermost "beingfulness" of *a* being, *this* being, the "human being." Man *is,* essences, *west,* for Heidegger, in ways that we are now in a position to hear and take seriously. To speak of the essence of man is to unfold the belonging to language. It is for this very reason that we spent so long examining on the one hand Heidegger's understanding of man as the being that has, and is held by, language (*zōon logon echon*), and on the other, Marx's extreme disdain for language—a disdain that enabled him to show up the power of ideology (and prepare many who followed in his name to become the most powerful ideologues). The dialogue that Heidegger believes Marx to open up, and in which his (Heidegger's) thinking also participates is not *between* Marx and Heidegger, but for the sake of the destiny of the Occident. In this, Marx and Heidegger speak of the same, and from the same, although in different ways. The dia-

10. See, for a discussion of this, Laurence Hemming, *Heidegger's Atheism: The Refusal of a Theological Voice,* 103–77.

logue opens up the possibility of naming the same of which they speak. As a dialogue, it is also a listening—listening for whom the Occidental has been and by whom and how it is about to be and is being addressed. This is how we must understand the turning out toward the approaching god.

Marx claims that "the thoughts [*Gedanken*] of the ruling class are in each epoch the ruling thoughts, which is to say, the class which is the ruling *material* power of society, is at the same time its ruling *spiritual* [*geistige*] power."[11] Normally this sentence is translated "the ideas of the ruling class . . . ," but this translation places Marx too close to an interpretation of Kant, who speaks constantly of ideas or concepts (*Begriffe*), or even Hegel, who speaks directly of ideas. Marx emphasizes here that what rules is the way the world is *thought*, but that at the same time all thinking is a "speaking to oneself" that in antiquity was described as the activity of the soul, and that shows the extent to which Marx speaks the *same* as is spoken in Parmenides's dictum, which we saw Heidegger cite in indicating the belonging together of being and speaking.

The essential connection of ideology and its structure is with *material* language, not with any kind of idealism. This passage of the *German Ideology*, whose meaning Marx amplifies in the sentences following it, encapsulates the contemporary understanding of power, as a controlling reserve in particular hands, establishing the regulatory "frame" of everything under its sway. As this, it is essentially something to be distrusted and exposed, in order to be overcome. The extreme nihilation given in Marx's understanding of language (of all speech) illustrates the extreme nihilism of the historical "condition" from out of which Marx writes, a nihilism taken for granted by Marx and which Nietzsche reaches forth to name. Marx knows well that the *word* will not uncover the phenomenon as the thing that it is, but becomes the means by which *every* ruling valuation is enforced, so that the word has rather been put into service *for the sake of:*—the bourgeois; the owners of the means of production; those who resist the inevitability of the forces of history (to which we can always add, "big business"; "the law of the father"; "white masculinity"; "heterosexuality"; and so forth); finally, "the (liberal) state"; *such that* the word itself must be taken over by the proletariat and put to use for history's triumph in communism. In this Marx both denies the word and accords it the strength of its highest power as a capability for action. Language, far from speaking man's essence, becomes both the instrument of his most

11. Karl Marx, *Die deutsche Ideologie* (*MEW*3), 46. "Die Gedanken der herrschenden Klasse sind in jeder Epoche die herrschenden Gedanken, d.h. die Klasse, welche die herrschende *materielle* Macht der Gesellschaft ist, ist zugleich ihre herrschende *geistige* Macht" (Marx's emphases). Near-identical statements can be found in *The Communist Manifesto* and throughout many other works.

extreme alienation and greatest hope *and possible enactment* of liberation. In showing up, and himself denoting, the extent to which the word has failed to speak, Marx is not wrong: and yet Marx is never able to exceed or evade that we are *bound* to speak.

Should we perhaps not have said more of *technē,* more than was said in the last chapter on the relation to the "plan"?[12] Certainly Kostas Axelos, in reading Marx, brings the understanding of *technē* to the fore in Marx's texts and argues that "industry constitutes the most completed form of labour";[13] in his book on Marx and Heidegger, Axelos devotes a significant section to "the planetary," subtitling this: "world-history of technology."[14] There is increasing interest in Heidegger's "critique of technology," which at the same time often betrays a failure to understand what is fundamentally at issue for Heidegger in it. The "critique" of technology is not at any stage an investigation of the "what" of technology—Heidegger pointed out that "modern technology is only what it is and how it is, from out of the essence of technology. One therefore says nothing of the essence of technology, if one conceives it as machine technology."[15] Heidegger himself spoke (translating literally) of "the question that goes out after technology."[16] The understanding of "the productive" which we have unfolded in these chapters is nothing other than the pursuit of the question of technology, since "the productive" as the placing into the hands of man and for the sake of his own manipulation "nature" or "the whole planet," and so the whole of being, is how the essence of technology manifests itself. However, Heidegger repeatedly says that the essence of technology, strictly speaking, is unknown—or rather more pertinently, "the essence of technology is in an elevated sense ambiguous."[17]

This ambiguity resides in the way in which *technē* has become appropriated to metaphysics. Aristotle is the first to give *technē* a formal, technical (philosophical) meaning, in distinguishing it from the other modes of "speaking the true" (*alētheuein*) in the sixth book of the *Nicomachean Ethics.* Aris-

12. See 253.

13. Kostas Axelos, *Marx: Penseur de la technique,* 80. "L'industrie constitue la forme plus achevée du travail."

14. Kostas Axelos, *Einführung in ein künftiges Denken,* 61–86, especially 61. "Das Planetarische: Weltgeschichte der Technik." I have translated throughout *die Technik* with the term "technology." The word "technique" is really a better translation than "technology," because although all technology is covered by the older English sense of "technique," there are certain aspects of "technique" which are indicated by *die Technik,* but not suggested by the term "technology." "Technology" is, however, a more accessible term to our modern ear.

15. Martin Heidegger, "Das Ge-Stell" (*GA*79), 33. "Die moderne Technik ist nur, was sie ist und wie sie ist, aus dem Wesen der Technik. Man sagt daher nichts vom Wesen der modernen Technik, wenn man sie als Maschinentechnik vorstellt."

16. Martin Heidegger, *Die Frage nach der Technik* (*GA*7).

17. Ibid., 34. "Das Wesen der Technik ist in hohem Sinne zweideutig."

totle distinguishes *technē* from *sophia, phronēsis,* and *episteme,* as the four modes of *noein.* Each of these has a corresponding person in whom they are located: thus *sophia* is that mode of *alētheuein* sought by the *sophistēs, technē* by the *technētēs,* and so forth. Heidegger examines the interrelationship of these forms of speaking-the-true in great depth, and with huge dexterity, in the Marburg lecture course given shortly prior to the publication of *Being and Time,* published as *Plato's Sophist.*[18] Heidegger demonstrates how Aristotle simultaneously interrelates and distinguishes all the modes of *alētheuein* from each other, and makes each dependent on the other, without grounding them formally in any external term. Heidegger does not put it in this way, but we might note that Aristotle's astonishing capacity for interrelating and distinguishing in the production of definitions and elucidations indicates a fundamental moment in the outset of metaphysical thinking: being disappears and is forgotten.

There is not the time, nor would it be necessary, to retrace either Aristotle, or Heidegger's remarkable and clear commentary on Aristotle's text. One thing only needs to be said: Heidegger shows that *technē* is distinguished from all the other modes of *alētheuein* in its temporal relation to being. Every other mode of *alētheuein* depends on being in some sense "drawn-off" or, in the phrase I have used throughout this book, "taken-off" from being in some way. Every mode of *alētheuein* is a mode of abstraction *from* world, to a greater or lesser degree. One mode does not abstract, however, but in fact orders and directs what is to be put *in* to being in some way: *technē.* Heidegger says:

> That dealing with a concern which is guided by *technē* is always a making-ready-for. The *theōrein* of the *technē* is no speculation, but it guides the dealing with a matter in the orientating towards a "for-what" and a "therefore." Thus the *manner of being of the technē is an esomenon,* such, that will only come to be.[19]

We note immediately how *technē* has the capacity to belong, not to being, but to a thinking of becoming, since it seems to concern what—*esomenon*—"will only come to be." This future part of the verb "to be" indicates the essential connection between *technē* and becoming, and shows how, as *technē* increasingly prevails over all the other modes of "speaking the true," why

18. Martin Heidegger, *Platon: Sophistes* (*GA*19), 21–64.

19. Martin Heidegger, *Platon: Sophistes* (*GA*19), 40. "Der von τέχνη geleitetete Umgang mit einer Sache ist immer ein Zu-richten für. Das θεωρεῖν der τέχνη ist keine Spekulation, sondern es leitet den Umgang mit einer Sache in der Orientierung auf ein Dafür und Dazu. So ist das *Seiende der* τέχνη *ein* ἐσόμενον, solches, das erst sein wird" (Heidegger's emphases).

speaking of becoming prevails over speech of being. However, the future in question is always one that is produced by the one having the future in view: it is therefore a future that does not befall the one whose future it is.

Heidegger's mention of *theōrein* is his drawing attention to Aristotle's technical term for the final truth, the formal "contemplation" of the things that are, but means really a "bringing to light" and bringing out into the open in which each of the modes of *alētheuein* are related to *a-lētheia,* truth as dis-closure. Because *technē* knows in advance what it *is to do,* its temporal relation to world (to being) is the reverse of all the others: it projects, and aims *at* the future (rather than having the future aim at the one who speaks the truth), from an unseen past which is not "in," and so not abstracted from, "world." Every other mode of *alētheuein* aims at what "is already here." *Technē* is vested by Aristotle in the *technētēs,* as the one who has perfected himself in this manner of *alētheuein.* As such, the one producing the plan for something, the *technētēs,* knows in advance what it is he is going to produce: he secures it in advance and brings it forth (he "manages" it): Heidegger speaks by example of the plan which the builder has in advance, and to which he works to bring forth in the building of the house.

What Heidegger does not argue, but which it is perfectly correct to infer, is that what is being demonstrated is a kind of elucidation of the structures within the polis, grounded in truth (what often now goes by the name of "hierarchy"), since not only are all the modes ordered to one another, but they are ranked (here is where in this discussion of Aristotle "being" makes its presence felt). Each of the modes of "being-true" is represented in a person. The implication is that, by extension, every relation to truth in the polis has a "person" in whom it is vested, one ranked in relation to others, and the one who, for each "personage" both is contemplating (*theōrein*) its truth and enacts it (through praxis the way he is concerned with, and oriented on, the *pragmata*). We should recall, in alluding to this, that Aristotle's *Nicomachean Ethics* and his *Politics* are really parts of a single body of thought:[20] they are better understood if considered as a single text. In this sense, Aristotle seems far in advance of Marx, in that for Aristotle thought and action have not yet come apart, such that an order of their relation—which one comes first and which later—has to be found. Moreover, we seem to have found in the way *technē* works the way that technology becomes the ruling and planning of the planet, exactly as Axelos describes in his work on Marx and Heidegger, and which forms the basis of so much of the description of Heidegger's "critique" of technology. *Technē* is therefore in a different temporal

20. Aristotle asserts that the material we know as the *Ethics* (within which the words ηθική, ἦθος are notably absent) in fact aims for the character of the political. See Aristotle, *Nicomachean Ethics,* 1095b12. ἡ μὲν οὖν μέθοδος τούτων ἐφίεται, πολιτική τις οὖσα.

relation to being to every other of Aristotle's modes of *alētheuein*. Whereas for the other modes, each is taken off from what is already "here," already to be encountered in the surrounding environment and in the world as such, *technē* is a putting of something into the surrounding environment, a certain ordering of the world.

However, to look here for the meaning or essence of technology would be to overlook the most subtle shift in the meaning of *technē* that Aristotle has undertaken. At the end of the 1953 essay *The Question Concerning Technology,* Heidegger remarks that "at one time not only technique bore the name *technē*. At one time *technē* also meant that disclosing which produces truth in the splendour of the apparent."[21] Heidegger makes explicit that there is a special character of this producing: "at the beginning of the fatedness of the Occident, the arts rose up in Greece to the lofty heights of their preserved disclosing. They brought the presence of the gods, brought the mutual speech of divine and human destiny to radiance."[22] He notes that the "arts" in this sense have nothing to do with culture and the "artistic."

What Heidegger lets us see here was less visible—perhaps also to him—in the lectures on Plato from almost thirty years before. For the question is *who* does the word *technītēs* name? By providing a technical meaning to *technē* worked out in relation to other modes of *alētheuein* and vested in types, Aristotle has already transposed the possibility of what it is *technē* speaks of, and *how,* from one place—not even the realm of the gods, but fate itself—into the resolutely and entirely human. From now on *technē* is the province of a solely *human technītēs.* In this sense the *technītēs* names what is every bit as much a "*typus*" as Ernst Jünger's "worker,"[23] and there is a more direct line between Aristotle and Jünger, or Aristotle, Nietzsche, and Marx, than between Aristotle and his "pre-Socratic" antecedents. In Greece, at the dawn of the Occident, not even the gods controlled or had power over fate and the fates. *Technē* as what was capable of placing the gods and men into dialogue, *also* unfolded from the fatedness—not even of man, or the gods—but the *kosmos* itself.

It is this placing of *technē* solely into human hands (and so taking it out of the hands of the fates and the disposing of the relation between gods and men) that gives birth to all thought of "becoming." When what *technē* names becomes the most decisive thinking of the whole of humanity, and "human-

21. Martin Heidegger, *Die Frage nach der Technik* (*GA*7), 35. "Einmals trug nicht nur die Technik den Namen τέχνη. Einstmals hieß τέχνη auch jenes Entbergen, das die Wahrheit in den Glanz des Scheinenden hervorbringt."

22. Ibid., 35. "Am Beginn des abendländischen Geschickes stiegen in Griechenland die Künste in die höchste Höhe des ihnen gewährten Entbergens. Sie brachten die Gegenwart der Götter, brachten die Zwiesprache des göttlichen und menschlichen Geschickes zum Leuchten."

23. See Ernst Jünger, *Der Arbeiter.*

ity's" whole grasp of being (nature, the planet, the whole of history)—the productive—only what is yet to come still has the power to bear truth to man. Everything that *is* falls short of what is yet to come: nor did Marx speak otherwise.

The "productive" takes on the particular form it does *not* because of the ambiguous essence of *technē,* but because it *also* has been restricted to the purely human: but this decisive restriction is to be found, not even in the hands of the violently gods-denying Marx, nor the "deicide" Nietzsche, but at the dawn of Occidental philosophy, in Aristotle, and indeed, prepared for in Plato. The ambiguity of the "essence" of technology is nothing other than the ambiguity of the subjectivity of the subject, which this book has attempted to trace in detail.

The word *technē* comes from the verb *tiktō*—"I beget, bring forth" into the world. In Marx's hands this "producing" (*pro-ducere,* "leading out before," German *her-vor-bringen*) becomes most formally understood as self-producing, the self-producing selfhood of man, both in general, and for every man and women taken one by one: indeed, the whole of Marx's thought (as we have seen) concerns how this "self-producing" can be considered through the formal equalization of the "in general" and the "in each case." It becomes clear and not difficult to see how in each case the "self-producing" is characterized by the labor, the *means* (or "scientifically" speaking, the "effort") and skill required for this self-producing to be driven to the highest degree. However, the equalization which Marx claims that "history" demands, which is, therefore, *demanded by the moment and overall* (the equalization is not only "spatial" but also "temporal" or historical) always remains ambiguous: it both is consumed with itself and is forced to contend with that which is beyond itself. Heidegger's understanding of the contemporary essence of technology (his use of the almost impossible-to-translate term *das Ge-Stell,* literally, "the gathered-positing," but with the sense of "the emplaced") is prepared for in the manuscripts of *Das Ereignis* through the discussion of "machination." In a note added for the 1961 edition of the 1941 essay "Recollection of Metaphysics," Heidegger refers to the (then) unpublished manuscript *Mindfulness,*[24] which says: "'machination,' the preparatory name for the *Ge-Stell.*"[25] The term makes its first public appearance in 1949, in the first of the Bremen lectures that marked Heidegger's return to public life after the war.[26]

In *das Ge-Stell* everything that is produced has at the same time to be managed and directed with the utmost and highest skill, both in the par-

24. Martin Heidegger, *Besinnung* (*GA*66).

25. Martin Heidegger, "Die Erinnerung in die Metaphysik" (*GA*6.2), 445, note a. "Manuskript 'Besinnung' 1938/39 ('Machenschaft' der vorläufige Name für des Ge-Stell)."

26. See Martin Heidegger, "Das Ge-Stell" (*GA*79), 24–45.

ticular and in general. Nothing can be left to chance (every risk must be calculated in advance, foreseen in its effects, minimized, and so accounted for). Everything becomes the site of the most extreme human management. This is the counter-position to Heidegger's pursuit of the question of being—the inquiry into the phenomenon, not as an object, but as *to phainesthai,* what in *phusis* appears for itself and brings itself forth into the light. We can see that as soon as *technē* becomes a predominantly or solely human affair, then every corresponding "*techtēsthai*" (there is no such Greek medial infinitive), which would mean "self-producing," becomes a matter, *not* of what can appear for itself (for only humans can bring it about), *but* a matter for the most extreme human anxiety and control. Inasmuch as every object must be subjected to this control, objectness as such must also be brought under this imperative of regulation and decision, of advance planning and rigorous management: nature "as such," the planet "as a whole," what now goes by the name "ecology," "the biopolitical," as names for "the whole."

Here is where to a certain extent we part company from Axelos and from much of the contemporary commentary, not only on Heidegger's understanding of technology, but also of Marx's. For the highest and most completed form of labor is not industry, nor the fact and character either of machines or of processes of management and control, but the total taking-over into control and the calculation of human thinking of self-producing itself: the human person as a perfected project and "type": the "perfect human being." It is impossible to understand Marx (or Engels) and the fundamental tendency of their thought without understanding how every formal difference between the types of human being (established as a possibility of the formal structure for reading "the political" in Aristotle), *including* sexual difference itself,[27] is to be resolved through the single, final "*typus*" which is not even the worker, nor the proletarian (and in this sense Jünger is behind Marx, demonstrating again how Marx's view of history can be understood as "superior"), but of species-being itself.

27. Engels understands bourgeois monogamy to be the final form of sexual *in*equality: "thus, monogamous marriage does not in history in any way mean the reconciliation of man and woman, even less as its highest form." It is quite clear from Engels's comments on the development of monogamy, and his extraordinary claim that in the proletarian family all the conditions for male domination have been removed, that a higher stage than bourgeois monogamy, based on sexual difference, has been reached: "in short, proletarian marriage is monogamous in the etymological sense of the word, but in no manner in the historical sense," which means the essential inequality of the sexes is in course to be overcome (in communism). See Friedrich Engels, *Der Ursprung der Familie, des Privateigentums und des Staats* (*MEW*21), 68: "So tritt die Einzelehe keineswegs ein in die Geschichte als die Versöhnung von Mann und Weib, noch viel weniger als ihre höchste Form"; and 74: "Kurz, die Proletarierehe ist monogam im etymologischen Sinn des Worts, aber durchaus nicht in seinem historischen Sinn."

Metaphysics is forced to oscillate between taking "man" in the most general, abstract sense (the "idea" of man, humanism, absolute subjectivity, species-being) and the most particular (*this* man or woman, the "leader"—be he Italian, Austrian, Chinese, Russian, or North Korean—"me"). To take the human being, and the future for humanity, in the most general and abstract sense is Marx's and Marxism's claim to internationalism, the counter-position to National Socialism and nationalism.[28] Hegel's positing of the relations between states, which approximates far more closely to the interrelationships that pertain today in global relations, indicates that the existence of the United Nations is possible only because it is already metaphysically foreseen.[29] It is in this context that Heidegger's own inquiry into the being of a people (*Volk*) must be understood. This is because Heidegger was acutely aware of Marx's own positing of the identity of the people: referring perhaps to a phrase in *The Communist Manifesto,* Heidegger says "by 'a people [*Volk*]' Karl Marx names the entirety of the workers, distinguished from the loafers and exploiters."[30] Heidegger does not provide an *answer* to the question "what is a people?," but rather seeks to show that the *question itself* has not been asked with sufficiently penetrating care (again, he has to be read here as rejecting the Nazi, "racial," "answers" to this question).

The very positing of a historically specific class *as* a people shows up the extent to which the character of what it is to *be* a people has been covered over *by historical events themselves.* It is no more possible to "make" a people or "decide" who is or isn't one of this people, or that "multiculturalism" supplies an answer: "we are all 'the people' now." A people is not self-constituting (nor, as in present gender politics, will "self-identification" suffice to decide). Every attempt to answer the question merely as a humanism has at least the potential (the danger that persists within it) to collapse into

28. Trotsky claimed that the theory of "socialism in one state" propounded by Stalin was in effect national socialism by another name. This was an extreme accusation, which does not adequately touch or describe the particularly hideous form of a self-consciously *racial* "socialism" as opposed to an ideological socialism with nationalistic overtones which better represents the peculiarity of the phenomena of the "national" forms of Marxist state that unfolded historically. In this sense Lenin's *The National Question* illustrates the speed and immediacy with which questions of nationhood arose in Marxist practice.

29. See 87.

30. Martin Heidegger, *Logik als Frage nach dem Wesen der Sprache* (GA38), 61. "'Volk' nennt Karl Marx die Gesamtheit der Werktätigen im Unterschied zu den Müßiggängern und Ausbeutern." This remark, made just after the period of the rectorate in 1934, immediately follows (among a multiplicity of other definitions of "a people") Heidegger's acknowledgment, without comment, of the Nazi goal in "the *völkisch* movement of bringing the people back to the pureness of their racial breed" ("Die völkische Bewegung will das Volk zur Reinheit seiner Stammesart zurückbringen"). For the reference in *The Communist Manifesto* to the proletariat as a 'nation," see 197.

the extremes of criminal horror or sentimental kitsch. Yet the question of the "nation" and "the people" cannot be evaded, nor need they in every case degenerate into the hideous racial pseudo-science of the Nazis, or the supreme self-election of the forms of "communist party." "Who are we?," "To whom do I belong?," recurs as a question because the question which the Greeks named with the naming of the polis is of the essence of the being of being human. It is here that a return would be required, not only to the word that both Marx and Heidegger use time and again—*Dasein*—"existence," but also to what the Greeks indicated with *sunousia,* and Heidegger translated as *Mitsein, Miteinandersein,* the antecedent "being-with-one-another" from which my individuality is always taken-off. It is impossible to understand the extant sections of *Being and Time* without gaining an understanding of the relation between *Dasein* and *Mitsein,* and how in that work Heidegger sought to open up the question of being beyond the subjectivity of the subject. Yet it is necessary to understand that this "opening up beyond" is not a "project" or a "move" that he makes, but *is itself only possible* on the basis of the thinking of Hegel, Marx, and Nietzsche—of the grounding experience of the "death of God" and the *political* unfolding of what Feuerbach's and Marx's thought of "species-being" ushered in.

Have we evaded Heidegger's discussion of the term *Weltanschauung,* "worldview," a most political term (a term frequently used by the Nazis)? In the case of "worldview" everything depends on *who* lays claim to the subjectivity of the subject. Nietzsche's "overman" represents the most abstracted form of the *Fürsprecher,* the "advocate," tangentially mentioned in the *Letter on Humanism* and which forms the basis of Nietzsche's presentation of Zarathustra and Heidegger's interpretation of that presentation.[31] What Heidegger draws attention to in this interpretation is the assumption of a voice: but in each case, it is a *typus* who takes up a voice, who *advocates* and so "speaks for" what is to become, by making the being of others correspond to that understanding of the will to power to which the *typus* has attained. In Marx (and especially in Marxism), however, the voice of the subjectivity of the subject is always located, not in species-being as such, since this ideal type has no voice, but in the party, and in that one who can speak for the party as a whole, who knows the "road" to communism and the attainment to species-being (in this sense Marxist politics is always actually realized through what Nietzsche foresaw, with the eventual promise that this "leadership" will cease to be necessary in the attainment of full communism). It is here that we must understand Marx's disdain for those voices that *cannot* attain to such a voice—from

31. See Martin Heidegger: *Brief über den Humanismus* (GA9), 346; "Wer ist Nietzsches Zarathustra" (GA7), 101; *Nietzsches metaphysische Grundstellung im abendländischen Denken* (GA44), 53 (= *Nietzsche I* [GA6.1], 270).

Bruno Bauer to the epigones against whom he wrote in the "Critique of the Gotha Program." Only the "subject" who attains to such a voice can take up a "standpoint"—over against the world—from which the evaluative height can be attained which asserts what has not yet become and so what is to be. This elevation of the subject, and the assembly beneath him or her of those who will take up the valuation given, establishes the "worldview" which will then be the object of the following striving. The very isolation of such a subject *over against* subjectivity in general exposes to the public gaze the ambiguity of the subjectivity which we have traced. It is for this reason that, Heidegger repeats in the manuscripts of *Das Ereignis,* "this 'worldview' is to be understood 'as the necessary un-essence of metaphysics'" and its possible overcoming.[32] It is here, once again, that what Marx has to say has the power to lead us up to the threshold of the overcoming of metaphysics.[33]

If *one* form of the resolution of the ambiguity of the subjectivity of the subject is the equalization of every difference (which is rapidly becoming the basis for every decision in liberal democracy at the present time, from the principles of international law and the laws relating to inequality to the practices of "human resources departments" and the education and employment policies of government), the other is the total taking into control of the human person. In the third Le Thor seminar, where Heidegger returns to Marx, America, and the Greeks, he addressed the question of "the transformation of biology into *biophysics.*"[34] Heidegger says of biophysics that "it means that the human being can be produced in pursuit of a definite plan like any technological object." Heidegger concludes that "the ground of this occurrence is far rather a modern relation to *power,* a political relation. In this regard must the emergence of a new form of nationalism be thought through, which is grounded upon technical power and no longer (just to name one example) on the particularities of peoples."[35] The production of the person as perfect self-reproduction, where original and copy are collapsed into one, would eradicate the need for every antecedent distinction, including sex or

32. Martin Heidegger, *Metaphysik und Nihilismus* (*GA*67), 113. "Die 'Weltanschauung' als das Notwendige Unwesen der Metaphysik."

33. It is easy to see and compare the "cult of personality" in which the essentially Romantic notion of "genius" is reproduced both in the various forms of Nazi, fascist, and communist politics. What is less easy to see is the extent to which all the forces of management and business are brought to bear, through the vast apparatus of patronage and political lobbying, to construct the necessary *types* for the production of worldviews in liberal democracy.

34. Martin Heidegger, *Seminare* (*GA*15), 358. "Die Verwandlung der Biologie in *Biophysik*" (Heidegger's emphasis).

35. Ibid., 358. "Grund des Geschehens ist vielmehr ein modernes Verhältnis zur *Macht,* ein politisches Verhältnis. Im Hinblick darauf müßte hier das Auftreten einer neuen Form von Nationalismus durchdacht werden, der auf technische Macht und nicht mehr (um ein Beispiel zu nennen) auf Eigentümlichkeiten der Völker gegründet ist" (Heidegger's emphasis).

gender (since this too could be altered with the appropriate manipulation of the technical means).

We acknowledge, therefore, that the "productive dialogue" turns out to be the preparation, over Nietzsche's whole two centuries, of a renewed inquiry into the hidden ground of that which the Greeks named by the word *polis.* Nor does this mean a "project" of our own, a "nostalgia," nor any of the other customary accusations that flood out to push aside the sheer scale and depth of the question. The question that went out after technology either remains in that province, and gets nowhere (and, as we have seen, does not touch the essence that it seeks, because that essence is ambiguous) or else, as Heidegger himself said at the end of the essay on technology and in many other places, ends up not confronting, nor allowing itself to be addressed by, the "danger" that he found named in Hölderlin's *Patmos,*[36] and to which he referred time and again. The question that goes out after technology comes to be the question *of* be-ing itself. Much of this book has concentrated on the extent to which Hegel's difficult word *Aufhebung,* which, for want of anything better, I have translated throughout with the term "sublation," is in Hegel himself, and as taken up by Marx and in Nietzsche, an indication of the most extreme nihilism of metaphysics as a whole. Human history, to proceed, must negate what went before and overcome it. In this, finite being is constantly overcome by the infinite possibility of becoming. It could be thought, therefore, that Heidegger rejects, and that I have been enjoining you the reader to reject, what "sublation" names.

The interviewers of the *Spiegel* exactly understood this question of the relation to technology to its overcoming and sublation when they asked Heidegger in 1966 "in exactly the place where the technological world originated, you mean . . ." to which Heidegger replied (we presume by interrupting) " . . . in the Hegelian sense, be sublated, not eliminated, but sublated, but not through man alone."[37] Heidegger explicitly sets aside the negating aspect of sublation, so that in overcoming the technological and its place of origination (the subjectivity of the subject) the full historical meaning of this place would also have to be taken up and into understanding. This is the "Hegelian sense" in its widest—as what in Hegel lets Hegel's own metaphysics be overcome for the sake of the understanding of the question of be-ing itself—the sense in which Heidegger himself negates the death of God, and

36. See 131.

37. Martin Heidegger, "*Spiegel*-Gespräch mit Martin Heidegger" (*GA*16), 679. "*Spiegel:* An eben dieser Stelle, wo die technische Welt entstanden ist, muß sie auch, meinen Sie . . . *Heidegger:* . . . im Hegelschen Sinne aufgehoben werden, nicht beseitigt, sondern aufgehoben, aber nicht durch den Menschen allein."

claims Nietzsche negated this death, by turning out toward that one who is yet to come, and promises to arrive.

Before we conclude the explication of this response, an important caveat must be sounded. For throughout this book there has been talk of gods and the Last God, and it is well known that this author, not unlike Heidegger himself, has a theological background. So strong is the grip of productive humanism in modern thought that all talk of gods is almost routinely simply set aside (and eliminated) as if nothing had ever been said (what is there left to say of gods, that could ever again be of any importance?), or interpreted as the smuggling in of a covert theology, or covert Christianity, or, worse yet, a covert sense of the "all," as that gesture toward totalization which we postmodern people have all learned to repudiate and hold our noses against with utmost disdain (we who live with Foucault "as if there were no universals"). Yet Heidegger's reference here is clearly to something other than the human, and to what the Greeks named with their gods, and what he names as the passing-by of the Last God. Nor is this a "theology" in either the overt or hidden sense. We seek to understand, rather, what speaking of the gods means, and what Heidegger understood by this.[38] Each *polis* was founded in, or by, or adopted by, a god, or founded from a city or region that was itself founded by a god. Entering into the encounter between Marx and Heidegger means opening up again, and from the very beginning, the origin and question of the political, although with no clear projection in advance of what the fate of this question is to be. This is what Marx and Heidegger speak *of:* they speak from this *same* place. This word "polis," which names, variously, nation, land, city-state, people, *Volk,* is always turned out beyond itself to something other than the human, something other, in which it sits, and which lets it *be.* We saw earlier in this chapter how *technē* poses the "who" of the preparedness it names, and in this preparedness *technē* lets into being a dialogue: not the *Gespräch,* the "common speaking" or conversation that a cheapened juxtaposition of Heidegger and Marx might have entertained us with for a while, but what Heidegger calls a *Zwiesprache,* an intimate exchange of two, belonging and betrothed, one to the other: what passes between gods and men. Fate is this *who,* that prepares and sets up the intimate exchange—the third voice that, having set the two together, with-

38. Heidegger is always enigmatic in this. About the closest he ever comes to naming what he means is in his schema for understanding "the history of be-ing," corresponding closely, but not exactly, to the structure of the *Beiträge* (*GA*65) in §114 of the text *Geschichte des Seyns* (*GA*69). Here we find in the last place, at the conclusion of the scheme for the discussion of the Last God, the sentence "earlier than *every* god is be-ing." (Martin Heidegger, *Geschichte des Seyns* [*GA*69], 132. "Anfänglicher denn *jeder* Gott ist das Seyn") (Heidegger's emphasis).

draws, as every matchmaker should, in the consummation of betrothal (this *is* the *event* of *das Ereignis*). Marx understood, and perhaps *is,* that fate that befalls humanity as humanity's wresting-forth and restlessness for something greater than itself, eliminating all idols and false gods along the way. The place of the origination of technology is overcome in *technē* itself, and fate alone, through no effort of mankind, will overcome it. In dialogue with the destiny of the Occident and what is yet to come, we deliberate when to act and speak, and when to await and hear what is, that is yet to arrive. If Marx takes us up to the threshold of this conversation, does Heidegger yet attune us to just what might be heard there?

Chapter 14

# Conclusion

IN OPENING UP A productive dialogue concerning Marx and Heidegger, a central question in this book has been that of the fate of Europe and that very *being* of Europe which has become a global affair. The taking into hand of the entire globe became a concern of the nineteenth century through the expansion of capital and production, and then through the political mastery of technology and its effects. Marx's understanding of that "taking in hand" as the positing of a humanity that steps into the productive place of God persists as the most powerful account of production and its effects. Marx's understanding of the subjectivity of the subject, and the persistent drive for equalization among subjects, is the persistent thinking of our age, whether we think ourselves to be Marxists or not. In this Marx's thinking, and his description of action, possesses an essential force.

As the management of the taking in hand of the whole planet, and the fate of the human person with it, has become an ever-more urgent drive, the postwar situation has given way to successive "crises"—financial, political, ecological, humanitarian. Counterposed to Europe has been Heidegger's discussion of the fate, and fatedness, of the Occident—of that thinking which he argues arises in the Greece of antiquity, and which was renewed in the voice assumed by Hölderlin, and which concerned the destiny of Germany. Although Heidegger has been attacked repeatedly for his nationalism, not only Heidegger, but also Marx (and even Lenin) also reserved a special place for Germany in relation to the fate of her neighbors (if without reference to Hölderlin). At the time of writing this book, a reluctant and resistant Germany has again been called to the fore to secure, if not the fate of the West, then the fate of the fragile unity of a faltering Europe. We can only ask: is the place occupied by Germany in this question only by accident? To this question, conventional "political science," "economics," and even contemporary philosophy has barely any answer. Both Marx and Heidegger have supplied one: they do not speak the same, but they speak *from out of* the same. This book has attempted to open up why that might be and how.

We have attempted to open up what Heidegger had named in relation to Marx as the dimension "within which a productive conversation with Marxism becomes possible." If on the one hand Marx has been understood as the founder of "communism," a politics now largely discredited by the history of its actual practice, and by the collapse of its Soviet forms, on the other hand Heidegger's politics have been almost always construed as a purely personal and individual affair, and discredits any understanding of him as a "political" thinker. With only one or two exceptions—Kostas Axelos would be one, Fred Dallmayr another (both only in brief or relatively short discussions)—what attempts there have been to place Heidegger and Marx into dialogue have already appeared within the domain of a very specific political thinking—most ordinarily the presuppositions of liberal democracy. This thinking already takes for granted that it "knows" or understands the ways in which Marx, or Heidegger, are to be understood, and it does so on the basis of a very specific understanding of the human being or human "essence." This thinking, as we have seen, has concentrated on interpreting Heidegger's word *Dasein* as a name for the individuality of the subjectivity of the (human) subject, rather than understanding the range of meanings the term *Dasein* has—used in the same way as Hegel, Kant, and Marx use it—of "existence." As we have seen, Heidegger adds to this the more specific interpretation of "here-being" (rather than "being-there").

The "politics" that has followed after Marx in the twentieth and in our own centuries has remained resolutely within the domain that Heidegger names as humanism. In this, as I have sought to show throughout, it remains within the province of "metaphysics"—that thinking that arises with Plato and Aristotle, and that finds its fulfillment in the thought of Hegel and of Nietzsche. Increasingly this manner of "political" thinking—of liberalism taken in the widest sense—is concerned with the freedom of the human subject. The struggle to define and defend this freedom oscillates between a negative conception, exemplified by the thinking of Rousseau and the notion of the radical individualism of the human subject who secures his or her freedom "contractually" in relation to the "general will," and (for both Marx and Heidegger) a higher and fully positive freedom unfolded through Hegel's philosophy of the relation of individual subjectivity to absolute subjectivity. The absolute freedom of the human subject is the freedom to become—to correspond—to absolute subjectivity. Hegel identifies the phenomenon to which individual subjectivity corresponds as the being of the state. In interpreting Hegel as the most resolute materialist, I have indicated the way in which the horizon of the fulfillment of the correspondence of individual subjectivity with absolute subjectivity is the state, a view that Heidegger briefly espoused in the period of his Hitlerism through his claim that the state is the "being of the people." This is what Hegel means in his claim, reported by Eduard Gans, that the state is the "path of God through the world."

Both Heidegger and Marx enter into the most radical confrontation with Hegel precisely at this point. Marx, because the state is only a transitional, not a final and absolute, form of subjectivity; Heidegger, in his rejection of the state as the fulfillment of the totalitarian claims of liberalism, and in his sustained critique of subjectivity that began even before the publication of *Being and Time* and which persisted in his thinking to the very end. Both Marx and Heidegger remain resolutely oriented to the question of the "all," the "political" question posed through Hegel's thinking in his identification of individual and absolute subjectivity through the being of the state. Marx, as we have seen, understands the "all" to be manifest in the concrete production of history itself, where humanity *is* its self-production of itself from the past into the future. This is to be understood as a fulfillment of itself as "species-essence," the fulfillment of the being of the human essence. Marx grasps the very essence of Hegel's thought, and shows how his radical materialism is not fulfilled *merely* in the state, but in and through the goal, the very *end*, of history itself. History itself posits the completion and fulfillment of "species-essence," of absolute subjectivity, not in the being of the state (an alienated being, a being in some sense estranged from and "other to" the being of the individual), but in the end to which the individual human essence is ordered. That essence is fulfilled in communism: in the equalization of difference, not through its annihilation, but through an exchange that is constituted by an equalization of social relations. Alienation, self-estrangement, is overcome through the receiving-back in equal measure that which through production itself is alienated from the self.

The politics of liberalism that has followed Marx appears to have abandoned any orientation to the "all," either of Hegel's state or of Hegel's understanding of absolute subjectivity. Through taking up the language of "incredulity toward grand narratives" and the imperative to live "as if there were no universals," it would appear that the "all" (as the merely hegemonic) has been abandoned in the pursuit of the politics of human freedom, as the resistance to every form of hegemony. The hegemonic "all," as the demand to succumb to the totality of what is present, where "presence" is understood to be the regulating and decisive force (in whatever terms—"the bourgeois," "international finance capital," "neoliberalism," "the law of the father," "masculinity," "heteronormativity," and so forth), is stalked and destabilized by the constant arising of new subjectivities, new political demands, new forces and standpoints, all of whom demand to be heard. As each new form of political demand arises, so it is included into the totality of presence. But the persistent arising *in itself*, the nagging absence of those who claim to have no voice (and shout all the louder for their claim to have been silenced to be assuaged), an absence constantly coming into presence, is never questioned or inquired into. This absently constant arriving is *in itself* the ungrounding of presence, the anxious appearing of *the* nothing, but in its concrete, material, particular, political, forms.

Every particular politics that announces itself does so by making a claim to advance and be the co-executor of the equalization between selves that Marx's humanism represents. In this, every particular standpoint remains ordered to the "all" as the very horizon of its realization. The *practice* of contemporary politics, either on the grand or the immediate scale, remains always oriented toward the goal of an equalization that realizes a higher humanity. In this sense it remains within the domain of thinking laid out by Hegel and fulfilled in Marx's thinking. This ever-increasing appropriation of the equalization of humanity to *overcome* difference in the name of freedom and equality is the material condition for the constant realization of the infinite: it is in the constant drive for the infinite to realize itself that the *nothing* itself is annihilated and canceled. It is here that we can hear the two different descriptions of "sublation"—on the one hand the nihilistic sublation of Hegel and Marx, that annihilates and destroys the past for the sake of the future and what is to come, and on the other hand Heidegger's sublation, that brings the past into its full meaning, as a preparation for the future that is yet to befall us. Yet, as Heidegger argues, his fuller understanding of sublation could never have arrived without first having passed through that which arrived through Hegel and with Marx. It is precisely this that the excursus into Hegel in our discussion has attempted to show. The "all" does not in any sense disappear, but manifests itself as an orientation which itself allows the particular to appear, and conditions the manner of its appearing. In this contemporary social, or "world," democracy is the authentic inheritor of the thinking which Marx thinks through. Heidegger's most radical argument is that this thinking—in Nazism, in Marxism, and in "world democracy"—is inherently always on the way to being totalitarian.

For Marx, the history of production is the production of history. Humanity, and it alone, takes over the self-production of the human self in its social relations as the final end of man: in this the materialism of every form of liberalism takes over and fulfills the "death of God" proclaimed by Hegel, by Marx, and by Nietzsche. This taking-over is the human assumption of the place of God as "the creative." For Marx, the history of humanity is an entirely human affair. In this Marx claims an activity (over against a thinking) that brings metaphysics to an end. It is here that Heidegger's own orientation to the "all" becomes most manifest. For Heidegger challenges Marx on the very ground which Marx himself identifies as the central question in both thought and action: the extent to which Marx and what follows from him has succeeded in that thinking which overcomes metaphysics. Heidegger's dialogue with Marx emerges at the point where Marx takes over the place of

God and supplants it with the absolute self-creativity of human subjectivity, as the history of man himself.

It is remarkable that there has been so little written of Heidegger's engagement with Marx, and so few attempts by those sympathetic to Marx to enter into a dialogue informed by Heidegger's thinking. Throughout this text I have constantly brought into view a Heidegger who is yet very little known, and not only to those who first know Marx. The Heidegger of the *Letter on Humanism,* as we have seen, is a Heidegger consciously taking up the language of metaphysics in order to engage with those who still ask, as Jean Beaufret asked Heidegger in 1946, "how to restore a meaning to the word "humanism?' "[1] The Heidegger of the manuscripts of *Das Ereignis,* the private notebooks of 1936 to 1948 and the Bremen lectures of 1949, the real "Heidegger II" of the "language that lies in the background" (the "Heidegger II" of whom William Richardson could not ever have spoken), is a Heidegger who is only yet emerging from the shadows of previous interpretations. This Heidegger is the Heidegger who decisively rejected Nazism (but privately), while refusing to embrace "liberal democracy." This Heidegger is the one who sets us the task of discovering how to think. Not "how to think Heidegger," but how to think at all.

We speak often of crisis, but without paying sufficient attention to what we mean. A "crisis" is not a moment of calamity so much as a moment of *decision* (from *krinein,* to judge or decide). The question is always *how well* we have been equipped already to be decisive, when we are put to the test. Crisis calls forth all that has been learned, and the way in which it has been learned, at the moment when judgment and decision are called for. How we act at moments of great import will very much be determined by how well we have been prepared. What is disclosed through our actions in moments of crisis is the thinking that is prepared for. In the face of every "crisis" the question "what is to be done?" is posed. It is in this question of action that Heidegger and Marx stand closest together, and, at the same, farthest apart. No one has yet advanced beyond Marx in securing a description of the self-production of the history of humanity as humanity's sole concern. The "all" as an entirely human affair, because humanly produced and controlled, comes into view most clearly in the thinking which Marx resolutely and rigorously lays out. Marx answers Heidegger's question "who are we now?" by calling forth the question of who, through our own actions, we are to become. It is here that "humanity" is called upon to attain consciousness, to organize itself around an *organ* of consciousness, to undertake the planning and deciding

1. Jean Beaufret, quoted by Martin Heidegger, *Brief über den Humanismus* (GA9), 315. "Comment redonner un sens au mot 'Humanisme'?"

for those actions necessary to secure man's fate. For Marx, man acts from out of the imperatives of history.

Yet the question remains, of whom, or how, it is that Heidegger, who is clearly not speaking of the Christian God, can speak of the Last God? Who is the God for whom Heidegger says we must be in waiting? If Marx lays before us the task of history itself, history is experienced here as the "all." Heidegger, in reply, asks, what of when a fate and a destiny befall us? A fate, *not* of our making, not produced by us, and yet which utterly concerns us and which we cannot avoid? For the fate of each man and woman individually is death. Men and women are *thnetoi,* beings ordered and oriented toward death. A god is, however, "always"; he or she does not die, and has no fate, even if he shares in the bestowal of fate upon men. But a nation, a people, a place, can die, but need not—and while without death, has a destiny and a fate. A nation, a people, a place, receives its fate and dwells with it—a fate and destiny *not* of its own making, and toward which it may rise up with force and strength and enthusiasm, or only reluctantly. To encounter and dwell within one's fate in a place, as a people, or a nation, requires that we think again, and are again encountered by the "all." It is in how the "all" befalls us that we experience the passing by of the Last God. Our fate is nothing human, and yet it concerns the essence, the unfolding of the being *of* our being that we *are.* It is here than man encounters both the appropriately ordered (that life that lives from *dikē*) and the tragic, as something that is other than, and yet given to us in, our history.

# Bibliography

The date given by each work is the date of publication of the actual work consulted. In cases where this is not the date of first publication of the work, this is supplied in parentheses immediately after the first date. For works not published in English, as far as possible details have been provided of one or more English translations, where they exist.

## WORKS BY MARTIN HEIDEGGER

All works are from the Heidegger *Gesamtausgabe* unless otherwise indicated. *Gesamtausgabe* volumes are prefixed in the text by the initials *GA* and the number of the volume. A year given in italics indicates the year of composition or first presentation. The first nonitalicized date given is the year of the edition consulted, a second date, if given (in parentheses), is the year of first publication (if different), and subsequent years of publication where there have been important additions to the text. Italicized dates ordinarily indicate the year of composition of the work referenced.


Heidegger, Martin. *Gesamtausgabe.* General editor Friedrich-Wilhelm von Herrmann. 102 vols. Frankfurt: Klostermann, 1976–.

*GA*2. *Sein und Zeit.* Edited by Friedrich-Wilhelm von Herrmann, 1977 (1927). Translated as *Being and Time:* (1) by John Macquarrie and Edward Robinson, London: SCM, 1962; (2) by Joan Stambaugh, New York: State University of New York Press, 1996.

*GA*3. *Kant und das Problem der Metaphysik.* Edited by Friedrich-Wilhelm von Herrmann, 1991 (1929, 1950, 1973). Translated as *Kant and the Problem of Metaphysics:* (1) by James S. Churchill based on the 1950 second edition, Bloomington: Indiana University Press, 1962; and (2) by Richard Taft based on the 1973 fourth, enlarged, edition, Bloomington: Indiana University Press, 1990. Developed from lectures given in the Marburg winter semester of 1927–28, the text of which is published separately as vol. 25 of the *Gesamtausgabe* (see *GA*25).

GA4. *Erläuterungen zu Hölderlins Dichtung.* Edited by Friedrich-Wilhelm von Herrmann, 1996 (1971, 1951). Translated by Keith Hoeller as *Elucidations of Hölderlin's Poetry,* Amherst: Humanity (Prometheus), 2000.

"Das Gedicht," 182–92. First added to the 1971 edition, and based on a lecture given in honor of Friedrich Georg Jünger's seventieth birthday in August 1968. Translated as "The Poem," 209–19.

GA5. *Holzwege.* Edited by Friedrich-Wilhelm von Herrmann, 2003 (1950). Edited and translated by Julian Young and Kenneth Haynes as *Martin Heidegger: Off the Beaten Track,* New York: Cambridge University Press, 2002.

"Die Zeit des Weltbildes (1938)," 75–113. Translated by William Lovitt as "The Age of the World Picture" in *The Question Concerning Technology,* edited by William Lovitt, 115–54, New York: Harper and Row, 1977.

"Hegels Begriff der Erfahrung (1942/43)," 115–208. From seminars and lectures given in 1937 and 1942–43. Translated as "Hegel's Concept of Experience" in *Off the Beaten Track,* 86–156.

"Nietzsches Wort 'Gott ist Tot' (1943), " 209–267. Translated by William Lovitt as "The Word of Nietzsche: 'God is Dead'" in *The Question Concerning Technology,* edited by William Lovitt, 53–112.

"Wozu Dichter? (1946)," 269–320. Lecture given before a small audience to commemorate the death of R. M. Rilke in 1946. (1) Translated by Albert Hofstadter as "What Are Poets For?" in *Poetry, Language, Thought,* 89–142, New York: Harper and Row, 1971; and (2) "Why Poets?" in *Off the Beaten Track,* 200–241.

GA6.1. *Nietzsche I.* Edited by Brigitte Schillbach, 1996 (1961).

*Der Wille zur Macht als Kunst,* 1–224 (= *GA*43). Freiburg lectures, winter semester 1936–37. Translated by David F. Krell, ed., as *The Will to Power as Art* in *Nietzsche by Martin Heidegger,* 4 vols., New York: Harper and Row, 1979, vol. 1.

*Die ewige Wiederkehr des Gleichen,* 225–423 (= *GA*44). Freiburg lectures, summer semester 1937. Translated by David F. Krell as *The Eternal Recurrence of the Same* in *Nietzsche by Martin Heidegger,* vol. 2.

"Der Wille zur Macht als Erkenntnis," 425–596 (= *GA*47). Freiburg lectures, summer semester, 1939. Translated by David F. Krell as "The Will to Power as Knowledge" in *Nietzsche by Martin Heidegger,* 3: 1–158.

GA6.2. *Nietzsche II.* Edited by Brigitte Schillbach, 1996 (1961).

"Die ewige Wiederkehr des Gleichen und der Wille zur Macht," 1–23. Translated by David F. Krell as "The Eternal Recurrence of the Same and the Will to Power" in *Nietzsche by Martin Heidegger,* 3:159–83. The two concluding lectures to all three of the Nietzsche lecture courses, written in 1939 but not delivered.

"Der europäische Nihilismus," 23–229 (= *GA*48). Freiburg lectures, first trimester, 1940. Translated by David F. Krell as "European Nihilism" in *Nietzsche by Martin Heidegger,* 4:1–196.

"Nietzsches Metaphysik," 231–300 (= *GA*50, 3–87). Translated by David F. Krell as "Nietzsche's Metaphysics" in *Nietzsche by Martin Heidegger,* 3:1–196.

"Die seinsgeschichtliche Bestimmung des Nihilismus," 300–361. Translated by David F. Krell as "Nihilism as Determined by the History of Being," in *Nietzsche by Heidegger,* 4:197–250. An essay composed during the years 1944–46.

"Die Metaphysik als Geschichte des Seins als Metaphysik," 363–416. Translated by Joan Stambaugh as "Metaphysics as History of Being" in *The End of Philosophy,* 1–54, New York: Harper and Row, 1973. An essay composed in 1941.

"Entwürfe zur Geschichte des Seins als Metaphysik," 417–38. Translated by Joan Stambaugh as "Sketches for a History of Being as Metaphysics" in *The End of Philosophy,* 55–74. An essay composed in 1941.

"Die Erinnerung in die Metaphysik," 439–48. Translated by Joan Stambaugh as "Recollection of Metaphysics" in *The End of Philosophy,* 75–83. An essay composed in 1941.

*GA*7. *Vorträge und Aufsätze.* Edited by Friedrich-Wilhelm von Herrmann, 2000 (1954).

*Die Frage nach der Technik (1953),* 5–36. Also published in *Die Technik und die Kehre,* Pfullingen: Neske, 1962. Based on the 1949 lecture "Das Ge-stell" in the series *Einblick in das—Was ist?* (see *GA*79). Translated by William Lovitt as *The Question Concerning Technology* in *The Question Concerning Technology,* 3–35.

"Wissenschaft und Besinnung (1953)," 37–65. Translated by William Lovitt as "Science and Reflection" in *The Question Concerning Technology,* 155–82. A lecture given to a small circle in Munich in August 1953.

"Überwindung der Metaphysik (1936–1946)," 67–98. Translated by Joan Stambaugh as "Overcoming Metaphysics" in *The End of Philosophy,* ed. Joan Stambaugh, 84–110, London: Harper and Row (Condor), 1975 (1973).

"Wer ist Nietzsches Zarathustra (1953)," 99–124. Translated by David F. Krell as *Who Is Nietzsche's Zarathustra?* in *Nietzsche by Martin Heidegger,* 2: 209–33. A lecture given to the Bremen Club.

*GA*8. *Was heißt Denken.* Edited by Paola-Ludovika Coriando, 2002 (1954). Translated as *Martin Heidegger: What Is Called Thinking?* by J. Glenn Gray, New York: Harper and Row, 1968. The text of lectures given at Freiburg in the winter semester of 1951–52.

*GA*9. *Wegmarken.* Edited by Friedrich-Wilhelm von Hermann, 1976. First published as *Wegmarken,* Frankfurt: Klostermann, 1967. Translated and edited by William McNeill as *Pathmarks,* New York: Cambridge University Press, 1998.

"Phänomenologie und Theologie (1927)," 45–78. Lecture given in Tübingen in 1927 and again in Marburg in 1928. First published in *Archives de Philosophie* 32 (1969), together with a French translation. Subsequently published separately as *Phänomenologie und Theologie,* Frankfurt: Klostermann, 1970. First translated by J. Hart and J. C. Maraldo (eds.) as "Phenomenology and Theology" in *The Piety of Thinking,* Bloomington: Indiana University Press, 1976. Reprinted in a revised translation in *Pathmarks,* 39–62.

"Vom Wesen der Wahrheit (1930)," 177–202. A lecture first given in 1930. Translated as "On the Essence of Truth" by (1) David F. Krell in *Martin Heidegger: Basic Writings,* 111–38; and in a revised translation by John Sallis and William McNeill in *Pathmarks,* 136–54. See also the translation by R. F. C. Hull and Alan Crick in *Existence and Being,* 292–324, Chicago: Henry Regnery, 1949.

*Was ist Metaphysik? (1929),* 103–22. Inaugural lecture given at Freiburg in 1929. First published as *Was ist Metaphysik?,* Bonn: Cohen Verlag, 1929. The fourth edition was published in Frankfurt: Klostermann, 1943, together with a *Nachwort* (*GA*9, 303–12). The fifth (1949) edition included an *Einleitung* (*GA*9, 365–84). First translated by R. F. C. Hull and Alan Crick as "What Is Metaphysics?" (including the *Postscript*) in *Existence and Being,* 325–61. Subsequently translated as "What Is Metaphysics?" by David F. Krell in *Basic Writings,* 93–110. Revised translation by David F. Krell and William McNeill in *Pathmarks,* 82–96.

*Platons Lehre von der Wahrheit (1931/32, 1940),* 203–38. Based partly on a Freiburg lecture course, winter semester 1930–31 (see *GA*34). First published as *Geistige Überlieferung,* Berlin, 1942. Subsequently published in *Platons Lehre von der Wahrheit mit einem Brief über den 'Humanismus,"* 5–52, Bern: Francke, 1947. Translated by (1) J. Barlow and E. Lohner as "Plato's Doctrine of Truth" in *Philosophy in the Twentieth Century,* ed. W. Barrett and H. Aiken, 270–302, New York: 1962. Retranslated by Thomas Sheehan and William McNeill as "Plato's Doctrine of Truth" in *Pathmarks,* 155–82.

"Vom Wesen und Begriff der Φύσις: Aristoteles Physik B, 1 (1939)," 239–301. First published in *Il Pensiero,* vol. 3, nos. 2 and 3, Milan, 1958. Translated by Thomas Sheehan as "On the Being and Conception of Physics: Aristotle's Physics B 1" in *Man and World,* no. 9 (1976): 219–70. Modified translation in *Pathmarks,* 183–230.

*Brief über den Humanismus (1946),* 313–64. First published with the subtitle *Brief an Jean Beaufret* in *Platons Lehre von der Wahrheit mit einem Brief über den "Humanismus,"* 53–117. English translations: (1) John Barlow and Edgar Lohner, trans., *Letter on Humanism* in William Barrett and Henry D. Aitken, eds., *Philosophy in the 20th Century,* 274–81; (2) Frank A. Capuzzi and J. Glenn Gray, *Letter on Humanism* in *Basic Writings,* 217–65; (3) Frank A. Capuzzi, *Letter on "Humanism"* in *Pathmarks,* 239–76.

*Zur Seinsfrage (1955),* 385–426. Originally published as *Über "die Linie"* in a *Festschrift* for Ernst Jünger, *Freundschaftliche Begegnungen: Festschrift zum 60. Geburtstag,* 9–45, Frankfurt: Klostermann, 1955. Published separately as *Über "die Linie,"* Frankfurt: Klostermann, 1956. Translated (1) by William Kluback and Jean T. Wilde as *The Question of Being* (bilingual edition), New York: Twayne, 1958; and (2) by William McNeill as *On the Question of Being* in *Pathmarks,* 291–322.

"Hegel und die Griechen (1958)," 427–44. A lecture given at the Heidelberger Akademie der Wissenschaften in 1958, first published as a contribution to the *Festschrift* for Hans-Georg Gadamer on his sixtieth birthday, *Die Gegenwart der Griechen im neueren Denken,* 43–57, Tübingen: Mohr, 1960. Translated into English by John Sallis and William McNeill as "Hegel and the Greeks" in *Pathmarks,* 323–36.

"Kants These über das Sein (1961)," 445–80. A lecture first given in Kiel in May 1961. Originally published as a contribution to the *Festschrift* for Erik Wolf on his sixtieth birthday as *Existenz und Ordnung* in *Festschrift für Erik Wolf zum 60. Geburtstag,* ed. T. Würtenberger, W. Maihofer, and A. Hollerbach, 217–45, Frankfurt, Klostermann, 1962; also published separately in Frankfurt: Klostermann, 1963. Translated by (1) Ted E. Klein Jr. and William E. Pohl as "Kant's Thesis About Being" in *Southwestern Journal of Philosophy* 4 (1973): 7–33; (2) translation revised by John Sallis and William McNeill and reprinted in *Pathmarks,* 337–63.

*GA*10. *Der Satz vom Grund.* Edited by Petra Jaeger, 1997. Lectures given in Freiburg, winter semester 1955–56; the final (extended) lecture was given in Vienna and to the Bremen Club in 1956. Translated by Reginald Lilly as *The Principle of Reason,* Bloomington: Indiana University Press, 1991.

*Vorlesung: Der Satz vom Grund,* 3–169. Translated as *Lecture Course,* 3–113.

*GA*11. *Identität und Differenz.* Edited by Friedrich-Wilhelm von Herrmann, 2006 (1957).

*Was ist das—die Philosophie?* (1956), 3–26. Lecture held at Cerisy-la-Salle, Normandy, on August 28, 1955. Published in a French translation by Kostas Axelos and Jean Beaufret under the title of the original lecture, *Qu'est-ce que la philosophie?* Paris, Gallimard, 1957. Translated into English by William Kluback and Jean T. Wilde as *What Is Philosophy?* Plymouth: Vision (Harper and Row), 1989 (1963).

"Der Satz der Identität" (1957), 27–110. Partially translated (from the 1957 edition) with an introduction by Joan Stambaugh as "The Principle of

Identity" in *Identity and Difference,* 23–41, New York: Harper and Row, 1969.

*GA*12. *Unterwegs zur Sprache.* Edited by Friedrich-Wilhelm von Herrmann, 1985 (1959). Translated by Peter D. Hertz as *On the Way to Language,* San Francisco: Harper Torchbook (Harper and Row), 1977.

"Die Sprache (1950)," 7–30. Translated by Joan Stambaugh as "Words," in *On the Way to Language,* 137–56.

"Aus einem Gespräch von der Sprache (1953/54)," 79–146. Translated as "A Dialogue on Language," in *On the Way to Language,* 1–54.

"Das Wesen der Sprache (1957/58)," 147–204. Translated as "The Nature of Language," in *On the Way to Language,* 55–108.

*GA*13. *Aus der Erfahrung des Denkens.* Edited by Hermann Heidegger, 1983.

"Zeichen (1969)," 211–12. Article first published in the *Neue Zürcher Zeitung* of September 21, 1969, no. 579.

*GA*14. *Zur Sache des Denkens.* Edited by Friedrich-Wilhelm von Herrman, 2007 (1969).

"Das Ende der Philosophie und die Aufgabe des Denkens" *(1964),* 67–90. Translated by Joan Stambaugh as "The End of Philosophy and the Task of Thinking" in *Martin Heidegger: On Time and Being,* 55–73, San Francisco: Harper Torchbooks, 1972.

*GA*15. *Seminare.* Edited by Curt Ochwadt, 2005 (1977).

*Vier Seminare* (1973), 271–400. Translated by Andrew Mitchell and François Raffoul as *Martin Heidegger: Four Seminars,* Bloomington: Indiana University Press, 2003.

*GA*16. *Reden und andere Zeugnisse eines Lebenswegs.* Edited by Hermann Heidegger, 2000.

"Die Selbstbehauptung der deutschen Universität" (1933), 107–16. Translated by Karsten Harries as "The Self-Assertion of the German University" in *Martin Heidegger and National Socialism,* edited by Günther Neske and Emil Kettering, 5–13.

"Die deutsche Universität (zwei Vorträge in den Ausländerkursen der Freiburger Universität)" (August 15–16, 1934), 285–307.

"Zu 1933–1945," letter to Marcuse of January 20, 1948, 430–31. Translated by Richard Wolin as "Letter to Herbert Marcuse" in *The Heidegger Controversy,* 160–64.

"Nachsinn über das Geschichtliche Selbstbewußtsein," letter to Rudolf Stadelmann of July 20, 1945, 370–71.

"Das Rektorat 1933/34: Tatsachen und Denken (1945)," 372–94. Translated by Karsten Harries in collaboration with Herrman Heidegger as "The Rectorate 1933/34: Facts and Thoughts" in *Martin Heidegger and National Socialism,* 15–32.

"Erläuterungen und grundsätzliches," letter to Professor Constantin von Dietze of December 15, 1945, 409–15.

"*Spiegel*-Gespräch mit Martin Heidegger," September 23, 1966, 652–83. A corrected and expanded version of the article originally published in *Der Spiegel,* May 31, 1976. The *Spiegel* published text is translated by Karsten Harries as "The Spiegel Interview" in *Martin Heidegger and National Socialism,* 41–66.

"Martin Heidegger im Gespräch" September 17, 1969, 702–10. First published in *Martin Heidegger im Gespräch,* edited by Richard Wisser, 67–77, Freiburg: Karl Alber Verlag, 1970. Translated by: (1) Lisa Harries as "Martin Heidegger in Conversation with Richard Wisser" in *Martin Heidegger and National Socialism,* 81–87; (2) B. Srinivasa Murthy in *Martin Heidegger in Conversation: Edited by Richard Wisser,* 38–47, New Delhi: Arnold Heinemann, 1977.

GA18. *Grundbegriffe der aristotelischen Philosophie.* Edited by Mark Michalski, 2002. Translated by Robert D. Metcalf and Mark B. Tanzer as *Basic Concepts of Aristotelian Philosophy,* Bloomington: Indiana University Press, 2009. Marburg lecture course, summer semester 1924.

GA19. *Platon: Sophistes.* Edited by Ingeborg Schüßler, 1992. Marburg lecture course, winter semester 1924–25. Translated by Richard Rojcewicz and André Schuwer as *Plato's Sophist,* Bloomington: Indiana University Press, 1997.

GA20. *Prolegomena zur Geschichte des Zeitbegriffs.* Edited by Petra Jaeger, 1979. Translated by Theodore Kisiel as *History of the Concept of Time: Prolegomena,* Bloomington: Indiana University Press, 1985. Marburg lecture course, summer semester 1925.

GA23. *Geschichte der Philosophie von Thomas von Aquin bis Kant.* Edited by Helmuth Vetter, 2006. Marburg lecture course, winter semester 1926–27.

GA24. *Die Grundprobleme der Phänomenologie.* Edited by Friedrich-Wilhelm von Herrmann, 1975 (1989). Marburg lecture course, summer semester 1927. Translated by Albert Hofstadter as *The Basic Problems of Phenomenology,* Bloomington: Indiana University Press, 1988 (1982).

GA25. *Phänomenologische Interpretation von Kants Kritik der reinen Vernunft.* Edited by Ingtraud Görland, 1995 (1977). Translated by Parvis Emad and Kenneth Maly as *Phenomenological Interpretation of Kant's Critique of Pure Reason,* Bloomington: Indiana University Press, 1997. Marburg lecture course, winter semester 1927–28.

GA29/30. *Die Grundbegriffe der Metaphysik: Welt, Endlichkeit, Einsamkeit.* Edited by Friedrich-Wilhelm von Herrmann, 1992. Translated by William McNeill and Nicholas Walker as *The Fundamental Concepts of Metaphys-*

*ics—World, Finitude, Solitude,* Bloomington: Indiana University Press, 1995. Freiburg lecture course, winter semester 1929–30.

GA31. *Vom Wesen der menschlichen Freiheit: Einleitung in die Philosophie.* Edited by Hartmut Tietjen, 1994 (1982). Translated by Ted Sadler as *Martin Heidegger: The Essence of Human Freedom: An Introduction to Philosophy,* London: Athlone (Continuum), 2002. Freiburg lecture course, summer semester 1930.

GA32. *Hegels Phänomenologie des Geistes.* Edited by Ingtraud Görland, 1988 (1980). Translated by Parvis Emad and Kenneth Maly as *Hegel's Phenomenology of Spirit,* Bloomington: Indiana University Press, 1988. Freiburg lecture course, winter semester 1930–31.

GA33. *Aristoteles, Metaphysik Θ 1–3: Vom Wesen und Wirklichkeit der Kraft.* Edited by Heinrich Huni, 2006 (1981). Translated by Walter Brogan and Peter Warnek as *Aristotle's Metaphysics Θ 1–3: On the Essence and Actuality of Force,* Bloomington: Indiana University Press, 1995. Freiburg lecture course, summer semester 1931.

GA34. *Vom Wesen der Wahrheit: Zu Platons Höhlengleichnis und Theätet.* Edited by Hermann Mörchen, 1997. Translated by Ted Sadler as *Martin Heidegger: The Essence of Truth,* London: Athlone (Continuum), 2002. Freiburg lecture course, winter semester 1931–32.

GA35. *Der Anfang der Abendländischen Philosophie: Auslegung des Anaximander und Parmenides.* Edited by Peter Trawny, 2012. Freiburg lecture course, summer semester 1932.

GA36/37. *Sein und Wahrheit. 1. Die Grundfrage der Philosophie. 2. Vom Wesen der Wahrheit.* Edited by Hartmut Tietjen, 2001. Freiburg lecture course, winter semester 1933–34.

GA38. *Logik als die Frage nach dem Wesen der Sprache.* Edited by Günter Seubold, 1998. Translated into English by Wanda Torres Gregory and Yvonne Unna as *Logic as the Question Concerning the Essence of Language,* Albany: State University of New York Press, 2009. Freiburg lecture course, summer semester 1934.

GA39. *Hölderlins Hymnen: "Germanien" und "Der Rhein."* Edited by Susanne Ziegler, 1989 (1980). Freiburg lecture course, winter semester 1934–35.

GA40. *Einführung in die Metaphysik.* Edited by Petra Jaeger, 1983 (1953). Translated by: (1) Ralph Manheim as *An Introduction to Metaphysics,* New Haven, Conn.: Yale University Press, 1959; and (2) by Gregory Fried and Richard Polt as *Introduction to Metaphysics,* New Haven, Conn.: Yale University Press, 2000. Freiburg lecture course, summer semester 1935.

GA42. *Schelling: Vom Wesen der menschlichen Freiheit.* Edited by Ingrid Schüßler, 1988 (1971). Translated by Joan Stambaugh as *Schelling's Treatise on the Essence of Human Freedom,* Ohio: Ohio University Press, 1985. Stambaugh's translation is of the 1971 edition: the 1988 (*Gesamtaus-*

*gabe)* edition organizes the material slightly differently and has additions. Freiburg lecture course, summer semester 1936.

*GA*43. *Nietzsche: Der Wille zur Macht als Kunst.* Edited by Bernd Heimbüchel, 1985 (= *GA*6.1). Freiburg lecture course, winter semester 1936–37.

*GA*44. *Nietzsches metaphysische Grundstellung im abendländischen Denken: Die ewige Wiederkehr des Gleichen.* Edited by Marion Heinz, 1986 (= *GA*6.1). Freiburg lecture course, summer semester 1937.

*GA*45. *Grundfragen der Philosophie: Ausgewählte "Probleme" der "Logik."* Edited by Friedrich-Wilhelm von Herrmann, 1984. Translated by Richard Rojcewicz and André Schuwer as *Basic Questions of Philosophy—Selected "Problems" of "Logic,"* Bloomington: Indiana University Press, 1994. Freiburg lecture course, winter semester 1937–38.

*GA*46. *Zur Auslegung von Nietzsches II: Unzeitgemäßer Betrachtung "Vom Nutzen und Nachteil der Historie für das Leben."* Edited by Hans-Joachim Friedrich, 2003. Freiburg lecture course, winter semester 1937–38.

*GA*47. *Nietzsches Lehre vom Willen zur Macht als Erkenntnis.* Edited by Eberhard Hanser, 1989 (= *GA*6.1). Freiburg lecture course, summer semester 1939.

*GA*48. *Nietzsche: Der europäische Nihilismus.* Edited by Petra Jaeger, 1986 (= *GA*6.2). Freiburg lecture course, second trimester, 1940.

*GA*49. *Die Metaphysik des deutschen Idealismus (Schelling).* Edited by Günter Seubold, 2006. Freiburg lecture course, first trimester, 1941.

*GA*50. *Nietzsches Metaphysik; Einleitung in die Philosophie—Denken und Dichten.* Edited by Petra Jaeger, 1990 (*Nietzsches Metaphysik* = *GA*6.2). Lectures prepared for the winter semester 1941–42, but not delivered, and lectures from the winter semester 1944–45.

*GA*53. *Hölderlins Hymne "Der Ister."* Edited by Walter Biemel, 1993 (1984). Translated by William McNeill and Julia Davis as *Martin Heidegger: Hölderlin's Hymn "The Ister,"* Bloomington: Indiana University Press, 1996. Freiburg lecture course, summer semester 1942.

*GA*54. *Parmenides.* Edited by Manfred S. Frings, 1992 (1982). Translated by André Schuwer and Richard Rojcewicz as *Martin Heidegger: Parmenides,* Bloomington: Indiana University Press, 1992. Freiburg lecture course, winter semester 1942–43.

*GA*55. *Heraklit.* Edited by Manfred S. Frings, 1994 (1979). Freiburg lecture courses, summer semester 1942 and summer semester 1943.

*GA*60. *Phänomenologie des Religiösen Lebens.* Edited by Matthias Jung, Thomas Regehly, and Claudius Strube, 1995. Translated by Matthias Fritsch and Jennifer Anna Gosetti-Ferencei as *The Phenomenology of Religious Life,* Bloomington: Indiana University Press, 2004. Freiburg lecture course, winter semester 1920–21.

*GA*65. *Beiträge zur Philosophie (Vom Ereignis).* Edited by Friedrich-Wilhelm von Herrmann, 1989. Translated by Parvis Emad and Kenneth Maly as *Contributions to Philosophy (From Enowning)*, Bloomington: Indiana University Press, 1999.

GA66. *Besinnung*. Edited by Friedrich-Wilhelm von Herrmann, 1997. Translated by Parvis Emad and Thomas Maly as *Mindfulness*, London: Athlone (Continuum), 2006.

GA67. *Metaphysik und Nihilismus. 1. Die Überwindung der Metaphysik (1938/39). 2. Das Wesen des Nihilismus (1946–48).* Edited by Hans-Joachim Friedrich, 1999.

GA68. *Hegel. 1. Die Negativität. 2. Erläuterung der "Einleitung" zu Hegels 'Phänomenologie des Geistes."* Edited by Ingrid Schüßler, 1993.

GA69. *Die Geschichte des Seyns. 1. Die Geschichte des Seyns (1938/40). 2. Κοινόν. Aus der Geschichte des Seyns (1939).* Edited by Peter Trawny, 1998.

GA70. *Über den Anfang (1941).* Edited by Paola-Ludovika Coriando, 2005.

GA71. *Das Ereignis (1941/42).* Edited by Friedrich-Wilhelm von Herrmann, 2009.

GA75. *Zu Hölderlin / Griechenlandreisen.* Edited by Curd Ochwadt, 2000.

"Zur politischen Mißdeutung des 'Vaterlands' bei Hölderlin" (1939), 277–78.

GA76. *Leitgedanken zur Entstehung der Metaphysik, der neuzeitlichen Wissenschaft und der modernen Technik.* Edited by Claudius Strube, 2009.

GA78. *Der Spruch der Anaximander.* Edited by Ingeborg Schüßler, 2010. The manuscript of an undelivered lecture series probably written in the summer and autumn of 1942.

GA79. *Bremer und Freiburger Vorträge. 1. Einblick in das was ist. 2. Grundsätze des Denkens.* Edited by Petra Jaeger, 1994.

"Das Ding," 5–23. First published in *Vorträge und Aufsätze* (*GA*7). Translated by Albert Hofstadter as "The Thing" in *Poetry Language Thought,* edited by Albert Hofstadter, 163–82.

"Das Ge-Stell," 24–45. Later developed and expanded into the lecture "Die Frage nach der Technik" (see *GA*7).

"Die Gefahr," 46–67.

"Die Kehre," 68–77. Originally published in *Die Technik und die Kehre,* Pfullingen: Neske, 1962. Translated by William Lovitt as "The Turning" in *The Question Concerning Technology,* edited by William Lovitt, 36–49.

GA86. *Seminare: Hegel—Schelling.* Edited by Peter Trawny, 2011.

GA88. *Seminare (Übungen) 1937/38 und 1941/42. 1. Die metaphysischen Grundstellungen des abendländischen Denkens. 2. Einübung in das philosophische Denken.* Edited by Alfred Denker, 2008.

GA90. *Zu Ernst Jünger.* Edited by Peter Trawny, 2004.

*Heidegger Jahrbuch.* Edited by Alfred Denker and Holger Zaborowski. Freiburg: Karl Alber Verlag, 2004–.

Vol. 1, *Heidegger und die Anfänge seines Denkens,* 2004.

Vol. 2, *Heidegger und Nietzsche,* 2005.

Vol. 3, *Heidegger und Aristoteles,* 2007.

Vol. 4, *Heidegger und der Nationalsozialismus I: Dokumente,* 2009.

Vol. 5, *Heidegger und der Nationalsozialismus II: Interpretationen,* 2009.

## WORKS BY KARL MARX AND FRIEDRICH ENGELS

All works are from the *Marx Engels Werke* unless otherwise indicated. *Marx Engels Werke* volumes are prefixed by the initials *MEW* and the volume number. The year given after each work is the year of first publication. A date given in parentheses after this is the year of first partial publication. In the case of *Das Kapital,* the first date is the date of the *MEW* edition consulted, followed by the date of original publication in parentheses.

Marx, Karl, and Friedrich Engels. *Werke,* Institut für Geschichte der Arbeiterbewegung. 43 vols. Berlin: Dietz Verlag, 1959–.

*MEW*1. *1839 bis 1844.* Edited by Erich Kundel, Roland Nietzold, Richard Sperl, Hildegard Scheibler, et al., 2006 (1981).

Karl Marx, "Kritik des Hegelschen Staatsrechts," 1927, 201–333. Translated by Rodney Livingstone and Gregory Benton as "Critique of Hegel's Doctrine of the State" in *Karl Marx: Early Writings,* London: Penguin, 58–198.

Karl Marx, "Zur Judenfrage," 1844, 347–77. Translated by Rodney Livingstone and Gregory Benton as "On The Jewish Question" in *Karl Marx, Early Writings,* 212–41.

Karl Marx, "Zur Kritik der Hegelschen Rechtsphilosophie. Einleitung," 1844, 378–91. Translated by Rodney Livingstone and Gregory Benton as "Critique of Hegel's Philosophy of Right. Introduction" in *Karl Marx, Early Writings,* 243–57.

*MEW*2. *1844 bis 1846.* Edited by Ludwig Arnold, Walter Schulz, et al., 1990 (1957).

Karl Marx and Friedrich Engels, *Die heilige Familie, oder Kritik der kritischen Kritik: Gegen Bruno Bauer und Konsorten,* 1845, 3–221. Translated by R. Dixon as *The Holy Family: or Critique of Critical Critique,* Moscow: Foreign Languages Publishing House, 1956.

*MEW*3. *1845 bis 1846.* Edited by Ludwig Arnold, Walter Schulz, et al., 1990 (1958).

Karl Marx, "Thesen über Feuerbach," 1845, 5–7. Translated as "Theses on Feuerbach" in *The German Ideology,* 569–71, Amherst: Prometheus Books, 1998 (1924).

Karl Marx and Friedrich Engels, *Die deutsche Ideologie: Kritik der neusten deutschen Philosophie in ihren Repräsentanten Feuerbach, B. Bauer und Stirner, und des deutschen Sozialismus in seinen verschiedenen Propheten,* 1932 (1845–46). Translated as *The German Ideology,* 25–478, Amherst: Prometheus Books, 1988.

*MEW*4. *May 1846–March 1848.* Edited by Ludwig Arnold, Walter Schulz, et al., 1990 (1959).

Karl Marx and Friedrich Engels, *Manifest der Kommunistischen Partei,* 1848, 459–93. Translated by Samuel Moore as *Karl Marx, Friedrich Engels: The Communist Manifesto,* Harmondsworth, U.K.: Pelican Books, 1979 (1888).

*MEW*8. *August 1851–März 1853.* Edited by Rolf Hecker, Martin Hundt, Erhard Kiehnbaum, François Melis, Manfred Schöncke, et al., 2009 (1960).

Karl Marx, *Der achtzehnte Brumaire des Louis Bonaparte,* 1852, 113–207. Translated by Daniel de Lion in 1897 as *The Eighteenth Brumaire of Louis Bonaparte,* New York: Mondial, 2005.

*MEW*13. *Januar 1859 bis Februar 1860.* Edited by Ludwig Arnold, Walter Schulz, Richard Sperl, et al.

"Zur Kritik der politischen Ökonomie," 615–41 (= *MEW*42, 19–45), 1897. Translated by N. I. Stone as an appendix to *Karl Marx: A Contribution to the Critique of Political Economy,* 265–312, Chicago: Charles H. Kerr, 1903.

*MEW*19. *März 1875 bis Mai 1883.* Edited by Ludwig Arnold, Käte Schwank, Christa Müller, Peter Langstein, Walter Schulz and Richard Sperl, 1987 (1962).

Karl Marx, "Kritik des Gothaer Programms," 11–32. Translated by Terrell Carver in *Marx: Later Political Writings,* edited by Terrell Carver, 208–26, Cambridge: Cambridge University Press, 2002 (1996).

*MEW*21. *Mai 1888 bis Dezember 1889.* Edited by Marxist-Leninist Institute, 1984 (1962).

Friedrich Engels, *Der Ursprung der Familie, des Privateigentums und des Staats,* 23–173. Translated anonymously as *The Origin of the Family, Private Property and the State,* Harmondsworth, U.K.: Penguin, 1985 (1972).

Friedrich Engels, "Ludwig Feuerbach und der Ausgang der Klassischen deutschen Philosophie," 1888 (1886), 259–307.

*MEW*23. Karl Marx, *Das Kapital: Kritik der politischen Ökonomie. Vol. 1: Der Produktionsprozeß des Kapitals.* Edited by Horst Merbach, Walter Schulz, et al., 2008 (1867). Translated by Samuel Moore and Edward Aveling as *Capital: A Critique of Political Economy. Vol. 1: The Process of Production of Capital,* London: Lawrence and Wishart, 1977 (1954).

*MEW*24. Karl Marx. Edited by Friedrich Engels. *Das Kapital: Kritik der politischen Ökonomie. Vol. 2: Der Gesamtprozeß der kapitalistischen Produk-*

*tion.* Edited by Horst Merbach, Walter Schulz, et al., 2008 (1885). Translated by I. Lasker as *Capital: A Critique of Political Economy. Vol. 2: The Process of Circulation of Capital,* London: Lawrence and Wishart, 1977 (1956).

*MEW*25. Karl Marx. Edited by Friedrich Engels. *Das Kapital: Kritik der politischen Ökonomie. Vol. 3: Der Produktionsprozeß des Kapitals.* Edited by Horst Merbach, Walter Schulz, et al., 2008 (1895). Translated by H. Kerr et al. as *Capital: A Critique of Political Economy, Vol. 3: The Process of Capitalist Production as a Whole,* London: Lawrence and Wishart, 1977 (1954).

*MEW*26. Karl Marx. *Theorien über den Mehrwert.* Edited by Rolf Dlubek, Erich Kundel, Richard Sperl, Horst Merbach, Artur Schnickmann, and Walter Schulz, 3 vols. Translated by Emile Burns (vol. 1), Renate Simpson (vol. 2), and Jack Cohen (vol. 3) and edited by S. Ryazanskaya and Richard Dixon as *Theories of Surplus Value,* Moscow: Progress, 1969 (1963).

*MEW*27. Karl Marx and Friedrich Engels. *Briefe Februar 1845 bis Dezember 1851.* Edited by Marxist-Leninist Institute (1965). A selection of the Marx-Engels letters is translated by Ewald Osers and edited by Fritz J. Raddatz, *The Marx–Engels Correspondence: The Personal Letters, 1844–1877,* London: Weidenfeld and Nicholson, 1981 (1980).

*MEW*33. Karl Marx and Friedrich Engels. *Briefe Juli 1870 bis Dezember 1874,* 1966.

*MEW*40. Karl Marx and Friedrich Engels. *Schriften und Briefe November 1837–August 1844.* Edited by Rolf Dlubek, Erich Kundel, Richard Sperl, et al., 1990 (1985).

Karl Marx, *Ökonomisch-philosophische Manuskripte aus dem Jahre 1844,* 1932, 467–588. First published in a redaction by David Riazanov of the incomplete and unfinished three manuscripts in vol. 3 of the first section of the *Marx Engels Gesamtausgabe,* Berlin: Dietz Verlag, 1932 (but see the edition published as *Nationalökonomie und Philosophie* [1844], also in 1932). Translated by Rodney Livingstone and Gregor Benton as *Economic and Philosophical Manuscripts (1844)* in *Karl Marx, Early Writings,* London: Penguin Books (New Left Review), 1992 (1974), 279–400.

Karl Marx, "Differenz der demokritischen und epikurischen Naturphilosophie," 1841, 257–365.

*MEW*42. *Ökonomische Manuskripte 1857/1858.* Edited by Erich Kunderl, Roland Nietzold, Richard Sperl, Hildegard Scheibler, et al., 2005 (1983).

Karl Marx, *Grundrisse der Kritik der politischen Ökonomie* (1939–41), 47–768. Translated with a "Foreword" by Martin Nicolaus as *Grundrisse: Foundations of Political Economy (Rough Draft),* London: Penguin, 1993 (1973).

Karl Marx. "Nationalökonomie und Philosophie" (1844). In *Der historische*

*Materialismus: Die Frühschriften*, edited by Siegfried Landshut and J. P. Mayer, 2 vols., 1:283–375, Leipzig: Kröner Verlag, 1932.

Karl Marx. *Le capitale, critique de l'économie politique: Livre premier, le développement de la production capitaliste.* Translated and edited by Joseph Roy and revised by Karl Marx, 2 vols., Paris: Éditions Sociales, 1969 (1872, 1875).

## WORKS BY OTHER AUTHORS

Aeschylus. *Fragments.* Translated and edited by Alan H. Sommerstein. Cambridge, Mass.: Harvard University Press (Loeb Classical Library), 2008.

———. *Prometheus Bound.* In *Aeschylus, I: Persians; Seven Against Thebes; Suppliants; Prometheus Bound*, edited by Alan H. Sommerstein. Cambridge, Mass.: Harvard University Press (Loeb Classical Library), 2009.

Anderson, Kevin B. *Marx at the Margins: On Nationalism, Ethnicity, and Non-Western Societies.* Chicago: University of Chicago Press, 2010.

Anderson, Perry. "The World Made Flesh: Review of *L'avènement du corps.*" *New Left Review* 39 (May–June 2006): 132–39.

Aristotle. *Metaphysics.* 2 vols. Translated by Hugh Tredennick. Cambridge, Mass.: Harvard University Press (Loeb), 1933.

———. *Nicomachean Ethics.* Translated by H. Rackham. Cambridge, Mass.: Harvard University Press (Loeb), 1934.

———. *Politics.* Translated by H. Rackham. Cambridge, Mass.: Harvard University Press (Loeb), 1998 (1932).

Axelos, Kostas. *Einführung in ein künftiges Denken: Über Marx und Heidegger.* Tübingen: Niemeyer, 1966.

———. *Héraclite et la philosophie: La première saisie de l'être en devenir de la totalité.* Paris: Les Éditions de Minuit, 1962.

———. "Le 'dialogue avec le Marxisme' et la 'question de la technique.'" In *Dialogue avec Heidegger*, edited by Jean Beaufret, 4 vols. Vol. 2: *Philosophie moderne*, 143–81. Paris, Éditions de Minuit, 1973.

———. *Marx: Penseur de la technique.* Paris: Éditions de Minuit, 1963 (1961). Translated by Ronald Bruzina as *Alienation, Praxis and Technē in the Thought of Karl Marx*, Austin: University of Texas Press, 1976.

———. *Vers la pensée planétaire: Le devenir-pensée du monde et le devenir-monde de la pensée.* Paris, Éditions de Minuit, 1964.

Bacon, Francis. *De dignitate et augmentis scientiarum.* Paris, Petri Mettayer 1624 (1623). Translated by Gilbert Wats as *Of the Advancement and Proficiencie of Learning: or, the Partitions of Sciences*, London: Thomas Williams, 1674.

———. *Of the Proficiencie and Advancement of Learning, Human and Divine.* Edited by G. W. Kitchin. London: Bell and Daldy, 1861 (1605).

Badiou, Alain. *L'hypothèse communiste.* Paris: Éditions Lignes, 2010. Translated by David Macey and Steve Corcoran as *Alain Badiou: The Communist Hypothesis,* London: Verso, 2010.

Barash, Jeffrey. *Heidegger et son siècle: Temps de l'être, temps de l'histoire.* Paris: Presses Universitaires de France, 1995.

———. "Martin Heidegger in the Perspective of the Twentieth Century: Reflections on the Heidegger *Gesamtausgabe.*" *Journal of Modern History* 64 (1992): 52–78.

Beaufret, Jean. "En chemin avec Heidegger." In *Cahier de l'Herne: Martin Heidegger,* edited by Michel Haar, 205–31. Paris: Éditions de L'Herne, 1983.

Bernasconi, Robert. "The Greatness of the Work of Art." In *Heidegger Toward the Turn: Essays on the Work of the 1930s,* edited by James Risser, 95–117. New York: State University of New York Press, 1999.

Blanchard, William H. "Karl Marx and the Jewish Question." *Political Psychology* 5 (1984): 365–74.

Blanchot, Maurice, and Paula Wissing. "Thinking the Apocalypse: A Letter from Maurice Blanchot to Catherine David," translated by Paula Wissing. *Critical Enquiry* 15 (1989): 475–80.

Brooks, Thom. *Hegel's Political Philosophy: A Systematic Reading of the Philosophy of Right.* Edinburgh: Edinburgh University Press, 2009 (2007).

Browning, Christopher R. *The Origins of the Final Solution: The Evolution of Nazi Jewish Policy, September 1939–March 1942.* Lincoln: University of Nebraska Press, 2005.

Burleigh, Michael. *The Third Reich: A New History.* London: Macmillan, 2000.

Carman, Taylor. "In and With: Flawed Efforts to Discredit Martin Heidegger's Philosophy," review of Emmanuel Faye's *Heidegger: The Introduction of Nazism into Philosophy. Times Literary Supplement,* September 10, 2010, no. 5606, 26–27.

Costigliola, Frank. "An 'Arm Around the Shoulder': The United States, NATO and German Reunification, 1989–90." *Contemporary European History* 3 (1994): 87–110.

Dallmayr, Fred. "Adorno and Heidegger on Modernity." In *Adorno and Heidegger,* edited by Iain Macdonald and Krzyztof Ziarek, 167–81. Stanford, Calif.: Stanford University Press, 2008.

———. "Heidegger and Marxism." *Praxis International* 3 and 4 (1987/88): 207–24.

———. "Heidegger on *Macht* and *Machenschaft.*" *Continental Philosophy Review* 34 (2001): 247–67.

Dascal, Marcelo. "Leibniz, Language, Signs and Thought." In *Foundations of Semiotics,* edited by A. Eschbach. Amsterdam: John Benjamin's Publishing Co., 1987.

Derrida, Jacques. *De la grammatologie.* Paris: Les Éditions de Minuit, 1967.

Translated by Gayatri Chakravorty Spivak as *Of Grammatology,* London: John Hopkins University Press, 1976 (1974).

———. "La main de Heidegger." In *Psyché: Inventions de l'autre II,* 35–68, Paris: Galilée, 2003 (1987–2003). English version as "Heidegger's Hand" in *Psyche: Inventions of the Other,* edited by Peggy Kamuf and Elizabeth Rottenberg, 2:27–62, Stanford, Calif.: Stanford University Press.

———. "La réponse de Jacques Derrida à V. Farías," interview with Didier Éribon in *Le Nouvel Observateur,* November 6–12, 1987. Translated by Peggy Kamuf as "Heidegger: The Philosopher's Hell," in *Points . . . Interviews 1974–1994,* edited by Elizabeth Weber, translated by Peggy Kamuf et al., 181–90, Stanford, Calif.: Stanford University Press, 1995.

Descartes, René. *Oeuvres publiées.* Edited by Charles Adam, and Paul Tannery. 13 vols. Paris: Vrin, 1996 (1965).

*Meditationes de prima philosophia,* vol. 7. Translated by John Cottingham, Robert Stoothoff, and Dugald Murdoch as *The Philosophical Writings of Descartes,* vol. 2, Cambridge: Cambridge University Press, 1993 (1985).

*Principiorum philosophiae,* vol. 8. Translated by John Cottingham, Robert Stoothoff, and Dugald Murdoch in *The Philosophical Writings of Descartes,* 1:177–291.

Diels, Hermann. *Die Fragmente der Vorsokratiker.* 3 vols. Berlin: Weidmannische Buchhandlung, 1922.

Dikötter, Frank. *Mao's Great Famine: The History of China's Most Devastating Catastrophe, 1958–62.* London: Bloomsbury, 2010.

Dorn, Walter L. Review of *Die Kommunistische Partei Deutschlands,* in *American Historical Review* 55 (1950).

Elden, Stuart. "Interview: Kostas Axelos, Mondialisation Without the World." *Radical Philosophy* (March/April 2005): 25–28.

Evans, Richard J. *The Coming of the Third Reich: How the Nazis Destroyed Democracy and Seized Power in Germany.* London: Penguin, 2003.

Farías, Victor. *Heidegger et la nazisme.* Paris: Éditions Vernier. Translated and edited by M. Benaroch and J.-B. Gras as *Heidegger und der Nationalsozialismus,* Frankfurt: Fischer, 1989; the German edition is an expanded and corrected version of a text originally in French. The English edition translated and edited by Joseph Margolis and Tom Rockmore is *Heidegger and Nazism,* Philadelphia: Temple University Press, 1989, with a foreword; this appears to be a version of the French edition.

Faye, Emmanuel. *Heidegger: L'introduction du nazisme dans la philosophie: Autour des séminaires inédits de 1933–1935.* Paris: Éditions Albin Michel, 2005. Translated by Michael B. Smith with a foreword by Tom Rockmore as *Heidegger: The Introduction of Nazism into Philosophy,* New Haven, Conn.: Yale University Press, 2009.

Feuerbach, Ludwig. "Grundsätze der Philosophie der Zukunft." In *Sämtliche Werke,* edited by W. Bolin and F. Jodl, 10 vols. Stuttgart: Frommann-Holzboog, 1959–64 (1903–11).

*Kritiken und Abhandlungen I 1832–1839,* vol. 2.

*Das Wesen des Christentums,* vol. 6. Translated by George Eliot as *The Essence of Christianity,* Mineola, N.Y.: Dover, 2008 (1841).

Flechtheim, Ossip K. *Die KPD in der Weimarer Republik.* Frankfurt: Europäische Verlagsanstalt, 1969 (1948).

Gagern, Michael. "The Puzzling Pattern of the Marxist Critique of Feuerbach." *Studies in Soviet Thought* 11 (1971): 135–58.

George, R. T. de. "Heidegger and the Marxists." *Studies in Soviet Thought* 5 (1965): 289–98.

Gillespie, Michael Allen. "Martin Heidegger's Aristotelian National Socialism." *Political Theory* 28 (2000): 140–66.

Goldmann, Lucien. *Lukács et Heidegger: Fragments posthumes pour une nouvelle philosophie.* Paris: Denöel/Gonthier, 1973. Translated by William Q. Boelhower as *Lukács and Heidegger: Towards a New Philosophy,* London: Routledge, 1977.

Gordon, Peter E. Review of Emmanuel Faye's *Heidegger: The Introduction of Nazism into Philosophy. Notre Dame Philosophical Reviews,* March 12, 2010, at http://ndpr.nd.edu/review.cfm?id=19228.

Hegel, Georg Wilhelm Friedrich. *Werke in zwanzig Bänden.* 20 vols. Frankfurt: Suhrkamp, 1986 (1970).

vol. 2, *Jenaer Schriften* (1801–07).

*Über die wissenschaftlichen Behandlungsarten des Naturrechts, seine Stelle in der praktischen Philosophie und sein Verhältnis zu den positiven Rechtswissenschaften.* First published in the *Kritisches Journal der Philosophie* 2, part 2 (November/December 1802) and part 3 (May/June 1803). Translated by T. M. Knox as *Natural Law: The Scientific Ways of Treating Natural Law; Its Place in Moral Philosophy; and Its Relation to the Positive Sciences of Law,* Philadelphia: University of Pennsylvania Press, 1975.

vol. 3, *Phänomenologie des Geistes* (1807). Translated by A. V. Miller as *Hegel's Phenomenology of Spirit,* Oxford: Oxford University Press, 1977.

vol. 7, *Grundlinien der Philosophie des Rechts oder Naturrecht und Staatswissenschaft im Grundrisse* (1821). Translated by T. M. Knox as *Hegel's Philosophy of Right,* Oxford: Oxford University Press, 1973 (1952). See also the translation by H. B. Nisbett, edited by Allen W. Wood as *Elements of the Philosophy of Right,* Cambridge: Cambridge University Press, 2003 (1991).

vol. 8, *Enzyklopädie der philosophischen Wissenschaften I (Logik)* (1830). Translated and edited by Klaus Brinkmann and Daniel O. Dahlstrom as *Georg Wilhelm Friedrich Hegel: Encyclopaedia of the Philosophical Sciences in Basic Outline, Part I, Science of Logic,* Cambridge: Cambridge University Press, 2010.

vol. 10, *Enzyklopädie der philosophischen Wissenschaften III* (1830). Translated by J. N. Findlay as *Hegel's Philosophy of Mind,* Oxford: Oxford University Press, 2003 (1971).

vol. 13, *Vorlesung über die Ästhetik* (1842 [1835]). Translated by Bernard Bosanquet with an introduction by Michael Inwood as *Hegel: Introductory Lectures on Aesthetics,* Harmondsworth, U.K.: Penguin, 1993.

vols. 18–20, *Vorlesungen über die Geschichte der Philosophie I–III* (1837). Translated by E. S. Haldane and Frances H. Simson as *Hegel's Lectures on the History of Philosophy,* 3 vols., London: Kegan Paul, Trench, Trübner, 1892–96.

———. *Glauben und Wissen.* Hamburg: Felix Meiner, 1962 (1802–03). Translated by Walter Cerf and H. S. Harris as *Hegel: Faith and Knowledge,* Albany: State University of New York Press, 1977.

———. *Politische Schriften.* Frankfurt: Suhrkamp, 1966. Translated by T. M. Knox as *Hegel's Political Writings,* Oxford: Clarendon, 1998 (1964).

Heinsohn, Gunnar. *Warum Auschwitz? Hitlers Plan und die Ratlosigkeit der Nachwelt.* Reinbek bei Hamburg: Rowohlt, 1995.

Hemming, Laurence Paul. *Heidegger's Atheism: The Refusal of a Theological Voice.* Notre Dame, Ind.: Notre Dame University Press, 2002.

———. *Postmodernity's Transcending: Devaluing God.* Notre Dame, Ind.: Notre Dame University Press, 2005.

Hitler, Adolf. *Mein Kampf.* Landsberg: Festungshaftanstalt, 1924. Translated by Ralph Manheim with an introduction by D. C. Watt as *Mein Kampf,* London: Pimlico, 2008 (1969).

Hölderlin, Friedrich. *Gedichte.* Vol. 1 in *Sämtliche Werke und Briefe,* 3 vols. Frankfurt: Deutsche Klassiker Verlag, 1992.

Hook, Sidney. "*Alienation, Praxis and Technē in the Thought of Karl Marx* by Kostas Axelos," review in *Journal of Economic History* 38 (1978): 744–46.

———. "Dialectic and Nature." *Marxist Quarterly* 2 (1937): 253–92.

Ioanid, Radu. *The Ransom of the Jews: The Story of the Extraordinary Secret Bargain Between Romania and Israel.* Chicago: Ivan R. Dee, 2005.

Johansson, Ingvar. "Searle's Monadological Construction of Social Reality." *American Journal of Economics and Sociology* 62 (2003): 233–55.

Jünger, Ernst. *Der Arbeiter: Herrschaft und Gestalt.* Hamburg: Hanseatische Verlaganstalt, 1932.

———. *Der Arbeiter: Herrschaft und Gestalt.* Frankfurt: Klett Cotta, 1981 (1932).

———. "Die Totale Mobilmachung." In *Krieg und Krieger,* edited by Ernst Jünger, 9–30. Berlin: Junker und Dünnhaupt, 1930. Translated by Richard

Wolin and Joel Golb as "Total Mobilisation" in *The Heidegger Controversy,* edited and translated by Richard Wolin, 119–39, Cambridge, Mass.: MIT Press, 1993.

Juvin, Hervé. *L'avènement du corps.* Paris: Gallimard, 2006. Translated by John Howe as *The Coming of the Body by Hervé Juvin,* London: Verso, 2010.

Kant, Immanuel. *Briefwechsel: Auswahl und Anmerkungen von Otto Schöndörffer.* Hamburg: Felix Meiner Verlag, 1986 (1924, 1873). Translated and edited by Arnulf Zweig as *Immanuel Kant: Correspondence,* Cambridge: Cambridge University Press, 1999.

———. *Kritik der reinen Vernunft* (1781, 1787). In Kant, *Werkausgabe,* 12 vols. Frankfurt: Suhrkamp, 1974 (1968), vols. 3 and 4. Translated by Norman Kemp-Smith as *Critique of Pure Reason,* Oxford: Clarendon, 1929.

———. *Kritik der Urteilskraft* (1790). In Kant, *Werkausgabe,* 12 vols. Frankfurt: Suhrkamp, 1974 (1968), vol. 10. Translated by James Creed Meredith as *The Critique of Judgement,* Oxford: Oxford University Press, 1952.

Kaufmann, Walter. *Nietzsche: Philosopher, Psychologist, Antichrist.* Princeton, N.J.: Princeton University Press, 1974 (1950).

Kellner, Douglas. *Herbert Marcuse and the Crisis of Marxism.* Berkeley: University of California Press, 1984.

Lachterman, David R. "The Ontology of Production in Marx: The Paradox of Labor and the Enigma of Praxis." *Graduate Faculty Philosophy Journal* 19 (1996): 3–21.

Lacoue-Labarthe, Philippe. *La fiction du politique.* Paris: Christian Bourgois, 1987. Translated by C. Turner as *Heidegger, Art and Politics,* Oxford: Blackwell, 1990.

Landshut, Siegfried, and J. P. Mayer, eds. *Karl Marx: Der historische Materialismus; Die Frühschriften.* 2 vols. Stuttgart: Kröner, 1932.

Leibniz, Gottfried Wilhelm. "Consilium de Encyclopædia nova conscribenda methodo inventoria." In *Opuscules et fragments inédits de Leibniz,* edited by Louis Couturat. Hildesheim: Georg Olms, 1961 (1903).

Lenin, Vladimir Ilich. "Critical Remarks on the National Question (1913)." In *Vladimir Lenin Collected Works,* 20: 17–51. Moscow: Progress, 1965.

———. "Political Report of the Central Committee, March 7, 1918." In *Vladimir Lenin Collected Works,* 27: 96–99. Moscow: Progress, 1965.

———. "The Proletarian Revolution and the Renegade Kautsky." In *Vladimir Lenin Collected Works,* 28: 227–325. Moscow: Progress, 1965 (1918).

Lévinas, Emmanuel. *Autrement qu'être: ou au-delà de l'essence.* Paris: Kluwer Academic, 1978. Translated by Alphonso Lingis as *Otherwise Than Being: or Beyond Essence,* Pittsburgh: Duquesne University Press, 2004 (1981).

Levine, Norman. "What Karl Marx Really Said." *Journal of Commerce,* Washington, March 18, 1999.

Losurdo, Domenico. *Hegel e la libertà dei moderni.* 2 vols. Naples: La scuola di

Pitagoria editrice, 2011 (1999). Translated by Marella Morris and Jon Morris as *Hegel and the Freedom of the Moderns,* Durham, N.C.: Duke University Press, 2004.

Löwith, Karl. "Les implications politiques de la philosophie de l'existence chez Heidegger." *Les Temps Modernes* 2 (1946): 343–60. Translated by Richard Wolin as "The Political Implications of Heidegger's Existentialism," in *The Heidegger Controversy,* 167–85.

———. *Mein Leben in Deutschland vor und nach 1933.* Stuttgart: Metzler, 1989. Translated by Elizabeth King as *My Life in Germany Before and After 1933—A Report,* London: Athlone, 1994.

Lukács, György. *Existentialisme ou marxisme?* Translated by E. Kelemen. Paris: Nagel, 1948.

Lynd, Robert. "Planned Social Solidarity in the Soviet Union." *American Journal of Sociology* 51 (1945): 183–97.

MacIntyre, Alasdair. "The Theses on Feuerbach: A Road Not Taken." In *The MacIntyre Reader,* edited by Kelvin Knight, 223–34. London: Polity, 1998 (1994).

Marcuse, Herbert. "Beiträge zu einer Phänomenologie des Historischen Materialismus." *Philosophische Hefte* 1 (1928): 45–68. Translated into English as "Contributions to a Phenomenology of Historical Materialism," *Telos* 4 (1969): 3–34.

———. "Briefe an Martin Heidegger" (August 28, 1947, and May 12 1948), published in *Pflasterstrand* no. 279/280 (1988): 465–80. Translated by Richard Wolin in *The Heidegger Controversy,* 160–64.

———. "Frühe Aufsätze." In *Schriften,* vol. 1. Frankfurt: Suhrkamp, 1978. Translated, together with two other short pieces ("Heidegger's Politics: An Interview with Frederick A. Olafson" [1977], 165–75; "Postscript: My Disillusionment with Heidegger," 176), by Richard Wolin and John Abromeit as *Heideggerian Marxism,* Lincoln: University of Nebraska Press.

———. "Beiträge zu einer Phänomenologie des Historischen Materialismus" (1928). In *Schriften,* vol. 1: 347–84. First published in *Philosophische Hefte,* 1: 45–68. Translated as "Contributions to a Phenomenology of Historical Materialism" in *Heideggerian Marxism,* 1–33.

———. "Über die Philosophischen Grundlagen des wirtschaftswissenschaftlichen Arbeitsbegriffs" (1933). In *Schriften,* vol. 1: 556–94. First published in *Archiv für Sozialwissenschaften und Sozialpolitik* 69 (1933): 257–92. Translated as "On the Philosophical Foundations of the Concept of Labor in Economics" in *Heideggerian Marxism,* 122–50.

———."Über konkrete Philosophie" (1929). In *Schriften,* vol. 1: 385–406. First published in *Archiv für Sozialwissenschaften und Sozialpolitik* 62 (1929): 111–20. Translated as "On Concrete Philosophy" in *Heideggerian Marxism,* 134–52.

———. *Hegels Ontologie und die Grundlegung einer Theorie der Geschichtlichkeit.* Frankfurt: Klostermann, 1932. Translated into English by Seyla Benhabib as *Hegel's Ontology and the Theory of Historicity,* Cambridge, Mass.: MIT Press, 1987.

———. "Neue Quellen zur Grundlegung des Historischen Materialismus." *Die Gesellschaft* 9 (1932): 136–74.

——— "Zum Problem der Dialektik I." *Die Gesellschaft* 7 (1930): 15–30. Translated by Morton Schoolman as "On the Problem of the Dialectic," *Telos* 27 (1976): 12–24.

McDonogh, Giles. *After the Reich: From the Liberation of Vienna to the Berlin Airlift.* London: John Murray (Hodder Headline), 2007.

Milchman, Alan, and Alan Rosenberg, eds. *Martin Heidegger and the Holocaust.* Atlantic Highlands, N.J.: Humanities, 1997 (1996).

Minder, Robert. *Hölderlin unter den Deutschen und andere Aufsätze zur deutschen Literatur.* Frankfurt: Suhrkamp, 1968 (1966).

Morat, Daniel. *Von der Tat zur Gelassenheit: Konservatives Denken bei Martin Heidegger, Ernst Jünger und Friedrich Georg Jünger 1920–1960.* Göttingen: Wallstein Verlag, 2007.

Neske, Günther, and Emil Kettering, eds. *Antwort: Martin Heidegger im Gespräch.* Pfullingen: Günther Neske Verlag, 1988. Translated by Lisa Harries as "Martin Heidegger in Conversation with Richard Wisser" in *Martin Heidegger and National Socialism,* edited by Günther Neske and Emil Kettering. New York: Paragon House, 1990.

Nietzsche, Friedrich. *Friedrich Nietzsche: Kritische Studienausgabe.* Edited by Giorgio Colli and Mazzino Montinari, 15 vols. Berlin: de Gruyter, 1999 (1968).

vol. 1, *Unzeitgemäße Betrachtungen,* 1873–76. Translated by R. J. Hollingdale and edited by Daniel Breazedale as *Nietzsche: Untimely Meditations,* Cambridge: Cambridge University Press, 2007 (1997).

vol. 2, *Menschliches Allzumenschliches,* 1880 (1878). Translated by R. J. Hollingdale as *Human, All Too Human,* Cambridge: Cambridge University Press, 1986.

vol. 3, *Die Fröhliche Wissenschaft* (1882). Translated by Walter Kaufmann as *The Gay Science,* New York: Random House, 1974.

vol. 4, *Also Sprach Zarathustra,* 1885 (1883). Translated and edited by Walter Kaufmann as *Thus Spoke Zarathustra* in *The Portable Nietzsche,* 112–439, Harmondsworth, U.K.: Penguin, 1976.

vol. 5, *Jenseits von Gut und Böse,* 1886. Translated by O. Levy as *Beyond Good and Evil,* Edinburgh: Foulis, 1909.

vol. 5, *Zur Genealogie der Moral,* 1887. Translated by Keith Ansell-Pearson as *On the Genealogy of Morality,* Cambridge: Cambridge University Press, 1994.

vol. 6, *Götzen-Dämmerung,* 1888. Translated and edited by Walter Kaufmann in *The Portable Nietzsche,* edited by Walter Kaufmann, 463–563.

vol. 11, *Nachlaß 1884–1885.*

vol. 12, *Nachlaß 1885–1887.*

vol. 13, *Nachlaß 1887–1889.*

———. *Der Wille zur Macht,* material ordered by Peter Gast and Elizabeth Förster-Nietzsche in a reworked edition. Stuttgart: Kröner, 1930 (1901). The edition cited is the 1996 Kröner (13th) edition. Translated by Walter Kaufman and R. J. Hollingdale as *The Will to Power,* New York: Random House, 1967.

Nussbaum, Martha C. *Liberty of Conscience: In Defense of America's Tradition of Religious Equality.* Philadelphia: Basic Books, 2008.

———. "Liberty of Conscience: The Attack on Equal Respect." *Journal of Human Development* 8 (2007): 338–57.

Ott, Hugo. *Martin Heidegger: Unterwegs zu seiner Biographie.* Frankfurt: Campus Verlag, 1988. Translated by Allan Blunden as *Martin Heidegger A Political Life,* London: Harper Collins, 1993.

Otto, Walter F. *Dionysos: Mythos und Kultus.* Darmstadt: Wissenschaftliche Buchgesellschaft, 1960 (1933). Translated with an introduction by Robert B. Palmer as *Dionysus: Myth and Cult,* Dallas: Spring, 1981 (1965).

Peters, H. F. *Zarathustra's Sister: The Case of Elisabeth and Friedrich Nietzsche.* New York: Marcus Wiener, 1977.

Petzet, Heinrich Wiegand. *Auf einen Stern zugehen: Begegnungen mit Martin Heidegger 1929 bis 1976.* Frankfurt: Societäts-Verlag, 1983. Translated in an emended and corrected edition by Parvis Emad and Kenneth Maly as *Encounters and Dialogues with Martin Heidegger 1929–1976,* Chicago: University of Chicago Press, 1983.

Phillips, James. "The Death of Hegel." Chapter 1 in *Heidegger's Volk: Between National Socialism and Poetry.* Stanford, Calif.: Stanford University Press, 2005.

Plato. *Euthyphro; Apology; Crito; Phaedo; Phaedrus.* Translated by Harold North Fowler. Cambridge, Mass.: Harvard University Press (Loeb), 1999 (1914).

———. *Republic.* Translated by Paul Shorey, 2 vols., Cambridge, Mass.: Harvard University Press (Loeb), 1994 (1930, 1935).

Pöggeler, Otto. *Der Denkweg Martin Heideggers.* Pfullingen: Neske, 1983 (1963). Translated by John Bailiff as *The Paths of Heidegger's Life and Thought,* Atlantic Highlands, N.J.: Humanities, 1997.

Richardson, William. *Through Phenomenology to Thought.* Dordrecht: Martinus Nijhoff, 1963.

Rochlitz, Rainier. "Lukács et Heidegger—suites d'un débat," in "Homme et la société" in *Revue internationale de recherches et de synthèses sociologiques* 43–44 (1977): 87–94.

Rockmore, Tom. Review of William Q. Boelhower's *Lukács and Heidegger: Towards a New Philosophy. Studies in Soviet Thought* 23 (1982): 342–46.

Safranksi, Rüdiger. *Ein Meister aus Deutschland: Heidegger und seine Zeit.* Frankfurt: Fischer, 1997 (1994). Translated by Ewald Osers as *Martin Heidegger: Between Good and Evil,* Cambridge, Mass.: Harvard University Press, 1998.

Santilli, Paul. "Marx on Species-Being and Social Essence." *Studies in Soviet Thought* 13 (1973): 76–88.

Sartre, Jean-Paul. *L'Existentialisme est un humanisme.* Paris: Nagel, 1946. Translated by Carol Macomber as *Existentialism Is a Humanism,* New Haven, Conn.: Yale University Press, 2007.

Sass, Hans-Martin. "The 'Transition' from Feuerbach to Marx: A Re-Interpretation." *Studies in Soviet Thought* 26 (1983): 123–42.

Schmitt, Carl. *Der Nomos der Erde im Völkerrecht des Jus Publicum Europaeum.* Berlin: Duncker & Humbolt, 1988 (1950). Translated by G. L. Ulmen as *The Nomos of the Earth in the International Law of the Jus Publicum Europaeum,* New York: Telos, 2003.

———. *Staat, Bewegung, Volk: Die Dreigliederung der politischen Einheit.* Hamburg: Hanseatische Verlaganstalt, 1933. Translated by Simona Draghici as *State, Movement People: The Triadic Structure of the Political Unity (1933), with the Question of Legality (1950),* Corvallis, Ore.: Plutarch, 2001.

Schweickart, David. "Heidegger and Marx: A Framework for Dialogue." In *Heidegger, the Man and the Thinker,* edited by Thomas Sheehan, 229–43. New Brunswick, N.J.: Transaction, 2010 (1981).

Searle, John R. *The Construction of Social Reality.* New York: Free, 1995.

Service, Robert. *Trotsky: A Biography.* London: Macmillan, 2009.

Shandro, A. M. "A Marxist Theory of Justice?" *Canadian Journal of Political Science–Revue canadienne de science politique* 22 (1989): 27–47.

Sheehan, Thomas. "A Normal Nazi," reviews of *The Heidegger Controversy: A Critical Reader,* edited by Richard Wolin (Cambridge, Mass.: MIT Press 1993); and *Martin Heidegger: Politik und Geschichte im Leben und Denken,* by Ernst Nolte (Berlin and Frankfurt, Propyläen, 1990). *New York Review of Books* 40 (January 14, 1993): 30–35.

Skerpan, Alfred A. "Aspects of Soviet Antisemitism." *Antioch Review* 12 (1952): 287–328.

Sluga, Hans. *Heidegger's Crisis: Philosophy and Politics in Nazi Germany.* Cambridge, Mass.: Harvard University Press, 1993.

Sokal, Alan, and Jean Bricmont. *Intellectual Impostures.* London: Profile, 1998.

Spengler, Oswald. *Der Untergang des Abendlandes: Umrisse einer Morphologie der Weltgeschichte.* Munich: Beck'sche Verlagsbuchhandlung, 1924 (1918, 1922), 2 vols.: vol. 1, *Gestalt und Wirklichkeit;* vol. 2, *Welthistorische Perspektiven.* English translation by Charles Francis Atkinson as *Decline of the West,* London: George Allen and Unwin, 1926–28, 2 vols.: vol. 1, *Form and Actuality* (1926); vol. 2 (1928), *Perspectives of World-History.*

Vallega-Neu, Daniela. "Poietic Saying." In *Companion to Heidegger's Contributions to Philosophy,* edited by Charles E. Scott, 66–80. Bloomington: Indiana University Press, 2001.

Warminski, Andrzej. "Monstrous History: Heidegger Reading Hölderlin." *Yale French Studies* 77 (1990): 193–209.

Weinberg, Robert. "Demonising Judaism in the Soviet Union During the 1920s." *Slavic Review* 67 (2008): 120–53.

Wisser, Richard, "Nachdenkliche Dankarbeit," 29–77, afterword to *Antwort: Martin Heidegger im Gespräch.* Edited by Günther Neske and Emil Kettering. Translated as "Afterthoughts and Gratitude," 89–124, in *Martin Heidegger and National Socialism,* edited by Neske and Kettering and translated by Lisa Harries.

Wittgenstein, Ludwig. *Bemerkungen über die Grundlagen der Mathematik.* Frankfurt: Suhrkamp, 1984. First published in the English translation of G. E. M. Anscombe as *Remarks on the Foundations of Mathematics,* Oxford: Blackwell, 1989 (1956).

Wolin, Richard, ed. *The Heidegger Controversy: A Critical Reader.* Cambridge, Mass.: MIT Press, 1993 (1991).

Wood, Allen. "Reply." *Bulletin of the Hegel Society of Great Britain* 25 (1992): 34–50.

# Index